Outcast Europe

Refugees and Relief Workers in an Era of Total War 1936–48

Sharif Gemie, Fiona Reid and Laure Humbert, with
Louise Ingram

continuum

Continuum International Publishing Group

The Tower Building   80 Maiden Lane
11 York Road   Suite 704
London SE1 7NX   New York, NY 10038

www.continuumbooks.com

First published 2012

British Library Cataloguing-in-Publication Data
A catalogue record for this book is available from the British Library.

ISBN: HB: 978-1-4411-1545-4
PB: 978-1-4411-0244-7

Library of Congress Cataloging-in-Publication Data
A catalog record for this book is available from the Library of Congress.

Typeset by Fakenham Prepress Solutions, Fakenham, Norfolk NR21 8NN
Printed and bound in India

OUTCAST EUROPE

County Council

Libraries, books and more . . .

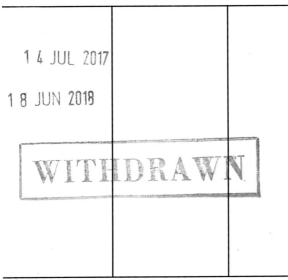
Please return/renew this item by the last due date.
Library items may be renewed by phone on
030 33 33 1234 (24 hours) or via our website
www.cumbria.gov.uk/libraries

Ask for a CLIC password

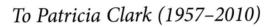

To Patricia Clark (1957–2010)

Contents

Preface

DEDICATION

To Patricia Clark (1957–2010)

To Pat, from Sharif

This is the first book that I've completed without Pat's help. She read six of the chapters and – as always – liked what she saw, but made some comments about what we could revise. I think she would have approved of the final result. She believed in helping people but, more importantly, as someone who'd taken some hard knocks in her own life, she admired people who tried to take control of their destinies.

Some episodes in this book now seem strangely prophetic: the rapid, unexpected separations, the common sense of trauma, and the lives which suddenly seem to lack a centre. Other passages seem to carry a different message. When I first read the works of Muriel and Harry (who appear in Chapters 6, 7 and 8), I was immediately reminded of Pat and myself. It's now rather comforting to think that there were people similar to us, in another time and place, coping with similar problems.

I'd like to thank all the people who've helped me get through the worst months in my life: the Clarks, Gemies, Parkers, Slapes, Weekes and so many others.

Pat was an agnostic, with no strong sense of any afterlife. It is certain, however, that something of her spirit lives on in the chapters of this work.

WRITING OUTCAST EUROPE

The project started in 2004, based on the idea of developing some of Sharif's previous research. The initial ideas were discussed by Sharif and Fiona. Laure was appointed as Research Assistant in 2007, and worked full-time on the project until 2010. Louise was appointed as a part-time Research Administrator for six months in 2010. Each of us developed their own specialisms. Sharif read Spanish-language texts, UNRRA diaries at the Imperial War Museum, and visited French archives. Fiona researched material in Friends' House in London, the Archives Nationales and the Institut d'histoire du temps présent in Paris, and in the International Red Cross archives in Geneva. Laure researched in French national, departmental and municipal archives, and in the UNRRA archives in New York. Louise researched film documentaries concerning refugees, and contributed to two 'spin-off' articles from this project.

Most of the writing was genuinely co-operative in nature: we would meet every week in Laure's office, report back on what we'd read, discuss possibilities and problems, and sketch out possible themes. The chapters were written by circulating digital versions, with each contributor working on the manuscript for two or three days, and then forwarding it on to the next. At our weekly meetings, we'd comment on the progress of the chapters. There are still some elements which each of us can identify as our own, but most of this book represents a real synthesis of our ideas and research. Sharif took final responsibility for drawing together a sometimes sprawling manuscript into what we hope is a coherent text.

Acknowledgements

This book represents five years' work involving four people. Along the way, we were lucky enough to have plenty of assistance and encouragement from friends, contacts and colleagues. In no particular order, we would like to thank:

The Leverhulme Trust, for their generous financial support, allowing us to pay for a full-time research assistant for three years

The History Division at the University of Glamorgan, for funding of research trips

Scott Soo, and all in the EXILIO network, who provided stimulus and encouragement

Mike Berlin, Stefan Berger, Gavin Edwards, Dee Gemie, Brian Ireland, Norry LaPorte, Susanne Schrafstetter, for their advice and assistance

On a personal note, Fiona would especially like to thank Norry LaPorte, Danu Reid and Joe Fenton for all their help and encouragement during the 'Outcast' years.

Every effort has been made to trace copyright holders and to obtain their permission for the use of copyright material. We would be grateful if any omissions or errors are brought to our attention so that corrections may be incorporated in future editions of this book.

Abbreviations

ADBRhin	Archives Départementales du Bas-Rhin
ADBRhône	Archives Départementales des Bouches du Rhône
ADHG	Archives Départementales de la Haute-Garonne
ADI	Archives Départementales de l'Isère
ADI&V	Archives Départmentales de l'Ille-et-Vilaine
ADM	Archives Départementales de la Manche
ADMM	Archives Départementales du Meurthe-et-Moselle
ADPO	Archives Départementales des Pyrénées-Orientales
ADR	Archives Départementales du Rhône
AML	Archives Municipales de Lyon
AMM	Archives Municipales de Metz
AMN	Archives Municipales de Nancy
AMR	Archives Municipales de Rennes
AN	Archives Nationales
COBSRA	Council for British Societies for Relief Services Abroad
FAU	Friends Ambulance Unit
FL	Friends Library
FRS	Friends Relief Service
ICRC	International Committee of the Red Cross
IHTP	Institut d'histoire du temps présent
IRO	International Refugee Organisation
IWM	Imperial War Museum
NA	National Archives
SHAEF	Supreme Headquarters Allied Expeditionary Forces
SHAT	Service Historique de l'Armée de Terre
UN	United Nations
UNRRA	United Nations Relief and Rehabilitation Administration
WL	Weiner Library

Introduction: Writing Refugees

- The Inner World of the Refugee
- Defining Refugees
- Writing Refugees
- Historians and Refugees
- The Great Journey: Transformative Movement and the Second World War

THE INNER WORLD OF THE REFUGEE

The story of George Orwell's conversion to patriotism in 1940 is well known. Following his experiences in the Spanish Civil War, Orwell joined the Independent Labour Party in 1938 and adopted far-left, frequently almost pacifist attitudes. He was pessimistic about the nature and consequences of a future war: 'How can we "fight fascism" except by bolstering up a far vaster injustice?' he asked in July 1939.[1] Then, as France fell and German armed forces occupied the French channel ports, Orwell discovered that he was 'a patriot at heart'.[2] He adapted well to the new circumstances. Like many British people, he responded willingly to the promotion of a common patriotic endeavour which marked so many of Churchill's early speeches. He joined the Home Guard in June 1940, and had great hopes for the new organisation's social and political potential. In later months he was frustrated by his inability to play a more prominent role in the British armed forces. One of the most curious aspects of this period is his eventual compromise with the British Empire. Orwell, the man whose first political stance was a heart-felt revulsion against the racket of imperialism, wrote propaganda to be broadcast by the BBC to Indian listeners, with the aim of restraining the development of Indian nationalism. Orwell's writing developed astonishingly during the war years. He became the master of the short essay and, a few years later, drew on his wartime experiences to write his fictional masterpieces, *Animal Farm* and *Nineteen Eighty-Four*.

In a sense, Orwell's experience was a typical one. From a position of isolation or scepticism, he found place and purpose within the wider war effort. This did not stifle his critical political and social thinking: his essay, *The Lion and the Unicorn* (1941), re-casts patriotism as a progressive, even revolutionary force, and his later novels included an acerbic satirical dimension, portraying the hollowing-out of British political culture by the totalitarian radicalism of the war years. But the final force of these wartime texts emphatically suggests Orwell's reconciliation with his nation – a perspective that certainly seems compatible with the commonplace images of united patriotic endeavour, social solidarity and joyful victory over evil that structure the popular British memory of the war years. This type of narrative highlights a sense of continuity throughout the period: while the nation was dangerously threatened, while exceptional efforts were demanded, again and again, from the population, while radical, innovative measures were enforced as a response to dire military necessity, the fundamental relationship between the citizen and the nation remained unchanged – and, perhaps, it was even strengthened by this most mighty of tests.

This book concerns people who had a different experience of the war years, and who experienced a deep alienation in their relationship to the nation state. One could compare Orwell's experience with that of his close contemporary, Victor Klemperer (1881–1960), a literature teacher at the Technical University in Dresden in 1933. For Klemperer, the years that followed 1933 were marked by a dreadful decline in his professional, political and even physical status. Although a committed, sincere Protestant, Klemperer was defined by the Nazi state as a Jew. He experienced repeated dispossessions, each in turn more horrific: he lost his job, his car, his house, his savings, his access to libraries, his books and even his ability to walk the streets or to eat adequately. He did, however, preserve his marriage, and this tiny micro-community of two frail 60-year-olds survived the repressive power of the Third Reich. Like Orwell, Klemperer defined himself as a patriot: 'I am a German forever, German "nationalist" … Liberal and German *forever*'.[3] His sense of patriotism was put to a far harsher test than anything Orwell faced. In 1937, Klemperer acknowledged 'I have not only outwardly lost my Fatherland … my inner sense of belonging is gone … Contempt and disgust and deepest mistrust with respect to Germany can never leave me now. And yet in 1933 I was so convinced of my Germanness'.[4] By May 1942, this question of identity grew increasingly bitter and desperate: despite the German government's denial of his national identity, Klemperer clung to his sense of nationhood by denying the 'Germanness' of the new rulers: 'I am fighting the hardest battle for my Germanness now. I must hold on to this: I am German, the others are un-German. I must hold on to this: the spirit is decisive, not blood. I must hold on to this: On my part Zionism would be a comedy – my baptism was *not* a comedy'.[5] Again, like Orwell, the war years bring forth his best writing: Klemperer himself notes that writing 'is the only antidote against the desperateness of the situation'.[6] Yet Klemperer, as an author, faced far more serious threats than Orwell. 'Always the same see-saw. The fear that my scribbling could get me put into a concentration camp. The feeling that it is my duty to write, that it is my life's task, my calling'.[7]

Unlike Orwell, Klemperer lived these years with a constant, immediate and dreadful sense of the fragility of his own life. As early as 1936, he wrote that 'I often very much doubt whether we shall actually survive the Third Reich'.[8] By 1939 he asked himself 'Will they come for me tonight? Will I be shot, will I be put in a concentration camp?'.[9] As the war progressed, Klemperer grew more pessimistic and fearful. In March 1942 he noted: 'The fear of the Gestapo: 90 per cent of all conversations among Jews revolve around house searches'.[10] 'I only think: When will it be *my* turn?' he wrote in May 1942, 'Shall I be beaten and spat upon today?'[11] and in December of the same year: 'Everyone around me is dying. Why am *I* still alive?'.[12] While Orwell could experience the war effort as a period of increasing social unity, Klemperer found the opposite. His isolation was a constant theme in his records: he writes of being 'increasingly isolated ... the greatest isolation ... we are alone, absolutely alone ... our absolute isolation'.[13]

While most of the German Jews were murdered during the Third Reich, Klemperer and his wife were fortunate exceptions. One reason for this is that, despite the appearance of isolation, helplessness and fragility, Klemperer deployed strategies which made his survival more likely. He avoided the streets that the Gestapo regularly patrolled; he volunteered for work in order to make it less likely that he would be deported to the General Government in Poland or to a concentration camp. What appears as his obsessive desire to record even the most trivial details of life in Dresden is part of this strategy: he wishes to observe in order to understand his predicament and therefore to predict and to control his fate. Richard Evans notes some striking features of Klemperer's writing: it was 'pedantic, with an attention to detail that was one of the qualities that make his diaries so valuable'.[14] But, in a sense, these comments miss the key point: Klemperer's observational skills are not some exceptional quirk of an odd literature teacher. Instead, his diaries reveal a common trait of a large section of the peoples of wartime Europe. Many considered that their futures, even their simple physical existence, depended on their ability to understand the direction and dynamics of the societies in which they lived, which no longer appeared as familiar, hospitable national homes, but as bewildering, threatening, alien structures. This point suggests a theme to which we will return frequently in this work: while external observers repeatedly characterize refugees' lives as marked by panic and chaos, in reality, the primordial feature in the process of becoming a refugee is an exercise in rational analysis during desperate, dangerous and confusing conditions.

While Eva and Victor Klemperer sat alone in their tiny flat in Dresden, fearing the arrival of the Gestapo, the Spanish republican Ana Delso suffered a similar type of dispossession following her flight from Spain to France in early 1939. She too was left without resources in a hostile environment, and had to make decisions about her future. How was she to survive?

> My school was that of exile. My life was like that of a grasshopper: full of fear, but also marked by a passionate desire to live and to survive the horrific slaughter which had been unleashed across Europe ... One thing is certain, only autodidacts learn the art of survival and no one can teach it.[15]

Klemperer is both exceptional and gifted in the manner in which he *records* the details of daily life, but he is *not* unusual in his quest to observe and understand. Like Delso and other refugees, he urgently wanted to learn the art of survival. This dimension to refugees' writing is one of the justifications for this book:

their writing is often exceptionally observant, for their lives depend on their powers of observation. For this reason alone, their records and writings deserve study.

Is it correct to describe Klemperer and Delso as refugees? Let us begin our discussion of this point by re-capping some of the differences between Orwell's experience and that of Klemperer. Orwell did not need to flee his home; he identified with his government, tried to support its war effort and could legitimately consider that he shared some important principles with the majority of the British population. Klemperer identified himself as a German, but the new, Nazi German government refused to accept him as a citizen. To his dismay, the majority of the German population accepted Nazi leadership, if not with enthusiasm, then certainly without protest. This implied that the German population – his erstwhile fellow citizens – had rejected him. He considered that he was a fragile, isolated individual. Turning away from these two positions, one notes that there was, however, another form in which these building blocks of wartime identity could be arranged: a dissident or protesting section of the population could consider that they represented legitimate sovereignty better than the existing government. On occasion, this could be based on a sense that the dissident group commanded the loyalty of the statistical majority of the population: arguably, the greatest achievement of the French Resistance was to work this miracle between 1940 and 1944, creating 'an immense and clumsy desire for union' in Sartre's words, and thus facilitating the swift creation of a new government in 1944.[16] More often, this sense of representing the majority was a matter of assertion and symbolism, particularly when the dissidents were physically separated from the homeland. Discussing German refugees present in Britain in 1940, François Lafitte perceptively argued that in previous months 'to be a refugee became an honourable profession … [they were] citizens of that other better Germany which Hitler is striving to destroy'.[17] In the same vein, exiled Spanish republicans like Delso proudly claimed that they represented an intellectual, scientific and even moral elite. While never constituting more than about four or five per cent of the Spanish population, they still argued that they represented the *real* Spain better than Franco's government.

This was an attitude which was something more than an assertion of a collective cultural superiority or a diplomatic challenge. It is noticeable that, for example, when the Spanish refugee Pépita Carpeña records her exile in France, she constantly uses the first person plural, even during the darkest moments. In 1939, 'we were always locked in, forbidden to leave our zone, by orders from above. This weighed on everyone'. Following the French defeat in June 1940 her little group of exiles, sheltering in a small village near the Mediterranean, suddenly had the unlikely idea of creating an anarchist library. She explains: 'For us, the right to culture was more important than the misery of our situation'.[18] The point here is not simply that Carpeña was less threatened than Klemperer – probably a valid point, but not as clear-cut as might be thought – but that the basis of her existence and exilic identity is quite distinct from that experienced by either Orwell or Klemperer. For Orwell, 'we' means the British nation or people; for Klemperer, usually himself and Eva, sometimes irregularly extended to those suffering like him. Carpeña writes in a different way: for her, 'we' means a large imagined community of dissidents; this forms the basis for her thinking, her political projects (or fantasies) and her writing. It is this sense of group feeling, which Klemperer sadly lacked, that first marks the difference between the refugee and the individual dissident.

DEFINING REFUGEES

Differences between dissidents, refugees, forced migrants and evacuees may seem clear in theory, but in practice it is often difficult to apply hard and fast distinctions to specific cases. In particular, there was a constant slippage between the terms 'refugee' and 'evacuee'. Throughout the 'long' Second World War (1936–48) new waves of outcast people were constantly created: each represented a different form of distance, dissidence and opposition to the nation state. Their existence can be monitored by the new terms coined to identify them. They were deportees, displaced persons, evacuees, voluntary evacuees, homeless, illegal migrants, infiltrees, internees, expellees, in *no-man's land* (an English language phrase used in France), persecutees, refugees, returnees, stateless, unassimilable aliens, unclassified, undesirables and uprooted. In nearly every case, these are terms devised by external authorities and relief agencies in an attempt to classify and control people living outside the physical or metaphorical boundaries of the nation state.

One telling example of the plasticity of these categories is the case of the 16 million Soviet citizens who were evacuated eastwards in the summer of 1941: classified by their state as evacuees, their movement was organized by the institutions of Soviet state planning. Yet these people quickly experienced destitution, hunger and homelessness. They soon called themselves refugees.[19] Should one challenge their right to use the term? Such common incidents of confusion show how misleading official classifications of marginalized peoples can be: they do not necessarily reflect the lived experience of these peoples.

To illustrate this point more fully, let us return to Klemperer's records. If one puts to one side the pleasure trips which he made between 1933 and 1939, his diaries record only three significant journeys. The first was after the fire-bombing of Dresden, in February 1945. Klemperer and his wife, Eva, joined evacuees from the city to travel a few miles northwards to the airport at Klotzsche. Along the way, they saw refugees from the east, returning to Germany as the Russians advanced.[20] Eva decided to rip the yellow star from her husband's jacket, and he then joined the other evacuees, no longer marked out as different from them. But rather than accepting the official guidance given to evacuees, in April 1945 they independently decided to travel to Munich, and then onto the villages to the north of the city. Following Germany's official surrender, in May 1945 they then tried to return to Dresden. At the beginning of this third journey, Klemperer reflected on the differences with his second journey: 'This is the pleasant difference compared with our situation on 3 April … one's life is no longer at risk. And this is the unpleasant one: then we *had* no choice, we had to leave, whereas this time we have to choose'.[21]

Klemperer's words are thought-provoking. The idea that making a choice might actually be *more* unpleasant than being ordered to leave challenges one to re-think the nature of these journeys and the travellers. Klemperer's observations also suggest one of the major interpretative problems that face the historian of refugee movements, for they imply that the status of a person as forced migrant, evacuee or refugee may well depend more on their attitude of mind and their decision-making capacity – their inner world – than on their classification by state administrative bodies. Some further observations about the nature of refugee experiences can be made here.

The origins of the word 'refugee' are Latin. The term started as a verb, *refugere*, meaning to retreat by fleeing.[22] It appears to have been re-invented between the twelfth and fourteenth centuries, creating first a noun meaning a place of shelter, then a noun meaning a person. The term was commonly applied to French Protestants who left France after the Revocation of the Edict of Nantes in 1685.[23] The exact meanings of the term, however, remained unclear. Governments themselves often made little precise distinction between refugees and emigrants. The nineteenth-century lexicographer, Louis-Nicholas Bescherelle, considered that a refugee was someone who arrived in a country: an exile was someone who left.[24] Often there was an unspoken assumption that the term could only truly be applied to a well-educated, cultured elite in exile: perhaps a last echo of the older aristocratic sense of membership to a trans-national elite, whose bonds of allegiance stretched over national frontiers.[25] Such elite concepts were challenged in the late nineteenth century as new types of refugees emerged: political fugitives like the French Communards of 1871, fleeing a bloody, politicized repression, and Jews driven out from Russia by state sponsored pogroms. In these decades, the political crises which were usually the causes of their changed situation were seen as exceptional events, to be resolved on an *ad hoc* basis. Each was particular and special, and there was little sense of the need for general legislation to govern their situation.

The later development of international laws to govern the treatment of refugees was an integral part of the legislation designed to manage and contain warfare as a whole. Throughout the eighteenth century war became increasingly limited to the fighting force itself and 'all Europe rejoiced at this development'.[26] General Trochu announced to his men in Alexandria in 1859: 'We will wage war in a manner humane and civilized'.[27] In post-enlightenment Europe, military and political authorities aimed to separate combat troops from civilians, and believed that this separation of spheres denoted civilized, humanized warfare. The citizen of nineteenth-century Europe had to be prepared for war: most

European societies introduced some form of conscription in this period. By the end of the nineteenth century, however, most citizens felt confident that the ugliness of warfare would not intrude into their homes. Modern European citizens expected to feel secure within their homes and their nations; conversely, being beyond the protection of the nation state was increasingly perceived as a dangerous position.

Legislation to control refugees' movement developed slowly. Certainly in Britain there were very limited restrictions on those foreigners seeking asylum, refuge or opportunity until the early twentieth century: the Aliens Act of 1905 limited the entry of those 'without means' but it was not until after the First World War that free entry was severely restricted.[28] As nation and home became symbolically – and actually – more important, the nation state suffered severe crises, and growing numbers of people were expelled from their countries and their homes. The flight of Belgian refugees signalled the beginning of the First World War in western Europe and the subsequent collapse of the German, Russian, Austro–Hungarian and Ottoman empires resulted in forced evacuations, fleeing populations and widespread homelessness in central and eastern Europe.[29] After the First World War, the post-war peace treaties and the League of Nations should have enshrined the principles of a world order based upon the internationally recognized nation state but – leaving aside the question of European empires – the re-drawing of national boundaries and the escalation of post-war conflicts such as the Russian civil war ensured the continuation of refugee crises. Those holding the 'Nansen passports' issued by the League of Nations were living testaments to the potential weakness of the nation state.[30] As a direct result of the First World War and its aftermath, modern forms of international voluntary relief work became established, and refugees came to be seen as a permanent 'special category' and so a subject of international responsibility.[31] Following the Second World War, relief work was professionalized, and new, permanent organisations to take of refugees were established.

Public opinion and state policy vacillated. Many felt a spontaneous sympathy for those in distress, while others feared the presence of strangers in the nation. Tragic contradictions abounded: in the 1930s, the French government was willing to accept those it considered were genuine political refugees, but not Jews fleeing the racist policies of the Nazi state.[32] As the modern figure of the refugee began to take shape within international law and European political cultures, some clear tendencies emerged. One senses a type of special relationship, a particular form of tension between the refugee and the nation state. Reviewing the recent decline in the international acceptance of refugees, Julie Peteet makes a pertinent observation: 'In its very usage, "refugee" once called for international action'.[33] In such cases, supra-national forces were required to compensate for the deficiencies in the policies and actions of incompetent nations. E. V. Daniel and John C. Knudsen capture the awkward nature of this moment when they observe that 'from its inception, the experience of a refugee puts trust on trial'.[34] Betrayal is often evoked as an integral element of the refugee's condition: refugees had been betrayed by their own nation states, to which others could retort that, on the contrary, it was the refugees who had betrayed their nations.[35] Furthermore, there exists a second layer of trust between the refugee and the new host community: can these people be trusted? Will they be good citizens?

Surveying the history of twentieth-century refugees, one can see three principal modes of interpretation.

a. Suspicion

The most loudly voiced attitude considered refugees as objects of suspicion. As a general rule, they arrive at the wrong time: moments of international crisis are more likely to stimulate xenophobia than solidarity among the makers of public opinion. The accumulated weight of patriotic schooling and nationalist history-making made many believe that each people should stay in their own nation state: under these circumstances, how could one accept the long-term presence of a large and potentially politically disruptive population within one's borders?

b. Compassion

Those initially attempting to defend refugees were usually humanitarian agencies within the host country. They tended to argue that the refugees were defenceless, innocent victims. Often, their case centred on images of mothers and children, terrified by processes beyond their control. Such impulses are often effective in mobilizing aid for needy refugees, and in moments when many were suffering real hardship, such charitable endeavours should be applauded, not scorned. There are, however, clear limitations in the 'compassionate' case: it tends to deny the political issues which formed the refugees' experience and – above all – ignores refugees' real abilities to run their own lives and even their own countries.

c. Admiration

This is the least frequently voiced attitude to refugees. Yet it is one which is sometimes prominent in refugee writing itself, and therefore worth noting as a distinct mode of interpretation. Here, the refugee is hero rather than villain or victim. The active courage of refugees, sometimes even their fighting qualities, are praised: often, when writing of women, their resilience in the face of hardship is celebrated.

Looking at these three modes of interpretation, it is noticeable that only one has stimulated influential legal definitions of refugees. The first – suspicion – works to deny any specific status to refugee people. According to this perspective, refugees (however defined) are merely rogues, subversives and opponents of the nation state; they deserve no more special status than tramps, thieves or other outlaws within the host nation. Such thinking merges refugees into a host of other imaginary enemies, and therefore does not stimulate articulate discussion. Curiously, the last attitude – admiration – also dissolves into a paradox. It celebrates refugees' achievements, but whoever heard of a 'successful refugee'? Can one imagine such a label being applied to the Pilgrim Fathers or the Bolsheviks? Yet the experience of both groups included episodes of refugee living and, significantly, it is also noticeable that the great world religions give prominent place to flight and exile. Adam and Eve were flung from Paradise and had to make their way in a hostile world. Judaism and Christianity both include reference to the exile of the Jews in Egypt as a formative experience in the development of two religions, while Islam gives similar status to the flight from Mecca to Medina. In the New Testament Christ leaves his home to wander the world and his disciples are urged to do the same. The medieval pilgrimage was based on the premise that one must forsake the familiar for unknown and sometimes dangerous places. Turning to the secular discourses of the nation state, one notices a similar prominence of travel-orientated literature, particularly in the early, formative stages of nation-building. Chaucer's *Canterbury Tales* is arguably the first text to be written in English. *Pilgrim's Progress* and *Waverley* both use travel as metaphors for the creation of a moral community. *Don Quixote*, *The Last of the Mohicans*, *Moby Dick* and *Le Tour de la France par deux enfants* – the 'little Red Book' of the Third Republic – all use the images of travel or flight as means to map their respective nations.[36] Such travel-orientated literature, however, changes its nature following the definitive establishment of the nation state, becoming dissident or alternative in nature; the dreams of Orientalists or the gentle self-parody of *Three Men in a Boat* replace more serious quests. Itinerant peoples similarly suffer a decline in status: no longer heroic pioneers, they are seen as inferior to the stable majority. Such qualities are then used to understand refugees: it is argued that their distinguishing feature is their *lack* of success, whether measured in terms of the re-creation of their homes, of their countries or their political victory. Given these points, the successful refugee is therefore normally not classified as a refugee, but is defined as something else altogether.[37]

The second mode of interpretation – compassion – has instead dominated the attempts to define and classify refugee experience by governmental and international agencies. Such definitions nearly always stress negative qualities as means by which to distinguish the refugees from the majority population; they are marked by what they lack. The experienced relief worker, Francesca Wilson, writing at the end of Second World War, spoke of 'the refugee proper, i.e. the person who by law, or in fact, has no protecting government'.[38] Jacques Vernant, an established authority on international relations and refugee legislation, noted in 1953 that 'In everyday speech a refugee is someone who has been compelled to leave his home … a helpless casualty'.[39] Finally, the often-cited words of the 1951 United Nations Convention on Refugees speak of 'a well-founded fear of persecution' as the refugee's distinguishing feature.

This mode of interpretation creates problems. Cultures founded on the nation state and the cult of the home fear the homeless, rootless and itinerant.

This fear is embedded in our language: the stranger is strange; the foreign body is dangerous and should be removed; the alien is not simply unfamiliar but unknowable. One way of making the stranger less fearful is to deny their agency, to focus on their pitiful state and to ignore the courage, endeavour and resourcefulness that have enabled them to survive in taxing circumstances. While compassion in itself is clearly a positive emotion – and refugees require both sympathy and assistance – an overly sentimentalized approach which defines refugees' lives according to these negative criteria of lack, deprivation and vulnerability risks creating two conceptual problems. First, there are thin borderlines between sympathy, pathos and repulsion. Some descriptions of refugees paint such a desperate picture that any sense of humanity is obscured: the images are often animalistic, horrific or alienating and human communication is therefore denied. Secondly, an exclusive focus upon the desperation of refugees encourages observers to marginalize the real factors which led to the development of refugees, and – therefore – creating unsuitable policies with which to aid them.

If approaches based on suspicion, compassion or admiration are inadequate as means by which to define refugees, what other paths are left for us? In this work, we have chosen to concentrate on the subjective experience of the refugee. All refugees act under the imperative of necessity: like the Klemperers after the bombing of Dresden, they normally consider that they *have* to leave; they rarely refer to any sense of choice, beyond the most basic dichotomy of staying or going. But this perception of necessity is, in itself, the result of a rational process, a decision to evaluate and to analyse the exterior world. In practice, foreign governments or international relief agencies have often taken on the role of official adjudicators of refugees' perceptions, and their judgement about the nature of the danger the refugee faces confers or denies the refugee's official status. But before such official judgements are reached, it is the refugees themselves who assess their situation. Here, the neat categories of international law are less important. What matters most is not so much the 'well-founded' nature of the fear, but the fact that a dissident group makes this judgement. In other words, a key point to consider is the one evoked in the previous citation by Klemperer, when considering his two journeys: the difference between those whose journey is ordered by external authorities, whether in the form of evacuation, expulsion or deportation, and those who decide for themselves that they *must* leave. During the course of the war, the distinction was constantly blurred by authorities, by observers, and by evacuees, deportees and refugees themselves, but it remains important, for it leads us to consider the inner world of the refugee.

This book will study three types of people: the first, and broadest, category could simply by labelled 'outcasts'. These are the people like Klemperer who find that the official government of their nation no longer represents them: their writing provides a critical perspective on authority structures, political cultures and daily life during the war years. Secondly, we will examine more closely the specific category of refugees. Thirdly, we study relief workers, who form a type of necessary partner to the refugees: the two interact, and it is from this process that the modern refugee camp is created.

Our working definition of a 'refugee' is based on the following characteristics: we study people who make rational decisions, even in the most difficult and terrifying circumstances. We study people in groups, often opposed to or separated from governments, possessing the potential to claim that they represent majority populations, if only symbolically. The most visible sign of this break is a journey from one's home, but – we will argue – this physical movement is not necessarily the most important characteristic of a refugee's life.

There is one further important point to make, relating to the scope of our research. We are studying the displaced, evacuated or fleeing peoples of the long Second World War. Over the centuries many refugees have felt compelled to leave their homes and have then formed settled and prosperous communities elsewhere: the French Huguenots who came to Britain are one obvious example, as are those English Puritans who left for America. Our concern is with refugees in a state of physical transit or emotional limbo: those who are literally seeking refuge. These states may have been temporary, but they also created enduring patterns: there were long-lasting psychological consequences for all those personally involved and there were long-term effects on political structures, welfare provisions and the idea of the nation state in Europe. Our research therefore leads us to consider questions of memory and legacy, stretching beyond the immediate experiences that occurred between 1936 and 1948.

WRITING REFUGEES

Writing and refugees seem, at first sight, to be almost opposite qualities. The act of writing implies leisure, rationality and freedom from immediate want; the lives of most refugees seem to be constrained by necessity, without easy access to the facilities needed for self-expression or analysis. Victor Serge gives a telling example: one day, while still working as a writer in Paris, he worked himself into a fury because he was unable to find a particular document in the papers on his desk; the next day, on the road: no documents, no papers, no desk.[40] The celebrated war journalist, Janine di Giovanni, even presents this contrast between the refugee and writing as the basis for her work. She was inspired by a simple imperative: 'Write about the small voices, the people who can't write about themselves'.[41] On occasion, the gap between refugees and the word can also be an expression of a voluntary retreat. John Knudsen, analysing Vietnamese refugees in the late twentieth century, notes how they would seek safety in 'silence and withdrawal'.[42] There are many significant obstacles which prevent refugees from being writers.

Yet there is substantial documentation concerning refugees' lives and a large
– if extremely varied – body of literature produced by refugees themselves. The
constraints on refugees usually mean that – in general – they are first *written
about*, and only subsequently do they pick up their pens and produce their own
images. During the first phases of their journeys, as the objects of others' observations, they tend to be depicted according to the three modes of interpretation
identified above.

There are some further interpretative issues in these outsiders' images of
refugees. Whether internal migrants within a single nation state, or trans-
national travellers who cross borders, refugees usually live outside the settled
structures of state or local administration. Aside from the obvious problems
posed by linguistic and cultural differences, there are many elements of
refugees' lives that external authorities fail to seize. It is often genuinely difficult
for outsiders understand them: thus French observers found it far easier to
characterize all Spanish republican refugees as 'rouges' rather than to attempt
to register the differences between – for example – the conservative, Catholic,
Basque Republican; the progressive, liberal Catalanist; the Socialist trade
unionist; the pro-Russian Communist; and the self-reliant anarchists. Equally,
in 1939 and 1940, British, Belgian and French authorities were suspicious of
all German and Austrian migrants within their nations. Some attempt was
made to gauge their possible degree of sympathy for the enemy after conflict
was declared, but this was done in an extremely poorly considered manner. In
each country, German-Jewish refugees were interned on the grounds that they
were likely to sympathize with the Nazi invasion. Similarly, post-1945 Allied
authorities needed time to understand the difference between Polish Displaced
Persons, Jewish Poles and Polish Jews – and, in a sense, it could be argued that
the distinctions between the three was never really appreciated. These distinctions were rarely appreciated because the observer tends to confer homogeneity
on the observed, who are often defined by criteria drawn from racial, political
or religious prejudice. This tendency towards homogenization is essentially
de-humanizing: *they* are all the same whereas *we* are highly differentiated
individuals.

A further dimension is introduced by the wartime media. When considering
refugees, what was the story? There were a number of possibilities available to
journalists: the reception of refugees could be presented as a heroic, uplifting
story of united national resolve by the host country, linking volunteers, civilians,
relief workers and generous soldiers in a single gesture of humanitarian munifi-
cence, a fitting demonstration of the maintenance of moral values in times
of crisis. Political lessons could also be drawn from the refugees' plight: was
their misfortune not the result of their feverish political passions, their lack of
foresight and unpreparedness? However, in the last analysis, the refugees were
inconvenient items for the media. The sight of the endless columns of exhausted,
filthy, hungry women, children and old men, each with their particular tale of
misery, was a diversion. The patriotic media was required to sustain the main

story: the armed forces, and their most immediate support. Press reports therefore often paid remarkably little attention to the plight of refugees, and the rare reports were often dictated by externally imposed considerations.

There are a number of forms of writing or documentation concerning refugees available to the historian. They can be classified according to the following criteria.

1. Outside Observers

As a general rule, refugees are written about in order to demonstrate some other point. In France, in May and June 1940, the numbers on the road could be taken as evidence of the collapse of the Third Republic. Similarly, when Berlin was engulfed by waves of refuges at the beginning of 1945, it was clear that the Third Reich was losing the war. In post-1945 Europe, the stubbornly high number of DPs (Displaced Persons) demonstrated the failure of the allies to create a stable post-war order. Citations in this manner usually depended on a social hierarchy or power relationship: it is the healthy who observe the sick; male leaders or journalists who watch the disorganized crowd of women; the politically successful who pass judgement on the defeated rebels.

a. Great Leaders, Generals, Diplomats

These texts form a minor sub-genre in the literature concerning refugees, which could be termed 'the refugee as seen through the windscreen of the diplomat's limousine'. For many in power during wartime, the refugees, evacuees, and even the civilian population as a whole, were simply unimportant. Civilians clogging up the roads were a distraction rather than part of the main story, and so many elite narratives largely ignore them. Refugees were in the wrong place because their presence challenged the fiction that combat troops and civilians should occupy different spheres. Such crowds appear as obstacles in the officials' path, and predictably, such writers' observations tend to be purely visual, with no effort to talk to the refugees. The descriptive scenes concerning refugees in such writing tend to be brief interruptions to the main narrative.

b. Soldiers, Officers in the Field

Such works are different from those by great leaders: if officers and soldiers in the field put pen to paper, it is not due to some assumption that they 'naturally' possessed a right to record the nature of war, but because they claimed that right. In some cases, genuinely gifted writers – such as Sartre or Georges Sadoul, a Marxist-influenced film critic – found themselves in the middle of unforeseen circumstances, and used their literary and observational talents to record their experiences.[43] In others, participants found themselves drawn to write, even despite themselves. Mariano Constante was a Communist who served in the republican armies during the Spanish Civil War: his autobiographical work begins with the supremely enigmatic phrase 'I am not a writer'.[44]

Once again, the first priority of these men is not to describe refugees, but to evaluate their military experiences. Their meetings with refugees are often unexpected, and sometimes unwelcome. Such encounters show that the division between the military and civilian spheres has not been respected: they are, in and of themselves, a demonstration that the war is going badly. Other considerations can also be in play. Soldiers can feel a sense of guilt about their own performance during military conflict and so seek to blame someone else for defeat. It was less challenging to shift the responsibility for setbacks and defeat on the helpless refugees than to undertake a rigorous examination of military policy. Such images, while resonant and interesting in their own right, are of little real use in understanding refugees' lives.

The contacts between soldiers and refugees sometimes can take a more disturbing form. Soldiers, even retreating soldiers, have power. They are always male, usually armed and have access to food and transport. Refugees in contrast lack these powers; most crucially they are often women. Horrific tales abound: on the French *exode* women reported being raped by French soldiers, others felt compelled to offer sex in return for food or transport. The mass rapes which accompanied the Red Army's advance through eastern Europe have now become infamous.[45]

On the other hand, soldiers can demonstrate more positive feelings. They can feel solidarity or compassion with these civilians who – after all – are not so different from their own wives, mothers, children and fathers. Sadoul and Gustave Folcher both clearly felt pity for the refugees they met. 'It was sad to see, and it made me feel bad. Poor people!' wrote Folcher.[46] This type of sympathetic external observer can provide valuable information concerning refugees, although even their accounts tend to begin with the assumption that refugees are victimized people 'in the wrong place', who need the advice of the more knowledgeable soldier.

c. Municipal Services and Civil Administrations
One might expect that massive movements of people, such as those discussed in this work, would be carefully monitored and directed by local authorities. On occasion, records were gathered. The Mayor of Rennes wrote to the Prefect of the Ille-et-Vilaine to explain that at the end of July 1940 the Refugee Service still had 5,103 files for refugees: fewer than the 8,000 they had in May and June, but still a considerable number.[47] Such records contain useful data concerning the movement of particular people, but they are weaker in documenting the inner world of the refugee: the displaced are registered and classified according to specific criteria, they are only rarely given the opportunity to speak for themselves.

Moreover, in practice, local administrations were often overwhelmed by the same disaster which caused the sudden population movement. Their priorities were to provide immediate aid, where possible, and perhaps even to organize their own evacuation. Documents by local authorities which record and evaluate unexpected refugee movements are therefore rarer than might be expected. There are some exceptions to this observation: for example, in January and February 1939, the French local administrations along the Pyrenees were quite separate from the wild influx of Spanish refugees, and the relevant municipal and departmental archives do provide useful observations.[48] Similarly, the epic story of the illegal immigration by post-Holocaust Jews to Palestine in 1947 and their subsequent forced return captured the imagination of many observers. In the little French Mediterranean port of Port-de-Bouc, local administrations were actively involved in recording their conditions: the subsequent documentation is a valuable resource.[49]

d. Press Reports

The words of refugees are rarely reported directly in the press, even when there was ample opportunity to do so. During January and February 1939 refugees from republican Spain made the arduous journey across the Pyrenees to seek refuge in France. *The Times* sent special correspondents to the border, who provided detailed accounts of the final section of the *retirada*. These accounts are generally sympathetic towards the refugees: they contain rich descriptions, detailed statistics, political analyses and even photographs, but they still marginalized the direct voice of the individual refugee. From 25 January until 27 February 1939, *The Times* carried daily reports about the Spanish refugees, yet on only three occasions did the journalists record the actual words of the refugees.

On the other hand, some journalists undertook lengthier and more challenging assignments. I. F. Stone's *Underground to Palestine* (1946) and Victor Gollancz, *In Darkest Germany* (1947) both began as columns for newspapers: both try hard to listen to the refugees' voices, to record them, and to represent them in a manner to gain the respect of an initially unsympathetic reader. Both are of some considerable documentary value.

Newspaper columns are useful accounts: they can document numbers and flows of people; they can record reactions by host communities and the activities of welfare workers. But, with a few notable exceptions, newspaper columns are rarely good guides for understanding the motivations of refugees themselves.

e. Novels, Wartime Memoirs

One finds similar tendencies in the great novels and memoirs of the Second World War. While Sartre's *Carnets de la drôle de guerre* contain some valuable observations concerning the experience of evacuees, in his *Chemins de la liberté* the experiences of the millions of refugees in France are squeezed out from the main story, which concerns the search for a form of political commitment during France's fall. One observes the same tendency across the various literary genres: an autobiographical memoir such as Miguel Ezquerra's *Berlín, a vida o muerte* includes dramatic passages about the apocalyptic collapse of the Nazi regime and some well-observed points concerning the deteriorating texture of daily life. But the tremendous flood of refugees coming in from east is barely registered: in some curious manner, it seems to spoil the flow of the narrative.

Once again, there are exceptions to the rule: the Breton writer Louis Guilloux remarkably produced two challenging sketches, *Salido*, concerning the escape of a Spanish refugee from French control and *O.K., Joe!*, which provides a critical, non-celebratory description of the 'liberation' of Brittany in 1944. Both break with the established grand narratives of struggle, unity and liberation: but both are mere glimpses, snapshots that briefly illuminate a shadow world.

f. Relief Agencies: UNRRA (United Nations Relief and Rehabilitation Administration) and the Red Cross

Our period is a turning-point in the history of welfare services: during these years many organisations consciously aimed to renovate their practices, transforming themselves from quasi-religious charities, dependent on the goodwill of committed volunteers, into more professional, well-planned institutions, employing trained staff. In Francesca Wilson's words, 'We have at last become planning-minded'.[50] The UNRRA was probably the most prominent model of the new practices. Part of this transition was a more rigorous approach to the registration, analysis, documentation and portrayal of the refugee experience. Some of the results are impressive. The documentary film *Seeds of Destiny* – sponsored by UNRRA – is credited with raising over $200 million for war relief programmes.[51] But in practice, the archives of these newly professionalized agencies are often disappointing. One simple reason for this is that such agencies were often run according to social-scientific and technocratic principles: they therefore monitored refugees by examining their calorific intake and incidences of tuberculosis, typhus and dysentery, rather through the documentation of their attitudes.

Documentation which addresses questions of history, experience and identity are usually produced by the less senior members of relief agencies. When reading these, one has reason to be cautious. Monnier's research, concerning the experience of refugees during official interviews in the 1990s, gives a necessary warning about the interviewees' understanding of the process. 'Is the "good asylum seeker" the one who tells the truth straightforwardly or the one who manages to lie well enough not to be detected?'.[52] A 'successful' refugee often has to be a good liar: one must therefore be sceptical of even the most apparently knowledgeable and sympathetic reports written by informed and experienced welfare workers.

More useful than the official reports of these agencies, whose priority was often to demonstrate to their paymasters that they were working efficiently and that all problems would soon be solved, are the memoirs written after the event by the relief workers. A small, steady stream of these problem-posing works have been written: these often challenge the established narratives of progress and resolution that dominated the agencies' official discourses. Some have achieved commercial publication, from Robert Collis's *Straight On* (1947), Margaret McNeill's *Rivers of Babylon* (1950), Kathryn Hulme's *The Wild Place* (1954), to Kanty Cooper's *The Uprooted* (1979). Others still linger as type-written, paperclip-bound manuscripts in archives, awaiting their publisher. Unusually, in this genre, women are relatively prominent as authors, even though they did not normally form the majority of employees in relief agencies. The classic male narrative of the 'long' Second World War centres on the battles, diplomacy and the struggle for liberation which structured the life-worlds of so many men: it downplays or underestimates issues outside these conflicts. The women's war looked different: they were often denied the opportunity to participate in active service. Relief work was therefore more likely to stimulate women's writing, for it was more likely to be central to their war experience.

There is also a narrow but rich seam of more informal writing by relief workers. Some kept journals and wrote letters, often full of the sort of detail omitted from official reports. Margaret McNeill kept scrapbooks in which she noted her daily observations and frustrations: she pasted photographs and she recorded the life stories of the DPs in her care. These sources are not compre-hensive, but they are illuminating.

There remains, however, a power relationship even in this type of work: the relief worker was in authority; she was trained, well fed, psychologically stable and – above all – she had volunteered. She could be working to a specific political agenda: to neutralize a threat, to encourage a 'return'. The refugee was under constraint, away from home, psychologically disturbed and often both mistrusting and ignorant of the external world. Such differences did not prevent communication and even friendship, but they formed a structure that inhibited any full revelation of the refugees' inner world.

2. Refugees Themselves

The paragraphs above have outlined some of the problems inherent in works by external observers. The solution now seems obvious: we must base our research on works by refugees themselves. In practice, this strategy is more difficult than it may seem. First, there are the obvious practical difficulties that refugees face in communicating. When Paul Burmetz, suddenly interned by French police in May 1940, wished to write to his wife, he had to borrow a pencil from another internee, and then push a note through the police-cell window to a co-operative passer-by.[53] But perhaps more serious still are the psychological problems that disturbed people experience in finding the words to illuminate their experiences. For many, like Jorge Semprun, the choice was literature or life.[54] Better to get on with living than attempt to consider the difficult, perturbing episodes of the past: Semprun lived by these rules from 1945 until 1962, when he felt almost compelled to write his challenging, uncomfortable text, *Le Grand Voyage*. These points suggest some serious difficulties which refugees experience when trying to transform their experiences into compre-hensible, coherent narratives.

a. The Tyranny of the Transcript: the Weakness of Oral History

For many working in these areas, oral history is the answer to the problems the historian faces. Certainly, one can find many good examples of oral history, such as Neil McMaster's *Spanish Fighters* (1990) or Scott Soo's sensitive, anthropologically informed work.[55] Here, historians have used the techniques of oral history in a sophisticated and self-critical manner to discuss issues for which orthodox forms of documentation are not available.

Alongside these works, however, there is a vein of less reliable material. One significant problem of this type of writing is that it is difficult to transform fractured, often inconclusive accounts into the clear narrative structure that readers expect. Pierre Miquel tried to surmount this problem by turning refugee narratives into a selection of short stories, all recounted in the third person.[56] This provides both coherence and engagement but it also removes the immediacy of the refugee's voice. Nélias has based his work on the French *exode* on a large collection of interviews but these interviews (collected many years after the event) seek to illuminate the author's story of the Fall of France: only rarely do the motivations of the refugees dominate.[57]

Pons Prades, Neus Català, Gabrielle Garcia, Isabelle Matas and Natasha Benjamin have all edited works concerning the Spanish republican refugees, which are principally based on transcripts of interviews.[58] The original model for such writing seems to be the earlier experience of post-Holocaust Jews. A work like *The Root and the Bough*, edited by Leo W. Schwarz in 1949, could be cited as pioneering such techniques. Schwarz's initiative must be applauded: European Jews had been condemned to silence and deceit as strategies for their survival, and in 1945 – without exaggeration – many survivors were in such physically weak condition that it was quite possible that they would not live for much longer. Schwarz's decision to record, to edit and to publish their words was an extraordinary and welcome challenge to the record of the Nazis.

Unfortunately, there is reason to doubt the real historical worth of records produced in this manner. In Schwarz's collection, it is noticeable that the contribution by the Buchenwald Kibbutz – an edited diary-form narrative – is a far more articulate, detailed and memorable contribution than many of the more spontaneous interview-based transcripts.[59] Why are the informal texts less useful? Their editors often seem to have underestimated the obvious problems suffered by disturbed survivors: are they able to find the words to express themselves? If Jorge Semprun, an experienced and talented writer, needed two decades to find the right words to tell his story, why should we assume that a chemist, an accountant, a flower-seller will be able to work the same miracle when a microphone is stuck under their noses? What could such people do when faced with 'the absence of words to describe an extreme reality'?[60] Secondly, the editors of such works have been caught in a methodological trap of their own making: by identifying their interviewees as *the* bearers of *the* endangered memory, they then treat the interviewees' words with a reverence which will permit no contradictions. If this is *the* memory, then it must also be *the* truth. In reality, people make mistakes. Memory plays tricks on everyone.[61] Such problems are exacerbated when survivors are asked to recall events that happened decades earlier. Furthermore, even the most dreadfully suffering victim of a dictatorship's crime can want to lie: they can still experience 'survivor guilt', and want to conceal elements of their past lives. For the editors of such works, these are non-questions: no doubts are permitted concerning the words of the interviewee. When such transcripts are gathered into edited collections, another feature emerges in these works, akin to that which Marx, with reference to the French peasantry, once identified as the 'sack of potatoes' scenario.[62] Each transcript stands on its own, unique and immaculate; each is an individual, integral contribution to *the* memory. The fault lines in the group usually remain unexplored: the collective tensions between radicals and moderates, women and men, religious and secular cannot really be examined in a context where each interview stands in its own right. Such records are therefore poor sources for understanding how a group identity developed, for they are merely larger or smaller collections of individual interviews.

For these reasons, while we make full use of some of the excellent oral histories which have been published, we have chosen to rely on written sources to structure and guide our analyses.

b. Immediate Correspondence to Administrations

It is often assumed that refugees are silent. In reality, there are a number of situations in which they will choose to write to local authorities, sometimes simply as part of bureaucratic procedures, sometimes on their own initiative, for more personal reasons. At first sight, such documentation looks promising for the refugee historian: here, refugees are not writing under any immediate constraint; on the contrary, they are taking the initiative to re-make their lives under difficult circumstances. Refugees will – for example – write to complain that they have not been accorded the correct allowance, or to dispute local regulations devised to order their lives. Thus Jacques Piette, a Belgian refugee in the Haute-Garonne in July 1940, wrote to the Sous-Préfet at Saint-Gaudens to challenge a local regulation forbidding journeys by refugees out of their host communes: he explained that there was no local shop, and therefore they needed to travel further in order to buy food.[63] On occasion, such notes involve a partial re-telling of the refugee's story, and therefore can give details of individual itineraries which are not available elsewhere. A second theme which frequently features in such correspondence is the separation of family members.

These sources are, however, of only limited use in interpreting the refugees' experiences. Refugees are not using them to recount their lives, but to state a specific case in a tightly defined bureaucratic context. Their lives and experiences are turned in to mere fragments to be cited to prove a case to an official. Such notes and letters can only give supplementary information. One could not imagine basing a historical analysis of these sources.

c. Immediate Correspondence to Family, Friends and Other Refugees

For obvious reasons, correspondence between refugees is less likely to be preserved in archives. However, some letters are available. Once again, they are less revealing than might be expected. 'Nadine is well' wrote Andrée to her mother in July 1940, 'Marcel has come to our house, he's looking for Guémené'.[64] In these desperate little notes, often determinedly upbeat, stuffed with enquiries about the health – even just the simple existence – of others, refugee life is reduced to a stark minimum of family, space and time. They resemble the censored and regulated letters that soldiers sent home from fighting fronts, which were principally designed to indicate that the writer was alive and to impart or elicit other limited pieces of information. They do not explore in detail the journeys they have undertaken or the causes that motivated them. Basic survival is the issue which dominates over all others.

Once again, valuable supplementary information can be gained from these letters, but they cannot form the basis for a historical enquiry.

d. Published Memoirs and Autobiographies

These are more challenging and sophisticated forms of writing. Genuine memoirs demand sustained commitment and literary talent from the refugee writers themselves, for this type of writing is often an attempt to create a bridge between two worlds. Luisa Passerini makes a memorable observation about the refugee's struggle in writing: the refugee possesses 'a memory that is a stranger to the world, which will not be able to become a house for human beings without accepting that stranger and his estrangement'.[65] It is easy to assume that telling the story must be a form of communication, and therefore therapeutic. This is not necessarily the case. Telling a story can entail the realisation that others are quite incapable of understanding it, an experience which serves only to exacerbate the writer's sense of alienation. The struggle to write is therefore difficult and even dangerous: one thinks of Semprun's injunction 'literature or life' and the tragic suicide of Primo Levi, one of the most gifted writers of the Holocaust, unable to carry the weight of his own words.

The forms of refugee memoirs vary enormously. 'El Campesino's' *Jusqu'à la mort* (1978) is principally an account of a political journey, from anarchism, through communism to arrive at socialism, as democratic parliamentary procedures were being re-established in Spain. Juan Goytisolo and Jorge Semprun both produced complex, sophisticated modernist narratives, as intricate as texts produced by Joyce or Proust.[66] Christine Morrow, an Australian post-graduate stuck in France in 1940, writes with less sophistication and polish, but her *Abominable Epoch* (1972) is a revealing and informative work. Ruth Kluger's *Landscapes of Memory* (2003) is a challenging autobiographical work, angry in places, a type of dialogue between the author, the legacy of the Holocaust and Jewish opinion.

While some of these works have achieved the fame they deserve, many have not. There are good reasons for this: often these refugee writers are inexperienced, naive and even obsessive, button-holing their readers with poorly structured, repetitive accounts. Just as refugees begin their exilic lives by deciding that they *must* travel, so, towards the end of their lives, some seem to decide that they *must* write.

Can one base historical research on the collective analysis of such works? At first sight, they seem extremely useful: these are texts which are written more freely, on the refugee's own initiative, according to their agenda. They are still constrained by the nature of the audience they address: Passerini's warning concerning the bridge-building role of such narratives must be taken seriously. These narratives also share some of the problems with the 'naive' oral history discussed above, in that they are marked by the necessary distortions and blurring of the memory process. In this context, 'a life history is not a story of a life but rather a conscious, or even unconscious, strategy for self-representation, a legitimation of moves and counter-moves and of projections for the future'.[67] But – we argue – when treated critically rather than reverentially, these apparent errors can be read as *part of* the refugee's life-world, rather than as merely faulty data.

e. *Testimonio*: the Refugee-Writer as Collective Autobiographer

The classic Western autobiography is 'the story of my success', reflecting the new sense of self that was celebrated in Western culture in the seventeenth century: it can be seen as an example of the ego document. Its basic plot is how the author, through their exceptional gifts, beat off adversity to achieve a well-deserved triumph. In recent years, such plot lines have been twisted into the misery memoir, which celebrates survival rather than success, but which is still structured in a similar manner.

The refugee texts that we have examined tend to follow a different structure, which John Beverly has identified as the *testimonio*.[68] Here, the writer writes not to celebrate their individual success, but the experience of a group. The 'we' recorded by Carpeña in the first section is an example of this. This form of writing does not preclude political bickering, score-settling, exaggeration and just plain inaccuracy, but it does mean that the refugee narratives are open to a different form of reading than classic Western autobiographies.

We have chosen to place refugee narratives at the centre of this work. They cannot provide us with all the needed information, so we have used them to set the agenda, to provide the basic conceptual building blocks on which this work is based. We have supplemented them with the other forms of information detailed above, principally the official and administrative correspondence of refugees, and the after-the-event accounts by relief workers. At first sight, this seems almost an obvious decision. Yet, curiously, our work seems to be the first based on such sources. Why is this?

HISTORIANS AND REFUGEES

We are analysing the long Second World War, from 1936 to 1948, an era dominated by military conflict, when there was no clear dividing line between military and political leaders, and when military sources – variously defined – seem to provide most straightforward entry point to the historical past, through detailed and moving accounts of battles and campaigns. Of course, such histories do not necessarily exclude the human stories of civilians en route. Antony Beevor's *Berlin: The Downfall* has received much acclaim precisely because it includes engaging and accessible human stories. Beevor also writes about refugees, and does so with much obvious sympathy. He criticizes the authorities for failing to care adequately for refugees and points out that Bormann, the Reichsleiter of the National Socialist Party, did not even bother to mention refugees in his diary.[69] Beevor does not dismiss the refugee experience, but he does attribute emotions to the refugees he observes. Describing the convoys of refugees from the east at the beginning of 1945, Beevor comments that 'most gave the impression of exhausted aimlessness'.[70] Yet many refugees were – quite sensibly – fleeing from the Red Army, or searching for family or for sanctuary. We can reasonably conclude that they were exhausted, but we do not know that they were aimless. Finally, one notes that Beevor's narrative ends in May 1945: the book is based on the assumption that the important events stopped at that date. We, however, are interested in precisely the issues which grew in importance after that date.

The history of refugees has also been presented as an aspect of the history of social policy.[71] Certainly in terms of primary documents, the papers of local social services or of welfare agencies provide one of the most obvious starting points: those who cared for refugees in wartime were often drawn from the same agencies that had cared for the vulnerable and excluded in peacetime. The Council of the League of Nations appointed Fridtjof Nansen as High Commissioner for Refugees in 1921: from this point on refugees had a specific legal status and the international community had a duty of care. In Wyman's words, during the twentieth century the international community began to develop 'co-ordinated systems of protection for those forced to flee their homelands'.[72] These systems of protection have been the subject of some recent academic scrutiny. A useful pioneering collection of studies, edited by Jessica Reinisch, were published in 2008 the *Journal of Contemporary History*, concerning the organization of relief in the aftermath of the Second World War.[73] These papers concentrated on developments in systems of welfare, and debated the development of 'planning-mindedness' during the war. With the field of social policy-orientated studies, there have been some more original studies. For example, the work by Gousseff, published in 2008, focused specifically on Russian refugees in the 1920s, and produced a more challenging model, stressing the collaboration between international institutions and refugees. The work argued that this was the point when the refugee ceased to be an independent actor and was placed more firmly under the guardianship of a state or of international organisations.[74] Gousseff's work reveals some of the weaknesses of the social policy-orientated studies: they inevitably focus on policy, regulation and restriction. The autonomous motivations of the individual refugee can easily become marginalized.

One can also cite specific case studies in which historians stress agency and individual autonomy. Writing about Jewish DPs living in the US zone of Germany after the war, Zeev Mankovitz emphasizes the way in which the Central Committee of the Liberated Jews in Germany actively sought to ensure the welfare of Jewish DPs. These are not passive subjects, but survivors motivated by a powerful desire to begin life anew.[75] In a similar vein, Atina Grossmann argues that the Jewish baby boom in DP camps was an affirmation of both life and femininity after the ordeals of war, holocaust and displacement.[76] Our aim is to follow these more original studies, and to highlight these qualities of agency and autonomy in a wider context.

THE GREAT JOURNEY: TRANSFORMATIVE MOVEMENT AND THE SECOND WORLD WAR

Many histories of this period have taken great battles as the landmarks around which one orientates research. Dunkirk, Stalingrad and El Alamein have become household names. This work is structured around the great journeys undertaken by large sections of the population of Europe and other linked countries. It starts with refugees leaving Spain in 1936; it ends with Palestinian Arabs fleeing Israeli forces in 1948. These twelve years witnessed some of the most arduous mass movements in history: each in turn seems to require new superlatives to describe them. We are asking: what if one chose to substitute great journeys for great battles?

The journeys we study are less well known. The first occurred during the Spanish Civil War (1936–39) when about a million refugees left Spain, the largest wave being the *retirada* of about half a million in January and February 1939. Fears of a large-scale European war provoked further population movements: in Britain about three and a half million people were evacuated from the south-east and from urban areas between June and September;[77] between September 1939 and April 1940 about three million people were evacuated from the north-east of France. In response to the German invasion in May 1940 about 10 to 12 million people moved from the Netherlands, Belgium, Holland and the north and the east of France to the south and the west of France. As the war expanded, so did refugee movements. In late 1941 the Soviet Union evacuated 16 to 17 million citizens eastwards; four years later there was a massive move westwards as about 10 million people returned to the newly redefined German territory after the war. The end of the fighting did not signal the end of vast population movements. The collapse of the British Empire resulted in the partition of India and the creation of Pakistan: at least 15 million people left their homes as a result. Journeys from Europe also had a direct impact on the wider world. About half a million post-Holocaust Jews travelled from Europe to Palestine/Israel, and in consequence almost a million Palestinians fled from their homeland, forming the *nakba* of 1948.

One must make some obvious qualifications to the details listed above. First, all the figures are mere 'guesstimates': one cannot be certain of the exact numbers involved in any of these movements, although the basic point that they were enormous is accepted by all authorities. Secondly, it could be argued that most significant figure might be the relative proportion of the population involved: on this basis, the Palestinian *nakba* might be counted as the most important of all these movements, for it represents approximately three-quarters of the Palestinian Arab population. Thirdly, one can question the extent to which these are compatible movements. For all its errors and tragedies, the evacuation of children from London in 1939, dutifully chanting 'Are we down-hearted? – NO!' is simply not of the same order as the starving, freezing republicans in the Spanish *retirada*.[78] Evacuees started their journeys in a different fashion from refugees, but then often came to look like refugees, and certainly experienced many of the same deprivations.

There were clear legal and practical distinctions between different types of outcast, whether refugee, evacuee, displaced person or asylum seeker. At the start of our research, we debated why – in practice – the people involved in each of these categories have become so easily confused. Why has each discrete term been so often used as a synonym for one of the others? As already stated, part of the answer lies in the indiscriminating, homogenizing gaze of the observer: outsiders always look the same. Yet there is something more important that links these disparate and distinct outcasts: they all take transformative journeys, which might better be compared to precedents such as the pilgrimage, the migration, and the diaspora rather than seen as mere side-effects of great battles.

There are three key characteristics to the transformative journey.

First, one cannot return as the same person. The difficulty of return is a crucial component of the refugee experience; every refugee is irrevocably changed by the experience, whether they eventually find refuge or not.

A second crucial aspect of the journey is the story. In the *Canterbury Tales* the pilgrims tell one another stories on the route – and the importance of telling one's own story is emphasized right at the beginning. Our understanding of mid-twentieth-century refugees is that they share something important with these medieval pilgrims. They recreate themselves through their journeys and they often wish to tell their tales.

Third, these transformative journeys changed the societies through which the refugees travel. The *retirada* established that there were – at least – two deeply rooted camps in Spanish society. The journeys of post-Holocaust Jews changed the state system of modern Europe.

Given the importance we attribute to refugee stories, it is pertinent to ask why we have not analysed all nine examples listed above. We can make two points in reply: first, we have chosen to concentrate on those travellers who most resemble refugees as defined in the second section: those who demonstrate decision-making capacities. Secondly, more mundanely, an analysis of all nine journeys would be a massive undertaking that would exceed the remit of this present volume. We have instead studied a select number of refugee journeys in detail: Spanish republican refugees in France in 1939, French people fleeing German invasion in 1940, Polish Displaced Persons, and post-Holocaust Jews seeking to travel to Palestine-Israel in 1945–48. For the sake of comparison, we also consider the French evacuees of 1939–40. Throughout these case studies we stress the interplay between refugee and relief worker.

The first part of our work concerns refugee peoples in France, as this country had the sad privilege of being the chosen destination of many anti-fascist refugees in the 1920s and 1930s, the site of two substantial refugee movements (the *retirada* of 1939 and the *exode* of 1940), as well as harbouring a range of charitable and welfare organisations. The second part concerns relief workers after 1945, largely in Germany, and examines the interplay between displaced persons and relief agencies. Throughout the work, we explore the 'inner world' of outcast people, following their journeys from their homes, through desperate conditions, to their difficult struggles to recreate homes.

PART ONE

The Midnight of the Century

Destruction threatens everywhere. But I increasingly feel that it is five to twelve. Only – shall we live to see twelve o'clock?

Victor Klemperer, Diary Entry, November 1940

Victor Serge used the term 'the midnight of the century' to evoke the sense of hopelessness felt by many in 1940. The moral authority of communism had collapsed, destroyed by the practices of Stalinism; the political power of the western democracies had been defeated by the rise of Nazism. This part of our book studies a series of defeats: the collapse of the Spanish Republic, the bungled attempts by the French government to anticipate the realities of twentieth-century warfare, and the desperation of successive waves of refugees seeking havens in an increasingly hostile world. We will study in particular the dichotomy between the authorities' plans, apparently coherent and confident, and the improvised strategies devised by refugees, apparently shaped by panic and fear, but often suggesting more perceptive understandings of the dilemmas and threats they faced than the pronouncements of the authorities.

1

The Retirada: Spanish Republican Refugees, 1939

- The Refugees' War
- Images of France
- Organizing the Retirada
- The French Reception: Watching the War
- The French Reception: Organizing Welfare
- The French Reception: The Spanish Experience
- The French Reception: Controlling the Flood
- Conclusion

The conflict that erupted in Spain in 1936 created successive waves of displaced peoples, first within Spain itself, then flowing out into Europe, before finally dispersing across the world. This chapter will concentrate on the mass flight of republican refugees from Catalonia in January and February 1939. It does not present a general survey of Spanish refugees, nor a history of the Civil War. It will first consider the formative experience of the Spanish republicans, before turning to evaluate their journey over the Pyrenees. The contrasting attitudes of Spanish refugees and French authorities will be analysed, and the chapter will end by considering the legacy and lessons of this episode.

THE REFUGEES' WAR

As the conflict progressed, mass flights and evacuations grew more frequent: approximately half a million people left the southern regions of Andalusia and Extramadura as Franco's forces advanced in 1936. Some settled in Madrid but, above all, they went to Barcelona. By 1939, there may have been a million refugees in the Catalan city.[1] A second wave of refugees fled when republican forces in the north were defeated in the summer of 1937: many made a difficult journey from south-western to south-eastern France in sealed trains which took them to Spanish republican territory. In 1937 the Republic organised care for refugee children: some were evacuated abroad, and by December 1937 it had created 560 centres for some 50,000 evacuated children within Spain.[2] The greatest of these refugee movements set out in January and February 1939, when the city of Barcelona fell to Francoist forces: half a million refugees sought shelter in France. By that time, some of them were already experienced refugees. Solano Polacio, travelling out of Barcelona in January 1939, briefly sat next to an

Asturian girl. She had been evacuated first to Aragon, then Barcelona, and was now heading northwards for France.[3]

The nature of the conflict in Spain was debated across Europe. Was this 'a civil war, an anti-fascist struggle or a social revolution' asked commentators?[4] Each political tendency could see its symbols and struggles in the Spanish conflict. Welsh nationalists, for example, were uncertain about which side to support: their regionalist sensibilities demanded that they support minority nationalisms such as those represented by Basque nationalism and Catalanism, but there were many Catholics among the Welsh nationalists, and such religious sympathies drew some towards Franco's nationalism.[5] Soviet diplomats swiftly became sceptical of the various international non-intervention agreements, and agreed that they had to intervene in the war: but were their actions to take the form of a diplomatic initiative or a revolutionary strategy?[6] French anarchists were initially delighted by the political prominence of the Confederación Nacional de Trabajo (CNT), the Spanish anarcho-syndicalists who controlled Catalonia in the summer and autumn of 1936, but then felt growing doubts as they saw their brother militants compromise, again and again, with an increasingly less radical Republican government. Should they voice their criticisms?[7] Even groups who were experienced in refugee welfare work, such as the Quakers, found that issues were not clear-cut. Given that refugees could be found on both sides of the conflict, should all be helped? Was it possible to distinguish the 'natural poverty' of rural Spain from the specific poverty of the conflict's refugees? American-based and British-based Quaker groups arrived at different answers and adopted divergent policies as they organized relief units in Spain.[8]

In Spain itself, forcible mergers created two wartime coalitions. Their awkward, forced nature was obvious: traditionalist Carlists had been forcibly merged with futuristic Falangists, Communist representatives of High Stalinism were allied to anarchists and bourgeois liberals, regionalist cultures conflicted with the urge to centralize on both sides ... But, finally, two camps were created, which could be termed 'Francoists' and 'Republicans'. The war was a struggle without mercy. For Francoists, it was not so much a war as an exercise in punishment, with the aim of annihilating the anti-Spain.[9] The units commanded by Franco took the military repression of Arab nationalists in Morocco in the 1910s and 1920s as their model. Their advance through Andalusia set the pattern. Here, 'they conducted rapid, direct and simple attacks, based on blind obedience, thoughtless towards the dangers they faced and those they presented to others, implemented with the most absolute cruelty'. The town of Amendralejo, in Badajoz, with a population of 15,000, was taken without resistance in August 1936: the invading force still chose to shoot 56 of the townspeople.[10] This brutal strategy compensated for the political deficiencies of the Francoist camp: unable to articulate convincing political arguments to persuade their opponents to join them, they chose to use 'the spectacle of terror and death as the unique means by which their message was transmitted'.[11] In March 1939, when some in the Republican government wished to negotiate for peace and a planned evacuation, Franco consistently demanded nothing less than unconditional surrender.

With hindsight, the progress of the war in 1937 and 1938 appears obvious: the neat black lines on the maps trace, almost month by month, the shrinking of Republican territory. For contemporaries, the course of the conflict was not so obvious. Temporarily evacuated to France in June 1938, the Communist Mario Constante still believed in 'the Republic and the final victory'. The 12,000 soldiers of his unit were offered the chance to leave for Francoist Spain: only a couple of hundred accepted. Not until later in 1938 was his 'naive confidence' challenged.[12] Prior to December 1938, recalled the experienced CNT militant Abel Paz, 'no one thought of defeat'. Then there were two terrible months of combat, marked by disasters, anxiety, hunger, constant bad news and 'always thinking that each day was our last'.[13] A series of heroic defences and re-organizations of the Republican army failed to transform the war. While the two armies were approximately equal in size – about a million soldiers each – the nationalist forces were better equipped, better trained, more generously aided by foreign powers and capable of fighting with greater ferocity.

Early in 1939, Republicans had to consider their future. This was an awkward, difficult moment. Some still hoped for further aid from the Soviet Union, or that the western democracies would finally intervene. Many remained uncertain about the nature of the Francoist advances: was it inevitable that they continue? Might they be slowed? Others, on the other hand, learned to read between the lines of the still-optimistic press reports.[14] Above all, 'we knew what would happen to us if we stayed', explained Pépita Carpeña.[15]

IMAGES OF FRANCE

Spanish Republicans admired France. Had it not been the first place of refuge for the long series of Spanish exiles which began in 1813, if not before? When in 1926 the fiery Catalanist radical, Macià, called for creation of two clandestine armies to fight the Spanish dictator, Primo de Rivera, had he not been based in the French Pyrenees?[16] Following the failed miners' revolt in Asturias in October 1934, Federico Gargello Edo saw new refugees from Spain arrive in his immigrants' quarter in Bordeaux. This was no surprise to him: France was 'the haven' for the uprooted of the world, for those living in dictatorships, whether Russian, Italian or Spanish.[17] Aside from political militants and persecuted refugees, many migrant workers had also taken this well-trodden path: there were 106,000 Spanish immigrants in France in 1911, 350,000 in 1931.[18] In the early 1930s, after the Second Republic was created in Spain, and as economic depression ended many businesses in France, the number of Spanish migrants in France declined: there were only 250,000 in 1936, before the conflict began. They were never the largest group of emigrants: in 1931, there were more Italian and Poles in France than Spaniards. But, nonetheless, economic migration to France had been a relatively common experience for Spaniards prior to 1936: many could reasonably consider that they knew the other country well.

The images of France that Spanish refugees cite in their memoirs form a coherent collection of positive stereotypes. 'El Campesino' could recall the crowds in Madrid spontaneously bursting into the La Marseillaise when they learned the results of the April 1931 municipal elections: they knew the Republic had arrived in Spain.[19] For the Catalan exile Moral, the red, white and blue tricolour was the flag 'of asylum, a guarantee of safety'.[20] Palencia, the wife of a Republican diplomat, recorded that France was 'the land of freedom, where years ago the triumph of a great revolution had spread the principles of Liberty, Equality and Fraternity'.[21] When Filomena Folch, a CNT member, walked with her daughter across the Pyrenean border into France in January 1939, she said to herself 'At last! We are free!'.[22] When she saw the first French village in January 1939, the Catalan peasant Dolores Torres thought to herself 'France is life'.[23] Arriving in France in 1948, Vicente Marti was thrilled to attend a 14 July festival, and was moved to tears when he heard the crowd singing the Marseillaise.[24] Isabelle Alonso, the child of two exiled Spaniards who grew up in France in the 1950s, could recall her mother's respect for France. 'France was the Republic, the rights of man, generosity: these high ideals were enshrined in law, they were everything that she had been taught to respect, and they floated in the air of this land, a model of revolution and joie de vivre'. Later, migrants came to doubt these myths, but there was always one clear limit to their scepticism: 'don't mock the school!'.[25] Such attitudes were probably reinforced during Franco's dictatorship, when dissident and oppositional groups in Spain looked to French contacts for inspiration and support.[26]

Almost without exception, Spanish Republicans imagined a faultless France as the embodiment of the ideals for which they fought. Even after July 1936, when they felt abandoned by the French Popular Front government's policy of non-intervention, they still respected and admired France as the source of their values.[27] In records relating to the years prior to 1939, it is hard to find signif-icant disagreement about such ideals. Almost alone, the anarcho-syndicalist historian Abel Paz records a discussion in a CNT centre in Barcelona in January 1939, in which one participant warned his comrades not to expect hospitality from the French: 'our exile will be tough, very tough'.[28] Such views were excep-tional. Idealization of and admiration for French political ideals are the norm in Spanish refugees' memoirs, transcending all the political and regional currents.

Such pronouncements lead to another question: if France represented the ideal of liberty, then what did the Spanish refugees stand for?

Here, the Spanish memoirs are less explicit. While there were strong political tensions in 1939, there were few debates about specific topics: correspondingly, refugee memoirs are an odd mixture of intense political idealism and discon-certing vagueness about practical policies. At the centre of their beliefs was the Republic. Torres recalled that 'for us, the Republic was something sacred, almost like a saint'.[29] But it is less clear what it represented. A type of answer emerges in some of the descriptions and evaluations of refugees. Looking at the crowd of Republican refugees leaving Barcelona on 22 January 1939, Capdevila thought of the loss that these people's flight represented for Spain: 'the most skilled workers, the most celebrated artists, the greatest idealists, the wisest intellectuals, the most prestigious scholars and all that was best and healthiest in the Spanish people were abandoning the land'.[30] Llorens gives a textbook-perfect illustration of the same thesis: he cites a Spanish poetry anthology, published in 1932, featuring the 17 best poets of that year. What was the fate of those 17 in the next years? One died suddenly after 1932, two died in the fighting that followed 1936, four stayed in Francoist Spain after 1939, one – Antonio Machado – died shortly after crossing the border into France in 1939 and, in 1949, nine of them lived in exile.[31] Given this evidence, who could doubt that poetry *was* republican? The refugees' loyalty to the Republic was something greater than a loyalty to a specific political regime, and still more than fidelity to a particular party: instead, it was a respect for values such as education and culture, qualities which were understood as ideals in and of themselves.[32]

We can learn more about this ideal Republic by contrasting republican and Francoist attitudes. 'Franco did not see any need for intellectuals', comments Jordi Gracia: correspondingly the best-known names of Spanish culture tended to support the Republic.[33] The savagely repressive military tribunals that tried to wipe out all traces of republican political culture in post-1939 Catalonia were driven by 'a phobia against intellectuals', argues Conxita Mir.[34] This contrast reveals an aspect of the self-image of Republican exiles, and also suggests how they maintained a type of consistent identity despite the shattered condition of their political institutions. They represented the finest parts of Spain, its 'best elements' according to Carpeña.[35] The anarchist leader Federica Montseny struck a surprisingly nationalistic note when discussing this point: in the exiles' memoirs could be heard 'the immortal spirit of a race which has enriched the world, discovered a continent, defeated the barbarians and lit the light of liberty during the Dark Ages'.[36] Fernando Pradal, an exile who became a researcher in France, expressed a similar pride in his fellow exiles: in the 41 years he had lived in France 'I have never seen a worker be so fascinated by books on physics, chemistry or history as were the Spaniards of [1939]. They were extraordinary people'.[37]

Refugees could also draw some political lessons from their experiences after 1936 that aided them in the creation of a collective self-image. Held in a miserable French concentration camp in 1939, the Communist Constante immediately turned to developing a clandestine organization, in order to 'maintain the dignity of the fighters of the Spanish Republic'.[38] Stuck in an increasingly repressive work environment in France, early in 1940, Delso reflected that 'Since my birth I have never been just a victim: I rebelled against all that, I fought to get my rights, for me, for my fair share, for my part of the sky'.[39] Carpeña had similar thoughts: 'having lived through this unique revolutionary experience, it was going to be difficult for us to accept being beaten'.[40] Such pronouncements are not the equivalent of a political programme, but they do suggest an important attitude: these people retained a pride in their political achievements. In libertarian collectives, regionalist institutions, Communist military units or republican schools, their political ideals had informed and structured their lives. Clearly there were dangers inherent in these memories: they could stimulate a sectarian bitterness, and their loyalty to one organization could blind them to wider issues and concerns. But there was also a great strength: they knew how to fight, and they had even won victories.

ORGANIZING THE RETIRADA

At midday on 22 January 1939, Andrés Capdevila sat down to eat lunch with his *compañera*, Antonia. It was a clear, cold day: weather that favoured the invading Francoists. The radio was on. The music ended, and a loud, strong voice called on all anti-fascists to throw themselves into the defence of the Catalan land. Outside, the air-raid sirens started again: they could hear the sound of more bombing. For most of their meal they were silent, commenting now and again on the bombs. Then, as they finished, Antonia asked 'What do you think we should do, Andrés?'.[41]

Across Catalonia, families, groups of refugees, units of soldiers and branches of political organisations were asking themselves the same question. Their memoirs record partial aspects of their preparations: Polacio looked for a pistol, Paz wanted to discuss evacuation, Carpeña wanted a truck.[42] Each was haunted by the same fear. They had lived through years of social disruption in which many established links between people had collapsed. This final crisis presented a still more serious threat of division and separation. 'During 1939,' recalled the anarchist militant Vicente Marti, 'my family burst apart. My mother disappeared, my father was in prison, my sister and my brother stayed with my grand-mother'.[43] Palencia notes that in January 1939 she and her daughter lived in Sweden, her son and her son-in-law were serving as doctors in the Republican Army and her husband was in Barcelona.[44] As Polacio was writing his account, a thought suddenly occurred to him: 'Where are my comrades now, as I write these lines in a cell in an old prison in Redon?'.[45] Carpeña only packed a small case when she left, so as not to frighten her parents: they would think she was only leaving for one of her usual journeys.[46] Would the fall of the Republic also mean the end of their friendships, families and groups?

In practice, departure usually meant the creation of new, improvised groups. One would never normally cite the anarchist ex-Minister, Federica Montseny, as typical, but in January 1939 she acted like many others, travelling over the Pyrenees in an improvised, quasi-familial group of her two sons, her mother, the mother of her *compañero* and her adopted brother.[47] Torres's departure meant her separation from her mother, but she took her children with her, they represented 'the future and hope'.[48] Capdevila warned his little group: 'we're living through some extremely dangerous, difficult moments: if we get separated from each other, it will be difficult to go back to find one other'.[49] Groups formed in these moments could become truly tight-knit units of solidarity. Montseny's comments on this point are perceptive. 'The groups, created from multiple links – ideas, interests, characters and regional identities – constituted solidly formed groups of people which would energetically refuse all attempts at separation'.[50] To some extent, this group-forming experience was gendered: young men, in particular, tended to cross the Pyrenees in their military units; older men tended travel with political organizations. In some cases, one finds analogous experiences among women in political groups such as Mujeres Libres, but for most women the *retirada* was an exercise in the improvisation of solidarity. Their writing demonstrates this contrast: men are more likely to stress the continuities, from revolution, through war, then *retirada*, to exile. Women are more likely to record the *retirada* as rupture, even as a new beginning. Certainly, there is noticeable tendency for the episode to feature more fully in women's accounts.

Refugees' memoirs tend to skip over their hurried, anxious meetings in January 1939, and jump to the conclusions, which are often presented as stark life-or-death decisions. 'Now the struggle took a new turn,' remembered the Mujeres Libres militant Sara Berenguer, 'It was about saving your life'.[51] Capdevila discussed matters at the CNT offices, and then reported back to his *compañera* and her mother: 'Staying would be an act of great madness: it would mean humiliation, torture and death'.[52] They packed their suitcases immediately. They then faced some extremely difficult decisions. Moral, retreating with his unit, noted a common refugees' dilemma as they considered their equipment: 'It was unthinkable to abandon this material. It was impossible to carry it'.[53]

Before leaving, many political militants destroyed the documentation recording their activities over the previous three years. Paz eloquently captures the tragedy of this moment. On 21 January his CNT group met.

> We burnt our minutes and the circulars of the organisation in our *ateneo* [meeting-room or centre]. Everyone who contributed to this act of destruction realized that living history was being turned into dust; it could never be reconstructed … It was a sad sight, the liquidation of the records of the past in an improvised frenzy, a bit like saying goodbye to life.[54]

The rushed meeting, the difficult decision and the tough journey were all part of the larger process of the defeat of republican authority but – paradoxically – also part of the preservation of republican legitimacy, embodied in the physical presence of the refugees themselves. Torres recalls staying overnight in a school in one village near the Pyrenees, but not talking to any of the villagers: 'Things were clear: those who were not leaving were for the enemy'.[55] When they started, many were still unclear of their objectives and the true sense of their journey. 'What will be the end of our odyssey?' wondered Capdevila.[56]

Political groupings made one last, unwelcome, contribution to the process: even in the last weeks of the Republic, there was still a hard-fought contest for power. In Madrid, in March 1939, this took the form of Casado's coup d'état, which ended Negrin's rule and the associated Communist domination of governmental authority. In Catalonia, in January and February 1939, there was no equivalent to Casado's coup, but there was bitter enmity between organizations. Paz recalls how he would only go out into Barcelona's streets with a loaded pistol, in case he ran into patrols by the new Communist-controlled police force, and needed to answer their questions with shots.[57] Moral recalled how vulnerable he felt as his military unit crossed the Pyrenees: nearly all the officers were Castillan and 'centralist'; he was the only Catalan officer. He spoke darkly about the mysterious, unexplained deaths of three Catalans in his unit.[58] Polacio was sitting in the back of a truck, three kilometres from Figueras, at 1.30 in the morning, when they were stopped by a lieutenant who shouted 'This truck can go no further!' Polacio commented bitterly that this man was 'one of those Negrinist heroes who gained their stripes in a cooperative or on a committee. They got so used to giving orders that, though far from the front line, they believed that they were heroes'.[59] Later, just three kilometres away from the border, Polacio noticed how the Assault Guards from Barcelona, a republican para-military police force, held brand new sub-machine guns, while the militiamen from the front had only old, heavy rifles.[60] The more unified images of republican idealism, evoked above, are an important, common form of self-image *after the event*, when exiles had to re-assess why they refused to 'return' to Franco's Spain. During January and February 1939, the refugees were still far from political consensus.

Few refugees had time to consider these questions: they all faced more immediate, more pressing problems. How were they to travel? Palencia makes the following generalization: a few travelled in cars, many in horse-drawn carts, but most walked.[61] In fact, their journeys were often more complex. Many record starting their journey in motorized vehicles, whether cars or trucks. At 5 a.m. on 25 January, Carpeña waited for a car: by 9.am it had not appeared, and she was growing worried. A phone call made matters clearer: the driver had fallen into a panic, and already left the city. He was persuaded to return, and so she was saved.[62] Paz's little group waited at the CNT Ateneo in the Clot suburb of Barcelona on 25 January: he was with his mother, his brothers, his *compañera* and her two brothers. It was cold, it was raining, they had not eaten and they had no bread. No vehicle arrived. They looked at the road, and prepared to walk. Then, at the last moment, a comrade arrived in a truck that he had seized at gunpoint.[63] Capdevila began travelling in a car, but after reaching Llansá he had to walk to the frontier.[64] Polacio felt bitter when he saw Comorera, a leading member of the PSUC, drive out of Barcelona in his own car: Polacio himself left the city in a crowded, uncomfortable van.[65] Delso simply records that she travelled by truck to La Junquera, and then walked to Le Perthus.[66] Some were less lucky: Filomena Folch recalls walking from Barcelona to Prats-de-Mollo with her daughter.[67] Consuelo Grande and her group walked from Campradón to Prats-de-Mollo: she commented 'Those who were unable to walk couldn't get away, they were trapped'.[68]

What should they take with them? The refugees' choices about what to carry reveal much about what they expected from the journey. When Arturo Barea crossed into France in January 1938, he and his partner carried three suitcases and a typewriter.[69] Paz records people taking just the clothes they needed and perhaps some valuables which could be sold in an emergency to get money.[70] Moral found that a choice had been made for him: he had left all his documents, notebooks, clothes and photos back at the barracks. They were all burnt.[71] But these basic attempts to preserve a sense of family and identity, and to anticipate employment in France, were frustrated by the nature of the journey. In an echo of Klemperer's declining autonomy in Nazi Germany, the refugees lost many precious objects as they travelled, often just dropping things 'from sheer weariness as they marched forward'.[72] As Torres's group reached the Pyrenees, they realized that they would not be able to take their little cart any further. They sorted out the things that were most vital to them – food and blankets – and put them on their mule. Torres decided to keep part of her trousseau, and to carry this herself. Later on, she realized that she had not the strength to do this, and had to abandon even these sheets. 'I left behind lots of things, and my eyes filled with tears as I did so … But what could you do? There was no other way'. Later she regretted that she had kept none of the little things that made up her daily life.[73] Maria Seco Mateo carried a case full of embroidery thread: as she walked up a track through the Pyrenees, her hands grew colder and colder, and eventually she had to let the case fall. She cried, and her tears froze on her cheeks.[74] Moral's unit were forced to surrender to the inevitable, and to burn their equipment as they ascended the mountain paths.[75] Consuelo Grande tells a similar story of dispossession: her group quickly dumped their suitcases. Then, as she climbed ever higher, she lost her sister, her case and her shoes.[76]

This was a tough journey. The remaining political organizations and aid agencies were simply overwhelmed by the numbers on the road, and so the travellers had to make their own arrangements. The quiet little town of Gerona suddenly became the nerve centre of the evacuation of 'a mad torrent of human beings' which streamed through it, heading northwards for the border. Many slept on the streets, while Capdevila and his little group were lucky enough to be able to sleep on the floor of a trade union office. All the shops and cafés were closed, as they had nothing left to sell.[77] Delso spent the night in a cinema in Gerona, but found it was impossible to sleep, as there was so much noise from people coming and going all night.[78] One bar in the town 'was full of people from evacuated towns, most of whom spent the night inside its walls: in the corners there were mountains of cases, mattresses and packages of all sizes;

on the wooden benches lay men, women and children who slept despite the constant noise: nothing could wake them'.[79]

External conditions made the journey still harder. It was cold and wet. Paz's group were wedged together on the back of a truck; the rain poured over them and chilled them to their bones. As he remembers it, no one had anything to eat.[80] Those who walked to the Pyrenees soon reached the snowline. Even the air itself seemed threatening: Capdevila was haunted by the sound of enemy aircraft as he travelled.[81] Many record aerial attacks; Delso passed through La Junquera immediately after it had been bombed, and saw the terrible massacre of people in that town.[82] Such conditions led to deep fears. Montseny notes that 'the terror of the fugitives, when they saw that they could not pass [over the frontier] and Francoist planes were flying over their heads, was something indescribable'.[83]

Despite these horrific conditions, the march continued. It became clear that this was not an exceptional decision by a few dedicated political idealists, but the collective experience of a mass of people. How did they record it? One common comment was that the episode was indescribable. Delso's words can be cited as typical of this attitude. 'It is impossible to describe this disaster, this human tidal wave, all those people, walking, in carts, on mules, in vans, painfully moving along the highway. These are unforgettable images, truly worthy of depiction by Goya, in whose pictures the sublime, the absurd, the grotesque and the pitiful are mixed'.[84] Unforgettable but indescribable: once these limits have been set, writing about the *retirada* almost seems like a contradiction in itself. Others reached for psychological metaphors to describe the journey. The episode was 'like a bad dream' from which they could not awake.[85] Montseny portrayed people as reduced to an almost animal-like condition. 'Nothing could be as terrible as this collective panic, like a bestial terror which crushes all human communities who, in such moments, are left without the ability to reason, the ability to consider, [a terror which] prevents all forms of order and caution'.[86] The thought that Franco's forces were advancing as they travelled led to a still greater sense of urgency. As they walked, and their journey grew harder, the refugees became pessimistic.[87]

Other participants and observers make more nuanced comments, often choosing to focus on a single sight or event as a means to represent the whole process. Outside Gerona, Polacio watched the snow fall 'on thousands of people, each carrying bundles of clothes over their shoulders, walking slowly along the road: the men carrying cases on their backs, the women each with bundles over their shoulders, the children with their packages, and the smallest holding hands with their exhausted mothers'.[88] Paz is more discriminating in his observations than Montseny: while noting the element of panic, he does not see it as characterizing the whole episode. 'The refugees were overwhelmed. Panic was general, but despite everything, they did not lose sight of their objective which – for many people – was to get out of this hell'. Certainly there was chaos, 'but there were no hysterical scenes'. Everyone was aware that 'our lives hung on a thread'.[89]

Among the travellers, many were simply too exhausted to argue or debate. Watching the line of civilian refugees pass through Puigcerdá, Constante was struck by their silence.[90] At times, however, arguments could flare up. In Polacio's truck there was a disagreement about which way to go. Among the people wedged in at the back, there was an armed Assault Guard. He drew out his machine gun, unlocked the safety-catch, pointed the gun at the driver, and demanded that the truck stop. The walking refugees on both sides of the road saw this happen: one tall, muscular man stopped, flung open his arms, and cried ' "Shoot me, and end our sufferings" … That tall figure, in the midst of the little world of misery, moral ruin, pain and suffering, seemed like some picture from the Bible'.[91]

Other aspects of the journey have been recorded. One point to remember is that these people were trying to find a route out of Spain: sometimes they simply followed the person in front, but often they had to make decisions. Polacio felt lost almost immediately: he had never travelled northwards from this part of Barcelona.[92] Capdevila preferred to walk at night, as this offered some protection against aerial attack.[93] Delso chose to walk across fields and hills, and to avoid the main roads, for similar reasons.[94] Mariano Puente and his wife tried to find a route over the Pyrenees: it was impossible to cross. They then spoke to a shepherd, who recommended a track to them that led to Port Vendres.[95] When considering the common images of 'chaos and panic', it should be remembered that these journeys usually took at least several days, and required both physical strength and some form of organizational capacity: to characterize the refugees as 'in a panic' for such a long period seems unconvincing.

Furthermore, within these stories of grim, difficult travelling, there are moments of relief, suggesting the maintenance of a type of republican ethic, even under these most difficult circumstances. Paz observed able-bodied men and women getting off trucks, in order to give their places to children, the wounded and the old.[96] Soldiers shared their rations with starving refugees.[97] Refugees talked to each other, attempting to gather news of recent events and therefore to plan the next step of their journeys.[98] Just before Figueras, Polacio walked into a group camped out in an abandoned tile factory. He greeted them with a confident 'Salud, comrades!' and was promptly served a dish of rice with sugar.[99] Torres records 'we got ourselves organized, we helped one another'.[100] And lastly, if these journeys were frequently marked by separation and loss, occasionally there were also reunions. Andrés Capdevila was separated from Antonia in Gerona: she went on ahead in an ambulance, and he wondered if he would ever see her again. Three days later he found her in Figueras. 'We ran to each other, we hugged each other with passion … Our hearts beat together, while our eyes filled with tears, such was our emotion'.[101]

They kept going, because they thought they would find more than just refuge in France: they believed they would be welcomed in the land of the Revolution.

THE FRENCH RECEPTION: WATCHING THE WAR

According to Pierre Laborie, for French people the conflict was not an 'exterior' event. 'French people lived and fought out their problems via images of republicans and Francoists. The Spanish mirror turned them into spectators of their own differences'.[102] The most important means of information was the press. We will first consider the reports of *La Dépêche*, a prominent daily paper, edited from Toulouse and linked to both the governing Radical Party and the Minister of the Interior, Albert Sarraut. As a paper with established contacts with Spain, this should have been a source of reliable information. We will then contrast this with the Brittany-based *Ouest-Eclair*, which one would have expected to be less well informed. Lastly, we review a broad spectrum of papers.

La Dépêche often sounded strangely optimistic about the Spanish Republicans' chances. On 2 January 1939 it announced the 'heroic resistance' of the republicans and 'remarkable calm' of the Catalan countryside. The Francoist offensive was losing force, reported the *La Dépêche* on 5 January. Better still: a new republican offensive in the south, in Extramadura, was gaining ground, while Spanish 'public opinion is more and more certain that the Italian-Francoist enterprise will be halted'.[103] Reports from 10 January 1939 sounded a different note: it was impossible to deny that the Francoists had launched a heavy offensive in Catalonia. But on 11 January, *La Dépêche*'s readers were once again reassured: Franco had to withdraw soldiers from Catalonia in order to fight the republican offensive in Extramadura. A French governmental delegation to Barcelona, led by François de Tessan, reported back in the *La Dépêche* on 13 January: they had found 'complete harmony' and 'internal order' in Catalonia, plus preparations for a 'heroic resistance'. Those who were sceptical when they arrived, now saluted 'the moral greatness and unshakeable spirit of the Spanish people'. Above all, after a week in Barcelona, they had hardly seen a single representative of the far left.

The subsequent reports developed the theme of the congruity of the Catalan authorities and French traditions. On 14 January, *La Dépêche* reported that, just like the French government in 1792, the Catalan authorities had proclaimed 'la patrie en danger': the fatherland was threatened. 'Patriotic enthusiasm in Catalonia will once and for all push out the so-called "red" ideologies. In Barcelona, national feeling is rising, supported by Catalan and Basque Catholics, who hold prayer meetings across the whole of Catalonia'. Aimé Berthot, a Senator, applauded these developments: Bolshevik influences had been swept out of the government; the International Brigades had been dismissed, and the Spanish Army was now composed of 'free patriots fighting for the independence of their land'.[104] Even on 17 January, *La Dépêche* announced that 'a wave of heroism has swept over Barcelona, in response to the appeals by President Negrin … Despite the exhaustion of 30 months of war, Barcelona seems to want to show that she will become a new Madrid'. On 19 January, Franco's advances into Catalonia were slowing; on 20 January, Franco was still far from victory, as he faced solid defensive lines; and on 21 January – according to the *La Dépêche* – the tide of resistance was growing in Barcelona, as women shouted in demonstrations 'Men to the front, women to the factories!'. Even on 25 January, *La Dépêche* reported the suggestion that General Miaja, who had organized the successful defence of Madrid in November 1936, would be appointed for the same task in Barcelona.

Ouest-Eclair was considerably more sceptical about the defenders' capacity, noting on 17 January the material superiority of the attackers, who possessed some 800 aircraft. It first mentioned 'the exodus of civilians' on 14 January, and reported whole families travelling by car to France on 19 January.

Was there no scepticism about the Catalan defence in *La Dépêche*? On 19 January, a short article did report that a few Spanish people had crossed the frontier, but assured readers that their numbers were falling, from 35 on 17 January to a mere 17 on 18 January. By 23 January, an article acknowledged that 'Barcelona, unfortunately, is threatened', and on 24 January *La Dépêche* reported long lines of carts, north of Barcelona. By 26 January, a reporter acknowledged that Barcelona's fate would be decided in the next 24 hours. (*Ouest-Eclair* had published a similar article three days earlier.) There was clear regret concerning Franco's success. 'Barcelona, for all our region, is like a well-loved sister'. But also, very quickly, the reporter turned to consider the issue of refugees. Here, the article leapt into capitals. 'THERE IS A HUMANITARIAN DUTY WHICH MUST BE FULFILLED, BUT WHICH IS NOT FOR FRANCE ALONE TO ACCOMPLISH'. What could be done for 150,000 refugees? 'Remember the difficulties caused by the expulsion of Jews from Germany and Italy', the reporter reminded *La Dépêche*'s readers.

On 27 January, the headlines were sombre: 'Barcelona taken without fighting'.

> Barcelona has fallen … Fallen like a ripe fruit, with no serious attempt at resistance…
>
> We remember the successive crises that have occurred in this city, the internal struggles which have devoured it, in which members of the POUM opposed communists and anarchists; [we remember] how it was impossible to constitute a strong government, to get *discipline* respected. Republican Spain has died because of this: the impossibility of founding *real, total, strong discipline*, as we feared in August 1936, and as can be verified by consulting our editions from those months.
>
> If Madrid held, it was because of its discipline. Barcelona never accepted this.

The inaccuracies of *La Dépêche* are strange: this was a prestigious French regional paper, with well-established cross-border links to Spain and some knowledge of and real sympathy for the Catalan people. Yet, at many moments the Brittany-based *Ouest-Eclair* seemed to be publishing more accurate articles than the Toulouse-based *La Dépêche*. The articles give us some insight into mainstream public opinion within France. The constant underestimation of the threat posed by the Francoist offensive, and overestimation of Catalonia's defensive capacity, which seems to have been almost general across France, constitute one explanation for the lack of preparation for the arrival of the refugees.

The sympathy for the Catalans, however, must be heavily qualified. First, in order to be portrayed in a sympathetic light, Catalans had to be shown to *be like* the French. Secondly, even as early as 27 January, one could see other interpretations emerging: weren't the Catalans to be blamed for their defeat? Hadn't they deserved it, for not being sufficiently like the French? These arguments would grow more bitter and more pronounced in the following weeks. Optimism about the Catalans' defensive capacity then came to be mocked as a left-wing illusion; French right-wing commentators could now stress their down-to-earth realism. The right-wing *Journal des Débats* noted: 'Although one could have foreseen the events a month ago, no one wanted to predict the collapse of the red front. You'd think that, until yesterday, we all half-believed the fantastic reports with which [the Communist] *l'Humanité* and [the Socialist] *Le Populaire* tricked the naive and the simple-minded'.[105] The far-right *Gringoire* criticized Léon Blum, the Socialist leader, for his lack of realism: 'In mid-January, our ever-so-clever Blum, demonstrating once again his astonishing ability to see the future, announced the definitive victory of the Catalan reds. You could guess what happened next: Franco's staff swaggered down the ramblas of Barcelona'.[106]

The arrival of the refugees was therefore a shock for French public opinion, which had been led to believe that there was no urgent problem.

THE FRENCH RECEPTION: ORGANIZING WELFARE

Little French Pyrenean villages like Bourg-Madame, Prats-de-Molo and Le Perthus usually only received one type of visitor in the months of January and February: rich people, coming for winter skiing breaks. These villages were unprepared for the flood of people who crossed to find refuge. The French authorities had made no attempt to prepare reception facilities, or even to alert local authorities of the possible dangers. Rather than considering how to receive refugees, from September 1937, the Ministry of the Interior had initiated measures to expel Spanish refugees from France. A secret circular asked prefects to invite all able-bodied, young male Spaniards to leave within a week, and then to take them to the frontier if they refused.[107] A later note from the same Ministry acknowledged the protests that the first circular had provoked, and introduced some qualifications. The previous circular was not intended as a break with 'our land's traditions of generous hospitality'.[108] If families or private associations wished to take care of refugees, then prefects should cooperate with them. A further circular from June 1938 explained that able-bodied male refugees could only stay if they possessed (or were given) sufficient resources to allow them to stay without engaging in paid work. Furthermore, they must 'of course, be the subjects of excellent reports in every respect, and they must not engage in any suspect activity'.[109] These reactions prefigure reactions after

February 1939: alongside an avowed willingness to help refugees, one finds a strong drive to push them out of France.

French public opinion was confused about the conflict in Spain. The first concern by many observing the debate was simply their surprise that France had become 'a land deeply divided against itself', in Georges Bernanos's words.[110] The right stressed the stories of republican atrocities, and soon came to support Franco. A confused centre supported the principle of non-intervention, and was most clearly expressed by the formation of a committee for Civil and Religious Peace in 1937.[111] A number of apparently apolitical humanitarian organizations offered help to refugees. On the left, there had been important differences between those who saw the conflict as an anti-fascist struggle, and those who believed it was a social revolution. However, by 1938 observers sympathetic to the Republican cause normally stressed the orderly and well-policed nature of the Republican sector.[112]

French attitudes concerning the first Spanish refugees are difficult to judge, and probably fluctuated rapidly. In general, left-wing papers were sympathetic to the plight of refugees and highlighted their humanitarian needs, recalling French republican traditions of France as a land of asylum for those in flight from repression.[113] On the other hand, right-wing newspapers were more sceptical or even openly hostile to these hordes of leftist revolutionaries. Alongside this political opposition, a third factor was also important: the fear of an oncoming war. Barea's observations on this point are pertinent: in 1938 French people 'began to look askance at foreigners who embodied an uncomfortable warning and the threat of political complications'.[114] The presence of refugees reminded French people of complex, difficult, destructive struggles taking place beyond their borders: many preferred to ignore them.

The key point here is that an opportunity to prepare communities and organizations for a severe test was wasted: official hostility, xenophobic mistrust on the right, and facile optimism on the left combined to create a humanitarian disaster.

The mass exodus of Spanish republicans made the headlines in all the French press in the last week of January 1939. At first sight the refugees seemed astonishing, heart-breaking and troubling. It took a few days for French press to realize the gravity of the situation, but by the end of January 'an army of reporters, photographers and radio journalists' were present in the mountain villages.[115] Soon all the local hotels were full.

The first reports suggest an immediate awareness of the refugees' suffering, and also their determination. Thus the Communist *L'Humanité* reported from Le Perthus:

Under a heavy, rain-filled sky a human torrent unrolled from La Junquera, the last Spanish village before the border. Thousands upon thousands of poor creatures, shelled in their towns, machine-gunned on the roads, without bread or shelter, left their native land. To escape the invaders' ferocity, these poor people have walked, through bitter winds and storms, for days and night ... Their bodies are broken and their feet are bleeding; hunger, exhaustion, pain have left deep lines in their mournful faces ... But they would rather suffer than face the rough justice which devastates Spain and massacres its peoples![116]

The centrist daily *l'Oeuvre* published a comparable description.

On the road which leads to Le Perthus, a real army is entering France: a pitiful army of the lame, the stragglers and the sick, in which civilians and soldiers are mixed in one fraternal mob ... They are starving, and these poor people literally throw themselves on the food that the French bring them ... Then, in the middle of incredible piles of luggage of all sorts, they camp with their children, wrapping them in blankets to protect them from the cold.[117]

Except a few correspondents from far-right papers, almost all journalists expressed immediate sympathy for the refugees. *L'Humanité* ran a headline 'refuge for these unlucky victims', accompanied by three large pictures of wounded soldiers, an exhausted woman and starving children at the border.[118] *Ouest-Eclair* noted the suffering of those who managed to cross the Pyrenees with only espadrilles on their feet.[119] *The Times* reported the following tragic dialogue between a Spanish woman and a French customs officer: 'A forlorn woman is carrying a bundle. "Let me carry that" says a customs officer, who recoils when he finds it is a dead baby. "Do not take him from me", pleads the woman, "I cannot leave him behind"'.[120] Such articles noted the dreadful experiences of Spanish refugees, insisting on simple, physical points such as their exhaustion, starvation and ragged clothes. They stress the experience of women and children, and terms such as 'les malheureux', 'les innocentes victimes' or les 'pauvres gens' were frequently used to describe them.

Alongside the widespread, spontaneous sympathy for the wretched refugees, press reports also quickly suggested other lines of interpretation. As early as 19 January, *Ouest-Eclair* was reporting the arrival of fugitives and deserters from republican Spain: people about whom one should feel suspicious, rather than victims worthy of sympathy. Its later reports highlighted the irrationality of the refugees.

The entire crowd of Spaniards who were gathered next to our border and who yesterday were still hesitating to cross, literally threw itself at France during the night ... Mothers cried when they lost their children in the hold-ups during this unbelievable, sudden flight, which seems to have surprised even the most knowledgeable of observers ... [They formed] the most incredible jumble: women with bare feet, old people, wounded people on crutches, the haggard sick, their clothes in rags, barely protecting themselves from the cold with tattered blankets from their miserable homes ... [This crowd] are not even able to explain the reasons for their mad flight.[121]

In the same article, *Ouest-Eclair's* Roulleau notes the contrast between the mad crowd and the Senegalese soldiers at the border. 'Standing upright under their trench helmets, the lines of Senegalese infantry, normally strict in their observation of any order, show themselves to be almost friendly to the crowd'. The soldiers, however, implemented the French policy of turning back young men. (The border was not opened to militiamen and soldiers until 5 February).

Roulleau's words are clearly influenced by ideas of crowd psychology: he sees the refugees as an irrational mass, throwing itself at the French border; he finds the heterogeneity of the crowd unsettling, even unwelcome. Because they seem so different, so strange, there is no identification with them or sympathy for them. They do not represent a cause, but some mysterious, subterranean movement, and so there seems little question of according them any type of formal political status. With the implied contrast between the disorderly Spanish crowd and the orderly ranks of French soldiers, we glimpse the beginnings of another argument, to which we will return below.

These first attempts to represent the refugees' movements are based on a strong sense of hierarchy: wretched, worrying Spaniards enter a superior French civilization. The pre-eminence of France is demonstrated in a variety of forms. First, observers noted the relief that refugees felt when they arrived. *Ouest-Eclair* described the 'swarming shadows … marching towards French peace. "Francia! Francia!" cried the mothers and children, like Columbus's sailors spying the American coast when they had thought that they were completely lost. "Saved! We are saved!" they whisper again, as if they were waking from the most dreadful of nightmares'.[122] At the end of January, journalists from *The Times* were driving from Le Perthus to Cerbère. A group of refugees hailed the car, and one of the reporters recorded the following dialogue: "'Where are we?" they asked. "In France," we answered. "Thank God," they exclaimed'.[123] These simple images of rescue and relief shaped a deeper argument, summed up in the headline in *L'Intransigent* on 30 January: 'France: Land of Asylum'. Here, France is praised in an almost abstract manner, as a nation which is of itself a haven: a point which even the wretched Spanish appreciate. By the simple act of crossing the border, they have entered into a different and superior civilization.

Yet the idea of France as a sanctuary had to be made more concrete. Receiving refugees did not mean just allowing their physical presence in France. In order to be meaningful, the haven had to provide some real aid. But providing drink, bread, shelter and other forms of immediate aid on the scale required implied a massive mobilization of agencies and services. The French press celebrated the many initiatives by charitable and municipal groups for the Spanish refugees. *L'Oeuvre* reported that 50 lorries were constantly occupied in transporting refugees to the thermal station in Boulou, where they were given bread, showers and shelter.[124] At Cerbère, the station café was feeding everyone who arrived.[125] French soldiers walked along the endless lines of chilled, exhausted women and children, distributing hot coffee.[126] Little children were vaccinated on their arrival.[127] Children were sent to La Tour-de-Carol in trucks, each with a young woman to look after them. 'They hold hands. They are clean … Many of them hold ragged dolls in their arms'. The reporter from *La Dépêche* saw 710 children eating at La Tour, 'under the paternal eye of the supervisors'.[128] When almost 1400 refugees arrived by train in Nantes, 'Nurses and nuns rushed into the wagons to comfort the mothers, many of whom burst into tears. Charities distributed warm clothes to the children and cigarettes to the militiamen … It was strange: these children, these militiamen who, a few hours ago, had been raising their fists, now took their hats off to the priests'.[129] The *Croix* informed its readers about the material assistance and welfare provided by the Le Comité National Catholique de Secours aux Réfugiés d'Espagne.[130] The Ligue Féminine d'Action Catholique Française asked readers to think of the 'poor little ones, who are not responsible for the conflict'. It was the duty of charitable people to care for them, to feed them, to clothe them.[131] According to *La Dépêche* there were many other similar initiatives: 'All the French people of the border have truly shown that French hospitality is not a vain phrase and that all unfortunate people, whoever they are, will always find relief in our land'.[132] The explicit concentration on the 'innocent' children and women in these articles is significant: the conflict in Spain was wrong, because it had destroyed the lives of these blameless victims; French charity could right these wrongs.

The success of these charitable efforts seemed obvious to newspaper reporters. 'Today, the refugees look calmer. They are still physically suffering, but they no longer have that worried, tense look that they had when they crossed the border'.[133] Once women and children had spent one night under a French roof, there was a 'real transformation in their faces'; they re-found their taste for life.[134] These endeavours attracted official praise. When Albert Sarraut, the Minister of Interior, and Marc Rucart, the Minister of Public Health, toured the border, they noted 'how the local authorities had met the challenge, and how they had coped with these unprecedented difficulties'.[135] Sarraut commented 'What a task! …Everything has been anticipated and, thanks to everyone's efforts, I am certain that everything will go well'.[136] By 7 February *La Dépêche* reported on its front page that France had acted with 'that admirable generosity which elevates the French soul, so noble, so understanding'; France had fulfilled 'the humanitarian duties of all civilized peoples'. On the same day, the editorial in *Ouest-Eclair* struck a similar note. 'This is not only a wonderful example of humanitarian feeling, but also a striking proof of the orderly spirit, the sangfroid, the alertness and the intelligence of our compatriots'.

Such sentiments were not confined to the columns of the press. Local administrations also understood their actions in the same manner. In March 1939 a police official in the Pyrénées-Orientales writing a review for the Prefect on the reception of the refugees concluded:

> I wish to second the well-merited praise that has been given to all those social services under your direction during those memorable days when, inspired by our land's legendary reputation for hospitality, by the border population's need for security, by

a sense of duty and by a heart-felt generosity, all the units of the border police and all those present in reception centres and concentration camps worked ceaselessly, in close collaboration, supervised by the prefectoral administration.[137]

These reports do suggest a creditable sympathy for an exhausted and battered refugee people: the idea that there is an instinctive xenophobia which will always be awoken by the presence of refugees is certainly challenged by them. However, there are clearly some important limits to this discourse. First, one notes the deep suspicions felt by some journalists: these doubts would grow stronger. Secondly, there is the curiously silent presence of the refugees. They are *seen* by the reporters; very rarely is their voice *heard*. In these descriptions, the refugees are reduced to their physical existence: they are bodies to be fed, watered, housed, managed and then moved on. Thirdly, many of these reports appear to be trying to prove two points at once: that the refugees merit aid, but also that France is to be praised for providing such assistance. As events would show, these two points were not always compatible.

THE FRENCH RECEPTION: THE SPANISH EXPERIENCE

Spanish refugees had a quite different impression of their reception from that proclaimed in the French press: 'The France that was waiting for them was not the one that they had believed in' notes Palencia.[138]

Almost unanimously, the refugees speak of the inefficiency and even the cruelty with which the French authorities treated them. Andrés Capdevila was held for three days in the railway tunnel leading to the border at Cerbère, while the French government re-considered its refusal to allow able-bodied men to enter. He remembered this as a time of 'physical and moral martyrdom'.[139] Constante crossed the border with his military unit at Bourg-Madame. Their arms were confiscated, even though Constante told the border guards that they wished to be returned to Madrid. They were starving, but there was nothing for them to eat, and no medical services for the sick or wounded. The Red Cross was not present, and they had to protest to get a Red Cross unit to arrive.[140] After crossing the border, Moral recalls living in the woods near Tech: it was cold, the ground was wet, it rained and all they had to eat was the sheep and goats they had brought with them. After two days, a lorry arrived with bread.[141] At Le Perthus, Delso was met by a line of policemen, looking at them impassively. 'I asked myself if they had souls or consciences'.[142] There were no medical services. They were taken by truck to Le Boulou, where some women had organized a canteen for the refugees but by the time that Delso arrived, nothing was left for them. One refugee began to shout 'Food! Food!': these were the first French words Delso learned. Torres remembers the hostility of the Senegalese soldiers at Prats-de-Mollo. She was then sent to a Red Cross canteen, where she was given bread and chocolate, with boiling coffee. She seems to be a rare example of a Spanish refugee who recalls the French relief agencies working effectively.[143] Jokin Gálvez Preito was 15 in 1939. He crossed the border with his father, and was sent to a 'type of camp' at Le Boulou. They slept out in the open: each night, children died of cold.[144] Francisco Bardes Font was separated from his wife when they crossed into Cerbère. He was transported to Argèles concentration camp: it was five days before he was given any food.[145] Consuelo Grande was helped by her friends to get to Prats-de-Mollo, where they were taken to a school, guarded by Senegalese guards. There, she was given hot coffee that made her feel sick, but then went without food for five days. When a bread ration finally arrived, its distribution was filmed.[146] David Grande crossed at La Tour-de-Carol. 'Everything was taken from us by the police: lorries, guns, horses, sheep, and after that you couldn't touch a thing ... The cold was terrible, it was like Siberia, and we had nothing to protect us but straw'. Each night there were suicides among the refugees.[147] Rather than being welcomed by benevolent, caring charitable agencies, Spanish refugees recall being bullied by policemen or guards, 'shouting like maniacs' according to Capdevila.[148] Carpeña laughed bitterly at her own naivety: she had thought that she would be safe in the land of the Revolution of 1789. Instead, she was being treated as if she was a delinquent: while in hospital, she was not allowed to talk to the other French people. When the refugees were led through the streets to the concentration camps, people shut their doors and windows. 'Following our odyssey, we suffered a long agony'.[149] Even the much praised charitable services could be experienced in a different manner by the Spaniards. Concha González de Boix arrived in Cerbère. One of her legs had been injured during a bombing raid in Barcelona, but she could find no one to take care of her in France. Instead, they were ordered onto a train that took them to Limoges. Once they had arrived at the refuge, they were ordered to undress, and 'without considering our ages, ignoring our modesty', they were forced into showers.[150] Rather than benevolence, the refugees remember indifference and hostility. 'People stared at us as if we were from another planet', noted Carpeña.[151] Montseny made the same point, and went on to say that the refugees had been met with 'the proverbial French contempt for foreigners'.[152]

Once they had rested and eaten, many refugees felt bitter. Capdevila was angry about the 'sadism' of the authorities.[153] Constante was amazed when he was taken to the 'camp' at Septfonds. Having been pushed through a line of barbed wire by Senegalese soldiers, he found that nothing was prepared. 'Not a building, not a tree: just bare earth. All we had to protect us from the cold were our tents and blankets. As for the toilets: a ditch'.[154] When Carpeña was taken from a train at Clermont-Ferrand into a hangar near the station, and saw 900 women and children huddling together in the bitter cold, she cried 'tears of rage and powerlessness'.[155] Palencia points out the absurdity within the French policies. 'On the one hand, they complained of the burden on France of the enormous cost entailed; on the other hand, they often arbitrarily refused to let people go from the camps'.[156]

The difference between French claims and Spanish experiences is clear and stark. In many cases, French observers confused working hard with working efficiently. The multiple and varied charitable initiatives are certainly impressive examples of a will to help, but they cannot hide the reality that many Spanish refugees never received the assistance they needed. Where French observers took pride in the generosity of their nation, Spanish refugees experienced indifference, hostility and cruelty. French observers usually only registered the physical conditions of the refugees; they failed to consider their psychology or their recent experiences, let alone their hopes of France. The journalists' reluctance to engage in dialogue with the refugees reduced them to wretched and pitiful others; they overlooked the crucial fact that the refugees were the ones who could best explain their motivations, their political ideas and their aspirations. Moreover, the concentration on the 'innocent victims' then led to an unfortunate dichotomy in the assessments of the Spanish experience.

THE FRENCH RECEPTION: CONTROLLING THE FLOOD

From the arrival of the first refugees, the French authorities attempted to introduce some form of screening. Before 5 February 1939, they aimed to screen the refugees. The Minister of the Interior explained: 'We will accept the women and children; we will care for the wounded and the sick; we will send back the able-bodied men, without exception, without making any special allowance for their position or their wealth. This is clear'.[157] This screening was an important aspect of the French relief programme, and quickly seemed to develop into something other than the simple separation of men and women. Reporters used a moralistic language, distinguishing between the good refugees – victims, worthy of pity – from the sinister, threatening figure of the bad refugee. According to the *Gringoire*: 'Next to the exhausted and the wounded, there are the violators of cemeteries; arm-in-arm with pregnant women, sadist stabbers, and following clear-eyed children, the most dreadful rogues, the cruellest torturers, the most cowardly politicians'.[158] Such dramatic language did not circulate throughout all the press, but the idea of making a strict distinction between good and bad refugees was clearly popular. 'They have to be screened,' noted *La Dépêche* 'We accept that we must become an asylum, at our expense. But we will not become a home for agitators to our cost'.[159] The *Journal des Débats* thought that France should expel the criminals:

> Some good souls will think that I am heartless. But my sympathy goes first to our over-worked *gardes mobiles*, carrying out some extremely demanding police work. I sympathise with the suffering civilians … But, as for these international criminals who, under a revolutionary regime, sprout like mushrooms on a rotten trunk, I only wish to sweep them out of our land.[160]

Some reporters took as much pride in the well-disciplined actions of the police as in the humanitarian initiatives. If the Spanish republic had fallen because of indiscipline, this display of discipline was a symbol of enduring French power.

> The evacuation methods are properly in place: they function with a fine rhythm and a satisfactory discipline.
>
> Surveillance, identification, the verification of the accommodation, the disarmament of the wounded militiamen, the strict refusal of able-bodied men, the transport of deserters seeking their repatriation via Hendaye to Franco's armies: these are fine-tuned parts working effectively, structured around three administrative principles: feeding, lodging and hospitalisation.[161]

Suspicions multiplied. As early as 28 January, *La Dépêche* signalled that able-bodied men were hiding within the lines of exhausted women, and then slipping over the border. 'Have [the guards] really … disarmed all these people? Some of them look quite threatening.'[162] The idea that these people might represent some valid political cause was quite simply denied. In Catalonia 'these is no more authority, and the worst indiscipline reigns everywhere. Catalonia has become a vast region in which countless crowds act without orders.'[163] The last soldiers to arrive were a sorry sight. 'They no longer have any unity, cohesion, discipline or chiefs … They are gunners without cannon … The whole day, this mixed, stinking, sordid and miserable stream flows down the hills … into generous France.'[164] In Prats-de-Mollo, reported *La Dépêche*,

> After the pitiful crowd of refugees, a militarized scum crossed the frontier. Real bandits in uniform … No matter how noble the regime's ideals, it dishonours itself by employing such soldiers, such sinister thugs. The crowd of terrified refugees tremble before their arrogance and brutality … Prats cannot, will not live under the threat of a mutiny by these madmen.[165]

After all, this was not even a proper army. 'The lower officers were recruited among the best Marxist speakers or from influential members of international organisations … this, in part, explains their defeat.'[166] For Léon Daudet, the exodus was an 'invasion of barbarians'.[167] In such scenes, the actions of the French soldiers, 'channelling this human flood' were once again stressed and validated.[168]

Reporters were disturbed by the refugees' attitudes. Their simple failure to show proper gratitude was resented. 'Among these refugees whom we accepted with such magnanimity, there are some who do not show the politeness that we expect of them.'[169] The *Journal des Débats* reported: 'People cite some of them … making completely uncalled-for remarks. We do not ask them for compliments, but we do request, simply and clearly, that they should not forget that they are in our land: we did not ask them to come here, and we will not stop them from leaving'.[170] Once again, this was not a theme that was specific to the far right: the image of the ungrateful refugee circulated widely, usually with the suggestion that therefore all these people did not deserve French compassion; there was something suspicious or fraudulent about them; they brought with them a threat. Jean Vidal reported arrogant looks in reception centres: refugees demanded cigarettes, and when a meal was served, it was met with 'cries of refusal: "if we have to eat that, then it wasn't worth leaving Spain".[171] 'The refugees' attitude is not always as polite as might be expected: sometimes one hears bitter complaints when one could have expected some gratitude'.[172] 'Some of the Spanish emigrants, above all the men, have no sense of discipline. They complain of the food they are given, and they refuse to help with the potato harvest, saying that it is beneath their military status'.[173] Refugee attitudes could also denote immorality as well as ingratitude: 'There are good-looking Spanish women … who do their make-up while our generous soldiers are occupied with their children'.[174] These women were not good mothers, a serious condemnation in pro-natalist France.

Worse than the failure to show appropriate gratitude were the signs of outright protest from the refugees. Some refugees did demonstrate about their treatment. For example, Filomena Folch initially walked to Prats-de-Mollo, and was then led to a camp at Arras-en-Lavedan. There she had to sleep in a stable and the children cried endlessly for three weeks. Finally, she and some other women protested by singing the *Internationale* together. 'What a reaction! Two days later, they organized a convoy to take us back to Spain'.[175] Legitimate protest was interpreted as rank insubordination, even as an outright threat. Reports indicate that the French were clearly fearful of these supposedly wretched refugees.[176] 'Already, in fact, one can observe not just some protests in the reception centres, but – let us speak the truth – a few isolated acts of indiscipline or political propaganda which, in the current circumstances, we cannot tolerate for any reason'.[177] After all, such disobedience could have sinister motives. 'And, really, what are their reasons for so stubbornly trying to hold onto their weapons, even after repeated searches? This morning a nurse at Bellegarde Fort found a group of so-called wounded men, hiding grenades and sticks of dynamite under false bandages'.[178] While some papers spoke of a moral transformation of the refugees as they received generous French aid, other stories circulated. 'Even in the hospital at Perpignan, the charitable services of the French Red Cross, who work ceaselessly, are meeting with every obstacle. *The Spanish wounded refuse to let religious workers care for them, and shout the worst of insults to their face*'.[179]

Before 1939, the right-wing press had circulated images of Spanish refugees as potential criminals, who could rob, pillage and even join with French communists in an armed insurrection. After the defeats of January and February 1939, these themes became widespread. These were no longer *potential* threats: the subversives were now active in France. The *Journal des Débats* warned its readers about the dangers of 'worrying hordes of agitators, militants of all sorts, professional rioters'.[180] 'Close your hen houses and don't wander on the roads at night', *Le Figaro* advised.[181] *Ouest-Eclair* was concerned about the number of refugees who remained outside concentration camps. 'Thousands of those men, not to mention some women who are even more threatening than their partners, are going to roam over the south-west. There is a real danger of a moral and physical contagion'. It was the duty of France to impose 'the strictest discipline on the refugees … We cannot keep or absorb this multitude. They already constitute a public danger'.[182] *Le Figaro* cited the case of a garage vandalized by refugees and the Mayor of Banyuls was horrified by the behaviour of Spanish refugees: 'These people are a bunch of rogues. They take chicken and wine, they threaten our women: we're forced to throw them out of our cafés. I've had enough'.[183] *La Dépêche* reported that forty fugitives had stopped a property-owner at Boulou, and demanded that he give them cigarettes.[184] Anarchists attacked a farm near Prats-de-Mollo when the owners were not quick enough to offer them hospitality.[185]

Such stories encouraged expressions of open hostility. André Tardieu described the refugees as 'murderous scum'.[186] *Action Française* echoed these xenophobic statements, warned that 'true France cannot become a dumping-ground for criminals and assassins'.[187] The far right's hostility towards the refugees was rooted in their fears of communism and Soviets; the entry of the refugees was seen as 'an invasion by red Spaniards'.[188] *La Croix* advocated the evacuation of these 'undesirables' to Soviet Russia, a land which is perfect for them, as it has realized their ideal, and they marched under its orders'. [189]

It was widely assumed that refugees would bring infectious diseases, notably diphtheria and typhoid.[190] Some journalists compared the medical and political problems the refugees represented. 'The retreating Spaniards bring into our homeland their scabies, typhus, fleas, arguments, hates, ideologies and explosives' observed the far right *Gringoire*.[191] *Ouest-Eclair* drew a similar lesson from the refugees' presence in France. An editorial from 26 February 1939 noted that France seemed divided, caught between the struggle against fascism and the struggle to preserve republican legality. The problem was that the two forces could sound the same – as had been seen during the French Popular Front. But now, there was a danger that the refugees could disrupt France, due to 'the passion that animates most of them, which could well provoke all sorts of problems' in France.

These arguments are important: they are not the ravings of some exceptional journalists; they constitute the basic building blocks from which French policies to the refugees were formed; they lead directly to the grim, improvised concentration camps in which the male refugees were housed and the unfriendly, unprepared villages to which women and children were dispersed.

There may be an element of truth in some of the reports. By the end of their journey the refugees were a repellent sight. Montseny herself spoke of 'Filthy soldiers, covered in dust, full of lice, with unshaven beards … Hunger poisoned them, madness lay within them'.[192] The refugees were desperate for food and shelter: when these were not provided for them, they took what they could. In

Prats-de-Mollo, the forests around the town were devastated: the men camping out in the open had cut down branches in order to make improvised shelters and to use as firewood.[193] Young militants like Paz did try to evade the French authorities and survive underground. These factual details, however, cannot disguise the lasting impression left by the press reports and the French policies. Reports were marked by exaggeration and caricature: some – such as the story of 40 armed bandits stopping a passer-by to rob him of cigarettes – are frankly unbelievable. Taken collectively, one is struck by the degree of hatred which emanates from these articles.

CONCLUSION

An anonymous report concerning the Spanish refugee camps concluded 'The general impression I got was that a great deal of suffering had been caused and was being caused by bad organisation'.[194] The French authorities had every opportunity to study the course of the Spanish conflict and to make appropriate preparations for an inevitable disaster. The press could have studied the conflict in greater detail and alerted public opinion to the real dangers in posed. Charitable and welfare organizations could have taken a more independent attitude, and criticized government inactivity. Looking at the activities of welfare agencies, one can certainly find evidence of a widespread compassion for the refugees, coupled with a frequent desire to undertake practical tasks to help them. But this creditable impulse was not well-organized. And, in fact, by identifying some as 'innocent victims', this compassionate impulse also prepared French people to consider others as belonging to another, less worthy category: the bandits, scoundrels and rogues. While efforts to help the 'innocent victims' were praised, this impulse did not stop the development of the second discourse.

As for the refugees themselves, their actions transformed their lives.

At a stroke, in a few minutes, we cut the umbilical cord that linked us to twenty past generations: with the furniture that we had inherited from our grandparents, with the familiar landscape into which are parents had awoken, with the toys with which we had played and with which our children would never play. We lost, perhaps forever, the right to be children of a land.[195]

They would remain lost children for decades to come.

2

At the Limits of the Nation State: French Evacuations, 1939–1940

- Planning Evacuation
- Evacuation in Wartime
- Preparing for the Evacuees
- Evacuation Stories
- Reception and a New Life
- Alsace and Lorraine after the Evacuation
- Conclusion

Mass population movements were an integral part of the Second World War. Some, as was seen in the previous chapter, were largely spontaneous movements by people attempting to make the best of desperate circumstances. Others, such as the examples in this chapter, were qualitatively different, and more typical of the mid-twentieth-century assertions of state power. The French and British evacuation programmes of 1939–40 were among the least sinister and destructive of such projects, but they shared an authoritarian impulse. Governments evaluated, decided and acted for their populations, usually without proper consultation and without explaining the rationale of their programmes. At first sight, such measures might appear as the actions of a benevolent, responsible state, but often – in practice – they were marked by a lack of concern for individuals' needs.

An examination of these planned population movements provides a comparative dimension to our study: one fascinating point is that, despite over 15 years of planning and the elaborate coordination of a range of experienced military agencies, municipal services and charitable organizations, the French evacuations of 1939–40 were not well organized. This meant that in practice, it was often difficult to distinguish meaningfully between 'evacuee' and 'refugee'. For example, Somerset Maugham watched the evacuations from the regions of Alsace and Lorraine, and then observed that the 'refugees' had been 'evacuated': a terminological confusion which aptly reflected many personal experiences.[1] In a similar manner, the index to Robert Gildea's *Marianne in Chains* instructs readers: for 'evacuees *see* refugees'.[2]

This chapter will therefore concentrate on administrative records, first studying the early plans for the evacuation, and then considering the experiences of evacuees.

PLANNING EVACUATION

Military demands, social and humanitarian concerns and a rather more intangible will to demonstrate the strength of the state all contributed to the formulation of the French evacuation programme.

As was noted in the Introduction, during the nineteenth century codes of war for armies on the move, designed to protect non-combatants, were developed into binding international legislation. Even the tough-minded Count von Moltke – actually opposed to the international regulation of warfare – conceded that 'a gradual softening of manners ought to be reflected also in the mode of making war'.[3] Yet this 'softening of manners' contrasted with the manner in which twentieth-century military technology was developing. After the First World War, it was clear that any future war would involve aerial bombardment, motorized weaponry, tanks, high explosives and possibly poison gas. Ordinary Europeans could easily learn how terrifying industrial war had become. Throughout the late 1930s, photographs and cinema footage of the 'horrifically modern' wars in Guernica, Madrid and Warsaw circulated widely.[4] The psychological impact of such images was profound and ideas like Von Moltke's 'softening of manners' suddenly seemed old-fashioned and even ludicrous.[5]

On the other hand, there were still widespread demands that the previously developed humanitarian programmes, designed to protect the civilian population, should continue and even be expanded. The unprecedented casualty rates of the First World War had produced a profound and lasting hatred of war in many sections of French society – most notably among the teaching profession, war veterans and students.[6] From 1929 until 1936 the bulk of defence spending had been committed to the Maginot line, partly because such a system of defensive fortifications reduced the army's need for manpower.[7] Even amongst committed anti-fascists, there was often a determination to avoid war. This anti-belligerence, coupled with concern about a shrinking population, ensured that military elites, politicians, and the wider public expected French troops to be used sparingly: Daladier argued that French blood was precious.[8] Public opinion repeated similar ideas: despite – or perhaps because of – the extreme physical threats inherent in industrial warfare, it was expected that the home front would be properly protected and that non-combatants would be sheltered from combat. Evacuation seemed – in part – a simple humanitarian gesture, an element of the modern state's duty to protect its citizens; it would therefore make a significant contribution to French morale. Soldiers would fight better if they knew that their families were safe; civilians would find it easier to endure the hardships of war if they felt loyal to the state.

Successful evacuations, however, could contribute in a more assertive manner to nation-building. By coincidence, the area which was at the centre of military planning was also a region which posed difficult questions about identity, autonomy and government in the early twentieth century. From 1871 to 1918, much of it had been ruled by the newly formed Germany. Alsatians and Lorrainers had wildly applauded the triumphant entry of French troops in 1918, but the return of the 'lost provinces' to France proved difficult. Conflicts over cultural identity remained acute during the interwar years. One important and divisive issue was language. Although the French government imposed the French language at school and in the administration, in 1926, only 192,842 people out of a total population of 1,153,396 spoke French at home, while 940,944 still spoke either German or Alsatian.[9] Faced with such massive opposition to the republican assimilation, the French government made concessions: it accepted the existence of a separate legal and religious system; the 1905 law on the separation of the Church and the State did not apply in the newly recovered provinces.

The evacuations of 1939–40 revived these questions. Sometimes evacuation could work successfully.

> Sylvia's mother was born in Alsace when it was part of the Second German Empire. When Alsace was returned to France in 1918 she was not happy because she had to use French at school and she had to start thinking of herself as French. It was a big upheaval. There was an even bigger upheaval in 1939 when, as a young mother, she was evacuated to the Dordogne. It really did not feel like home. Living in a strange province may have been uncomfortable but the family's Jewish heritage would have guaranteed them a far darker experience had they all remained within German territory. During the war this family became committed French patriots because French evacuation policies had saved their lives.[10]

This example shows that evacuation could not only save lives but could also perform a yet more ambitious task: the transformation of half-hearted citizens into enthusiastic patriots, thus assisting the French government's long-term goal of ensuring that people along France's contested eastern frontier made a final and irrevocable decision to become – and to remain – truly French. However, as will be seen, Sylvia's mother was unusual: in most cases, evacuation did not stimulate patriotism.

Finally, evacuation was a military tactic. The Maginot line was intended to protect France from invasion from the east: troops had to be deployed close to the line and it was important that civilians did not impede their manoeuvres.[11] The Maginot line could not promise complete security, but it constituted a major deterrent that protected France from a surprise attack and ensured that any enemy would be held at bay until French troops had mobilized. French strategists were confident that any invader would have to be prepared for a long and difficult war.[12] Part of the planning for the north-eastern regions also involved consideration of the local civilian population. The fear of enemy occupation was especially strong in these areas, many of which had been occupied in 1914–18. Following the German invasion of 1914, waves of refugees had fled these departments, and there had been a similar mass movement in response to the German offensive of spring 1918.[13] It seemed likely that they would behave in a similar fashion in any future conflict. Alongside the older fear of enemy occupation – and of associated atrocities – civilians now worried about aerial bombardment. No one wanted to stay in a town that was going to become a second Verdun.[14]

French governments began discussing evacuation policies in February 1922. During the 1930s there were repeated rehearsals and planning exercises. Experts studied the Spanish Civil War and other conflicts, and the preparations for war made in other countries.[15] Plans were debated, disseminated and rehearsed. For example, early in 1939 a series of secret studies in Rennes considered how best to organize the circulation of vehicles during the mobilization of soldiers, while similar studies in Cherbourg aimed to devise a coordinated evacuation plan for 20,000 people from the town and seven neighbouring communes using 15 trains.[16]

Yet despite much detailed discussion, French evacuation preparations left important questions unresolved. For example, there was the awkward question of whether official evacuation plans would fuel panic by encouraging people to think that invasion was imminent. Up to September 1938 (the Munich Crisis), plans were discussed relatively openly: thus Parisians learnt of the administrative division of their city into sectors, sub-sectors and quarters.[17] Afterwards, a fear of public panic justified a code of official secrecy as a plethora of evacuation plans was developed between September 1938 and May 1940.[18] There was also the difficult question of who was to be evacuated. Were industrial centres of population the most obvious targets for enemy action? If so they needed to be evacuated first, but this would have serious repercussions for industrial production, which was reliant upon established production and distribution networks. It was even possible that industrial areas might be relatively safe. There was a widespread belief that Germany would not attack large urban centres because there would be no military or strategic benefit in doing so.[19] Others were concerned about how the German authorities would interpret evacuation. Would they see it as the beginning of a capitulation? This was certainly possible, and explained Camille Chautemps's commitment to a strictly limited evacuation plan. At a meeting of local regional authorities in February 1940, he argued that only children should be evacuated, and that healthy adults should be free to make their own decisions.[20] Effective evacuation therefore relied upon a thorough understanding of the enemy's offensive strategy and civilian attitudes.

There were clear signs that citizens lacked confidence in these preparations. During the Munich crisis of September 1938, there was widespread alarm in the Moselle and about 10,000 people tried to leave by train.[21] The government also faced the opposition from some Alsatian Deputies. In February 1939, M. Burrus, a deputy for the Haut-Rhin, spoke against the evacuation plans, warning that the evacuation would leave the evacuees without adequate food supplies, and would expose their homes to pillage by French soldiers.[22]

At first sight, it seems obvious that evacuees are not comparable with refugees: evacuees are sheltered and supervised by a benevolent state and their fellow citizens. They do not flee; they do not run panic-stricken into the night. Evacuees are given clear instructions, even orders: they know when to leave, they are allocated specific trains; they usually have travel warrants, food vouchers and money; their journey is punctuated by breaks for food; they are greeted at well-staffed, organized reception centres, given a daily subsidy and welcomed into new communities. For example, Paul Burmetz was an Austrian asylum-seeker interned in France in the spring of 1940. In June 1940 he was evacuated from his camp near Paris to Albi in the south of France. 'We received detailed instructions as to what to take and what not take with us. We should have to march at high speed in order to get a train, and, therefore, should not carry anything that was not absolutely necessary. We were to wear only dark clothes as a protection against air attacks.'[23] The contrast with the nervous improvisations of the *retirada* is obvious: Burmetz made no decisions about his journey, he merely followed instructions.

The evacuation programme as a whole, however, required active civilian cooperation. Frequently government agencies would appeal for a type of voluntary, patriotic response from administrators, officials and citizens. A circular from the Minister of the Interior in 1939 informed prefects that evacuation procedures were 'an absolutely central question for the morale of our land. Let each of you show total devotion, constant concentration and fraternal sympathy for those peoples who certainly deserve the greatest compassion.'[24] Planning for evacuation was integrated into the Défense passive programme, which was designed primarily to protect civilians from aerial bombardment or gas attack. One lecture on the risk of bombing explained that the programme aimed 'not to end the risks encountered during aerial attack, but to limit them ... through an appropriate organisation of aid.'[25] Evacuation policy was clearly vital to this programme: an audience of Défense passive instructors in Metz were told that evacuation's primary purpose was to protect the civilian population by transporting them to a distant department.[26] The programme was largely implemented by municipal authorities, and required the cooperation of civilian volunteers. The authorities in Brest began to study air-raid precautions from 1929 and the French Red Cross organized rehearsals for responses to air raids in Paris in 1935.[27] From 1936, pamphlets and information leaflets were being distributed throughout France to advise on the construction of shelters, the dangers of gas, and the procedures to be followed in the event of attack.[28]

Défense passive included consideration of civilian morale and public order. One pamphlet explained:

The loss of sang-froid and discipline is the greatest danger.
   In every disaster, it is panic which causes the more serious damage, and not the disaster itself.[29]

Such references illustrate the complex nature of the evacuation programme, which required the coordination of many different agencies, and which combined important military, social and even psychological considerations.

French governments tried to learn lessons from the First World War and other conflicts, to plan in a rational and coherent manner and to prepare their citizens. They considered that evacuation was not simply a useful military tactic: it could also function to maintain social structures and national unity in adverse circumstances.

EVACUATION IN WARTIME

In September 1939, the plans were put into practice. With the declaration of war, a series of exceptional measures transformed the lives of French people. Observers in Paris noted how quickly and how dramatically the city changed. Shops were closed, people carried gas masks, theatres were briefly closed (but usually re-opened in late October), air raid shelter signs were prominent along the roads, paper strips pasted on windows to protect against bomb blasts, sandbags piled up in the streets, the cafés closed at 11 p.m., identity cards were needed to use a phone in a post office, women stopped using make-up or dressing their hair, the blackout imposed, and the news was subject to an 'unprecedently strict censorship': one had to listen to American radio stations to learn of the progress of the war, for the French and British stations carried almost no clear news.[30] The city seemed quieter, more serious: emptier of noise and people. But the French government demanded still greater changes. Prefects were ordered to cut back on unnecessary expenses. 'All our effort must now be directed to one goal: Victory'.[31] Prefects in turn made demands of local officials. The Prefect of the Haute-Garonne instructed the mayors of the department:

Consider yourselves on state of alert.
Be vigilant and diligent.
I am counting on the sensitivity and the spontaneous, heart-felt élan of our people.
As for you: you know your duty.
I am confident that you will accomplish it with a determined, firm and lucid will.[32]

One striking innovation from this period was the new ability of local military authorities to issue exceptional orders. In Rennes, General Etienne forbade all political and trade union meetings, and General Marrasse wrote to the mayor to complain about the widespread evasions of the regulations on night-time black-outs.[33] But perhaps the most far-reaching measure was the right to requisition material judged essential for the war effort. For some, these seizures were a necessary, even welcome, part of the war effort with which all patriots should cooperate: 'self-serving resistance' to such measures was to be condemned, for 'today, more than ever, all French people should be united by the most ardent feelings of national solidarity'.[34] The range of objects and buildings seized in this manner is memorable. Denyse Weiller was on a family holiday in Préfailles (Loire-Atlantique) in September 1939. Her first war memories are of the baker passing by each morning, his little van full of bread for the evacuated Parisian children staying in a requisitioned hotel.[35] Mayors in the villages of the Haute-Garonne complained that buses, coaches and even horses had been seized: this meant that their region was almost denuded of all forms of transport.[36] Some businesses in the Rhone collapsed when lorries were requisitioned as the government did not compensate the owners adequately.[37]

Mass evacuations from the anticipated conflict zone took place in a tense, confused context. France was 'the last asylum' in Europe, taking in a higher proportion of refugees than any other country in the world.[38] In spring 1939 numerous groups of foreigners living in France, such as Poles, Czechs, Austrians, even Italians, demonstrated their loyalty to France by raising funds for French armaments and thus publicly committing themselves to the defence of the nation.[39] Yet the declaration of war in September 1939 did not awaken a wave of socially inclusive, popular enthusiasm: France had not been invaded, there was no clear cause to defend, no revival of the *union sacrée* of 1914 and military morale was often low.[40] Rather than celebrating its status as the last major democratic power in western Europe, French society was marked by a exaggerated fear of traitors, spies, foreigners and an organized 'fifth column'.[41] While such attitudes often originated among the far right, they seemed to be becoming almost ordinary in 1939–40.[42] Suspicions towards foreigners in particular were exacerbated by a new concern that they were dragging innocent France into a costly war.[43] Victor Serge, exiled in France during this period, lists French grumbles about both actual and metaphorical outsiders during the *drôle de guerre*: Jews, foreigners, strikers, communists, pacifists, Germans (les Boches) and fascists were all resented.[44] These suspicions produced a surprise: often the first people to be evacuated from the border regions were not the native French, but those who were suddenly classified as 'undesirables' following the announcement of war.[45] The internment of 18–20,000 foreigners between September and November 1939 – including many German Jews who had fled the Third Reich – was part of the evacuation programme.[46] Among their number was Arthur Koestler, imprisoned with 2,000 others in the Le Vernet camp (Ariège) in October 1939. He found the conditions in the camp were harsh, constituting 'an undramatic everyday torture'. Nearly all the internees had previously been in Nazi jails or concentration camps for at least 18 months.[47]

Examples provided by military reports from the Franco–Belgian border show that there were also suspicions about those who seemed insufficiently French. For example, Mlle Bruxer had German relatives and apparently had commented that Hitler had done a lot of good in Germany: her presence in the same zone as the French army was deemed 'unsuitable'. Mme Grossmann, 'une miséreuse', was questionable because of her strange life, although the official report concluded that she should not be considered as suspect from the 'national point of view'.[48] Both women had been reported to the authorities by anonymous letters, presumably from their near neighbours.

September 1939, therefore, initiated a cycle of anxiety and suspicion within French society. Rather than facilitating national unity, the evacuation programme introduced a further severe strain on French resources and morale.

The evacuation programme of 1939 involved transplanting entire communities and their political representatives into another area. This was unprecedented. As Sartre observed, in 1914 people moved in direct response to the circumstances of war: these movements were usually spontaneous and sometimes haphazard. In contrast, in 1939–40 French Alsatians and others were moved methodically, commune by commune, village by village along with their municipalities and their administrations.[49] Minister of the Interior, Albert Sarraut, had earlier explained the rationale behind such plans.

> The central theme to this policy is the reconstitution of each evacuated commune in their host department. This will, to a large extent, attenuate the suffering of the people torn from their homes by the war; it will develop into a form of 'cousinship' between evacuated communes and host communes which will aid considerably the organization of aid and will strengthen the feeling of national solidarity.[50]

Yet Sartre argued that this policy was partly responsible for the failure of French evacuation in this period because it meant that two or more local authorities had to co-exist in the one place.

Prefects appealed to those living in the new host communities to assist in the process. In the Haute-Garonne, the Prefect's circular suggested an open-ended commitment.

> The department of the Haute-Garonne is 'in reserve': in other words, it will receive refugees as and when people are retired from departments from which no official evacuation is currently planned. It is impossible to know in advance when this measure will be implemented: it goes without saying that as soon as I learn of the arrival of convoys [of evacuees] I will inform those among you who will be receiving them.

Among the evacuees there would be Poles. 'Of course, they must be treated exactly like French refugees'. (One notes that even in these official documents, the term 'refugee' swiftly replaced 'evacuee'.) The circular ended by warning that buildings for the new arrivals would be requisitioned.[51] Another circular berated anyone who opposed the requisitioning of their buildings.

> *This attitude is intolerable.*
> While convoys of unfortunate people are arriving each day in their new departments, the duty of those living in the rear is clear and formal. Everywhere, refugees

must meet with a fraternal welcome, and must be lodged in the best accommodation possible.

Our fine soldiers are at their post, demonstrating their unshakable determination, forged by the union of their hearts and minds: they are already engaged in the first struggles with enemy: a fight to defend France's moral and material traditions...

The same spirit of sacrifice must unite all French people.[52]

In Rennes, the Mayor demanded that the city prepare to receive some 20,000 evacuees. 'It is our duty to do our best to receive them, and to help them to the best of our abilities'.[53] The Prefect of the Ille-et-Vilaine sounded a similar tone as he called on mayors to prepare to receive evacuees.

It is not possible to reduce the number of [evacuees] that you will receive. This is an absolute duty of national solidarity...

[Any difficulties] can be easily overcome because at all levels of organisation there are citizens charged with a mission which they will accomplish with devotion, even with abnegation: they will wish to serve their nation at a moment when she requires that everyone contributes towards the common good with all their forces.[54]

In these official pronouncements by ministers, prefects and mayors, one sees the characteristic blending of social policy, military requirements and heady patriotic idealism that constituted the evacuation policy. It is clear that evacuation was understood as a test for the entire nation, in the fullest sense of the word, and not the simple physical transportation of a large number of people from the north-east to the south and west of France.

PREPARING FOR THE EVACUEES

An invaluable file of letters preserved in the Haute-Garonne archives shows how mayors responded to these appeals.[55] In general, they present a disappointing picture: mayors produced long lists of reasons to explain why they were unable to accept evacuees. For example, in Arbas, there was no butcher, baker, grocer, cooperative store or public transport system. Following requisitioning,

we are all resigned to return to the primitive lifestyle of the disinherited countryside: boiled potatoes, crêpes, milk foods and other plain dishes ... Of course, for better or worse, we will survive and we will adapt to these shortages without complaining. But it would be a sad thing to make people who had abandoned a better lifestyle share our misery.

The Mayor of Encausse was equally sceptical.

Today ... we lack everything: there is one baker for eight communes. Some of his family has been mobilized, and he can't produce more bread.

We only have one elderly butcher who is not able to do tiring or intensive work.

I was mayor of Encausse during the last war. We lodged twenty refugees from the Somme then, and so I know the nuisance and bother that their arrival created in the commune and I remember the many problems that I had to solve.

My age and my health will not allow me, at this moment, to do the same again. So I request that you do not insist on Encausse receiving a large number of refugees.

The Mayor of Benque wrote one sentence in reply. 'I am sorry to inform you that, despite my exhaustive investigation, I have not been able to find a single building which could be used by the people withdrawn from the border'. Payrissas had been too battered by hail and frost to take refugees. There were only 16 houses and 60 people in Moustajon. They had already accommodated 20 Spanish migrants; in the whole commune, there were only two empty rooms left. These belonged to Parisians, who were expected to arrive soon. Artigue was high in the Pyrenees, and suffered frequent snow storms that cut it off from the market at Luchon, some ten kilometres away. The people of the commune could only get there by horse. Benque-Dessous-et-Dessus suffered similar problems.

Buying food is difficult: the nearest station is at Luchon, some six kilometres away, on a steep hill, at a 1 in 6 gradient. Since mobilisation, there are no more buses or horses, and the commune's women have to walk to Luchon, and bring back their purchases in their arms. When it snows in winter, I don't know what we're going to do. Despite my goodwill and that of the commune, if we get sent refugees, I don't see how we're going to lodge them.

There was equally little welcome from the mayor of Fougaron.

This year, the harvests have been disastrous in our region: persistent rain over many months has rotted the potatoes, and no other vegetable has grown well.

The population has good reason to worry about winter in these conditions. So how can one consider taking in more people? Who can give them what they need, when we're short of everything?

Finally, he conceded that they might be able to take about 35 refugees.

The Moncaup Mayor was more measured, but hardly welcoming. His commune could take 20 refugees. 'It will be easy enough to lodge them, but feeding them will be difficult, because we're 30 kilometres from the nearest market, and the local people find things difficult enough'. The Mayor of Eoux could only take five or six refugees, but did add an interesting comment: 'Could you send us some farmers? Someone who could work the land would be very useful for our commune'.

Some mayors did respond more positively. The Mayor of Aubas estimated that his commune could accept at most 25 refugees, and the Mayor of Arguenos could take 20. The Mayor of Aulon first warned of the difficulties: all the available accommodation was in extremely poor condition.

> But it shall not be said that my commune, despite these valid objections, refused to carry out its duties of charity and solidarity, which all French people must carry out today. I appealed to the population, to the feelings and good will of my fellow citizens. This was not in vain, because now I am pleased to tell you that it will be possible to receive a hundred refugees. They will be placed in empty houses: the furniture, supplied by the devotion of those I administer, will be basic but sufficient.

One cannot escape the conclusion that the most typical response from these mayors was negative. Alongside a basic reluctance to accept refugees, mayors made more specific points: mobilization and requisition has left their communes stripped of the resources needed to accommodate refugees. The picture that emerges is of an old, poor, exhausted France, knocked back by the strains of war preparation, sceptical and unwelcoming – if not actually hostile – to newcomers, and unable to meet the challenges of evacuation. Other evidence – to be reviewed below – demonstrates that this hostility to evacuees was not some regional peculiarity of the Haute-Garonne.[56]

EVACUATION STORIES

The mobilization of French soldiers and the evacuation of civilians both began on 2 September 1939. Two vast population movements, both involving millions of people, swirled round each other. Despite the years of planning and the array of contributing organizations, the evacuation did not proceed smoothly.

In practice, 'spontaneous' and 'voluntary' evacuees merged with 'official' evacuees in a manner that made precision impossible. The Weiller family illustrate this confusion: after the summer of 1939, they stayed in their holiday home near Nantes instead of returning to Paris, and began to call themselves 'refugees'.[57] Mayors in the Ille-et-Vilaine expected evacuees from the Lille after September 1939. Were they to treat non-returning tourists like the Weiller as the first evacuees? What of the handful of 'voluntary' evacuees who arrived in the first days of September? Were they entitled to the official subsidy?[58] Because of this type of overlap, it was difficult to estimate exactly how many people were involved in the evacuation: we have found some useful 'snapshot' estimates of particular moments. By 15 October 1939, 365,000 people had been evacuated from the Bas-Rhin, Haut-Rhin and the Moselle.[59] A report from the end of October 1939 spoke of 2.37 million people evacuated to 64 departments.[60] By May 1940, half a million people had been evacuated from the 'première zone' around the Maginot line to reception areas in south-west

France.[61] The weak, sick, ill and elderly also featured in evacuations. By February 1940 the hospital at Angers was overflowing, having received all the patients from two hospitals in Paris.[62] Overall, it seems likely that several million people were involved in the various evacuation programmes of 1939–40.

Some initial reports noted the success of the operation. On 2 September the Prefect of the Moselle reported that 100,000 of 145,000 planned evacuees had been transferred. 'There is nothing to signal. The evacuation proceeded in calm and order, and the people were admirable'.[63] Juliette Droz spoke of 'a triumph' for the train services and the social services.[64] Folcher, mobilized in September 1939, was relieved to see Red Cross nurses at railway stations, giving bread and jam to the evacuees, and ensuring that they had cool drinks in the hot, crowded railway carriages. At times, he even envied the evacuees. He only had the haziest idea about where he was going and what he was to do: he thought that, in contrast, the evacuated civilians seemed to inhabit an ordered world. At least knew where they were going.[65]

The evacuees themselves were often more critical about their experiences. Reviewing past events on 25 February 1940, Mr. Schuman, a deputy of the Moselle, admitted that the authorities were badly organized in September 1939: villages were evacuated in less than two hours. Often, evacuees did not have time to pack their bags, and left without warm winter clothes. Changes of itinerary and program were frequent.[66] The citizens of Strasbourg were given one day to evacuate the city.[67] Other official reports detailed one train arriving for the refugees that had no indication of its destination, open carriages with no roofs, and no food and no medical facilities, while another train took evacuees on a four-day journey during which some of the older travellers died of stress.[68] Many evacuees left on foot, carrying up to 30kg of luggage.[69]

Some extremely perceptive records of the process have been left by the Vallotton family, a group of philanthropic French Protestants from Alsace. According to Pierre Vallotton, this evacuation was carried out with admirable calm. Yet his friend, Emile Rupp, a church organist, felt differently. He and his wife left Strasbourg on a bicycle. Rupp subsequently noted: 'This exodus is the most painful and saddest day of my life'.[70] The experience did not make him less patriotic. On the contrary, he called on God to wreak vengeance on Hitler and the Germans.

At Schillik, just outside Strasbourg, evacuees also complained. Evacuation notices were only posted on the evening before the evacuation, leaving little time to prepare. Like the Spanish refugees of the *retirada*, they faced some difficult decisions. A young woman and her mother agonized over what they should take. Should they carry souvenirs with them? Or photographs? Would it be sensible to take valuables? Finally, they decided to take mainly clothes: this seemed like the most practical decision.[71] Others came to different conclusions. Dr Pautrier was determined to take his medical instruments.[72] This practical decision also had an emotional aspect: by maintaining his professional status the doctor was also maintaining his sense of self. Keeping hold of possessions is not simply a material issue: belongings also denote status, professional lives, and family histories. Choosing what to take, and what to leave behind, was therefore a painful process.

Evacuation left many feel confused and alienated. One common argument was that as there was no real fighting, there was no good reason to evacuate. In Colmar and Mulhouse (Haute-Rhin) the Prefect reported 'a categorical refusal' to follow instructions to evacuate. Worse still: by 10 September, some were already returning to their houses.[73] One young woman was at 'the end of her strength' after only one day. She arrived at Barr (Bas-Rhin) on a bicycle: one of her children was on the front, the luggage was on the back and her two other children were in the trailer.[74] An officially designated evacuee, she had cycled almost 35 km in one day. Would she have felt that she was enjoying the protection of a state? Similarly, in Nancy, Mme Lafleur had little reason to thank a benevolent state. By May 1940 her husband had been mobilized and she was living alone and suffering from tuberculosis. Her weakened state meant that it was difficult for her to reach the air raid shelters when the alarms sounded and so she requested government help for transport to family in the Haute-Saône. Yet the state would only support evacuation to specific locations despite the presences of relatives in other areas, and her request was refused.[75]

The evacuees' arrivals in their new communities often proved difficult. One report tells us a group from Alsace who spent a fortnight in trains, 'without guides or advice' before finally arriving in the Haute-Vienne.[76] Droz noted that frequently reception committees found that they had been misinformed about the time of the evacuees' arrival and their number.[77] Eugene Muller, a senator for the Bas-Rhin, spoke movingly of the men, women and children who had been forced to leave. It was a 'painful sight', and one which he would never be able to forget. One particular episode dominated his memory. A 'lost ghost train', full of evacuees, travelled down the Midi network. There should have been a station with a reception committee, food, medical care and someone to arrange accommodation but the driver was unable to find it. The idea of a train, loaded with 'its human cargo' and passing aimlessly across France in the dark suggests a powerful metaphor for the whole process.[78] Mayors found that they lacked the resources to help evacuees.[79] The Mayor of Hablainville (Meurthe-et-Moselle) was baffled when 48 evacuees arrived unexpectedly from Nancy. 'This is embarrassing and complicated for a little commune like ours which had never been involved in anything important'.[80] The mayor of Pierre-Percée (Meurthe-et-Moselle) was puzzled by the instruction that he should only help the poor among the evacuees. 'All of them say that they lack everything'.[81] The number of 'voluntary' evacuees posed further problems: as they had not arrived in the officially designated place, they also had no right to any official subsidy. The Prefect of the Meurthe-et-Moselle told mayors to advise them to continue their journey to the correct department.[82]

Formal complaints about the process were soon heard. For example, in

November 1939, the Chambre d'Agriculture for the Bas-Rhin pointed out that evacuation was paralyzing the region's economic life, and confounding the Alsatians' 'love of their family homes and rural work'. It requested that any further evacuations should be cancelled or at least delayed for as long as possible.[83]

This first stage of the programme did not work well. The process of transporting millions of people was more complex than had been anticipated. But these journeys only took days – or, at most, weeks. They were only the first stage of a longer process.

RECEPTION AND A NEW LIFE

Mme de Chaise-Martin, a wealthy woman from Limoges, was enjoying a stroll with her daughter in January 1940. She noticed something strange on the horizon and commented 'my goodness, what a lot of sheep!' As they grew closer, she realized that they were not sheep, but a large crowd of over 1000 evacuees, all loaded down with bundles.[84]

The arrival of evacuees placed an immediate strain on their host communities. Sometimes, there was sympathy and genuine care for evacuees. Gauthier Cros, writing from the Creuse in October 1939 acknowledged that there were problems caused by the evacuees, but that there was also much pity for them.[85] Similarly Annie Vallotton described a dreadful example: Alsatian refugees had arrived at Périgueux (Dordogne), nearly 900 km from Strasbourg, to find that nothing was ready for them and they had to sleep ten to a room. The people of Périgueux were genuinely sympathetic and very willing to help.[86] Great efforts were made to ensure the provision of blankets, foods, stoves and lodgings, and government agencies were supplemented by charitable and philanthropic networks. This voluntary help was much needed as in some places the first evacuees were sleeping on straw and being bothered by rats.[87] In response the Comité Mosellan and the Comité d'Entr'aide du XVeme Corps d'Armée distributed tens of thousands of blankets, warm clothes and knitting wool to evacuees during the winter of 1939–1940. Extra support came from the Solidarity Committee of the United Associations of Great Britain and France.[88]

These basic, physical problems should not be underestimated. In September 1939, 80,000 people were evacuated from the Bas-Rhin to the largely rural Dordogne over a period of three weeks, and nine-tenths of those evacuees were from Strasbourg. Their presence placed a great strain on local food supplies.[89] The evacuees often found that as they arrived, local prices rose. Civil servants of Strasbourg evacuated to the Perigueux complained bitterly that their salaries no longer covered costs, and accused local people of profiting from their presence.[90] Others were just unhappy. 'Their accommodation is in lonely farms, far from any town. Many evacuees seem miserable, physically and morally lost, feeling – unfortunately accurately – that they have been abandoned'.[91] Two evacuee women from Metz presented some specific complaints. Each had just given birth. Their journeys to Poitiers took place without incident, but the food in the new hospital was insufficient. After a week, they were both taken to a rest home in which Spanish refugees were also lodged. The two French women complained that Spanish refugees were better treated than them: unlike the Spaniards, they had no access to hot water, and the food that they were given was of inferior quality.[92]

While charitable agencies, municipal organizations and local groups tried to accommodate the evacuees, it is obvious that hostility and suspicion still circulated. This can be seen at almost every stage of the evacuation. Approaching the Nivernais by train in September 1939, Folcher saw carriages full of evacuees from Alsace. He then witnessed a mysterious incident: there was a tremendous uproar on the platform. Local people accused the evacuees of holding up blankets decorated with swastikas to the train windows.[93] Similar hostility was expressed in Calvados after the arrival of evacuees from the 4th arrondissement of Paris. According to the Prefect, local people complained that these apparent Parisians were not in fact French but were 'Israelites, Poles, Rumanians' and unnamed – but clearly foreign – others.[94] Tereska Torres, a French Pole, visited Lectoure (Gers) in October 1939, and found it 'invaded' by refugees from the Haut-Rhin; one only heard German on the streets.[95] Alsatian evacuees in particular were often the targets of accusations: one repeated claim was that they celebrated Hitler's birthday.[96] In place of sentiments of national solidarity, the new host communities often distrusted evacuees, seeing them as different, foreign, disloyal and potentially threatening.

With reference to the British evacuation experience of 1939, a Fabian pamphlet noted that while transport was relatively easy to organize, the absorption of evacuees into a new area was far more challenging.[97] Similar points can be made about evacuation in France. Often, accommodation was inadequate. In the Haute-Vienne, families of six to twelve people were placed in one-room or two-room flats without adequate heating. The children did not have enough clothes or shoes, and were not attending school.[98] In Périgueux, evacuees lacked wood, coal and coffee.[99] In the Dordogne, one report found that 'the two populations do not mix, and mistrust each other'. Local people resented the fact that the evacuees did not contribute to agricultural work.[100] For the Alsatians, most of whom came from an urban environment, life in rural France seemed primitive rather than bucolic. In the Limousin, the local people offered them Jerusalem artichokes and chestnuts to eat: the Alsatians were horrified, for at home these foods were fodder for the pigs. The Alsatians thought that the Limousins were dirty because they did not wash much; yet to the Limousins the Alsatians were dirty, because they put toilets inside their homes.[101] Evacuees and local inhabitants also had different attitudes to work. Alsatians were shocked by the primitive agricultural tools and practices in the south. Alsace was a more modernized, more technological region and one evacuee reflected bitterly 'perhaps we've been sent here to teach *them* how to work'.[102] The British

Consulate General of Strasbourg neatly reflected popular prejudices by arguing that cultural difficulties stemmed from the fact that 'a naturally hard-working people, whose morale is under considerable strain ... have been placed among people more disposed to idleness and with a normally lower standard of living'.[103] These cultural and social differences fuelled rumours and innuendo in local communities, which were also visible in official discourse.

Sometimes, the previous arrival of Spanish refugees complicated the situation. Evacuees in the Lot-et-Garonne certainly complained bitterly that they were being treated like Spanish refugees: both groups were undesirable outsiders.[104] There were few attempts to bridge this gap. An editorial in the *Journal du Loiret* distinguished between 'the unfortunate French evacuees' and 'foreign evacuees' (namely Spanish republican refugees), stressing that, despite superficial similarities, there were profound differences between good French citizens and the suspect Spanish.[105] Ultimately, these comparisons simply serve to illustrate the extent to which French evacuees were often seen as outsiders. The category of outcast trumped that of official nationality, leaving national solidarity as 'a term devoid of meaning'.[106]

Early in 1940, a number of reports attempted to draw conclusions about the process. Some struck a moderately optimistic note: the two populations were now getting on better, rural people from the north-east in particular were beginning to assimilate to the lifestyle of the south-west, the over-concentration of evacuees in main towns had been alleviated by their dispersal to the countryside, and so the most serious problems were over.[107] Somerset Maugham observed that evacuated Lorrainers were making a positive material impact in the under-populated, dilapidated Charente: they mended leaking roofs, cleaned houses and so made them into comfortable homes.[108] Monsieur Ott, a civil servant from the Bas-Rhin, noted that evacuees were routinely being described as refugees, and insisted that this was not the case. The people from Alsace had not fled – he argued – they had left in good order, they had made a sacrifice for the sake of national defence and, had the order been to stay, they would have stayed. He presented the evacuees as part of a military strategy: they were in the Dordogne because they had followed orders and therefore they should be treated with respect.[109]

Some conservative commentators actually welcomed the new situations created by the evacuations, which presented opportunities for national reconciliation and regeneration. The presence of evacuees allowed people to demonstrate Christian compassion. The Jeunesse Ouvrière Chrétienne (JOC – Christian Worker Youth, a social-Catholic organization) worked with evacuated Alsatians in the rural Dordogne. It ensured supplies of food and clothing arrived, and supervised the smooth running of the postal service.[110] *La Croix*, a staunchly Catholic publication, saw this forced population movement as providing the impetus for re-creating a unified, Christian, rural, traditional France. According to this interpretation, the evacuees were not really leaving home; instead, they were part of a process which would re-establish the real roots of France. Pierre

Lermite, writing in *La Croix*, highlighted what the evacuees had brought with them, namely their strong sense of religious devotion. One village was quite indifferent to religion before the arrival of the devout Alsatians; afterwards, the church was full on Sundays. Lermite also records a conversation between a local peasant and a pious Alsatian evacuee:

> 'So, you're still praying to God? But he's been pretty rough with you'.
> An Alsatian woman, with black ribbons in her hair, raised herself forward.
> 'God? But He's the only treasure that we've kept'. [111]

In this exchange the homeless, helpless evacuees are seen as contributing something substantial to their new community: religious devotion. Conservative commentators had long bemoaned the demise of traditional, rural France and had insisted that France would be in real peril if the countryside continued to deteriorate. [112] Now, Catholic welfare groups and evacuees were using the opportunities of the evacuation to regenerate the authentic France.

These optimistic accounts were probably outnumbered by more critical reports. Some expressed concern that unhappy evacuees could be a suitable base for defeatist propaganda, whether Nazi or Soviet in origin. [113] Police reports carefully monitored any signs of subversion, even in the form of a single letter denouncing a 'capitalist war', or a meeting of 30 evacuees in a café. [114] The publication of bi-lingual papers for the evacuees was criticized. [115] Most reviews of their situation, however, concluded that 'no propaganda aiming to encourage alarmist rumours' and no propaganda of a pro-German, Communist or autonomist nature circulated among them. [116] However, the same reports did note the evacuees' deep bitterness. A police report concerning the Landes paraphrased the evacuees: 'we've been made to leave our land, and so we deserve to be given all we want'. [117] In Auch, the evacuees showed 'the most profound egoism'. [118] A visit by a Strasbourg municipal official in the Charente-Inférieur was greeted by cries of 'at last! At last you've come to see us'. [119] Police officials were more sceptical, and one dourly noted that the official's visit only encouraged the evacuees to complain. [120] One is left with a strong impression of the extent to which the evacuees were objects of suspicion for both local people and police agencies.

An official review found that while the evacuees had certainly demonstrated their patriotism, feelings of 'sad resignation' and 'bitterness' were common among them. [121] A final report, drawing on nine surveys, painted a still more pessimistic picture.

> Anyone travelling through any reception-department will note points which rightly worry all clear-thinking people and authorities concerned with the evacuees' morale. On the roads, around the villages, in the squares of the places where the refugees from Alsace and Lorraine are lodged, groups of idle women stroll about all day long, showing all the signs of an unchanging and complete boredom. All the men and some of the

young people crowd into the cafés, drink all they can afford, play cards, shout and sometimes quarrel. For seven months they have lived in a state of complete idleness.

The young people in particular were actually refusing to work, although there were some more positive signs of the employment of evacuees in the Lot-et-Garonne, Gers and Landes. The dialects of Alsace and Lorraine were an obstacle to assimilation: many of the local people thought the evacuees were speaking German. While the communists were inactive, and while the evacuees showed a 'sincere and spontaneous' attachment to France, this report suggested that evacuation had not been a success.[122] Folcher's peculiar story about the swastika-blankets indicates how easy it was to suspect the patriotism of the Alsatian evacuees.[123]

During Christmas 1939 there were substantial attempts to recreate a sense of community: to be outcast at Christmas would demonstrate that there really was no national solidarity. Hippolyte Giraudoux, the head of French propaganda, called on inhabitants from rural areas to extend a fraternal welcome to Alsatian refugees, and explained that Alsatian German-speaking refugees were patriotic *French* citizens. He invited some Alsatian children to sing in their dialect at the end of his 1939 Christmas radio broadcast.[124] Gritou and Annie Vallotton's letters indicate the extraordinary measures taken to ensure that all the evacuees shared in the festivities. They bought huge quantities of sweets for the children; they bought candles, presents, and clothes; they distributed layettes to new mothers. French social services ensured that the evacuated new mothers had 'godmothers' in the same way that soldiers during the First World War had had godmothers to care for them and to send them parcels. Those who volunteered for these duties were usually relatively wealthy women from Paris, and their gifts were designed not just to provide practical help but also to dissipate suspicions and create national solidarity. If the evacuated new mothers felt alienated in rural France, they could at least comfort themselves with the thought that they had friends in Paris and that the nation had not abandoned them.[125] In addition, although evacuees were scattered across many departments, welfare workers put up the famous 'Giraudoux Christmas trees' wherever evacuees could be found. The Alsatian Foyer in which Annie Vallotton worked held a big Christmas party for evacuated children and distributed gifts in hospitals and sanatoria.[126] Police reports confirm these impressions, and tend to record positive results for this effort.[127]

Yet underneath these celebrations, there were still tensions and conflicts. 'Evacuee' is not a homogenous category; some were more in need than others. Annie Vallotton was worried that too many sweets had gone to the 'spoilt village kids' and that others had been left out: divisions among the evacuees were often overlooked.[128] Furthermore there was much concern when the Parisian committee wanted photographs of Christmas parties which would be suitable for American magazines: a demand that was more about satisfying benefactors than creating national unity.[129] The needs of the philanthropic donor certainly intruded. Annie Vallotton complained about their complicated requirements. She described 'mad letters' in which they insisted that their gifts went to very specific cases: to a child born on a particular date, to a boy if possible, to a Catholic, to a child with a particular name, and so forth.[130] Similarly *dames d'oeuvres* [charitable ladies] often wanted to play the part of Lady Bountiful. Annie Vallotton provides a withering description of a lady benefactor receiving the thanks of the children after the Christmas party. She revelled in her role to an extent that some of the welfare workers found distasteful.[131] Of course, it was inevitably elite women who had the time and resources for this type of charity work, and these criticisms do not mean that they achieved nothing. The British Consulate General of Strasbourg commended Mrs Crawshay for the efficient distribution of 'splendid and useful articles' to the evacuees.[132] Mrs Crawshay's two brothers had been killed in the First World War: a point which motivated her to act in 1939. Yet she was from an aristocratic family and her reports about the 'English ladies' personally distributing gifts to women and children from eastern France certainly suggest a sort of grandiose benevolence.[133]

This was a vast process that unfolded over several months. It is therefore difficult to reach a simple judgement concerning its success or failure: in particular, one could debate exactly which criteria should be used to reach such a judgement. But, in the final analysis, one is struck by the amount of hostility and prejudice that it revealed. While several million people were moved from the north-east to the south and west reasonably effectively, it is hard to find significant, convincing evidence that this move stimulated a sense of national unity. It is therefore telling that the only sustained optimists were conservative Catholic commentators, ever willing to welcome a blow against urban, modern France.

ALSACE AND LORRAINE AFTER THE EVACUATION

Evacuation plans assumed the wholesale movement of large communities, yet some people simply would not, or could not, go. Rupp described some terrible scenes in Strasbourg when those who did not want to leave were evacuated by force, and noted that elderly men in their sixties and seventies became Red Cross volunteers and volunteer firemen to avoid evacuation.[134] Why did people want to stay in a danger zone? Some did not believe that the threat of war was serious. In Paris, for example, two-thirds of the population who had voluntarily evacuated in September 1939 had returned by March 1940.[135] A similar pattern had been observed in 1938 before the Munich conference: people had left, and then returned when international affairs seemed calm and fears waned. France had been mobilized in September 1938 and March 1939, and so when yet another mobilization began in September 1939, it seemed to many that the declaration of war had not signified the beginning of a *real* war. Weiller had been tormented by visions of fire and blood at the outbreak of war but several weeks later the horror had disappeared and, as far as she was concerned, the war was imaginary and its impact was slight. Denyse, her mother and her brother stayed in their holiday home but her father returned to Paris, reluctant to neglect his shop.[136] Many, like M. Weiller, were genuinely worried about losing their businesses or were anxious about living on a small allowance in a strange place. For them, it seemed more sensible to stay at home. In addition, those whose sons or brothers or husbands had been enlisted were sometimes hostile to evacuation because they wanted to keep a home for the soldiers returning from leave. Lastly, many were worried about leaving their homes in wartime, and correctly guessed that French soldiers might damage houses as much as any foreign invasion.

War and evacuation raised questions about the extent to which Alsace and Lorraine were considered as really French: the provinces that had been so symbolically French before the First World War were often seen as insufficiently French afterwards. Soldiers found the evacuated areas strange places. Some noticed the region's wealth: with its cows and pigs, its flans and butter, it seemed 'the land of milk and honey' to Barlone.[137] Other were struck by the sight of its empty villages, populated only by abandoned cows.[138] Somerset Maugham visited Strasbourg during the *drôle de guerre* and described it as 'a fairy-tale' city 'wrapped in a magic sleep'. Houses, streets and lanes were empty, but there were women's stockings and fashionable hats in the shops, domestic pets strolled the streets, and little cakes and sweets were still on display in pastry-cooks' windows.[139] The abandoned town seemed eerie and still after its too rapid evacuation. In addition, soldiers' letters indicate the difficulties of being billeted in evacuated areas. In operational terms it made sense for an army to operate in de-populated areas, but in terms of military morale this may well have been counter-productive. Soldiers' letters indicate that they were bored because they could not see civilians – a boredom that was especially significant given that there was no fighting.[140]

Certainly billeted soldiers caused much damage in the region during 1939–40. Amand Boulé, posted near Nancy, recorded with shame the sight of drunken soldiers acting like madmen, restrained only by a pistol-wielding officer.[141] Reports from Sarreguemines (Moselle) tell of soldiers damaging homes and destroying furniture, even attacking wardrobes with hatchets.[142] Near the Maginot line, Folcher found that soldiers had pillaged villages as soon as the evacuees had left, despite the many posters forbidding such behaviour: 'Everything was stolen, everything was pillaged'.[143] Raymond Guérin observed similar scenes: 'Cupboards smashed and emptied, animals with their throats slit, harvests wasted, buildings made filthy, and all done with that calm that characterizes the soldier-vandal [soudard]'.[144] Habrioux described comparable scenes in the evacuated village of Saint-Erme (Aisne) in northern France. He noted that it was not only ordinary soldiers who were responsible for acts of serious vandalism; officers also had looted.[145] A parliamentary mission visited the affected areas in November, and confirmed the extent of the damage. Cellars, apartments, cupboards are been smashed open; money, jewels, watches and linen had been stolen; chicken and other birds had been taken to feed the units.[146]

Why had this happened? One simple explanation was boredom. Soldiers were fed up because they could not see civilians: their boredom was especially oppressive given that there was no fighting. Alongside complaints about rats and bad food and the cold desolate countryside, soldiers grumbled about the lack of civilian diversions. According to one soldier, 'although we are billeted in a village there is not another human being here. There are only men in uniform, and what men!'.[147] Soldiers complained that citizens from the borders were not really French patriots, not really French or German but 'Alsacien'. 'We were too soft in 1918' commented one soldier to Sartre, 'we should have made them into Frenchmen'.[148] Feldman, also posted to the area, suggests another factor: for soldiers from outside, these rich, ambiguous, half-German, half-French areas were seen as one of the causes of the war. Looting was a form of revenge by a resentful, scared conscript army.[149] Others saw looting as normal: in Folcher's cynical words, it was just 'one of the laws of war'.[150] Lastly, circumstances seemed to give would-be looters the opportunity they were looking for. At the beginning of the war, Sartre noted, many soldiers expected a cataclysm of artillery shells and aerial bombardment to devastate the area: it would erase all the signs of their pillaging.[151] Despite the discourse of national solidarity, French soldiers stole from, and damaged, the homes of those they should have been protecting.

The evacuees were appalled by the news of pillage. Many wrote in to complain: they repeated stories of soldiers sending back large parcels of looted goods, of the insufficient attention of the authorities, of the shame that these acts brought to the French army, and of their wish to return to examine the damage and protect their properties.[152] According to the Prefect of the Bas-Rhin, the incidents of looting were immediately exaggerated by those who wished to spread unfavourable propaganda.[153]

CONCLUSION

Of all the movements to be studied in this book, the evacuation of 1939–40 should have been the best organized. It had been discussed for 17 years; it had been planned by professionals; and it had even been rehearsed. It did not take place during a military crisis. The evacuees were not refugees: they did not spontaneously decide to leave their homes – they left as they instructed to do so. At first sight, their movement therefore seems quite different from that of the Spanish refugees: among the evacuees, no political groups engaged in significant activities. However, as one studies their experiences more closely, one notes some surprising resemblances. The first is simply semantic: government organizations, outside observers and the evacuees themselves all readily applied the term 'refugee' to those who were moved from the north-east. More importantly, their experiences trace out the condition of France in 1939–40. Some substantial charitable and philanthropic drives are certainly present, but the final impression is of an embittered, grumbling society, suspicious of outsiders, resentful and sceptical about central direction. Vigorous state action was not sufficient to create national unity. Like refugees, evacuees were 'people on the move'. Like refugees, they often came to feel like outcasts from their own country.

The French evacuations of 1939–40 present a model for the action of relief agencies: while they attempted to combine clear planning and humanitarian concern, in the last analysis they failed. In the second half on this work, we will turn to consider whether the post-1945 agencies were more successful.

3

The Exodus: French Internal Refugees, 1940

- The Broken Hinge
- May 1940
- Soldiers and Civilians: Encounters on the Road
- Images of the Crowd: The Mindless Underworld
- Making Sense of the *Exode*
- Solidarity on the Road
- Conclusion

In mid-June 1940 Georges Friedmann, mobilized into a French medical corps, visited the station at Niort.

> The railway workers and the station managers arrived and threw themselves into their work. They did not sleep or eat; they responded to everyone. Refugees came from everywhere: of course, for days before, there had no longer been any question of a plan. It was everyone for themselves, heading for wherever they could.[1]

Active combat began on French territory on 10 May 1940, when the Nazi blitz-krieg began and the *drôle de guerre* ended. As Nazi troops poured into the Low Countries and France during the following six weeks, civilians moved out in an unplanned and impulsive 'exode'. Friedmann's observations bring to light the sharp contrast between the previous, relatively well-prepared evacuations and the chaos of June 1940. This type of dichotomy has structured many contemporary accounts and secondary analyses, to the point where it has formed the dominant paradigm of interpretation. Thus, for example, the respected French historian Jean-Pierre Azéma insists that the evacuations of 1939 worked smoothly, whereas the *exode* was a 'monstrous migration' characterized by drama, anxiety and lost children.[2]

The previous chapters have concerned large population movements: about half a million people in the case of the *retirada*, and two to three million in the various evacuations. In this chapter, we move onto a different scale: it seems quite possible that as many as twelve million people, French, Belgian, Dutch and Luxembourgeois, plus assorted exiles, took to the roads in May and June 1940, probably representing about a quarter of the population of France. This was an unprecedented population movement, almost certainly the largest of its kind at that date, only to be dwarfed by the still-larger movements after 1945. The *exode* definitively demonstrated the failure of the carefully prepared French war plans and yet, curiously, it has often been ignored or side-lined from the historical agenda. In this respect, Claire Chevrillon – a Resistance militant – is quite typical. When she came to write her memoirs of the period, she told her readers that this would be a narrative of her life during a time of great historical events: defeat, occupation, collaboration, resistance and liberation.[3] The flight of 12 million people is subsumed into the more general category of defeat: it is not recognized as an episode in its own right. But detailed analysis of the *exode* leads us to question this historiography: why has this vast movement has been almost written out of the history books?

The term 'exodus' was originally used to describe Moses leading the Israelites out of slavery: it was not a heedless movement but one with a clear purpose. Rather than assuming that the millions of voyagers of May and June 1940 were victims of some mass psychosis, can one find similar, positive unifying themes in the myriad journeys which composed the *exode*? Was the *exode* an example of blind panic, or is it possible to assign meaning to it? We argue that rather than a thoughtless flight, the *exode* was a series of journeys, prompted by realistic fears and punctuated by diverse interactions, encounters and confrontations. Sometimes *exodiens* had a clear destination in mind, sometimes not, yet they all knew that they needed to escape from the occupying forces and bombs. On these journeys, civilians mixed more and more frequently with soldiers. The planned demarcation lines between the two grew blurred.

The following sections are primarily based upon soldiers' accounts of the *exode*, supplemented by observations from *exodiens* and administrative officials.

THE BROKEN HINGE

French evacuation plans and the passive defence programme were designed to contribute to military victory, to keep civilians away from direct military action and to preserve a patriotic sense of unified French identity. Unlike early modern wars, with their baggage trains and civilian observers, these plans allotted the army a specific sphere, separate from civilians. During the German invasion of May-June 1940, the barriers broke down. In the Low Countries and north-eastern France, millions left their homes and headed for the south and west, mingling with the mobilized soldiers, seeking safety somewhere – anywhere – else. Some of these travellers had very brief, uneventful journeys. The Moison family travelled the 4km from Templeuve to Geneche (Nord) and then back again. Their *exode* – probably the shortest on record – lasted for only one hour.[4] Other travellers planned their journeys carefully. For example, Andrée and her mother prepared to leave Beauvais on 26 May. They had little time, but they packed a few valuables and some potatoes, and they killed and cooked their last rabbit for the journey.[5] They were anxious, but they had not lost all sense of reason. At the other extreme, some *exodiens* were killed by enemy aircraft on the road, some stayed away for years and some never returned. Once again, like the evacuees of 1939-40, these travellers were usually described as refugees.

But unlike the Spanish refugees of the *retirada*, most of them had not left their country; instead the structures of their nation state collapsed around them. To understand this movement we need to step back and to consider, once more, the context of 1939-40.

The events from September 1939 to May 1940 could not be represented by the French government as outstanding military successes. But French people could be reassured that, if this was an odd sort of a war, *un drôle de guerre*, at least everything was as anticipated in the official projections. The right people were in the right places. Georges Sadoul, mobilized in 1939, swiftly became a bitter and perceptive critic of the French military policy. But even he seemed to feel a moment of optimism when he was sent to a warehouse near Nancy on 5 September. He observed a long procession of Lorrainers leaving, while he collected supplies for his unit. 'Here, everything seems to work perfectly, like a well-oiled machine'.[6] And, initially, most French people were confident about the capacities of the French Army.[7] They were bombarded with propaganda showing the impenetrable Maginot Line and robust soldiers. In 1938, Loubignac's film *Sommes-nous défendus?* provided this reassuring conclusion: 'France can ... at any moment, close the doors and turn the lock ... Today, the Maginot Line protects us from all evil projects'.[8] In September 1939, Paul Reynaud gloatingly announced that 'We will win because we are the strongest'.[9]

Few had any doubts about France's eventual triumph. Roland Dorgelès, working as a war reporter in 1939-40, could later recall: 'Defeat? That word was not something that worried us. If we felt the slightest concern, someone from Headquarters popped up to reassure us ... We had no doubts about the victory, we just wondered about its date'.[10] Friedmann reported the same degree of confidence. Looking back at the period before May 1940, he recalled that 'For months, despite weaknesses and failures, one could have faith in – and I'll say quite honestly I did – the construction of a vast structure of defence and attack, in the organization of a whole land for war'.[11] Similarly, Léon Werth acknowledged that he simply could not have imagined the defeat of the strong, well-prepared French troops.[12]

During the *drôle de guerre* the media celebrated the qualities of French soldiers, proof of the continuing solidity of France. Dorgelès himself wrote of their 'manly confidence. Invincible hope shines in their eyes'.[13] 'Ready Everywhere' the headline of the *l'Est Républicaine* proclaimed on 5 May 1940, 'Of course, victory is guaranteed'. On 9 April, *La Dépêche's* headline read 'Paris will Fall on 1 June', which was presented as a laughable example of German propaganda: it was assumed that its readers would readily see how ridiculous it was. More movingly, some officers seemed to feel similar emotions. Barlone recorded the following description of his soldiers.

> The heart of France is what it has always been – clean, honest, brave. I realize this all the
> more because through my men I can always put my finger on what is the true France.

All of them, humble folk, country folk, workpeople, small business proprietors – how patriotic, upright and worthy they are in every sense of the word.[14]

Henri Sautreuil was ten in 1940, and lived in Le Havre. His memoirs recall a similar confidence during the *drôle de guerre*.

> Of course, everyone said that victory was certain: did we not have the best sailors in the world? And as for planes, we had fast, manoeuvrable fighters ... Our English allies were the undisputed masters of the seas, and they had one the best fighters of the epoch, the Spitfire. And nobody could see how Hitler could overcome our famous Maginot Line.[15]

Such records illustrate the dominant discourse during the *drôle de guerre*.

Some suffered a more harrowing start to the war. Edith Thomas was a writer and a journalist who had reported on the Spanish Civil War. She describes a darkened, sombre Paris in the days before the invasion. There were no students and no children playing; French officers paraded themselves like conquering heroes and an old man in the metro told her that 'if I were in a concentration camp, at least I'd have something to eat'.[16] Foreign exiles complained of an increasing xenophobia, a 'war psychosis', that seemed to be gripping the French: a point to which we will return. Such dissident voices were usually ignored. No one wanted to be accused of defeatism; doubts were suppressed and expectations remained buoyant.[17]

For many, the previous 'Great War' served as a model for the conflict in 1939–40. The First World War had been a great victory for France, but it had come at a heavy cost: huge swathes of French territory had served as the battleground, about a million and half men had died and another million had been permanently mutilated.[18] It was not a straightforward victory, as Clemenceau recognized by entitling his memoirs *Grandeurs et misères d'une victoire* (1934). References back to the Great War were omnipresent. Blondeau, a boy during these years, recalled: 'in between the two wars, the war of 14 was at every meal!'.[19] Georges Gendreau, growing up in Brittany, recalled the same point. 'I was only ten [in 1940] ... but I already knew about war for the good reason that I had heard people talk about it every day since I was born'.[20] It has been argued that such conversations encouraged a sort of pacifist spirit in France, even amongst old soldiers.[21] Werth identified a slightly different, more worrying, response; he saw the French contemplating war 'like peasants watching hail fall', implying not pacifism but fatalism and passivity.[22] Paul Reynaud worried about this attitude, and as early as December 1939 he insisted in the Senate that 'It's not patience that we need, but courage'.[23]

During the seven months following the declaration of war, analyses, debates and information concerning the nature of war in general and the conflict of 1939–40 in particular circulated in France. It is impossible to summarize the mood of the entire population in a single phrase: while a clear confidence in France's military capacity was certainly dominant, this did not exclude some doubts and worries. French people certainly knew about the threats they faced: whether they were well prepared, or whether they learned the right lesson, are different questions. To paraphrase Reynaud, did the hinge break in June 1940?[24] The defeat seems to demonstrate conclusively that all the preparations were ineffective, but it is possible to put forward other perspectives.[25] The more significant point for our study is to consider why so many considered that flight was a rational and reasonable response to a serious military crisis.

MAY 1940

'Suddenly, there was war', Dorgelès observed.[26] With 4.5 million Frenchmen called up and the Nazi armies advancing, it was clear that the peculiar static war was now over.[27] A sense of urgency transformed newspaper headlines: 'Holland, Belgium, Luxemburg have been invaded'; 'The Barbarians shall not Pass'; 'Battle Rages from the North Sea to the Moselle'.[28] The Mayor of Cherbourg issued an appeal to the city's population, noting how the situation had changed: 'the bombing of towns by enemy aircraft is now no longer something which is merely possible. Events have proved to us that is a reality'.[29] A clear indication that the *drôle de guerre* was turning into a 'real' war was the radicalization of the previous emergency measures of September 1939. 'In these exceptional circumstances, you must not hesitate to use exceptional measures' ordered the Ministry of Supplies.[30] Countless small changes were implemented. In Rennes, cinemas, theatres and dance halls were all to close at 11.pm.[31] The city's school-teachers unanimously proposed that their annual school prize day should be cancelled due to the danger of aerial bombardment – after all, a similar measure had been implemented during the previous war. The Mayor also wrote to the religious authorities to tell them that their traditional ceremonies on 23 May and 3 June would be cancelled.[32] In Nancy, all football matches and horse races were banned; all cinemas, theatres, dance halls and concert halls were closed.[33]

The French began this war of movement as the observers of another wave of refugees. French evacuees were joined by hundreds of thousands of refugees from Belgium, Holland and Luxembourg: at first, these newcomers travelled down the established routes, through north-east France and onto the south and west. Belgians constituted the largest section of this new wave of refugees. There were some two million of them, of whom about 1.4 million managed to reach southern France.[34] The Prefect of the Pyrénées-Orientales alerted his mayors: 'These circumstances will certainly lead me to ask you to lodge a far greater number of refugees that originally envisaged … The resulting additional difficulties must be met by a stubborn will to succeed'.[35] The town of Evreux (Eure), with a population of fewer than 20,000, was told to prepare for the arrival of 45,000 refugees. 'What could one do with these thousands of human beings, lost as they were in a whirlpool of terror and misery?' wondered the American socialite, Consuelo Vanderbilt: she had volunteered to help.[36] Large numbers of French people then began to appear among the crowds of refugees. Various 'snapshot' statistics illustrate the flight of people from the north-east to the south and west. By 27 May the population of Lille had fallen from 200,000 to 20,000, and that of Roubaix from 122,000 to 15,000.[37] Conversely, the population of Bordeaux had been 258,348 in 1936: it contained more than 1.5 million people at the end of May 1940.[38] Pézenas (Hérault) housed evacuees, refugees and exiles from 16 nations in May 1940: the town's 30,000 French residents found that they had become a minority within this new population.[39] Georgette Guillot, secretary to the Ministry of Interior, first felt embarrassed as she stared at passing refugees from the comfort of her fashionable Parisian café, and then realized that she might be joining them in the very near future.[40]

Images of the French *exode* now emphasize speed, danger and a certain recklessness. The opening scenes of *Casablanca* (1942) and *Jeux interdits* (1952) portray desperate crowds rushing away. More recently, *Les Egarés* (2003) begins with people running down roads and across fields. Leaving aside the simple fact that is impossible to run for days on end, especially when carrying children or pushing a cart, in reality refugees' movements were more hesitant, more considered and less heedless than these images suggest. Françoise Meifredy, a Red Cross nurse, recorded the following conversations with an *exodien* in Lyon on 19 June.

> 'Aren't you leaving?' someone asked me early one morning.
> 'Why bother? We'll see what happens'.
> 'You're right. I would have stayed as well, but it was my wife … You see?'
> Another added: 'It's stupid to leave. It's like you're scared. But my old father is by himself, in a house in the south. I've got to be by him'.[41]

Chevrillon remembers leaving her Parisian school in May 1940: she had to pack in thirty minutes. One of her colleagues refused to leave: 'she was an officer's daughter, and was not going to flee before the enemy'.[42] The French–Polish Teseska Torres, 20 in 1940, recorded her criticisms of her parents' plans to leave in her diary. They sound almost like teenage pique. 'The spirit of this family: "run away from danger", instead of facing it … Leaving Paris now is *lunacy*. Incredible lunacy'.[43] These references show that there was something potentially embarrassing, even dishonourable about fleeing recklessly. Refugees discussed their movements, and rationalized them: running away was not an acceptable option, but leaving to support a wife or to look after an aged father was a different matter altogether. These comments may have been disingenuous, but they were not careless or inattentive.

Other accounts of the *exode* suggest a sense of civic entitlement. Refugees often trusted the efficacy of French authorities. Even after the invasion, many still thought that the French state was capable of organizing evacuation programmes, and expected to be treated as French citizens. After the first aerial bombardment of Nancy, the Mayor received a series of requests from citizens who wanted official help with their evacuation plans. On 22 May, Madame Haller asked him for a lorry so that she could take her children to Grenoble and stay with her uncle.[44] Monsieur Keller made a similar request: he wanted the Mayor to find him a car so that he could drive to Limoges.[45]

Haller and Keller clearly expected an extension of the benevolent state to accompany war and invasion. After all, such dire circumstances should have prompted generosity and sympathy. Instead, authorities reacted to the invasion by implementing the repressive policies of September 1939 more firmly. The editor of *Ouest-Eclair* provided an emphatic justification for such policies to his readers:

> Our children's lives are at stake. We see this more clearly now, after the four days [since the invasion], than in the last eight months! ... There is a fifth column in France, divided into different brigades ... There are communists, trotskyists, anarchists, false nationalists, with their chiefs, assistant chiefs, propagandists, officials and their accomplices, who act out of weakness or cruelty. Obviously, here, we cannot give details or figures. But the government has decided...
>
> Now, we must hit, and hit hard. There is a terrible struggle in the Low Countries and Belgium: are we going to hesitate to terrorise the internal enemy, to fight fire with fire throughout France?[46]

Similarly, *Le Temps* warned its readers about fifth columnists disguised as refugees. 'Extremely strict measure must be implemented so that an enemy which tramples over the most holy feelings of men does not, once again, exploit the generosity and natural pity of our land'.[47]

One important new measure demanded that all foreigners from enemy nations (a categorization which included German–Jewish exiles) were to be placed in internment camps.[48] Paul Burmetz, who had fled Austria with his Jewish wife and disabled daughter, tried to protest as he was locked in a police cell: his words provoked an extraordinary outburst from the nearest policeman: 'Dirty Boche ... One more word, and I'll smash your head ... You dirty Boche! There were a thousand children in Rotterdam! You understand? A thousand! Ten thousand! Ten thousand children and babies! You have burned them all! You have burned them or buried them alive!'.[49] Curiously, most of his new companions regarded such aggression with equanimity, hoping that it indicated that the French would fight determinedly against Nazi Germany. Others were less forgiving. Hans Fittko, a Jewish anti-fascist from Prague, followed a long line of internees from an open-air stadium into a truck that would take them to a more permanent camp. The waiting police hit each man in turn with their truncheons. Fittko himself was thumped on the head, and suffered a headache which lasted a week. 'It was small consolation to know that the blow was intended for Nazis'.[50] Soma Morgenstern, an east European Jew exiled in France, was still less generous. He noted this 'xenophobic psychosis' growing in France, and commented despairingly that the Georges Mandel, the new Minister of the

Interior, was doing what all 'strong men' do: hitting the very weak very hard.[51] In all, about 700,000 foreigners were interned between May and June 1940.[52]

Many new measures related, directly or indirectly, to population movement. The new refugees had to be directed and 'monitored rapidly' the Prefect of the Ille-et-Vilaine informed his mayors.[53] In Toulouse, the Prefect warned motorists that the city's accommodation was now full, and asked travellers to follow police directions to outlying communes.[54] During air raids, the citizens of Rennes were forbidden to walk along the pavements, and all private cars, trams and buses were to stop.[55] *Ouest-Eclair* explained: this was an example of a far-sighted municipality encouraging some less sensible citizens to be wise and cautious.[56] The announcement on 13 June 1940 by a Sub-Prefect in the Haute-Garonne was the logical conclusion of a long process. He bluntly ordered: 'Belgians must not circulate'.[57] In the south and west, an increasingly static, controlled France anticipated the arrival of refugees: in the north-east, a different tension was developing.

SOLDIERS AND CIVILIANS: ENCOUNTERS ON THE ROAD

In this section we will first consider an established account of the *exode*, and then suggest some other interpretations.

In mid-May, early descriptions of the war noted how combatants and refugees travelled in different directions. Henry Bordeaux, a prestigious French writer, described two groups passing each other: 'On this fine French road, two processions met ... One was slow and pitiful, the other fast and almost cheerful'.[58] More prosaically, Christian Habrioux, a 35-year-old artillery man, described a common scene in northern France, on 14 May. On one side of the road there were lines of troop lorries and tanks, heading north-east, while on the other side there was an unending, lamentable column of refugees from Belgium and Luxembourg.[59] Dorgelès suggests a similar contrast: he noted the 'sang-froid' of the soldiers, and then he turned to the refugees: 'Always the same stories of the dreadful bombing of defenceless homes ... At the station, trains following, one after another. Full of evacuees. Old men, women with uncombed hair, crying children'.[60] Friedmann met an unruly refugee crowd on 13 June: his unit had act to organize and reassure them.[61] Barlone felt sorry for the refugees but doubted some of their awful stories: were they telling them 'because they want to justify their plight?'.[62] Feldman was sympathetic to them, but also felt something like the awakening of a warrior spirit:

> They are everywhere: in the squares, by the river, along the roads; they've walked for 48 hours, they're half-starved, and they flee, flee, with their little identity card holders on their chests, their wheelbarrows and prams riddled with bullet-holes. When you see them, when I see them, I don't feel full of pity: it really is rage that fills me.[63]

He was left with a desire to fight the German invaders more fiercely. These comparisons emphasize the difference between soldiers and refugees: the two groups occupy different places because of their respective qualities. By distinguishing themselves from the crowd, the soldiers were asserting their superior status.

The Germans had advanced but – at first – the distinct spheres of civilians and soldiers were kept apart. French soldiers saw refugees as incidental to the real focus of the war; they were merely another good reason for fighting. Therefore these soldiers' accounts stressed the differences between civilians and combatants. They depict civilians gripped by panic and calm soldiers; the vulnerable are contrasted with the strong and well-armed; the civilians going in one direction, the troops in another: everything apparently proceeding to plan.

Later descriptions strike a different tone. British observers were probably the first to challenge the previous consensus. As German advance continued, the distinction between civilians and soldiers broke down, and the fleeing civilians were seen as culpable. Freeman and Cooper, part of a British ambulance unit in the north of France, blamed 'undisciplined hordes' for clogging the roads near Provins (Seine-et-Marne) and hindering troop movements. These people were 'oafish, stupid, uncomprehending'.[64] The magnificently pseudononymous 'Gun Buster', a British artillery officer, used similar terms for a comparable scene.

> Thousands and thousands and thousands of refugees, all pressing in the other direction, driven on by ceaseless terror, without order and without control. And struggling to force a passage in the opposite direction through this panic-stricken army were all the machines of war, British and French, tanks, guns, mortars, companies of mitrailleuses with motor cycles, their heavy machine-guns in side-cars, and trucks upon trucks of infantry. The confusion and shouting and screaming and cursing was a war in itself. Often a farm-cart would decide to pull out and try to pass the vehicle in front. Then the entire military column was held up till the chaos died down a bit. That sometimes took half an hour. This in a speed-war when every minute was precious, and an obstreperous farm-cart might lose us a lump of France![65]

Such analyses of refugees obstructing the war effort were accepted as accurate even by contemporary leaders. Churchill telegrammed General Ismay on 23 May 1940: 'The refugees should be driven into the fields and parked there, as proposed by General Weygand, so that the roads can be kept clear'.[66]

French soldiers also began to make similar complaints: as early as 15 May Barlone found that the increasing numbers of refugees 'jam all the roads and prevent the movement of military convoys'.[67] Miquel, basing his research on soldiers' oral testimony, noted that his interviewees even reported that this confusion was a deliberate German strategy. The Nazi bombers had one clear aim: 'to throw the civilian population onto the roads to hinder the movements of the French army'.[68] French military authorities were certainly troubled by the presence of civilians on the road. On 13 May officers instructed local police to forbid civilians from using the road to Chagny (Saône-et-Loire) for fear that they would hinder military manoeuvres.[69] On 18 May General Gamelin signed an order forbidding the non-authorized flight of civilians: its justification was the need to keep the roads free for troop movements.[70]

Most historians now agree that the refugees of May–June 1940 were caused by – and were not the cause of – the rapid success of the Nazi advance. As early as 1957, Vidalenc argued that sometimes soldiers had created the panic in the first place. At Flavy-le-Martel (Aisne) soldiers had encouraged the local population to evacuate by ringing on door-bells and shouting 'Sauvez-vous!'.[71] In addition, not only is there little convincing evidence to indicate that the crowds of refugees seriously blocked the armies' manoeuvres but – as Vidalenc points out – the many histories of the motorized and mechanized units of this period attach little importance to the *exode*.[72] Had these units been trapped by fleeing refugees, they would have noted it. Later historians such as Rioux also insist that the civilian *exode* had little effect on military operations, while Ollier notes that the refugees did not appear to hinder the French armies at all. If they really had blocked the roads then all troops – not just the French armies – would have been affected.[73] Alary clarifies: 'the *exode* followed the withdrawal of troops, and not the inverse'.[74] Yet the older interpretation is still repeated: Wyman has insisted that 'swarms of refugees' complicated the Allied efforts to 'thwart the German invasion in May and June 1940', and Marrus similarly refers to refugees becoming 'tangled' in military operations.[75] Such analyses reflect the anxieties of the military command at the end of the Second World War. They were convinced that civilians had impeded military progress and – rightly or wrongly – they were determined to ensure that it would not happen again. As a result, much established military and historical commentary rests on the difference between the uniformed, fighting soldier and the fleeing refugee: the refugee is the 'other', sometimes a victim, sometimes a rogue, but always other.

In contrast to this established interpretation, based on a sense of binary opposition, one can read the narratives from this period in a different manner: they portray a series of encounters between soldiers and civilians, and between men and women. In order to present this different interpretation, we will first review soldiers' experiences during the *drôle de guerre*.

The Third Republic had a system of compulsory military service, yet despite this preparation many men did not want to go to war in 1939, and many wives protested. Jean de Baroncelli, mobilized early in the war, describes the period immediately preceding September 1939 as one when men were anxious and in denial, and their wives simply refused to acknowledge the realities of conscription.[76] From September 1939 to April 1940 the mobilized but inactive soldiers were celebrated by French propaganda, but there is no doubt that the soldiers themselves were experiencing something different from the patriotic solidity such accounts evoked. The aimless wait of the *drôle de guerre* was unexpectedly difficult for many soldiers. One could cite the letters of Paul

Nizan, a conscript in 1939–40: 7 October, 'nothing to report', 21 October, 'nothing to record', 30 October, 'nothing new to record', 16 November, 'nothing to record', 28 December, 'nothing's happened since yesterday: this phrase sums up the life I'm living here', 6 March 'I'm really fed up'.[77] Other soldiers record similar feelings. On 17 October 1939, Sartre wrote in his diary 'I hate war' and two days later added 'I have no idea why I'm here. In any case, it's not to defend the nation, nor civilization. At best, it's to defend my freedom (above all, as I can't do anything else)'.[78] Georges Sadoul faced an awkward problem: how to keep a diary when nothing was happening. He gave up writing soon after Christmas 1939. Then a thought occurred to him late in January 1940: 'I was wrong to use the pretext that nothing happened to stop writing. That's true in an operational sense. But notes made day-by-day are the only way to get the atmosphere of this funny sort of war'.[79] Boredom sometimes turned into real depression. In April 1940, Feldman wrote of his profound despair, noting that 'this life is more and more exhausting'. The war just wore him down.[80] Using far more literary language, Friedmann recorded similar feelings in March 1940:

> O you who I love, with your sweet faces and dear looks, you who have some nobility, some real goodness, some love … I think of you this evening … All the sadness of this day, of this world, from dawn to dusk, all this awful stupidity, hangs heavily on my shoulders tonight. There is no light tonight, not even a sense of hope in your faces. I am so sad I could die: I feel so weak, this evening, in the middle of chaos.[81]

Some of these writers were undoubtedly unusual men: could Sartre ever be cited as a typical French soldier? Yet the congruity of their accounts is remarkable, and points to a general malaise. The *drôle de guerre* was a disillusioning experience, leaving soldiers feeling useless and incompetent. Perhaps most importantly of all, some began to doubt whether they were really contributing anything to the defence of France.

Ideally, such soldiers should have clearly differentiated themselves from civilians. Yet for these inactive soldiers, the civilian refugee was not always the 'other'. Sometimes they recognized their friends and family members amongst the crowds of evacuees and refugees; elsewhere, they could feel an easy identification with people like their friends or neighbours. Most French soldiers were not professional military men removed from the realities of civilian life and civilian worries: until recently they had been part of that world. When Father Boulé was posted to Haussonville (Meurthe-et-Moselle) in October 1939, he helped the local farmers, noting that 'their lives were like ours in Brittany'.[82] As Folcher was travelling through France during the *drôle de guerre* he often commented on the local agriculture and the condition of the farms he passed. Sometimes he seemed more interested in the farming than the soldiering: certainly he appeared to be as much of a peasant as a soldier.[83] Similarly, Sartre, stationed in Alsace, felt sorry for the Alsatian evacuees, and often commented on their tragic situation.[84]

For some, this strange compatibility ended on 10 May 1940, as soldiers were thrown into active combat, and civilians took to the roads. As we have seen, there are many accounts which stress the difference between the two groups. But, alongside these, other accounts continue to note the links, affinities and similarities between military and civilian lives. For many soldiers the *exode*, despite its horrors, was a welcome reminder of the foibles and comforts of domestic life. Henry de Montherlant was what we would now describe as an embedded journalist. He enjoyed the suspension of bourgeois norms which characterized the military life of the *drôle de guerre*.[85] For him, the retreating crowd of refugees was a bizarre mirror of the world the soldiers had only recently left, full of images of bourgeois life at its most absurd. 'A little cart leaves the town, full of refugees, and stops in front of us. On an old lady's knees is a cat with a collar. One of the soldiers says "That's a fine collar!" And the old lady replies, "Yes, we put it on him because it's Sunday"'.[86] Montherlant is clearly aware of the incongruity of the situation but – nonetheless – one cannot escape the conclusion that the soldiers enjoyed the episode. The scene may have been mildly ridiculous, but the lady was familiar: as far as these soldiers were concerned these refugees were certainly not 'the other'. Baroncelli's account gives a similar example, centred on the naïve romantic relationship between troops and a young woman they nicknamed 'Snow-White'. There is nothing unusual about soldiers falling in love with women whilst on campaign, but the French Army formalized this type of innocent romance through the 'marraine de guerre' (godmother) system. A woman of any age could become a soldier's godmother, and she would then write him letters, send him parcels and presents, and generally care for him in the way that a mother or wife should. One of Baroncelli's troop proposed that 'Snow-White' should be godmother to them all.[87]

The oft-noted chaos and confusion of the *exode* was hardly something that would have seemed new to soldiers. When Barlone described the first movements of his unit in September 1939, he remembered thinking: 'On to the next stop? Why does one stop? No one will ever know'.[88] Baroncelli described the chaotic movements of his motorcycle troop during the *drôle de guerre*, sometimes lost and often confused. Feldman's comments suggest a bitter exhaustion: for every order, a counter-order eventually arrived. 'Nine orders out of ten are aimed at correcting the stupidity of the tenth'.[89] Even the doggedly patriotic Marc Bloch complained in a similar manner of the stream of orders and counter-orders after 10 May, while Folcher recalled 'an avalanche of orders' in the same days.[90] There was little clear information; soldiers operated in a world of half-truth, rumour and hope. Friedmann described his frenzied evacuation: '6.am, 16 May: "Order for immediate evacuation". "Evacuation"? How? The men left on foot, with barely any time to pack ... Everything's upside down. The actions and plans of all the orders are usually torn up, shredded, in pieces'.[91] Near Vimy, 'Gun Buster' was appalled by the sight of the refugees he met. His comments are interesting: at first, they sound like familiar statements of British despair at French inadequacy and of military superiority over nervous civilians. However, another theme emerges at the end.

> The total absence of any sign that these poor wretches had received any assistance accentuated the horror … It was typical of the utter breakdown of the French civilian relief services all over the northern invasion area … Certainly there was never a hint of refugee camps, mobile canteens, or civilian casualty stations…
>
> The miserable refugees received no instruction where to make for. There was never a gendarme to be seen controlling and directing them. They just wandered along in a dumb panic, bombed here, machine-gunned there, imploring any troops they met to tell them a safe route to take to get away from the Germans. To proffer advice on such occasions was dubious assistance. So quickly did the situation change that it was quite easy, without knowing it, to shepherd inquirers straight towards the German tanks.[92]

In this account 'Gun Buster' starts to assume an approximate equality between soldier and refugee. The oft-cited opposition between the well-ordered military machine and the chaotic crowd seemed more and more unconvincing, for military movements were frequently disorderly. Civilians and soldiers shared similar experiences. After her own harrowing *exode,* Guillot felt that she understood military manoeuvres more; she became less inclined arbitrarily to judge the army and its generals.[93]

As military plans broke down, soldiers returned to the notorious *Système D*, which in this context meant forced requisitioning and looting. During the revolutionary and Napoleonic wars soldiers had done this because there were generally no established supply chains.[94] This sort of random supply method – one relying heavily on the civilian world – should not have featured in a modern European theatre of war. Initially civilians were usually happy to help their own soldiers, as the warm relations between Baroncelli's motorcycle troop and the local farmer indicate. Later, as the threat of invasion became real, civilians were often prepared to give supplies to French troops so as to prevent German troops from seizing them. Habrioux described drinking large glasses of pernod in a town in the north of France on the 14 May. The inhabitants were desperate to leave before the Germans arrived and so the bistrot owners were giving everything away.[95] Claud Jamet, stationed near Thionville (Moselle) tells a similar story about bistrot owners giving free beer to the soldiers.[96] This can be seen as a patriotic gesture of support for French soldiers or even as a sort of scorched earth policy. However, it could also be a justification for looting. In areas which had either been invaded or were on the verge of invasion, French soldiers could justify looting by telling themselves that they were at least preventing the Germans from doing so.

As the war progressed, soldiers and refugees no longer formed two streams of movement, heading in opposite directions. Instead, soldiers were heading in the same direction as civilians, and moving in an equally unplanned, unprepared manner. On 11 June, Friedmann grumbled about his evacuation orders:

I found my comrades of the High Command once more, at Château-du-Loir: they were unhappy, even a bit ashamed. Although I obeyed my commander's orders and I know that the medical service must follow the army's withdrawal, I feel that unhappiness of all those who are 'going down' [southwards]. If, by some miracle, the war continues in France, I'll ask for a post in forward unit.[97]

His comments suggest disappointment: rather than staying to fight, his unit was heading in the same direction as the civilians. Sautreil met soldiers in Lisieux (Calvados) who had been told 'go as far as you can', and who were therefore heading for the south.[98] Kermadec's unit travelled 'along the route of the *exode*', and soon became mixed up with the refugees. After ten days of continual travel, with little food or sleep, his unit looked like 'zombies', carried by their machines rather than driving them.[99] During the hasty retreat Baroncelli describes soldiers going through the process of deciding what to keep and what to throw away.[100] Soldiers are normally instructed to carry particular kits for specific purposes but the defeat made them act like the evacuees and refugees around them. Similarly, soldiers and civilians were alike in their thirst for accurate information. 'Maps were the most precious things one could possess in those days' observed Major General Sir Edward Spears.[101] Soldiers also wanted newspapers, letters and access to the radio. Much has been made of the chaos and panic of the *exode*, of civilians fleeing like a disorderly rabble in fear of the Nazi invaders. Yet there was also disorder and confusion amongst the retreating troops: the two groups were more similar than has previously been acknowledged.

While retreating from the fighting in north-east France, there was also a growing realization among soldiers and other observers that this was a war which would be won by effective, fast, coordinated action. 'Gun Buster' summed up the main rule of the campaign: 'Move, move, move all the time … [this was a] moving war. Moving at top speed'.[102] It was precisely this war that the French Army seemed to be losing: Bloch found that the Germans had fought a modern war, 'ruled by speed'.[103] 'A war of boldness, speed and surprise; just the opposite of what we had foreseen', noted Dorgelès.[104] Years previously, De Gaulle had warned of the dangers of making passivity – symbolized by the Maginot Line – the main principle of the French defence.[105] By June 1940, many were echoing his observations. Boulé noted that while the Germans travelled in cars and lorries, the French soldiers walked.[106] 'The Germans believed in action and surprise', concluded Bloch, 'we placed our trust in immobility'.[107] As it became clearer that France had lost the War of Speed, another vital distinction between the well-prepared, trained soldier and the panic-stricken civilian also disappeared.

One further point to be considered here is the clear decline of the army's prestige. During the evacuations, there was the scandal of French soldiers looting French villages. By June 1940, the army also carried the stigma of losing the war. Baroncelli was keenly aware of the change in civilian attitudes towards him. During the *drôle de guerre* soldiers had been warmly welcomed but by the end of the war civilian disdain was palpable: he was not served properly in a café because he was one of those 'little bastards who lost the war'.[108] Chamson later wrote of the officers in their best uniforms, driving away from the battle-field with their girls [poules].[109] On 16 June, Folcher participated in the last movements of his unit at Saint-Dizier. Civilians watched them: 'Many women cried, and the men hung their heads as they watched the last pathetic scraps of the French Army pass by: covered in mud and blood, their uniforms in rags: it was pitiful to see'.[110] There was little obvious difference between beaten soldiers and deserters. A carpenter near Beauvais did not even attempt to make the distinction: 'Deserters', he said, eyeing up the bedraggled French soldiers. 'In 1914 they would have been shot. But now there are no more military police'.[111] François Goutalier, watching French soldiers in the Marne on 12 June, made a similar observation: 'The disbanded soldiers, without their weapons, joining the refugees in little groups of two or three, looked more like deserters than a fighting unit'.[112]

In stark contrast to the haggard, undisciplined remnants of the French Army, the German soldiers appeared orderly and sometimes even helpful. They set up soup kitchens when they reached Paris. They did loot but they also distributed food to the refugees. Werth recalls his mixed emotions after he accepted a tin from a German conqueror: he realized that the tin was French![113] There appear to have been no atrocities similar to those of 1914, and it is certainly the case that the Nazi invaders were more restrained on the western front in 1940 than they had been in Poland in 1939 or than they would be in Russia in 1941. In the words of Thomas Kernan, the American editor of French *Vogue*, 'If the German was going to rule with an iron hand, it was at least tidily gloved'.[114]

These growing similarities between soldiers and civilians explain some soldiers' reactions to the crowd of refugees. As noted above, some soldiers resented refugees who got in the way of straightforward 'soldiering'. On 19 May, in an attempt to control civilian movements, Weygand forbade all further evacuations. Those moving without evacuation orders, however, could still be admired by soldiers for taking the initiative. Certainly new refugees were disobeying orders, but these soldiers knew that in war, improvisation was often necessary when events move faster than official commands. They understood that refugees were trying to escape German occupation, and that many of them had memories of German atrocities during the Great War; a few refugees even remembered the German invasion of 1870. On 29 May Sadoul was stationed near the Amiens (Somme). He met an old couple in their sixties: the woman walking with a stick, the man resting a parcel on a bicycle. They told him that this was their third evacuation: they had left before in 1914 and 1918.[115] He was clearly moved by their story: in a sense, he was learning from them. Folcher was most affected by the sight of refugee families struggling for weeks to bring their cattle with them, before finally being forced to leave them behind.[116] Baroncelli's troop helped to evacuate people from a hospital.[117] Such sympathy was reinforced when soldiers realized that the *exode*, far from being peopled by 'the other', was made up of recognizable individuals, similar to their own sisters, mothers, wives or girlfriends. Kermadec was constantly looking for his wife and mother-in-law in the crowds.[118] Habrioux gave bread to two women in a crowd and noted that they reminded him of his mother and his sister.[119] Montherlant describes soldiers who were worried for their own families, and of one soldier in particular who tried to search for his wife and child after hearing that they had left Paris and were on the road somewhere.[120] Other soldiers were worried about those who were not on the road. Baroncelli talked to an anxious soldier who insisted that there were worse things than being a refugee, and that those who had stayed in their homes risked more than hunger or tiredness.[121] The soldier was obviously hinting at rape and at the understandable fear that invasion would be accompanied by atrocity. This soldier seemed to ignore the sexual attacks that women suffered from French soldiers during the *exode* itself.[122] Nevertheless his comments describe the *exode* as a place of relative safety for women: a memorable and positive statement about the *exode* in particular and the refugee crowd in general.

IMAGES OF THE CROWD: THE MINDLESS UNDERWORLD

Vidalenc, the first historian of the *exode*, regretted the lack of personal accounts of this great drama. His observation is only partly true: a very small proportion of those on the *exode* produced direct accounts of their journeys, but personal descriptions are not as meagre as was first thought. A more important factor inhibiting analysis of this monumental event has been the tendency to dismiss it as simply rowdy, disruptive and mindless.

While the crowds of *exodiens* never attracted the same hatred as the Spanish refugees, few observers viewed them with respect. Gustave Le Bon's work on the irrational crowd was influential in the Third Republic: he had argued that the crowd formed an irrational, feminine collectivity, dominated by unconscious rather than conscious considerations.[123] Echoes of such ideas structure many descriptions of the *exode*. It seems that while desperate people can provoke sympathy, they rarely meet solidarity; they provoke revulsion more often than compassion. Hence Ollier's pitiless phrase: for some observers the refugees were part of 'a mindless underworld'.[124]

As we have seen, a common attitude was that the fleeing refugee was an inevitable counterpart of the purposeful soldier. For such observers, the refugee crowd was a loose element, a potential challenge to the tightly disciplined wartime community celebrated in newspaper editorials and official announcements. The State was there to 'organise, coordinate, evaluate', wrote L.-A. Pagès in *Ouest-Eclair*: ordinary citizens needed to develop similar discipline in their own lives.[125] At a moment when mastery of movement was becoming the central issue in the war – fast or ultra-fast for soldiers, slow or static for civilians – the itinerant *exodiens* could even be seen as rebelling against the patriotic policy required for the survival of the nation. For these reasons, there developed a sense of shame about participation in the *exode* even as early as the summer of 1940: a point which partially explains the relative paucity of accounts by participants.

Many contemporary accounts present the *exodiens* as irrational and helpless without the guidance of a state which had failed to act on behalf of its citizens. André Morize insisted on their madness: 'France was mixed-up, tangled like some immense ball of wool which had been mistreated by some malign superhuman power'.[126] Dorgelès gave a description of the scene at Cambrai (Nord) station: 'Terrified by the bombing, thousands of people fled, holding onto bundles, dragging their kids behind them, not knowing where to go. "Head for Ailly-sur-Noye, there are trains there!" someone shouted to them'.[127] Fabre-Luce, a collaborator who wrote one of the first French interpretations of the *exode*, also uses concepts of crowd psychology: this was a movement 'driven by fear and famine' which hindered the French Army and pushed people out to the Pyrenees.[128] His words suggest a crowd which is not quite human: through losing their rationality and autonomy, the crowd had lost their own humanity. Bestial images also occur repeatedly in other descriptions. Irène Némirovsky's interesting but over-praised account of the *exode* falls into this category. She depicts it as a type of sub-Darwinian struggle for existence. 'This miserable multitude no longer had any human features,' she wrote, 'it was like a herd that had been put to flight'.[129] For Friedmann, *exodiens* did not even deserve the name of 'refugee'. They were more like beasts, living in accordance with Kipling's rule of the jungle.[130] Ollier compared them to 'blind insects'; St Exupéry likened them to ants scattering from their anthill; Guillot thought of them as sheep.[131]

There was something pathetic and ridiculous about these strange convoys. Mexandeau, observing refugees passing through his village of Wanquetin (Pas-de-Calais) in mid-May, could even laugh at them. 'Nobody has ever tried to list those little domestic items that they thought were essential or valuable. Furniture, sheets, plates, blankets, cutlery: everything for a house removal that was both incomplete and absurd'. They took their cows and 'everyone had their dog'. They stopped every 200 metres, already too tired to carry on, but unable to leave anything behind. The funniest of all was a tall bearded cyclist, who passed by calmly, his hands firmly gripping the handlebars. He had a six-pound loaf tied round his neck, and he regularly bit off pieces as he cycled.[132] *Exodiens* themselves were acutely aware of the strains and tensions of their journeys. Werth, stuck in a vast traffic jam somewhere near the Loire in mid-June, travelling at a maximum speed of four kilometres an hour, observed the mounting resentment of those around him. 'The convoy, which had been quite patient until then, became bad-tempered, rocked by waves of fear, mistrust and hate. Those in cars complained that the carts were slowing them down, those in carts complained that the people in cars thought that they could do anything. "It's us who feed you"'.[133] Georges Filoque's account of his *exode* raises an important question about the rationality of the whole enterprise. He returned to his house in Les Andelys (Eure) on Monday 19 August: the army had been defeated, the Republic had collapsed, France had been occupied. While he had lived in other people's houses in the south of France, his own home been occupied by a homeless family.[134] Reading this account one can easily wonder: what was the point of this *exode*?

This image of the irrational crowd – the mindless underworld – could be manipulated in several ways. It could be used to target elites, implying some sort of social desertion. Freeman and Cooper clearly blamed the collapsing and culpable French authorities. They lamented the lack of governance that had enabled the *exode* to take place, so that for want of leadership, sane people had been allowed to become insane.[135] Women, children and the elderly were on the roads of France, unprotected from enemy bombing: there could be no better symbol of an ineffective regime.[136] Louis Mexandeau voiced similar criticisms: France was sliding into anarchy because 'those who should have given an example and continued to exercise public authority had themselves fled, often in their official cars'.[137] Koestler noted something similar: his comments sound positively spiteful. 'It was a peculiar sadistic irony of Fate, to have turned the most *petit-bourgeois*, fussing, stay-at-home people in the world into a nation of tramps'.[138] Taking a different approach to the same theme, Fabre-Luce's easy reference to a frantic minority who – in September 1939 – could afford to flee from Paris at 100 kilometres an hour, or Dorgelès's brief evocation of the 'luxury refugees' who, early in July 1940, could still afford to buy petrol, meals and hotel rooms in Limoges, suggest that the *exode* was a form of social decomposition, led by irresponsible elites.[139] Such examples show how the image of the *exode* could be exploited politically.

There is good reason, however, to doubt whether 'fear and panic' is sufficient explanation for the *exode*: rather than using social psychology as a means to explain the movement, such accounts frequently seem to refer to social-psychological concepts in order to argue that the movement was inexplicable. One can easily understand that any attempt to generalize about a movement without a clear centre or directing organization, involving over 10 million people, and spread out all over France, is challenging. But it remains true that there is something too easy, almost lazy, in these analyses.

MAKING SENSE OF THE *EXODE*

The first point towards understanding the *exode* is to note that there were observable rules in its movements. One unusual document which demonstrates this comes from Fougères (Ille-et-Vilaine), where a record of all refugees requesting a petrol allowance from 18 May to 15 June 1940 has been preserved.[140] In sum, 83 such requests were made, involving some 213 people: 93 women, 49 men, 50 children, plus 21 people who cannot be precisely identified. This impression of the participants – half women, a quarter men, a quarter children – is probably a reasonable representation of the *exode* as a whole. They tended to travel in groups. Only 24 travelled alone; there were 30 groups of 2 people, 14 groups of 3, 9 groups of 4, 4 groups of 5, and single groups of 11 and 20 people. Often these groups are based on families, but only 29 of the 83 requests are from married couples: instead, groups of mothers and children, or grandmothers, mothers and children, are more common. Like the refugees of the *retirada*, they formed in improvised groups. The departments from which they originate are predictable: about a quarter are from Belgium, more than half from the north and east of France, and eighteen are from the Paris region.

This data covers 30 days, which can be divided into five six-day periods. For the first 24 days the relative proportions of the numbers of women, men and children stay approximately constant, but in the mid-June there is a sudden surge in the number of women travelling, often originating from Paris.

Days	women	men	children	totals
1–6	18	12	10	40
7–12	9	7	3	19
13–18	13	6	9	28
19–24*	11*	7*	3*	41
25–30	42	17	25	84
totals	93*	49*	50*	212

* incomplete data
Table One: Petrol Voucher Requests in Fougères, 18 May – 15 June 1940

Travellers were also required to declare the destination to which they intended to travel.

Days	Most Popular Destination	Second Most Popular Destination
1–6	Haute-Garonne	Finistère
7–12	Haute-Garonne	No clear pattern
13–18	Ille-et-Vilaine	Côtes-du-Nord
19–24	Vendée	Indre
25–30	Morbihan	No clear pattern

Table Two: Listed Destinations of Travellers making requests for petrol vouchers.

In the first 12 days, Toulouse was the most popular destination: these were travellers who thought of their arrival in Brittany as merely the first stage of a longer journey. The southern city may have been popular due to its access to the Spanish border, as a staging-post to Marseille or simply because it seemed as far away as possible from the invasion. The majority of these travellers, however, were planning far shorter journeys, usually to friends, relatives or other contacts nearby. One simple point here is that, obviously, anyone who has the time and ability to plan a journey and request a petrol voucher does not sound like someone in the grip of irrational panic.

Rather than structured by irrational panic, many *exodiens'* journeys required forethought and real resilience. In descriptions of the *exode,* it is cyclists who come closest to presenting a positive, almost glamorous, image. Alongside the old carts, lumbering lorries and over-heated cars, they could seem light, free and fast; in the queues of blocked traffic and frayed tempers, only they 'moved easily, shouting to one another almost cheerfully'.[141] Victor Serge described a young man being sent off by bicycle from Paris to the Midi. The family jewels were sewn into his clothes, making this a dangerous as well as an arduous expedition.[142] A clerk from La Samaritaine, one of Paris's plushest department stores, achieved an even more startling feat. He cycled from Paris to Grandcamps-les-Bains (Calvados), a distance of nearly 300 km, in order to look for his family. Failing to find them, he cycled back to Paris where he found a letter telling him to return to Grandcamps-les-Bains as his family were waiting for him: he departed immediately. Each stage of his journey took approximately 20 hours.[143]

Women demonstrated a similar resilience. Alda Stasse was living in Ferté-Bernard (Sarthe) in May 1940. Her husband was away in the army and she listened intently to the radio to follow the news of battles and troop movements. Stasse was afraid when the first bombing raids began. She, her sister and all their children decided to leave. They had no idea where to go but they realized that they had to move away from the fighting and from the threat of bombardment. They eventually settled in Sarran (Corrèze), a village almost 550 km from their home: they had not had access to clear information, they had often been afraid but they still made coherent decisions and they did move their children to a place of relative safety.[144]

These are not heroic stories in the classic wartime mode. These people did not perform extraordinarily daring deeds; they did not run unnecessary risks with their own lives. Nevertheless, they demonstrated courage, commitment and endurance: they were not 'blind insects'. When they were bombed, they were obviously terrified; when the roads became one enormous traffic jam, they grew irritated. Yet fear and frustration were not their only emotions. We have long accepted that soldiers' memories of war are complex: they invoke terror, horror, boredom, joy, excitement, satisfaction and frivolity. The *exodien* experience was similar, and one basic error by most previous analyses has been their concentration only on the most negative themes. In reality, other aspects have been documented. Morize compared the atmosphere of the *exode* to that of people camping, or of going on a picnic.[145] When Sautreuil followed the lines of people leaving Le Havre, he was reminded of going on a pilgrimage.[146] Travelling near Vendôme in mid-June, Dorgelès was surprised by the mood of the crowd around him. It seemed like a 'compulsory holiday ... This unnatural phrase kept coming back to me'. People were fleeing danger, but they did not seem scared. Dorgelès was amazed when he saw how this vast, tense, heterogeneous crowd would obey the commands of a single boy scout at a crossroads. 'What surprised me above all else was the meekness of this crowd ... People repeat how furious the crowd was as if it was a line from a catechism: I saw the opposite. The behaviour of these poor people was the saving grace of those dreadful days'.[147] Edmond Delage, writing in *Le Temps* made some similar observations.

> There was no panic, just some signs of sadness on these wild faces. A whole people is migrating – they say that more than seventy thousand Belgian cars passed over a single bridge at the Loire – and there is hardly any sign of sadness under this fine summer sun. One senses, among these pursued people, their liberation, like something soothing: they are now driving on fine French roads.[148]

Near Lisieux (Calvados), a woman gave Sautreuil's family some water to drink. His mother offered to pay, but she refused, remarking 'we've got to help each other'. On reflection, however, she accepted their heavy bags of sugar in lieu of payment.[149] Werth's account records a mechanic who repaired *exodiens'* cars for free.[150] With one or two notable exceptions he met no one who could accept the idea of a peace dictated by Hitler.[151] Alongside misery, bravery, desperation and distress, there was also calm courage, good humour, mutual aid and a will to live.

In an early analysis of the *exode,* Vidalenc insisted that its participants had been motivated by more than basic self-preservation. The *exodiens* refused to accept enemy domination: their journeys symbolized refusal of collaboration and of co-existence with the enemy.[152] His point is valid. For all the descriptions of chaos and anguish, we need to remember that the refugees were motivated by a will to live and a rejection of Nazi power.

There was also a rational, decision-making element in the *exode.* Alda Stasse was not the only one who remembers listening intently to the radio, considering her options. Edith Thomas did the same, as did Mary Jayne Gold, an American heiress who fled to Marseilles to avoid the Nazis in 1940.[153] Many French people thought they knew what German occupation would entail. The peasants in the north were in no doubt: 'The Germans will arrive and they will burn everything like they did in 1914'.[154] The atrocity stories of the First World War still circulated, as did tales about the more banal aspects of life under foreign rule: the poor currency exchange, the collapse of property prices, the devaluation of money. Some French people seemed quite naïve about the possible impact of German rule. Werth met some women who seemed quite sanguine about the approaching Germans: 'It will be a protectorate like in Morocco ... we won't be any worse off, we'll work as before'.[155]

Such judgements were clearly mistaken: one must note that – nevertheless –
they are evidence of people attempting to make rational decisions based on the
information that was available to them. Often this information was unreliable
or, given the speed of war, it had become out of date. People could no longer
rely on the telephone system or radio broadcasts; the newspapers appeared
sporadically, if at all; letters sometimes arrived but not with any regularity.
For Thomas, this was one of the key characteristics of the *exode*: there were
no letters.[156] Sautreuil's mother complained that after moving so often, she no
longer knew which day it was.[157] Sadoul had time to laugh at two tearful ladies
he met near Sully (Loiret). He advised them to get away from the Loire, and
to head south. 'But where is the Loire?', they replied, 'Which way is south?'.[158]
Even when newspapers appeared it was sometimes hard to decipher the information. Was a 'brèche' [breach] better than a 'défaite' [defeat]? When one read
of a 'repli' [withdrawal], was this less serious than a 'retraite' [retreat]?[159] In
the absence of clear, accurate news, people had to rely on haphazard informal
communication systems for information about significant political events,
from which they could make decisions about their journeys. Morize happened
to bump into an officer he knew, on the street. The officer had come from
Tours and so could tell him that the government had recently left Tours for
Bordeaux.[160] Lisa Fittko looked out for other German exiles on the roads. She
claimed that she could always recognize them: they would stop and exchange
news about the people they'd met, and then record the information in little
notebooks.[161]

Exodiens had to rely on word of mouth and chance encounters. This
encouraged the spread of rumours. They heard that the Russians had declared
war on Germany; that they would be safe beyond the Loire; that revolution had
broken out in Germany; that Hitler and Goering had fled; that the German
advance had been stopped; that the Belgians had defended themselves magnificently.[162] These stories were inaccurate, but not completely implausible. During
previous invasions the German armies had not ventured south of the Loire;
despite the Nazi–Soviet pact, there remained a possibility of war between the
two, deeply hostile powers. More significantly, rumours like this have a clear
emotional function. They reassured people that all would be well in the near
future: as soon as the Russians or the Belgians arrive or when one has crossed
the Loire, then – it was said – there will be no more danger. Werth believed the
rumour that Russia had declared war on Germany, and then later recorded:
'Historians may laugh at my naivety, if they want. But we so needed to hear
this!'.[163] Other rumours seemed to exacerbate alarm. People feared rape, pillage
and strangulation; they told stories about clandestine radio stations, fifth
columnists or stray parachutists.[164] These stories were a way of expressing fears,
fears that were certainly exaggerated but not unfounded because one expects
spies in wartime, and pillage had already taken place. Moreover these were the
very dangers that authorities and newspaper editorials had urged citizens to
look out for. The rumours of the *exode* do not indicate that French people had

lost all sense of reason, merely that official information was unreliable and not readily available.

Another factor affecting people's decision-making powers was that sometimes they had to make decisions when it was beyond their powers to calculate the consequences. Refugees wanted to escape bombardment and occupation, but deciding on a safe route or a safe haven was genuinely difficult. Were German planes really attacking the trains? If so, it might be safer to travel by road.[165] Georgette Guillot thought that she would be safer in a town than in an isolated, rural spot; Hans Fittko advised his wife to look for a safe place to hide in the countryside.[166] Neither could be certain: refugees made guesses; certainty would have required a detailed familiarity with Nazi war plans.

Some refugees, however, did not merely claim that they were in a good position to make educated guesses: some went on to claim that they possessed a specific experience, of greater value even than the French memories of 1871, 1914 and 1918. This gave them a type of superior status to ordinary refugees. This elite were the foreign exiles. 'Going underground was nothing new for us; we'd been experts at it since 1933' noted Lisa Fittko.[167] Serge depicts 'Ortiga' watching the *exode* and remembering the *retirada*, and then bitterly noting he had now become 'an expert in defeats'.[168] Morgenstern even felt a brief moment of pity for the terrified French soldiers. 'These soldiers were more scared than us because there was more room for fear in their hearts than in ours. For days, our hearts had been filled with the fear of the Gestapo'.[169] In particular, Spanish accounts often claim a particular expertise. Leading his little group of Basque refugees to the French–Belgian border on 10 May 1940, Aguirre had time to note how the Basques were not gripped by 'the whiplash of fear ... We were calmer only because we had more experience ... We had seen it all before'.[170] Elsewhere, Spanish memoirs include a distinct 'I-told-you-so' streak: they were not surprised by the outbreak of war; they could see the fear on the *exodiens'* faces but they knew it was not a true tragedy, like the *retirada*, for many *exodiens* left without knowing what they were doing; they were not surprised by the fall of Paris.[171] At first sight, these comments may sound like nothing more than expressions of a sort of wounded pride. However, it should also be noted that of all the accounts of this period, it is the Spanish accounts which have the strongest claim to be realistic and coherent.

The common stereotypes of chaos and panic are not adequate to represent the full variety of *exodiens'* experiences: rationality and resilience in tough circumstances also need to be remembered.

SOLIDARITY ON THE ROAD

In a sense, this chapter and the previous two chapters have been considering appeals for solidarity. While the Spanish refugees met some compassion in France, they also faced sustained hatred. While the government promoted the cause of the evacuees, and made explicit appeal to French patriotic ideals, the evidence is clear that evacuees were often met with indifference, carelessness and sometimes resentment. How did the *exodiens* fare?

In a curious manner, at first they were often ignored. The movement of Belgian refugees was reported briefly in the French media: there were some references to the 'pitiful convoys', 'the anguished exodus of [Belgian] refugees' who were 'fleeing Teutonic barbarism'.[172] Such references could be integrated into the interpretative structures previously noted: the anguish of the refugees was merely the backdrop for the steadfast bravery of the professional soldiers; the refugees' experience was merely another justification for the war. Sometimes the plight of the *exodiens* conferred a sort of moral authority on them. At the end of May 1940, Doctor Limouzi was a refugee in Orleans. Limouzi, an *ancien combattant* who been wounded in the Great War, complained that each evening he and the other refugees could hear an orchestra playing frivolous tunes from a building in the Place de Martois. The *Journal du Loiret* agreed that this was 'indecent': the suffering of the *exodiens* was making the rest of the population face up to the grave realities of war.[173]

However, as the movement of refugees grew, and as more and more French people joined their ranks, the reports on them became less frequent, and were often re-categorized as merely local news, in which 'the story' was reduced to 'many examples of devotion', in other words to the generosity and the efficiency of the French reception.[174] This choice appears to have been an example of self-censorship. There was no formal government ban on reporting the movement of French refugees, although there could be problems with articles which gave details of the areas from which refugees originated, for this could allow readers to map the extent of the German advance.[175] The main problem was that newspaper editors found it difficult to see how this mass exodus could be integrated into the hyper-patriotic discourse that dominated. Instead, the headline news consistently following the progress of the fighting, and French papers struggled manfully for six weeks to transform this into a good news story. When people realized the contrast between these public, confident expectations and the real nature of the oncoming disaster, they were often stunned. Georgette Guillot was taken aback to learn that that Germans had crossed the Maginot Line. 'Ever since Paul Reynaud told us that "the hinge has snapped", I can see that nothing is working. What's going to happen to us?'.[176] The physical presence of refugees was often a first convincing sign that the optimistic press reports were false.

In the last weeks of the fighting, however, some reporters did note the *exode*. And here, surprisingly, one finds some examples of a real spirit of solidarity. When fishermen arrived in Brittany from Belgium and northern France, 'we immediately recognized them as our own people' reported *Ouest-Eclair*.[177] Paul Cressard's article on 'The *Exode* of the Country People', published in *Ouest-Eclair* on 6 June, was both genuinely moving and perceptive. These caravans of peasants were an 'example of bravery'. They had walked, trudged and stomped their way across France for weeks, even for over a month, some carrying three generations in their carts. They had been attacked by 'the barbarians'. They travelled from sunrise to long after sunset, stopping at midday to eat hard bread, with a bit of chocolate or cheese. They had left behind their fields, their crops and their cattle: 'Anyone who's a countryman at heart will understand the anguish'. Cassard cleverly blocked the most common objection to refugees: that they were lazy people, looking to live off government subsidies. These people 'bring us their arms', they want to work. 'Yes, country folk, welcome your comrades from the fields, just as the townsfolk have welcomed their colleagues from the offices and workshops'.

Some similar expressions are present in the accounts by *exodiens*. Stanley Hoffman, the respected historian, has presented a vivid description of his *exode*. His family arrived in the little southern town of Lamalou-les-Bains (Hérault), and found that over 10,000 refugees had overwhelmed the town's hotels.

> The most striking point, however, was the harmony that reigned within this apparent chaos ... Everything took place with a good humour tinged with sadness, with a dignity created by compassion and shame, in a climate of solidarity in face of a challenge that restrictions and bitter divisions had not yet spoilt.[178]

Sautreuil's family left Le Havre and, after days on the road, found themselves lost, and almost penniless in the La Mayenne. On 15 June they heard that a nearby aristocratic estate had opened its doors to the refugees, and were delighted to find that there was still room for them in its hunting lodge. His mother delicately raised the issue of payment. The *baronne* replied 'My dear woman, who said anything about paying?'.[179] They stayed until the end of July, surviving on the daily consumption of the cheapest meal in the town: ham and noodles at the railway café. Kermadec recorded his wife's lucky meeting with a generous old lady who served her coffee and food, and who took the time to talk to her.[180] Rupert Downing described the warm welcome of Mr and Mrs Pinault-Gignard in Entraigues. This couple offered him a meal and a bed. 'One of my ambitions in life is to return to Entraigues and meet again our friends M. and Mme Sylvain Pinault-Gignard'.[181] The most powerful of these examples, however, is that left by Léon Werth, whose two long encounters with Abel Delaveau, a farmer in the Loiret, almost take the form of a quasi-religious experience, as he re-discovers that 'I am in France'.[182] Such themes echo the pervasive ruralism and regionalism that developed in the 1930s and which were later exploited by the Vichy government: they positioned a 'real' France of the villages and farms as a healthy counter to the frenetic, artificial life of the cities. Such images were not original. What is surprising, however, is to see them re-interpreted in the context of the *exode*. Where the dominant interpretation had only seen a mindless chaos and a shameful panic, some participants found a sense of meaning, an education, a transformation, and even a sense of the basic decency of French people which allowed them to survive the hard years which were to follow.

CONCLUSION

The real flaw in the dominant historical interpretation of the *exode* is not so much that it has been interpreted negatively, but that it has *not* been interpreted. Reduced to an episode of chaos and panic, it has been overshadowed by the apparently more important 'big stories': military defeat, Occupation, collaboration, resistance and liberation. On the other hand, it is probably true that more people took part in the *exode* than became mobilized soldiers, willing collaborators or active resisters. Why has their experience been ignored?

One reason for the persistently negative descriptions of the *exode* is that it ended in disaster. As General Weygand reported to Prime Minister Reynaud on 13 June: 'the French armies were exhausted. The line was pierced in many places; refugees were pouring along all the roads through the country, and many of the troops were in disorder'.[183] The report does not present the relationship as one of cause and effect, but one cannot help seeing the two issues, flight and defeat, as intrinsically linked in such references. Individuals and their families may have escaped bombardment or capture, but the *exode* itself ended with France's capitulation to the Nazis.

Yet other similar catastrophes have been integrated into national narratives in a more positive manner. The dreadful British defeat at Dunkirk is now deeply embedded in the national story: it has been transformed into a tale of a nation pulling together in adversity, of the underdog as eventual victor. Slipping briefly into 'virtual history', one could imagine the Vichy government sponsoring some form of celebration of 'the return', which would have welcomed *exodiens* back to their communes, and publicly recognized their resilience and their efforts. But this was not to be. Montherlant's writing illuminates this problem. He heard a fellow soldier's anguished story about his lost wife and children after the Fall of France. The man had no idea how to find his family: they had been on the *exode* but he did not know whether they now lived in Occupied or Vichy France. Montherlant listened sympathetically, but realized that if he had spotted the soldier's family in the crowd, they probably would have struck him as shameful or abject.[184] His response was dismissive, not because he was unsympathetic, but because he found it hard to identify the human in the unruly mass. The *exode* became an experience was extremely hard to communicate afterwards.[185] Outsiders – primarily the soldiers who were close observers of the *exode* – imagined terrible horrors for their family members. Yet not long after returning home, many children appeared to have forgotten their traumatic flight and the associated miseries of homelessness, hunger and fear. Had these experiences been forgotten or repressed? Unlike the Great War, the *exode* of 1940 was decidedly not present at every meal.

It was also easy to scapegoat the *exode*. For British commentators, criticizing the *exode* was a means to signal frustration with the French war effort, without actually calling into question the French government itself. For French commentators, *exodiens* were more difficult to classify: they were not brave soldiers, generous welfare workers, willing collaborators or heroic resistors. Above all, they were primarily a female crowd: it was easier to laugh at them (asking where was the Loire!), to use them as backdrop for a determined defence of France, or to cite them as some vague example of moral decay, than to analyse them.[186] Finally, faced with the difficulty in placing them in a national narrative, it was still simpler just to ignore them.

Yet the *exode* achieved something. Rather than just the backdrop to France's military defeat, *exodiens* were active interlocutors, existing in dynamic interplay with France's soldiers, and thus raising those awkward questions about military status and the culture of the army. Their flight carried multiple meanings: it was at once definitive proof of defeat *and* of a will to refuse defeat. It was an astonishing experience for many of its participants, from which they drew lessons about the nature of French society and human nature. In some cases, it provoked a genuine solidarity: not in the form of a patronizing compassion towards the unfortunate victim, but a recognition of oneself in the other.

Perhaps the greatest difficulty in the interpretation of *exode* is the simplest one: no one was responsible for its organization. In the case of the *retirada*, there were a range of governmental and political agencies active in its instigation. With the evacuations, the French government took responsibility, although it constantly appealed for municipal, charitable and local assistance. Because of these authority structures, records were kept, and there are archives to consult. In comparison, no one organized the *exode*: it 'just happened', and therefore it left little documentation and no dedicated archives.

'Heroes are more popular than victims' is Dienke Hondius's chilling summary of immediate post-war interpretations of wartime experiences.[187] Even before 1945, the concepts of hero and victim were perhaps more plastic than Hondius allows: the wretched, defeated British soldier in the Nord can be transformed into the resilient, determined Tommy of Dunkirk. No one attempted such a transformation of the *exodiens*' story: the last government of the Third Republic, Vichy, the Resistance authorities and the British government all refused to speak for this female crowd.

4

After The Exodus: Return, Expulsion and Escape

- The Challenges of Return
- Returning Home
- Other Journeys: Continuing Southwards
- Other Journeys: 'Visa: A Hundred-Act Vexation'
- A Second *Exode*? The Expulsions of Alsatians and Mosellans
- Conclusion

On 2 July 1940 the Prefect of the Rhône received an unsigned letter from a mother in Lyon. She presented a list of complaints.

> Exactly two weeks ago, a notice in the evening paper instructed all young people aged 17, 18 and 19 years to leave Lyon as quickly as they could. I did the same as thousands of mothers: I put some of the supplies that I'd kept in reserve in a bag, I borrowed some money to buy a bicycle, and I gave my child as much money as I could. He left – with so many others – under beating rain…
>
> Yet brand new lorries were available … It would have been so simple to use them, and it would have saved our children a lot of trouble, and we could have kept some of our supplies.
>
> But you weren't satisfied with having inflicted this tragic loss on us: you made our pain worse by ending the postal service … No news … Our children might be ill, crushed by a car, lying exhausted in some ditch, even buried: for a fortnight, we've heard nothing.
>
> And the worst thing is that they're forbidden to return. Instead of helping them to come back home, there is obstacle after obstacle: they're forbidden to travel this way, they need a passport, or a permit to travel that way, and if you ask for one, you're just told that they can't be issued. It's only in France that this could happen. Yesterday I met a young man from Avignon who had returned to care for his sick mother. To get here, he had had to break all the rules, to hide during the night, to travel like a thief, and to cross via a half-wrecked railway bridge, as all the other routes were closed. Monsieur Bollaert, Prefect of the Rhône, you are DESPICABLE, you are a CRIMINAL, and the mothers of Lyon curse you.[1]

This letter suggests some new themes to study. Most obviously, there is a strong sense of bitter resentment and betrayal: the people we will examine in this chapter are first, angry about their government and then – subsequently – fearful. Secondly, the previous chapters have considered mass movements which retained or created some sense of unity among their participants: a unity which might be provisional, fragile, and rapidly changing, but which was at least based on some sense of common purpose and direction. In this chapter, there is no such obvious pattern. In the months that followed the *exode*, there was no single mass movement of refugee people, but something more akin to a series of waves and ripples running in contradictory directions: some echoing the original impulse of the *exode*, others running counter to it, and still further exilic journeys being produced by new disasters occurring on French soil. The borders of nations seemed less clear than ever: international events were smashing into the small world of French internal politics; the nation's frontiers were re-drawn by the new demands of the German invaders; these new borders were resented by French people and evaded by new waves of exiles, seeking to flee a haven which had turned into a trap.

In this chapter we will follow a series of strange journeys: voyages which took the travellers not only through physical space, but also through psychological realms and symbolic landscapes. The most common of these journeys was 'the return' northwards, which often did not lead the traveller back to the beginning point they expected. At the same time, usually travelling south, were a diverse group of refugees, exiles and dissidents, desperate to escape Nazi power.

THE CHALLENGES OF RETURN

On 17 June 1940 Marshall Pétain announced on French radio that hostilities would cease. He referred directly to the *exode*: 'During these painful hours, I have in mind the unhappy refugees who are crossing the country in a state of utter destitution'. Pétain was determined that their suffering would be swiftly ended: their repatriation was a priority.[2] For the new authorities, it was important that French people went back to work as soon as possible, in order to prove that the new government could organize people's homecoming better than the republican state had managed their flight in May–June 1940. The Armistice with Germany was signed on 22 June. There had been no second Verdun, no repeat of the unbearable casualty figures of the First World War, but the defeat was rapid and devastating, and had caused serious losses. After barely six weeks of fighting, the French Army – hitherto considered the strongest in the world – had been forced to surrender. The right-wing commentator Fabre-Luce observed that the *exode* formed the 'the moral foundation of the armistice', for this lost and shattered crowd seemed to want nothing more than peace.[3]

The simple shock of defeat affected many. The French economist Charles Rist, who had found refuge in Switzerland, noted in his journal:

> The dreadful point about the current situation is the strange suddenness with which it was produced. In just one day we passed from complete confidence in our invincible resistance to the great despair of defeat. Following this, it is difficult to believe in reality.[4]

The reverse movement after the *exode* was not simply a move back from the south and west; it also aimed to be a journey back to normality, represented as the cessation of movement.

> By their nature, the French are not nomads: they only become so against their will and when forced to do so. Builders, masons, stone-cutters, peasants: they love the trades that are linked to the earth. When they travel, when they leave, they are immediately thinking of their return. For them, a journey is a necessary task for their trades, or a break from their settled lives: for them, a journey is a minor madness, a temptation to sin.[5]

Organizing the orderly movement of millions of people would be a difficult task at any moment. It was exceptionally difficult in the summer of 1940. The fighting had stopped, but the damage of war remained. Roads had been destroyed by bombing; at least 2,500 road bridges had been completely blown up, and a further 500 were out of use; 5,200 kilometres of railway track was unusable and 1,300 railway stations had been destroyed.[6] Towns and villages which had been in the fighting zone were often devastated. The Deputy Mayor of the eastern town of Rethel (Ardennes), writing in September 1940, explained that it was still impossible for the population to return: 70% of the town's buildings had been completely destroyed, and many of the rest needed structural repairs. There was no electricity, running water, trains or barges.[7] Across France, banks had been evacuated and so people had to rely on the money and the valuables that they carried with them. Even those who had left their homes with well-laden cars were often in a precarious position by the time the Armistice was signed. Cars had crashed or had suffered bomb damage, some had over-heated in the immense traffic jams and some simply ran out of petrol. Georgette Guillot was appalled by the sights along the roads in Dordogne: 'We entered a crazy world. As the road curved, we found burnt vehicles everywhere: some had been driven into ditches; there were overturned lorries, a great mass of scrap iron.'[8] It was not just the modern vehicles that had collapsed. A refugee from northern France was struck by the stink of dead corpses and the sight of the drowned horses in a river.[9] Another refugee who had run out of petrol tried to buy a horse so that he could go home, but had to abandon his plan because there were not even any oats left: 'A litre of oats is just as rare as a litre of petrol', he observed.[10]

Postal, telegraph and telegram services had been disrupted.[11] The establishment of the Demarcation Line, dividing France into two parts, worsened communication problems. This new internal frontier disrupted roads, trains and postal communications.[12] On 18 June 1940, there were no postal, telegraph or telephone services at all in the Meurthe-et-Moselle. By 24 June, cars were being used to offer a limited postal service, but it was not until 20 August that all post offices in the department were re-opened.[13] Unfortunately, this was the moment when postal services were needed more than ever: the number of telegrams quadrupled in 6% of post offices and doubled in 44% of post offices.[14] These communication problems remained chronic for many months.

A new, heterogeneous population of evacuees, refugees and international exiles remained unevenly crammed into the towns and villages of the south and west. The figures below are from the western department of the Ille-et-Vilaine, which was probably not the most crowded in France. They show that while the numbers of this new population peaked in June and July, and then declined, it is also clear that the refugees did not simply disappear.

Arrondissement	Fougères	Redon	Rennes	St-Malo	Totals
28 July 1940	295	22	46,832	4,724	51,323
15 August 1940	3,497	3,656	23,575	11,347	42,075
25 October 1940	1,450	788	5,260	463	7,971

Table One: French Refugees Resident in the Ille-et-Vilaine, 1940, by arrondissement (NB: statistical inconsistencies are present in the original chart).[15]

Alongside the French refugees, disparate groups of foreign nationals were seeking shelter. In Lyon, the refugee centre of the 'Palais de La Foire' housed 5,800 refugees on 15 September, including 70 Belgians, 10 Portuguese and Spanish, 25 Jews, 70 Italians, 45 Luxembourgeois, 256 Polish, 600 French gypsies, 6 Russian and 56 Yugoslavs.[16] While Belgians were clearly the largest single group of foreigners resident in France, a wide scattering of people from other nations were also present. Furthermore, one notes how Jews were increasingly listed as a distinct category in their own right.

One hundred thousand civilians are estimated to have died during the May and June 1940, and about 90,000 children were missing.[17] Re-uniting families was difficult, and for months the newspapers printed notices from separated members of families seeking to find one another.[18] The *Figaro* of 13 August 1940, nearly two months after the end of hostilities, reported the continuing search for 740 children lost during the *exode*.[19] In the same edition, a Parisian doctor told how he had found and then taken care of a lost child. While he was working in a hospital in Nevers, he treated a young boy who had been seriously wounded in an air raid. The boy's mother had died in the same attack, leaving the child an orphan. The only thing that this doctor knew about the child was his name and town of origin: Alain Maréchal from Beauvais.[20] In the Loiret, police reported groups of children wandering around looking for their parents.[21] These lost children were deeply troubling: incapable of looking after themselves, they were perhaps the most potent and sentimental symbol of the horrors of war. Arguably, aberrant infant behaviour and the breakdown of the family caused particular anguish in France because of the long-standing governmental commitment to increase the French population.

The movements of people created by the war and *exode* continued to cause problems throughout the summer. One revealing sign of this is the number of unusual letters that were sent to prefects, sub-prefects and mayors, asking for basic information or assistance. For example, a local government official wrote to the Prefect of the Pyrénées-Orientales to ask an apparently simple question: where is the Préfecture of the north-eastern department of La Meuse? In normal times, the answer was obvious: it was in the department's main town, Bar-le-Duc. In June 1940, the question was more complex. Like other official facilities, it had been evacuated, and the writer thought that it had been re-constituted in the south. The Prefect was not able to give her any information about its location.[22] Another asked him where the gunpowder factory of Bourges was now located: once again, the Prefect was not able to help.[23] 'Where is my factory?' asked Joseph Lassardo. 'As everyone had to work out for themselves how to leave Paris as fast as possible, I was not told to which town the management would be transferred.'[24] Sapper Kavanagh, writing from the Dordogne, had a similar request, but was more worried: he thought his wife and son were probably in Rennes during the air-raid of 17 June: had they been killed? Were they registered as refugees?[25] Kiebhe knew that her husband was at the military hospital in Lille, and had written the address in her address book. Unfortunately, her suitcase (containing the address book) had been stolen. Not only had she lost the address, she was also certain that the hospital had moved: could the Mayor help?[26]

Following the defeat, many looked for someone to blame. As in Germany in 1918, when defeated Germans explained the military collapse by the fictional 'stab in the back' theory, a common reaction to the defeat in France was to blame elements of the Fifth Column,[27] or republican leaders and the Allies.[28] Rist recalled reading a letter from an acquaintance in the Nord, which spoke about well-organized spies operating in France, including German officers disguised as French officers.[29] Arthur Koestler heard rumours of French soldiers being attacked by Jewish refugees: he later described these weeks as like being surrounded by 'one ubiquitous, all-embracing conspiracy of betrayal'.[30]

The various refugees and exiles shared a deep, urgent need to communicate with family and friends. Paul Burmetz, a refugee from Austria, was interned in Paris in May 1940. He advised his wife, Alice, to get to the south of France: they then considered how they could keep in contact. They decided that each would send postcards to the *poste-restante* sections of the post offices in eight major European cities.[31] Surprisingly, this system worked, and the two went on to live in Albi (Tarn) later in 1940. The importance of even the most minor communications would be almost impossible to over-estimate. Paul, in the internment camp near Paris, heard nothing from Alice for several weeks. Then, suddenly, a postcard arrived from her. 'Within a single moment my whole world had changed. The void has disappeared. It had content now. There was meaning. There was purpose. There was a task to be accomplished. There was a future.'[32] Werth recorded how he and his wife anxiously waited for news from their mobilized son. 'I'm sure that my wife is less and less able to put up with this worry for our son. And, as for me, each day I'm finding it more difficult to disguise my feelings.'[33] Women feared the worst. Guillot noted: 'Women suffer terribly as they wait without news from their men: they get no letters, usually. We know they're prisoners, but where are they? There must have been a hundred thousand deaths: who's going to be grieving? This uncertainty breaks your heart'.[34]

It was in these difficult circumstances that the first evaluations and commentaries on the *exode* circulated. They suggest a surprising disparity between official discourse and refugee experience: while Pétain had, at least, recognized 'the unhappy refugees', the last officials of the Third Republic and the first officials of the Vichy state often seemed unwilling or unable to comprehend the urgent needs of a displaced population. In one announcement addressed to the refugees, the Prefect of the Ille-et-Vilaine recommended 'sang-froid and discipline. Strict discipline is necessary: the French people will accept it'.[35] As noted in the last chapter, there was no official attempt to commemorate, discuss or celebrate the adventure of *exode*. This means that the only immediate discussions concerning the *exode's* meaning and significance were fumbling, haphazard notes.

Two types of communication concerning the *exode* developed in the weeks after the Armistice: both contributed to forming the first, spontaneous interpretations of the experience. Refugees wrote to prefects and mayors, and refugees wrote to each other. In the first case, the most frequent motivation was to complain about mistakes in the allocation of the subsidy to which all registered French and Belgian refugees were entitled: it had been set too low, it had been delayed or it had not been paid at all. This situation usually put the refugee in the defensive position of having to make a case for the legitimacy of their claim. Where possible, they noted that they had been officially evacuated: 'I left my house on 17 May following the Prefect's orders' states one.[36] In other cases, they stressed how the pressure of events forced them to act, thus side-stepping the issue of whether they ought to be classified as 'official' evacuees or mere unofficial travellers, seized by panic: 'I was forced to leave Villiers-le-Bel'; 'we left Paris because it was impossible to get into the shelters'; 'I had to leave Andelys while it was bombed'; 'I left Joeuf after eight days of shelling'; 'Things happened so quickly that, on my departure, I was only able to bring a small sum of money'. As one reads these letters, one can hear an unmistakable note of defensive apology in them: these people know they are in the wrong place, and they find it difficult to explain to the Prefect why this has happened. A slightly fuller note from a woman refugee in the Pyrénées-Orientales rehearsed similar arguments.

> I shouldn't have left my post without an order from my supervisors, but I didn't think about that at all: after the events, I decided to take my two children to safety in your department. I left with the intention of returning straight away, but events moved too fast, and it was impossible for me to get back to Paris ... As I'm a manager in the alimentation sector, perhaps I could be included in the first group of refugees to return?[37]

In the absence of any official recognition of the *exode*, these terse statements of individual misfortune constitute an important element of the first interpretations of the *exode*.

Examples of correspondence between refugees are harder to find. While few in number, they are remarkably consistent in their concerns. An unidentifiable correspondent to 'Dear Audrey' states that

> I've just learnt that the post to Rennes is now working. Here's a quick word to say what became of me, and what I'm thinking of doing. All three of us are in the same position, aren't we? ...Of course, there's no news from Jean, but we mustn't get worried: as yet no one has any news of anybody.[38]

Andrée wrote to her mother:

> Nadine is well; she's with Marthe and the grand-parents. Marcel went to look for us in Guémené. I'm getting worried. Have you got enough money? I don't know your address. Come back when you can. Or go to Guémené: Ernest is still there.
>
> Marguerite and Jeannette are at rue de la Fontaine. I've had no news from René since the 9th. Where is he? My God, what an ordeal!
>
> I'm well, and I'm thinking of going to St-Cyr.
>
> The children are well.
>
> I've sent a note to the barracks.
>
> We all send kisses to our poor little mother, and we hope to see you very soon.
>
> A kiss from your daughter who's thinking from you.[39]

A soldier writing to his 'dear little wife', speaks of the retreat of the army, and ends by looking forward to 'a nice little celebration which, after the week we've been through, will do us good ... I send you my best and sweetest wishes'.[40]

These letters do not attempt any serious analysis of the invasion and *exode*: they are short, urgent, emotional communications. Defeat, surrender and flight are reduced to 'the events' or 'the ordeal'. The points which occupy these writers are the location and condition of their loved ones. Desperation is ever-present: what was the point of Andrée writing to her mother if she did not know her address? The explanation can only be the burning *need* to re-make contact and so re-make the family.

As Stanley Hoffman has already observed, few diaries and literary accounts present immediate French responses to the defeat.[41] Mitterand summed up his feelings later on: 'I had lived through 1940: no need to say more'.[42] For some, it was too painful to describe; for others, there was a real difficulty in finding the words for such a devastating experience. On 28 June, Georges Friedmann wrote in his diary:

> It is still difficult for me to describe, in its totality, how France has looked in the last

fortnight, to understand and to arrange such haunting images. They are still too full of all I feel and suffer; beyond their immediate appearance, [it is too difficult] to evaluate what they mean for the present and the future'.[43]

More prosaically, one *exodien* told the historian Pierre Miquel: 'we drank a hot chocolate … the war had ended'.[44] This statement was not intended to trivialize the experience; it was simply a recognition that the hostilities were over and that there was little that one could do about it. Finding the words to express a greater depth of feeling was beyond this interviewee. The last sentences of Léon Werth's lyrical and sophisticated account of the *exode* strikes a similar note, suggesting Werth's sense of his inability to describe adequately such a momentous and significant episode. 'We left Paris on 11 June. Now, it's 13 July. I've found once again my son, the peace of the familiar fields, earth and sky. I'm back with newspapers, human error and what we must call history. But history and newspapers … that's another story'.[45]

The difference between the literary outpourings of the First World War and relative silence surrounding June 1940 is striking. The battles of the western front were traumatic and the French army had been practically bled white at Verdun, but these traumas led to victory in 1918. Governments, propagandists and professional commentators led the public into discussing, even celebrating, the events. This was not the case in 1940, when defeat met with a relative silence. No one spoke publicly to celebrate or to defend the *exode*. But, if there was no formal commemoration, there were monuments, of a sort, to the *exode* on many roads. On 4 September 1940, Jean Gehenno was on his way home to Paris. Horrified by what he saw, he noted in his diary: 'We crossed the demarcation line at Moulins, having waited our turn for hours at Saint-Pourçain. I saw no sign of the fighting, but everywhere they were the marks of panic: abandoned, pillaged cars. There was no fighting. Fear made it impossible'.[46]

In the absence of any positive discourse, it was therefore negative and dismissive attitudes which seemed to predominate. The historian Marc Bloch, a bitter and perceptive observer of the defeat of France echoed this point in his clandestine text. He condemned French fearfulness.

> The timidity of the nation at large was, no doubt, in many cases but the sum of the timidity of individuals. There were cases of officials leaving their posts without orders. Many instructions to evacuate were issued before they need have been. A sort of frenzy of flight swept over the whole country. It was no rare thing, along the roads crowded with refugees, to come on complete local fire-brigades perched on their engines.[47]

While the new Vichy government certainly did not explicitly condemn the *exode*, it frequently understood history in terms of shame and punishment. Pétain argued that French men had fought bravely but that France could not possibly fight Germany because France suffered from 'too few children, too little arms and too few allies'.[48] From within such a moralistic structure, it was easy to see the *exode* not simply as a contributing factor to the defeat, but also as a punishment for having believed in the intrinsically dishonourable Republic. It was not simply that the refugees had impeded the movement of the armed forces but that these crowds had lacked the 'education of courage'.[49] Echoing the previous Catholic and conservative responses to the collapse of 1870–71 and the drama of the Paris Commune, the leaders of Vichy France insisted that everyone had played a part in the collapse and that everyone needed to expiate their past sins.

RETURNING HOME

After communication and information, the *exodiens*' next most urgent need was to return home. This simple demand proved difficult to put into practice. France itself had changed shape. France was divided into different areas, some occupied by German forces, and some unoccupied.[50] In addition, the two northern departments of Nord and Pas-de-Calais were attached administratively to Belgium, some territory in the south-east was given to Italy, and certain northern and western coastal and border areas were designated as 'Forbidden zones'. The unoccupied zone – also known as the free zone – was formed in the south-east from about two fifths of the territory of the defunct French Republic: it was this part of France which had been the destination point of so many *exodiens*. Consequently, when the fighting ended, many found that they were in the unoccupied zone, while their homes were in occupied France. What were they to do? Those who had lived in the occupied north-east of France during the First World War knew that life under enemy occupation would be hard. Did it make sense to go home to German rule? On the other hand, these stranded people had jobs, families, schools, homes and communities in the occupied zone. Surely it made no sense to stay away once the actual fighting was over?

Agnès Humbert, an eminent art historian and a future resistant, eloquently described in her diary on 20 July how difficult it was to decide.

> Should I go back to Paris, or should I resign from the museum? What should I do? I wrote to Mrs Orosio. Why not leave for California? Palo Alto, where she lives, has a University: I could teach courses on the history of art. And find a job in a museum or library. Or would it be better to live off our savings in a village in some part of south-east [France]? Sometimes I think that anything would be better than living under the swastika and then, suddenly, I can only think of going back to Paris, to be close to Pierre … It's the simplest solution, and the least dangerous (or is it the most dangerous?). It's quite possible that I'll be quickly dismissed … The radio is my only source of pleasure… This morning, I learnt that the German posters had been defaced and pulled down as soon as they were put up. The Parisians are already kicking out … Okay, that's it, I'm going home![51]

Like Humbert, most *exodiens* decided to return to their homes, but there were some important exceptions. Refugees from the 'Forbidden zones' were forced to wait several months before the German authorities allowed them to return home. Leon Werth's epic journey southwards took him out of Paris and to the south-eastern region of Jura. He preferred to stay there, in his holiday home, rather than face what he considered the dangers of occupied Paris. Some also decided to stay in the south for financial reasons. Camille Hanilis, a mechanic from Troyes, joined the *exode* on 15 June, with his wife and two daughters. He found refuge in Charavines (near Grenoble) and then learned that his house, garage and all his possessions had been destroyed by an air raid.[52] His only remaining source of income was the allowance for refugees. He therefore decided to stay and work in Charavines, while he was waiting for the repairs of his garage in Troyes.

Jews – and people who might be classified as Jewish – faced a particularly fateful dilemma. Of the approximately 100,000 Jews who joined the *exode* in May and June 1940, only about a third returned to their homes in occupied France.[53] Those who returned were often concerned that they should not appear unpatriotic. They had a strong sense of national identity and felt that, by choosing southern exile, they were betraying their country, as Joseph Weill later explained.[54] On the other hand, German initiatives made their return more difficult. In September 1940, a German law denied French Jews the right to return to their homes in the occupied zone.[55] On 11 September 1940, the Minister of the Interior wrote to all prefects in the unoccupied zone. He instructed them to prevent 'Jewish, black and mixed race' refugees from travelling. He explained that this instruction 'was in their own interest' as information from the demarcation line showed that the Germans were refusing to allow such refugees to cross.[56]

A further factor which complicated the refugees' decisions was the establishment of Pétain as French leader. Some *exodiens* believed that they could trust Pétain: this could even be a reason for staying in the unoccupied zone. While queuing for food in Toulouse in October 1940, Australian refugee Christine Morrow found that 'one still heard far too often "Notre Pétain". It was said with a break in the voice. It is easy to build up myths, especially perhaps in moments of great trouble.'[57] One point which we need to stress here is the multiple divisions developing among the refugees: in place of a single, shared refugee history, we are now examining many strands, sometimes overlapping, sometimes running in parallel, but also sometimes contradicting each other. Pétainism formed one line of division, separating those who thought they could trust the Marshal from those who rapidly became sceptical. This point is nicely illustrated by a further example from Morrow: walking in Toulouse in December 1940 she saw some chalked graffiti: 'Down with the Jews! Long live Pétain!'. She rubbed out the reference to the Jews, but left the Pétainist slogan.[58]

Despite the obvious difficulties, many refugees seemed confident about the authorities' abilities to organize transport. Georgette Guillot was relieved that her traumatic journey on the jammed-up and bomb-stormed roads was over, and expected a well-organized home-coming. On 26 June, she wrote in her diary: 'To my great surprise, I learn that the repatriation of the refugees is being organized. Everyone wants to get back to normal. After the chaos of the *exode*, they're taking people to their homes, methodically, convoy by convoy: this is a great change'.[59] At the beginning of July 1940 Gold heard that the trains were about to start running properly so as to repatriate everybody. Assuming that everything had returned to normal, without a moment's hesitation she decided to make the journey from Toulouse to La Bourboule to fetch her dog. The chaos of the *exode* was, she hoped, to be followed by a well-ordered, thoroughly-managed return.[60]

One good reason for returning to the occupied zone was the difficulties of life as a refugee in southern France. Refugee centres were often overcrowded, savings were running out and living conditions could be poor. In Lyon, three French women refugees wrote a joint letter to protest about the Palais de la Foire, the main refugee reception point in Lyon. They complained that there were 'stones in the beans; all the meals are badly cooked, the cod is too salty, and the morning soup is like dish-water'; they were horrified about 'filth of the buildings and the toilets'.[61] The streets and the cafes of Toulouse were full to bursting, and the Vallotton sisters described a typical scene in Clairvivre at the end of June 1940. 'A mad world. Queues outside all the food stores. You can't find any butter, milk, cakes, croissants, biscuits or cigarettes. The papers are growing smaller and smaller, and they only say what the German radio wants to tell us'.[62] Another refugee wrote to the Préfet of the Ille-et-Vilaine: 'I had hoped to return once the armistice was signed, but as I have no car, and as there's no train for Paris, I had to put up with staying. Anyway, we're forbidden to leave. I don't know how long this dreadful situation is going to last: my savings are running out'.[63] This transient, heterogeneous and disgruntled population was also potentially disruptive, and Jacques Bardoux, Senator of the Puy de Dôme, was struck by the absence of law and order in Clermont-Ferrand.[64]

Given these circumstances, it is understandable that refugees became frustrated while waiting – apparently for no good reason – in central and southern France. They wanted to discover what had happened to their homes and businesses, and they also felt what Guillot described as a 'nostalgie de Paris'.[65]

Despite the official commitment to repatriation, the majority of refugees could not return home immediately. Prefects were well aware of their eagerness to return home, and had to caution them. In the Haute-Garonne, the Prefect told the department's mayors on 4 July 'you must forbid any refugees in your commune from leaving for the occupied zone'.[66] There then followed a series of staged movements: after the 13 July refugees could leave for destinations in the unoccupied zone.[67] French and Belgian refugees with cars or horse-drawn carriages were told to leave for destinations in the occupied zone after August 1940.[68]

One reason for the delay was the demarcation line between occupied and unoccupied France. This was relatively easy to pass before 1 July, when the regulations were more firmly and consistently applied. By September, crossing became much more difficult.[69] In the first few weeks after the Armistice, few people had a clear idea of the demarcation line's position, or of the procedures required to pass it.[70] Just as during the early days of war and invasion, refugees still lived in a world dominated by rumour and half-truth, and it was difficult to make rational, well-informed decisions. Newspapers sometimes published misleading information, for example inaccurately identifying the crossing points on the demarcation line.[71] Even when one did receive accurate information, there was no guarantee that it would not change, as a *Le Figaro* journalist observed. 'What was true on 11 July might no longer be the case on 14 July. We have seen this so many times'.[72] Refugees who could not present the right documentation were stopped at the border, resulting in severe overcrowding in the towns and villages immediately to the south of the demarcation line.[73]

Georges Filoque is one example of a refugee who successfully returned home, yet even he seemed uncertain and confused throughout the process. Since the beginning of July priority had been given to civil servants, doctors, nurses and farmers, that it to say to those considered vital for the reorganization of the country.[74] Filoque however, was unaware of this development and remained in the Corrèze where he was well fed and comfortable, but worried about his home and business in Les Andelys (Eure). By chance, at the beginning of August, he read that people who worked with agricultural machinery were receiving priority repatriation papers and he immediately applied to the local mayor for permission to travel. When he went to collect his certificate a municipal official tried to talk him out of returning, arguing that no one knew what was happening on the other side. To pass the line he had to fulfil certain conditions: his papers had to be in order, he had to be demonstrably not a Jew, he was not allowed to carry arms and he had to have enough petrol to travel 200 km. Although he satisfied these conditions Filoque still could not cross on the expected date, because the German soldiers were operating within the German time-zone and had shut their offices two hours earlier than the French had expected. Once across the line Filoque was constantly stopped and checked by German officials. Poignantly, he only realized one consequence of his journey after his return: he could no longer contact his friend Charles who had remained in the non-occupied zone.[75] What had once been two parts of the same country now seemed like two separate states.

Filoque was one of many successful returnees in August 1940. In some ways he was luckier than most in that he had his own car and did not need to rely on the rail network, and he was not trying to return to Paris. Obtaining papers for return to the capital was more difficult and, as during wartime, a black market rapidly began to operate. It was possible to obtain an authorization for Paris in only two hours 'avec bakchich' but it took three weeks by the proper procedures.[76]

Returnees often felt humiliated. It frequently seemed that they would have been more sensible to stay home. Reflecting on a return which had been more difficult than the original *exode*, one interviewee described their reception in Paris, a return to a daily life amongst people who had thought it wrong to run from the invasion. 'You caught the underground, watched by mocking Parisian women in their bright, clean dresses and gentlemen in impeccable suits who had not been on the *exode*'.[77] In July 1940, the *Nouvelliste*, a local Lyon newspaper, condemned the 'heartbreaking collapses' and 'incomprehensible failure of will' of some refugees, but the journalist nevertheless invited the city's inhabitants who had 'bravely remained' in their homes, to avoid 'mocking smiles … and gloomy words'.[78] Unlike the exiles, who had left their homes for political reasons, it seemed as if the returning *exodiens* might as well have stayed. Their flight had not achieved anything, as their return indicated.

There had been no epidemics and, usually, the refugees did not starve. Given the scale of the problem, this was an impressive achievement. Predictably, the new French government trumpeted their successes. In December 1940, *La France de ce mois*, a Vichy propaganda magazine, stated with pride:

> The government was thus able to organize in a remarkably short time the return of more than three million people to their homes. A few figures show the speed with which these journeys were organised: in July [1940], 200,000 returned, in August 1,700,000 (including a million train journeys), and in September 850,000.

However, many French families remained separated for many years. The majority of prisoners of war only came back in 1945. Moreover, some refugees stayed in the unoccupied zone.

Refugees' Origins	Assisted Refugees	Non-Assisted Refugees	Totals
Occupied Zone	8,236	85,297	93,533
Forbidden Zone	61,462	79,746	141,208
Alsace-Lorraine	90,734	47,340	138,074
Foreigners	9,477	19,614	29,091
Totals	169,909	231,997	401,906

Table Two: Refugees in the Southern Zone, October 1942[79]

The figures above demonstrate that the 'return' was an incomplete process: while many did travel back to the north and east, a substantial minority stayed in the unoccupied zone.

Even those who did 'return' often failed to find the normality or stability they sought. Some found that their properties had been ransacked or pillaged: they had even more reason to regret their *exode*. One refugee from northern France described the wanton destruction of warfare in his commune, and blamed British soldiers.[80] The situation was similar in Lyon, where many refugees reported that their houses had been vandalized during their absence.[81] Pierre Gourd, a mechanic from Legny, described the damage to his house in great detail and listed all his losses. He was quite clear who was to blame: 'From what people say, those who robbed me were French soldiers and refugees.[82] For such householders, the *exode* had clearly been a mistake.

Practical difficulties aside, the return was humiliating for many French people because it was so bound up with defeat, the dismemberment of France and the establishment of a long, brutal occupation. In particular, crossing the demarcation line seemed degrading, because it was a German-imposed border on French soil. As Alary observed, the establishment of the demarcation line flagrantly insulted French pride and honour.[83] The right-wing commentator Rebatet was horrified by the sight of 'this map of France cut by a black line at Chalon-sur-Saône'.[84]

These returning refugees were finding that there was no return in the fullest sense of the word. The mental, political, cultural, administrative and even geographic context had changed around them. A physical journey of a few hundred kilometres could not erase these changes. Having left home, there was no return.

OTHER JOURNEYS: CONTINUING SOUTHWARDS

While many attempted to return to their homes in the north and east, and some remained in the south, a few decided to continue the journey southwards. Political considerations influenced them: this was a minority which became rapidly sceptical or hostile towards Pétain and who – still more unusually – often felt swift identification with De Gaulle as the representative of the true France, or who feared for their lives. The article 19.2 of the Armistice Convention stipulated that French authorities were to hand over any German refugees that the Germans required. Nazi authorities were given the list of German refugees who found refuge in France since 1933. Thyssen, a businessman resident in Nice, was one of the first to be handed over to the Gestapo and then interned in Dachau.[85] It soon became clear that the Vichy regime was hostile to the foreign Jews who had taken shelter in the unoccupied zone to escape German persecution. The Vichy law of 22 July 1940 established a commission charged with reviewing naturalizations that had been completed since 1927. A number of naturalized Jews, originating from eastern Europe lost their citizenships.

These persecuted groups faced the immediate problem of how to leave France: all routes to the east merely led to Nazi-controlled Europe; routes to the south-east, to Fascist Italy; routes to the north and west, via the Channel and Atlantic ports, led through the forbidden zones, strictly controlled by the German occupation forces. How could they leave?

Some headed for the Pyrenees. Here, we encounter a strange geo-political relativism: in January 1939, refugees fleeing fascism left Spain; after June 1940, they tried to enter Spain, usually in order to get to Portugal. In 1936, the new, authoritarian Portuguese state, headed by President Salazar, had sympathized with the Francoist cause and supplied some indirect aid. In November 1939, following a sharp rise in the number of visa applications, it issued the notorious Circular 14, which instructed all consuls to refuse visas to all stateless aliens (a category into which most German Jewish exiles fell), all holders of the League of Nations 'Nansen' passports, and all foreigners with no good reason to enter Portugal.[86] On the other hand, the Salazar government became markedly more sceptical about the Third Reich. Politically ambiguous, it became a chink in the armour of the New Order. Marcel Junod, a Red Cross official, observed that in 1940 'there was only one port in Europe still open: Lisbon'.[87]

In May 1940 the Portuguese Consulate in Bordeaux was flooded by requests for visas. A permanent queue developed, as refugees waited for what appeared to be their last chance to leave Europe. The Consul, Aristides de Sousa, appreciated their plight, and requested that the government authorize a relaxation of Circular 14. The government refused this request, and Aristides then seemed to experience a type of nervous breakdown: he saw that the people requesting visas were not ordinary refugees, but 'people under sentence of death'.[88] He decided to ignore his government's instructions, and to implement his own new policy of 'no questions asked'. The number of visas issued in this way is not known, but may well have reached tens of thousands. In July 1940, Aristides was dismissed from his post.

An exile community developed in Lisbon during the summer of 1940, some 200,000 strong.[89] It included Arthur Koestler, Jean Giraudoux and Erich Remarque. Their initial impressions of the city were often quite favourable: almost universally, they commented on the freedom of living in a city without any night-time blackouts. All were desperate for visas to almost any other place on earth; all were scared that the Portuguese authorities might hand them over to the Spanish, who in turn would deport them back to France, where they would be handed over to the Germans. Remarque quickly learned to spend his time visiting museums and churches: not because he was particularly interested in Portuguese culture, or because he felt any strong religious sentiment, but for a more practical reason: 'simply because in churches and museums no one asks for your papers'.[90]

Five international refugee agencies attempted to assist this variegated collection of the lost, the panic-stricken and the desperate. In theory, it was possible for them to apply for entry into the United States; in practice, demanding administrative practices meant that very few ever entered. In the summer of 1940, many left for Thailand, the only country which was prepared to accept them. 'This chaotic world was one of great arbitrariness and total unpredictability,' noted Quaker relief worker Howard Wriggins. 'I could never see any rhyme or reason why some people managed to stay all right and others ran into nothing but trouble.'[91] Remarque's comments on the same topic were markedly more bitter. He noted how strongly most of his fellow refugees wanted to reach the United States, and how few succeeded.

> If you couldn't reach it, you were lost, condemned to bleed away in a jungle of consulates, police stations, and government offices, where visas were refused and work and residence permits unobtainable, a jungle of internment camps, bureaucratic red tape, loneliness, homesickness, and withering universal indifference. As usual in times of war, fear, and affliction, the individual human being had ceased to exist; only one thing counted: a valid passport.[92]

This huddle of people in Lisbon represents a different type of refugee community than the ones we have previously studied. While relatively large, it possessed little sense of unified identity: no common language, religious culture, political values or even common history. They shared, at most, a common dilemma. 'The coast of Portugal had become the last hope of the fugitives to whom justice, freedom, and tolerance meant more than home and livelihood.'[93] Worse still, the refugees were in competition with each other: there were limited resources available to them in Lisbon, and few visas. Rather than thinking as a group, the refugees made their cases as individuals or – at most – as families, each applying separately for their visas.

After the final collapse of the Third Republic, however, the route to Portugal grew steadily more difficult. Southern French departments began to see some unusual travellers. Some headed first for Toulouse. In 1939, the city had become an informal centre of exiled Spanish organizations. In 1940, these bodies no longer had any legal status, but they still retained some influence. Moreover, the new political stresses proved to be a great stimulus for the expansion of the ancient Pyrenean profession of *passeur*: experienced guides who could take travellers through safe passes and avoid French and Spanish border controls.[94] From Toulouse, these refugee-militants headed southwards, often to the Val d'Aran, a small Spanish enclave lying directly north of the Pyrenees.[95]

Attempts to cross into Spain by this route began with the declaration of war in September 1939: police estimated that about 20 people had tried to cross in the September, October and November 1939.[96] The local authorities knew of the area's long history as a crossing point for refugees, spies, smugglers and political militants, and had grown weary of the constant governmental demands to assure the 'impermeability' of the frontier. 'All borders are permeable' noted one.[97]

In the 11 months between October 1940 and August 1941, police in the border arrondissement of Saint-Gaudens arrested 32 people for attempting to cross the border.[98] We can consider this sample as a picture of the 'extreme *exode*', of those for whom the flight from the German armies did not end when they reached the Loire. Inevitably, it probably gives a distorted picture of the would-be travellers: it over-represents the young, the inexperienced and impetuous, and those without good Spanish contacts. Unlike the *exodiens*, they are overwhelmingly male: only two of our sample of 32 are women. None of them are accompanied by children. Twenty-five give details of their origins within France: while seven are from relatively nearby southern departments (Bouches-du-Rhône, Herault and Lot-et-Garonne), the majority – as on the *exode* – are from the north. Sixteen came from the Nord, Pas-de-Calais, Somme and Bas-Rhin, or the Parisian region. They also included one Belgian and three British people. They were extraordinarily young: of the 30 whose age is known, the youngest was 16 and the oldest 46; their average age was just under 21, and the largest age group was the 18-year-olds, of which there were seven. Sixteen of them give their professions: the largest category is of seven students, but a waiter, an engineering apprentice, a clerk and a schoolmistress were also included.

Police interview records have been preserved for some of them. The arrests of Alexis Nouvel (17 years old) and Georges Colle (22) in March 1941 provide us with some further details of their experiences.[99] Nouvel had been born in the Nord, and then left for Nantes during the *exode*. Colle was born in Casablanca, but lived in Tours. Like all of those arrested, the two denied any links with organized oppositional groups: this may be the simple truth (and an explanation of why they failed to cross the frontier) or it may be that the two young men considered this the best tactic to employ during a police interview. Certainly, the police often doubted these claims of solitary heroism. Both were worried by the news of German round-ups of young people. Exactly how they knew each other is not explained in their interview. (Were they already friends? Or, like so many *exodiens*, did they meet on the road?) Nouvel and Colle seemed to have had no difficulty in crossing the demarcation line, and they then met in Limoges. They decided to head for the American Consulate in Marseilles. They travelled together by train, again seemingly without difficulty. However, when they got to the Consulate, Nouvel and Colle found it was guarded, and they could not enter. They then tried to find a boat that would take them to Africa, but failed. So they turned round, and headed for the Pyrenees. By this point they had almost no money left. They wanted to cross the border, reach Portugal, and then head to Britain. (Their records do not refer explicitly to the Free French, but some of the other interviewees do.) They managed to climb the Pyrenees, but were stopped by Spanish guards, and sent back to be arrested by the French police.

These people were the extremists of the *exode*. Young and healthy, they travelled without the baggage of the older *exodiens*. They were resourceful and determined: they outwitted border guards and police checks and – even in unfamiliar environments – they attempted to contact *passeurs* and guides.

They were motivated by a more focused desperation than that which drove the *exodiens:* they had a far more lucid idea of what they were running from, although even here they are often extrapolating an image of France's immediate future from the fragmentary information they possessed of its present. They were rarely motivated by genuinely political concerns: often, they had heard of De Gaulle, and they clearly had a preference for life in the countries free from Nazi domination, but beyond these simple themes, they cannot be seen as genuinely politicized by their experience.

OTHER JOURNEYS: 'VISA: A HUNDRED-ACT VEXATION'

In May and June 1940, some refugees managed to get out from France to Portugal. In retrospect, they may be considered to have been lucky. Following them were a series of less mobile, maybe more cautious refugees who acted less quickly. For example, Soma Morgenstern, held in an internment camp in Brittany, was frustrated by the absence of clear information in mid-June 1940. 'Terrible rumours ran through the camp. There were no more newspapers, as they were no longer being published'.[100] The Germans arrived and took control of the camp. Like almost every observer, Morgenstern comments on how surprisingly good-natured and polite they seemed. A young lieutenant spoke to them, outlining some of the changes that would be implemented, but without once using the word 'Jew'. Then the camp was divided into two sections: Christians and Jews. Many who had considered themselves as Christians, found they were categorized as Jews. Morgenstern assumed that this separation had been ordered by the new Nazi camp directors: he was dismayed to learn that, no, it was the camp inmates themselves who had demanded it.[101] As an Austrian Jew who had worked as a journalist, he had a good idea what Nazi rule would mean for France: he therefore know that he had to escape from the camp. But what then? Spain? Syria? Palestine? The American Consulate in Bordeaux?[102] He managed to get out, and then trekked across France with another Jewish camp inmate, observing a strange country that was changing before his eyes. They devised their own rules: they walked most of the way, sometimes accepting lifts from peasants in carts, never travelling on the main highways. Like so many others, they found that Toulouse was full, so went on to Marseilles. [103] Morgenstern records that he arrived in the city at 7.00 p.m. and was promptly arrested at 7.05 p.m.[104] Swiftly released, he remained uncertain about how to understand the city: the connecting point of Europe, Africa, and the Orient, was this the last free port, or the final trap?[105]

For a brief period, southern French towns like Toulouse, Albi and Marseilles became cosmopolitan cities: alongside Lisbon, each could claim to be the hosts of the last, pathetic, remnants of democratic Europe. Some found a warm welcome, and took comfort from it. Paul and Alice Burmetz attended a New Year Party in Albi, and came back delighted. `It did Alice and me good to hear again the "Marseillaise" sung by the large audience, with obvious confidence and pride, and it was reassuring to see, hear, and feel this imponderable Being called France. Here she was, right here, this living France, confident, reassuring, proud and dignified'.[106] The Mayor of Albi insisted that refugees were to be made welcome. Committees for housing, food, finance, medical aid and tracing families helped them. Paul, Alice and their daughter were placed in a one-room apartment: the ladies of the housing committee visited, and insisted that they be given a larger residence. They were offered a choice of six places, and eventually chose to live in cabin in the middle of vineyard, where they could grow their own food.

> Here was a town taking good care of a population that had more than doubled within a few weeks, and doing so without the elsewhere mandatory red tape and without infringement of individual freedoms. How could it be done? To me the secret lay in the Frenchmen's deep-rooted regard for human values and human dignity.[107]

Burmetz was delighted by this reception, but knew that it could not last. 'Below the surface of this normal life I constantly felt looming the threat inherent in the general situation'.[108] Burmetz threw himself into applying for visas, and in December 1941 was confident that they would soon be travelling out to the United States. Then came the attack on Pearl Harbour, and the American entry into the war. Trans-Atlantic travel was impossible and – worse still – police had started to arrest refugees in Albi. Burmetz then acted with breath-taking simplicity: he bought two maps of Switzerland, and planned to travel there. Astonishingly, he, his wife and their disabled daughter managed to walk over the Alps and to outwit the Swiss border guards; they remained in Switzerland for the rest of the war.

The Burmetz family, outside Albi, were relatively fortunate. Most of these international refugees arrived in exhausted towns which had seen too many refugees. 'How tired of it we grow!' one citizen of Toulouse told Morrow, 'They don't go away. More [refugees] come, [with more] requests still when there's nothing more to give. Congestion everywhere, home, street, restaurant, no air to breathe … they are locusts stripping the town bare'.[109] It was good news for those who wanted to rent rooms, bad news for everyone else. Asking for a place to stay, Morrow was bluntly told: 'Lodging impossible, employment impossible, go back where you came from, where you ought to have stayed, you never ought to have come here'.[110] Like Burmetz, she then devised her own solution: she caught a tram to the furthest suburb, and found somewhere to stay. She later explained her method of dealing with bedbugs and lice: 'The best way of dealing with vermin in the bed is not to go to bed'.[111] Lisa and Hans Fittko were not so lucky: they lived in an unfinished villa near Montauban, and then in a seedy hotel in Marseilles, mainly used by prostitutes, which they had to leave for an hour every time a ship reached port.[112]

Burmetz, Fittko, Morgenstern and Morrow found themselves trapped in a bizarre bureaucratic maze. Legally, it was possible for foreign nationals in 1940 and 1941 to leave France. This did become considerably more difficult after December 1941, and finally impossible after December 1942, when the German Occupation was extended across France. But … they needed to obtain authorizations for each stage of their journey. Could they find a country which would accept them? If so, they needed to provide documentation of this. Then they needed to plan their journey. Leaving France required an exit visa. Travelling across Spain and Portugal required transit visas. The increasingly suspicious Spanish and Portuguese authorities demanded to see proof that would-be 'transit' travellers actually had the means to leave: therefore, they demanded to see valid tickets for a ferry. To complicate matters, most visas were only issued for a specific period: thus, just as the refugees obtained the last needed document of the chain, they could find that the first was now out-of-date, and the whole process needed to be started again. Just to stay in Marseilles or Toulouse, they needed a residence permit, which – once again – was only granted for a limited period of time. Foreigners travelling to a consulate in another town also required valid travel permits. The frustrations suffered by the refugees were frequent and predictable: Morrow burst into tears when the Spanish Consul refused to issue her a transit visa. He then relented, and said he could issue one if she produced a recommendation by three Spanish citizens living in Madrid.[113]

Almost week by week their status was deteriorating. The constitutionality of the Third Republic was being replaced by the brutal authoritarianism of the Vichy regime. Sometimes neighbours and local officials would do their best to alert and to assist: the Burmetz were warned by a local policeman to expect a visit from the national police force shortly.[114] The true meaning of 'collaboration' was becoming clearer. 'We were sitting in a trap and must find a way out. The trap was France; we had to get out of France', commented Lisa Fittko.[115] In practice, getting out meant queuing at Embassies and Consulates. The Spanish Consul in Toulouse opened at 10.00 a.m.; the queue started forming at 6.00 a.m. 'One kept on going there at 6.am and still never saw the Consul, but in the queue one made friends and told them one's troubles, thus wiling away the hours sociably'.[116]

A few organisations tried to help these cosmopolitan exiles. The Rockefeller Foundation financed an *Emergency Program for European Scholars*, offering bursaries for intellectuals trapped in France.[117] Varian Fry, a member of the Emergency Rescue Committee, arrived in Marseilles in August 1940 with a list of about 200 intellectuals to save. This organized exile was extremely selective. It was reserved for exceptional intellectuals who could prove that they were in extreme danger. Daniel Bénédite, Fry's principal assistant, noted how those they refused to help hated them.[118] Of the 89 bursaries offered by the Foundation, 31 were not distributed, whether because the person to whom it was granted refused it or because they did not obtain authorization.[119] Gustave Cohen, a professor of medieval literature at the Sorbonne, and a beneficiary of the Committee, commented sarcastically: 'If Christopher Columbus had

had to obtain so many documents, he would have given up trying to discover America'.[120] Thanks to Fry's efforts, about 2,000 refugees – artists, intellectuals and their families – went to America.

Some refugees coped better than others. Looking at the Spaniards queuing at the Mexican Consulate in Marseilles, Anna Seghers could not help admiring 'the unbreakable hearts of these passionate beings that nothing ever made bitter: not wars, not concentration camps, not the terror of thousands of deaths'.[121] Morrow marvelled at the Polish Jew in the 'Spanish queue'. He handed round biscuits and cigarettes, and translated forms. 'Unlike the rest of us, he listened to troubles without giving expression to his own. Being a Jew probably summed them up sufficiently. This having to leave countries was more or less his routine'.[122] On the other hand, she noted how withdrawn and unfriendly others became. 'They had been refugees too long and had developed a refugee attitude. This often means getting what you can, where and in whatever way you can. Since you are an outcast, you have no social feeling, and unless you live unscrupulously, you cannot live at all; or so it appears often'.[123] She herself often grew depressed with her situation, commenting how she could write a 100-act play, entitled *Visa: A Vexation*.[124] During the winter of 1940–41 she, like so many other international refugees, spent her time sitting in cafés, making a single coffee last three hours. 'The coffee is acorns, dried peas and possibly mud, plus one bean of coffee per 50 cups, – or thereabouts. There is no milk. For sugar there is saccharine'.[125] The shops had no eggs, no milk, no fruit, no handkerchiefs and no envelopes; the bread upset her tummy, butter was only available if she queued for hours, the rice was for children. Morrow was lucky enough to have a wood stove – but no wood. Then, one day, she found three green sticks to burn. Looking at their weak flames, she thought: 'It was an Ersatz fire. Ersatz coffee, Ersatz bread, an Ersatz government and now an Ersatz fire!'.[126]

Morrow finally left Marseilles on 25 June 1941, a year after originally travelling southwards.

A SECOND *EXODE?* THE EXPULSIONS OF ALSATIANS AND MOSELLANS

Above all else, the returning *exodiens* wanted a return to what they remembered as normality. At first, the Pétain government seemed to offer them this, but quickly events demonstrated that no easy return was possible. In the summer of 1940, without any preliminary discussions with the French authorities, the Germans began a process of expulsions from the eastern French territories which had been conquered by German armies in 1870–71, and which had remained under their control until 1918. For the Nazis, these areas contained about 1.7m of the 30 million Volksdeutsche who had been living outside German borders in 1933.[127] Although the Armistice Convention contained no provision for such a move, the three departments of Haut-Rhin, Bas-Rhin (in the region of Alsace) and Moselle (in Lorraine) were annexed to the Reich and subjected to a brutal 'Germanization'. This included eradicating the use of French, destroying local administrations and 'cleansing' the territories of undesirable elements. Over 70,000 inhabitants who had fled Alsace in the *exode* (including 17,875 Jews) were barred from returning home.[128] On 2 July 1940, the German security police in Alsace ordered that all Jews, gypsies, foreigners, professional criminals and 'asocials' be expelled into the unoccupied zone.[129] Republicans, Communists and French patriots were soon also targeted. The other inhabitants of the annexed area were offered a choice: they could declare themselves German, in which case they would be sent to the new areas under German control in conquered Poland, or if they chose to consider themselves as French, they would be expelled in 48 hours.[130] The vast majority of the inhabitants chose to declare themselves French.

Outside the annexed zone, this episode created shockwaves: in the little town of Pont-à-Mousson (Meurthe-et-Moselle), people were horrified. Rumours multiplied: many wondered whether the same treatment would be extended to their department.[131] The Vichy government protested vigorously against the expulsions, but was forced to accept them. In total, 270,000 inhabitants from Alsace-Moselle were expelled and 130,000 refugees did not return home from the *exode*; they represented approximately a fifth of the population of the three annexed departments.[132]

The expulsion of Alsatians and Mosellans was carried out with brutality. The transport conditions were harsh: trains were overcrowded and there was little food. On 3 September 1940, Grenoble police reported one train of gypsies who had had no food for 24 hours.[133] In many instances, the expellees were given just a few hours to pack, and were allowed no more than 50kg of luggage per person.[134] The rest of the expellees' possessions, including savings and jewellery, were confiscated or simply looted.[135] Sometimes expellees were not even authorized to take luggage.[136] Eugène Dreyfus, an Alsatian Jew, was one expellee.

> On 16 July 1940, at 12.10pm, when he came back to the house that he shared with his mother, a Gestapo lieutenant and a German policeman were waiting for him. The officer told his 'You've got to leave in fifteen minutes'. He then read him a statement in German, which – in summary – said that in 1919, 150,000 Alsatians were expelled from Lorraine by the French authorities; 1940 was the revenge: the German authorities were going to clean the German soil, beginning with the expulsion of the Jews.[137]

Dreyfus was taken to a school where 200 Jews were gathered. The next day he was transported with his coreligionists in a lorry and dropped off at the demarcation line crossing point.[138] Police reports note some gruesome details about the inhuman conditions that prevailed during the forced removal, observing that German and French policemen in the annexed zone seemed to compete in inhumanity.[139]

People were expelled without notice, sometimes because their sons had served in the French army, or because they had refused to join Nazi organisations.[140] No preparations were made for the transport of disabled and mentally ill patients.[141] Families were separated. 'Wives found themselves separated from their husbands, mothers from their children, with no appeal possible against the arbitrary decisions that destroyed families by dispersing their members according to racial considerations which had been previously unknown in this country'.[142] Trains arriving in Lyon were covered with anti-German graffiti slogans.[143] Expellees sang *La Marseillaise* and proudly waved the French flag.[144] Sometimes they were met by anti-Pétainist groups who shouted their opposition to Vichy's policies.[145]

These expulsions were traumatic. M. Wursteisen, a railway employee from Mulhouse, found refuge in Saint Germain au Mont d'Or (Rhône). Although he found a job in Lyon, he could not cope with his forced removal. He had lost all his possessions. He grew depressed, and 'only saw the worst in everything'.[146] Police reports detail the anger, desperation and hatred among the expellees. 'Hatred of the Germans can be heard in all the conversations by those thrown out by the conqueror'.[147]

However terrible may have been the fate of the refugees of the Retirada, the evacuees of 1939 or the *exodiens* of 1940, it does not compare to the tragedy of the expellees of 1940–41. Expellees, especially Jews, gypsies, Communists or foreigners, experienced greater arbitrariness, political violence and alienation than the refugees. During the Retirada, the evacuations and the *exode*, participants were bound by some sense of common purpose and enjoyed a certain degree of autonomy, albeit a limited one. The expellees were singled out, brutally expelled in order to make room for newcomers and could not expect a swift resettlement in the unoccupied zone. Vichy France provided some assistance to French citizens, but not to foreigners, Jews, gypsies and criminals. An official circular from 17 August 1940 instructed prefects in the unoccupied zone that foreigners were forbidden to circulate without safe-conducts. They were to be divided into three categories: the rich would be given a residence; the poor placed in a refugee centre, and the dangerous were to be sent to a French concentration camp.[148]

During a time of severe economic hardship, the government was reluctant to provide assistance for expellees.[149] Legislation governing their lives grew increasingly restrictive: many were therefore reluctant to apply for the government benefits to which they were entitled, for fear of being sent to an internment camp.[150] Many refugees declared they were receiving assistance from Jewish organisations just to prove that they expected nothing from public fund. Jews were increasingly dependent on their own financial resources and on the help of charitable organisations. Forced to live in semi-clandestinity, they were under growing threat of arrest, confinement in internment camps or assignment to residence.

The experiences of Jews, gypsies, foreigners and Communists constitute the worst aspects of the expulsion. For them, forced removal meant alienation, persecution and, in some instances, deportation. The situation of those classified as French citizens from Alsace and Moselle in Vichy France was different. Their expulsion was carried out with brutality; their resettlement into new homes and jobs was slow and, for the majority, their arrival in the unoccupied zone inaugurated a period of uncertainty and waiting. Yet they received financial and material assistance from the state. The government of Vichy set up two administrative services to facilitate their resettlement. Like the previous republican authorities, Vichy's authorities appealed to their new host communities to assist in the process. Official circulars encouraged prefects to develop 'propaganda in favour of the refugees'.[151] This publicity was to

> create what one might term a 'psychology of mutual aid', to spread a movement of solidarity and hospitality, to persuade all those with a room or a house [available] to give it to the refugees, so that they may find in the free zone, not only an official reception, but also a 'human' welcome, a continuation of their home, a replica of the place they left.[152]

There were substantial attempts to recreate a sense of community for this new wave of refugees. An official brochure explained: 'Thanks to the press, the age which one French writer defined as "When the French people no longer loved each other" has passed'.[153] At Christmas, celebrations were organized and all the refugees invited to the festivities.[154] Associations and newspapers were created to help expellees to rebuild their lives. For example, *Les dernières nouvelles d'Alsace et de Lorraine*, a newspaper edited in Montpellier, kept refugees informed about what was happening in their region and what their friends and families were doing.[155] René Mer, the government's General Controller of Refugees, noted with pride the cooperation of charities and youth groups in assisting and integrating the expellees.[156]

The experience of the expellees was to some extent comparable to those of the evacuees (see Chapter Two): although the transfer of expellees was carried out with brutality, both evacuees and expellees made no decision about their journey and followed instructions; both were affected by a lack of food provision and changes of itinerary during their journey; both felt confused and alienated because their reception in their new communities proved difficult; but both benefited from the assistance provided by a benevolent state at their arrival. One point which we need to stress here is that, however, the expellees, unlike the evacuees, knew that they would be replaced by newcomers. Whereas evacuees and *exodiens* could hope that their homes were left intact and undamaged, expellees knew that German families were going to occupy their homes and often take their possessions. In their case, the trauma of displacement was exacerbated by the trauma of robbery. Henry Frenay explained:

> Refugees from Alsace and Lorraine arrive in the region. They are still overwhelmed

by the trials they have undergone ... They relate how in the days following their departure, German families occupy their homes ... And what is the government doing about it? What is the Marshall doing? This annexation is a violation of the Armistice convention. It is not enough to offer these unhappy expelled people hot tea in the stations. Public opinion should be alerted, but our press remains quiet on all of this.[157]

Expellees bitterly resented Nazi policies but also suffered from Vichy government's indifference. They often considered that the annexation of their region was a violation of the Armistice Convention and they fiercely condemned Vichy's collaboration with Nazi Germany. For example, in May 1941 one expellee wrote to General Huntziger, to complain about the policies of Pierre Laval, a committed proponent of collaboration:

Where will the betrayal of the great deaths of the 1914–18 war end? We must accept that we have been conquered, yes; but when people try to find despicable excuses for such a dreadful situation, this goes beyond what one could expect. A real challenge has been thrown in the face of the two provinces ... According to which law are we being treated in this manner?[158]

Police watched the expellees carefully. Their reports record the expellees' bitter sense of betrayal.[159] Many refugees felt that their reception in Vichy France was inadequate. One group of women, for example, considered that the organization of their reception in Lyon was as bad as the Germans' organisation of their departure from Cernay (Haut-Rhin).[160] In March 1941, a confidential report instructed prefects to implement special policing measures for the expellees, after first identifying particularly suspect individuals.[161] Such suspicions were not unfounded. Expellees from Alsace-Lorraine provided an important base for the Resistance.

Like the arrival of the evacuees, the expellees placed an immediate strain on their host communities; a strain was certainly exacerbated by the fact that shortages and living conditions worsened after the defeat.[162] In the Isère, Alsatians complained bitterly.

We're treated like pariahs: we're in their way, we're *calotins* [an insulting slang word for priest] and more and more often they call us *boches* [Huns] ... When we arrived here, there was nothing for us, not even if we offered to pay; there was a food shortage everywhere, in the shops and at the peasants' farms. People said to us: 'What do you expect? We've got nothing, and now they expect us to carry more refugees'. ...Twice a week we have to travel to get food, often to places ten or fifteen kilometres away ... Towards 15 June [1941], the village still had nothing. But then, after 20 June, the village was mobbed by tourists. And suddenly, as if by magic, there was food for these people. I understood straight away: they'd kept back everything for the tourists ... They told us 'we'll sell stuff to the tourists, not the refugees' ... The shopkeepers run a black market, and sell things at incredible prices to the tourists; we can't buy anything with our meagre allowance, and so it's always 'tighten your belt, tighten your belt'.[163]

Concern about food supplies became a daily obsession, as the rationing became more restrictive. In Isère, expellees complained about the shortages of potatoes and felt disadvantaged because, unlike the farmers, they had no chickens to complement their inadequate meat ration.[164] Food and material concerns dominated the expellees' complaints: they lacked coal, potatoes, meat and vegetables.[165] On the other hand, local people blamed the expellees for food and housing shortages. Like the evacuees in 1939, expellees were often called 'les boches [Huns] from the Nord'.

Vichy authorities soon realized that the expellees' experience – expulsion, mistreatment by the Germans, and hostility from their new host communities – made them natural recruits for anti-Nazi and resistance activities. They were therefore carefully watched. Former Communists and trade unionists were the object of special attention. For example, Voirin, an expellee from Moselle, was a former Communist. Although he had left the Communist Party, and showed no signs of political activity, he was still closely watched by the police in Lyon.[166]

CONCLUSION

This chapter has analysed the diverse experiences of a range of outcast people travelling through France in the 12 months after the *exode*. Many were trying to return from the *exode*, in a search for normality. The other journeys reveal that new stresses were developing: some continued their *exode* to Portugal, Spain, Thailand, Mexico or the United States. Others were forced out of their homes by the policies enforced by France's new Nazi rulers.

Of all the movements studied so far, the expulsion may well have been the most humiliating and violent. The expellees were neither refugees – they did not spontaneously decide to leave their homes – nor evacuees – they were not instructed to do so to protect their lives. Unlike the evacuation, forced expulsion was not motivated by military demands. On the contrary, it was based on an objective that can be explained only in terms of 'ethnic cleansing', a practice which often accompanies a process of national homogenization. Expulsion 'refers to the very physical violence of police batons or the military's gun, to the violence executed in the name ... of state authorities'.[167] It targeted individuals rather than entire villages and communities. The Alsatians and Mosellans who were expelled lost not only their homes and most if not all their belongings, but also relatives and friends in the course of their forced resettlement, and social networks and communities were destroyed.

While these different journeys were caused by quite different stresses, they had some points in common. All the participants were termed, quite indiscriminately, refugees. Within their numbers, Jews were growing more and more distinct: the category was even being imposed on people who had previously thought of themselves as Christian, French or free-thinking. The states of the New Order were demanding and enforcing an ethnic homogenization of their populations with little regard for an individual's sense of their cultural identity or religious faith. The new authorities also took a radically critical view of these diverse movements: its model was a 'rooted' population, in which location, identity and authority were neatly and forcefully mapped onto each other. Those who did not meet these criteria were simply expelled. The practice of government was brutalized in this period: minorities suffered a radical decline in their status, and this was frequently marked by violent forms of forced movement.

While the term 'refugee' was applied to all these movements, we must insist that it was being used imprecisely. Clearly, the various movements overlapped: we recall Morrow's observations about the diverse people queuing outside the Spanish Embassy. But our original model of a refugee, which stressed a decision-making capacity, a group consciousness and some potential claim to represent a majority experience, is increasingly less relevant to these exceptional individual militants and expellees. Forced migration, under tough, difficult conditions, as part of an anonymous mass, was becoming the norm. While the people of the *retirada* could claim to be the basis for a political project to represent the 'real' Spain against that led by Franco, the diverse groups studied in this chapter have no such solidity: their experiences divide them against each other; they adopt different attitudes to Pétain; they are defined as Jewish, French, foreign or refugee in a manner that short-circuits any collective consciousness.

PART TWO

FALSE DAWN

...when the day of military liberation comes, it will be the dawn of a newer and fuller liberation.

Mr Greenwood, MP for Wakefield, 25 January 1944[1]

Victory over want, confusion and despair must be as clearly kept in mind as victory over the enemy.

UNRRA publication, 1944[2]

On 2 April 1945 Susan Pettiss, an American volunteer relief worker, arrived in Southampton. Her ferry was the first passenger ship to arrive in the harbour for over two years. Pettiss was appalled by the sight of the town.

> The effect of war struck us with a bang. Destruction was evident everywhere. Fortunately for me, it was not quite so raw because rains and weather had washed it and moss and flowers were trying to hide it. Churches were skeletons. Buildings were just walls, window panes were out everywhere.[3]

Many people arriving in Europe in 1945 felt similar emotions as they saw its devastated towns and cities: this latest world conflict had produced destruction on an unthinkable scale.

Yet many – like Susan Pettiss – also felt other emotions. They looked forward to a better future, as if immense devastation had somehow prompted an equally vast wave of hope and idealism, a type of new dawn, like some brutally emphatic demonstration of Blake's observation that 'Without Contraries is no progression'.[4] The rehabilitation of the homeless, the outcasts and the refugees were integral parts of this re-building of the future. This argument was power-fully illustrated by Stuart Legg's 20-minute documentary, *Now – the Peace*, produced for the National Film Board of Canada in 1945.[5] This important film taught a clear lesson. It starts by discussing the end of the First World War and the creation of the League of Nations, presented as a missed opportunity to create a better world. It then turns to the conference held at Dumbarton Oaks, near Washington, in August and September 1944, which established the United Nations. This is seen as a second chance, allowing the great powers to learn from earlier mistakes and to create a new system of international cooperation. The first error that needed correction was the League of Nation's failure to prevent war, and the film rapidly moves from the Japanese invasion of China in 1931, through the Italian attack on Ethiopia in 1935, to German and Italian interventions in the Spanish Civil War. Viewers are given a brief summary of the structures of the United Nations, and pointedly reminded that the new organization will be able to intervene militarily. The point that turns this film into something more than a last example of wartime propaganda is introduced almost exactly half-way through, when the voice-over states that peace cannot only be based on effective military intervention: it must also rest on 'those mighty material forces that shape the intercourse of nations'. The succeeding images challenge the viewer to think on a world scale. Turbaned men are shown as pilots in enormous four-engined planes; armed soldiers patrol a seemingly endless pipeline; several shots of stock markets suggest the extent of international commerce. Then the viewer is introduced to UNRRA, the United Nations Relief and Rehabilitation Administration, which will serve a 'task of common world interest'. Its immediate role was to care for the approximately 20 million people made homeless by the war. Here, the film reaches a moment of supreme optimism. While showing an unspecified camp, presumably of refugees, the voice-over celebrated 'that forward-looking spirit that turns each campers' town into a self-governing community preparing its citizens for the day when they will take their place in the new community of nations'. The last minutes of the film propose a coordinated global economic policy, based on a single global food pool and an international bank. The film ends with a fine example of political balancing: while calling on the 'great powers' to take initiatives to bring about this future, it also notes that any project to establish 'true peace' must involve all the nations of the world.

In the chapters that follow, we will consider UNRRA's record in more detail, alongside the experiences of other relief agencies. We will concentrate on some lesser-studied aspects of UNRRA's activities: we are not proposing a global history of its vast international record; instead we use the experiences of some of its minor employees, like Pettiss, as means to guide us through important post-war issues. Our focus remains on refugees: while the first part of this work analysed the problems encountered, here we turn to consider some solutions, and the next two chapters will study how relief agencies interacted with refugees. In particular, we will study a new figure, the professional relief worker. While some previous works have analysed relief organizations, they have normally been presented in the context of international diplomacy or as studies of the institutions of social policy. As will be seen, there are good reasons for considering that such 'top-down' perspectives miss or underestimate important issues. Our analysis will consider how the interaction between relief workers and refugees produced a new 'outcast' identity.

In the next chapters, our geographical focus will also change. We will no longer to be referring to France as a type of laboratory for a variety of refugee experiences, but instead basing our discussions and analyses on the experiences of UNRRA's relief workers, among whom Britons and Americans were prominent. We will start by considering the British experience in some detail, because for a few years Britain played a vital mediating role. Britain had suffered far more war damage than the USA, and therefore British people had some comprehension of the destruction suffered by continental Europe. On the other hand, democratic and representative structures had survived in Britain during the war, allowing space for open debate, particularly concerning the future post-war world.

5

Lessons Unlearned: Wartime Debates and the Creation of UNRRA

- Ending Another War
- Neutrality and Commitment: the Red Cross and UNRRA
- Planning UNRRA
- Criticizing UNRRA, Defending UNRRA
- Recording UNRRA: Beyond Bureaucracy
- Joining UNRRA
- UNRRA at Granville
- Zones and Organizations
- Conclusion

The Allies' debates on the nature of the post-war world began surprisingly early: a British government-sponsored meeting of Allied representatives on 12 June 1941 could be cited as the first official body to address such issues.[6] The Council of British Societies for Relief Services Abroad (COBSRA) was formed in 1942 and COBSRA-affiliated staff were working in areas of liberated Europe as early as March 1944.[7]

In this chapter we will discuss why UNRRA was created. We start by sketching out some prominent themes that emerge from memoirs of wartime experiences, in order to re-construct the context from which UNRRA emerged.

ENDING ANOTHER WAR

During the Second World War, Allied commentators demanded urgent reforms to the way their countries were governed and the way in which war was conducted. The astonishing *Blitzkrieg* victories of 1939–40 had produced 'the most gigantic revolutionary ferment in history', according to the American publisher, veteran and commentator William B. Ziff, who argued in order to win the war 'the direction of the entire war effort should be handed over to a single man who has the strength to create one single vital, inspired war machine'.[8] 'The world cannot afford to repeat the experience of 1918–1919' insisted that an editorial in *The Times* in April 1944.[9] Even a natural conservative like General Sir Frederick Morgan (the European Director of UNRRA in 1945–46), could echo such vitalist rhetoric. Celebrating Churchill's leadership of the war effort, he noted that 'one could feel that the country was really at war, at last, and that the paralysis of national lethargy might, even at this late hour, be overcome'.[10]

These calls for radical change echoed earlier debates from the epoch of the Great Depression, when unplanned markets seemed to have produced a catastrophic disaster; these wartime debates share the same will to strengthen, to coordinate, to unify and to plan that marked critical economic thinking in the 1930s. Yet despite the near-universal consensus concerning the need to revise and re-organize the war effort, the results were curiously varied. For all the talk of scientific planning, real warfare remained a messy, bodged-up and often brutal affair, in which mistake followed mistake. For example, Norman Lewis, a British intelligence officer who took part in the Allied landing in southern Italy in September 1943, recalled attending a 'purposeless' intelligence lecture before the landing, and noted that 'we had been given no briefing or orders of any kind'. He was then appalled at the next instructions to soldiers: 'not only to take no German prisoners, but to use the butts of their rifles to beat to death those who try to surrender. I find this almost incredible'.[11] Grigor McClelland worked with the Quaker Friends' Ambulance Unit (FAU) in Germany in 1945: most Allied soldiers would certainly have identified his passing comment on 'the mass bungling inseparable from army administration'.[12]

Aside from the unsurprising shortcomings in the conduct of warfare, Allied commentators often made important conceptual errors. The real destructiveness of fascism was often underestimated or misrepresented.[13] Churchill's famous radio broadcast of June 1941, which responded to the German invasion of the Soviet Union, sounds more like playground caricature than an informed understanding of the nature of victorious Nazism.

> [They are invading Russia] where there are still primordial human joys, where maidens laugh and children play. I see advancing upon all this in hideous onslaught the Nazi war machine, with its clanking, heel-clicking, dandified Prussian officers, its crafty expert agents fresh from the cowing and tying down of a dozen countries. I see also the dull, drilled, docile, brutish masses of the Hun soldiery plodding on like a swarm of crawling locusts.[14]

Similar images were still circulating in 1945, when British soldiers entering Germany were informed that Hitler was more despotic than King John before the Magna Carta.[15] Such statements might galvanize the British public: a docile brute and 'bad King John' could both appear as manageable enemies. Nevertheless, they show that in Britain at least, commonplace views of 'the Hun' were similar to the propagandistic clichés of the 1914–18 war. Despite the increasingly accurate information concerning the death camps that circulated after 1942, many seemed unable to register the depth of the tragedy.[16] The British government consistently avoided direct reference to the issue, apparently judging that information about the mass slaughter of Jews would be exploited by anti-Semites, allowing them to argue that the war was fought on behalf of the Jews.[17] Public opinion seemed to follow. Brian Stone, captured by the Italians in 1942, was dismayed that his prison only contained four English-language novels. He immediately dismissed two of these as not worth reading: they were merely 'violently anti-Nazi novels by prominent Jewish writers'.[18] Jane Leverson, a British Jew, decided to join the Friends' Relief Service rather than a Jewish-based relief service, reasoning that Jewish persecution could not be 'as bad as all that' in Nazi Germany. She joined the team that liberated Belsen, and was the first Jewish relief worker to enter the camp. Her subsequent feelings of guilt were to have a lifelong impact on both her and her family.[19] Explicit anti-Semitism remained a force in British society during the Second World War. After June 1940, pro-Nazi groups could no longer operate, but four anti-Semitic weeklies continued to be published, and anti-Semitic rumours and stories circulated: Jews were the first to be evacuated from London, as they were the most cowardly; terrified, panicky Jews were responsible for the horrific crush at the Bethnal Green tube shelter in March 1943, in which 173 people died; Jews were the most active contributors to the black market.[20] While some felt a deepening sympathy for European Jews, there remained many who were indifferent or even actively hostile to such news.[21]

Beneath the common rhetoric stressing innovation, energy and unified effort, there is much convincing evidence to suggest continuities in structures and cultures. In Britain, one of the most important of these was the perpetuation of an imperial mindset: the public was persuaded to understand and to support the war effort in imperial terms.[22] This disparity between innovative, dynamic rhetoric and conservative practice is perhaps most obvious when we examine women's experiences of the war effort. This point is of some particular relevance to the chapters that follow, for women made a prominent contribution to UNRRA and similar agencies, and produced some of the most articulate accounts of their activities. On the one hand, one finds evidence for profound changes in attitudes and experiences. When Joan Rice, a volunteer in the Women's Auxiliary Air Force (WAAF), was posted to Egypt in January 1942, she reviewed the past two years. 'Before the war I should have gone mad with excitement and joy if circumstances had gratified the greatest of my aspirations and set me on a Channel steamer; now here I am en route for Africa and I feel no excitement at all'.[23] As well as participating in the excitement of war, women also found new positions of genuine responsibility. In January 1944 Herbert Lehman, Director General of UNRRA, appointed Miss Mary McGeachy as Chief of its Welfare Division. McGeachy was the first woman with an executive post in UNRRA with far-reaching powers, being responsible for the organization of relief for distressed persons, including specially dependant groups, such as the aged, children, and nursing mothers in liberated areas.[24] She was the only woman at executive level, however, and her post related to stereotypically feminine work. Welfare remained a low priority in UNRRA budgets and her division was subjected to severe and constant criticism.[25] In May 1946, the Welfare Division was merged with the newly created Displaced Persons and Repatriation Division, and her post was cut.[26] She was relegated to the position of Liaison Officer with the voluntary agencies until her resignation in August 1946.[27]

Women's roles within the armed services also indicated a level of continuity. Initially the WAAF seemed to mark an important change in women's wartime service. Its recruits performed jobs previously undertaken by men, they lived and worked close to men, and they wore similar uniforms to men. But: 'whatever the extent and the nature of substitution, men's tasks would, it seemed, always be defined as "more active"'.[28] One could also cite the striking example of British women's service in anti-aircraft batteries. In 1941, it was reluctantly accepted that due to the shortage of men, women would be allowed to serve in this sector. Many were keen to volunteer, and by all accounts performed their demanding tasks in a professional manner, confounding the initial doubts by older male officers. Yet despite this record, there was always one task reserved for male soldiers: while women could maintain and load the guns, while they could even aim them, only servicemen were allowed to fire them. It was argued that the British public would never accept women performing such an important *military* task. By actually firing guns women would be trespassing on the male role, aping masculine behaviour and emasculating men.[29] Gerard de Groot's study concludes: 'The mixed battery experience provides yet more evidence that war does not liberate women. The reassertion of traditional gender values during wartime outweighs their erosion in some quarters'.[30] During the upheaval of total war, the authorities judged that the maintenance of stable gender norms were crucial.

One last point relating to common wartime experiences needs to be made: in narratives from this period one can find many examples of heroism and of a common sense of uplifting participation in a unified national community. But it is also important to remember the grinding misery. John Guest, an officer responsible for an anti-aircraft unit sent south-east of London in 1941, recorded the stultifying routine and the feeling of being watched all the time. A friend compared their present and past lives: 'in civilian life one looked back on the day at evening with almost a touch of sadness, remembering what was past; here, one wrung the neck of each day with vicious satisfaction and flung it on the dung-heap'. As an officer, he was pestered with requests for leave that he could not grant: he was dismayed by his soldiers' easy acquiescence. Was this the pity of war? 'I had always been inclined to think of it in terms of violence, loss of life, rather than this inconspicuous sadness'.[31] Barbara Todd's exceptional, visionary novel, *Miss Ranskill Comes Home*, can be read as a type of female equivalent to Orwell's *Nineteen Eighty-Four*. She writes with despair of women's participation in the various semi-military and pseudo-military organizations that developed, and her work evokes a society made up of 'a little petty people, strangled by red tape, nagging along, intent on their own tiny quarrels, fretting over the fat ration, playing at war and pretending to be important in their [Air Raid Precautions] uniforms and gardening dungarees'.[32] Todd's response seems to be a conservative one: a return to a traditional, wholesome femininity based on family and home.[33]

Planning for the post-war world developed in these difficult, exhausted circumstances. By 1944–45, British opinion was growing more confident in the certainty of victory and the moral justification of their campaign. But the lessons they drew from six years of warfare remained confused, incomplete and sometimes simply inaccurate. While encouraging a substantial, activist minority to volunteer for organizations such as UNRRA, such people were ill-prepared for the challenges they would face.

NEUTRALITY AND COMMITMENT: THE RED CROSS AND UNRRA

To create a better post-war world, free from want, confusion and despair, UNRRA had to be and appear to be a new, impartial, moral force, free of links to the great interest groups. Yet in its origins, UNRRA was not neutral: it was a product of the Grand Alliance of Allied powers. This was not a new question for relief groups. The Red Cross, best represented by the Swiss-based International Committee of the Red Cross (ICRC), had previously considered it. The ICRC policy was not to discriminate: it offered 'humanitarianism, not justice' to all.[34] UNRRA, however, was both judgemental and discriminating: it aimed to help the victims of Nazi and Japanese aggression, but not the soldiers or civilians of the ex-Axis powers, or any criminals, quislings or traitors associated with them. In comparison with the Red Cross, there was a real danger that UNRRA might become nothing more than the conquerors' relief wing.

Neutrality could be difficult in wartime. For example, following successful military action against the Nazis in Greece, in December 1944 British troops were fighting the Greek National Liberation Army (ELAS) in Athens. *The Times* published the following story about one of the voluntary medical teams present:

> The leader, H.E. Dromard, was stopped and asked by a Greek to help a wounded British soldier. He walked down a side road between the fire of both parties, protected by the Greeks' Red Cross flag. At the same time two of his companions, who were in the truck, ran the gauntlet of British fire across a street corner and dressed the wound of an ELAS man.[35]

This particular team was led by a Royal Army Medical Corps officer, but was staffed by the FAU and UNRRA. It assisted both sides, and so faced the risk of being fired on by both parties. When it became clear how dangerous this situation was, UNRRA withdrew its medical teams from Greece.[36] This episode suggests the problems that post-war planners faced: they could not assume that an initial Allied victory would secure a lasting peace, and simply proclaiming neutrality was no protection from military attack. Lastly, UNRRA could not achieve anything if it had to withdraw from every difficult situation.

A policy of neutrality could lead to inaction. Activities in a combat zone or in post-war Europe demanded political negotiations with the dominant authorities: thus, for example, COBSRA's plans were based on the assumption that the Allies would win.[37] The ICRC, a self-proclaimed neutral organization based in neutral Switzerland, refused to make such commitments. Reviewing the establishment of UNRRA, an internal memo from the Swiss government's political department stressed the importance of Swiss neutrality and argued that Switzerland would have to be 'reserved' in its initial responses. The note accepted that Switzerland should play a significant role in post-war reconstruction, but argued that the government could not publicly attach itself to one group of belligerents while fighting continued. In particular, Switzerland could engage in no action which presumed the victory of one or other side.[38] The ICRC demonstrated a similar caution. In August 1944 UNRRA's Director General, Lehman, met with Alfred Zollinger, the international delegate of the ICRC. Lehman wanted the ICRC to cooperate with UNRRA. While Zollinger was willing to discuss UNRRA's use of their index of Displaced Persons, he remained hesitant about other forms of cooperation, asserting the over-arching importance of ICRC independence and neutrality vis-à-vis Allied organizations. Zollinger only agreed to attend the forthcoming UNRRA conference at Montreal as an impartial observer: he would play no active part for fear of compromising his organization's neutrality.[39]

The ICRC did not foresee a major role for itself in post-war relief work. The committee outlined its carefully limited aims in a draft memorandum at the end of the war.

> The ICRC does not wish to help displaced persons in the sense of providing teams of welfare, nursing or other personnel, except in exceptional cases, each of which will be raised and negotiated separately. Nevertheless, the Committee wishes to have access to camps and assembly centres in the person of its delegates and representatives … The Central Agency for prisoners of war of the International Red Cross Committee has been called upon by UNRRA to act as Central Tracing Bureau for Displaced Persons, and it is essential for this work alone that the Committee's delegates and representatives can enter camps and assembly centres.[40]

The problems faced by relief agencies in post-war situations are complex. The ICRC's carefully framed position of 'neutrality' provided one model: UNRRA, almost by default, adopted different policies.

PLANNING UNRRA

Some great claims were made for UNRRA. In one of its last publications, issued in June 1947, Richard Ford argued that UNRRA 'was a living example of the first post-war international organization doing the job for which [the United

Nations] was created'.[41] The first historical survey of its work, commissioned by UNRRA itself, argued that 'out of good-neighborliness and good-will, and in fulfilment of pledges given during the war, UNRRA was born'.[42] Given the extent of these claims, perhaps it was inevitable that the new organization also faced widespread criticism. General Morgan, one-time European Director of UNRRA, provides a useful introduction to some conservative objections.

> I left the Foreign Office bound for that 'greatest and most successful international organisation of its kind in the world', as it called itself, that adventitious assembly of silver-tongued ineffectual, professional do-gooders, crooks and crackpots, according to some other authorities, that operated under the title of UNRRA ... All said and done, some food went to some of the hungry, help was brought to some of the helpless, no mean achievement in existing conditions.[43]

Morgan suggests three points: first he notes the great idealistic claims made for UNRRA; secondly, he contrasts this with the people it actually attracted; but, thirdly, he does concede that UNRRA achieved something worthwhile.

UNRRA's own publicity highlighted the massive international scale of its operations. Gene Fowler's highly successful 1946 documentary on UNRRA's work, *Seeds of Destiny*, included brief shots of boxes of sardines, rice, tea and blankets being unloaded. Viewers could read their destinations as the boxes flashed past: Calcutta, Poland, Canada, Czechoslovakia and Greece.[44] In official publications, impressive figures suggested the vast scale of UNRRA's work: UNRRA spent $3.5 billion by the end of June 1947;[45] $168 million was spent on health work before January 1947;[46] 44 nations, representing 80% of the world, attended its founding meeting;[47] 48 governments sat on its policy-making council.[48] In 1945 the Nobel Peace Prize was awarded to Cordell Hunt, the American statesman, for his work in the creation of the United Nations. Representing the Peace Prize Committee, Gunnar Jahn's citation of UNRRA as an example of Hunt's success followed the same pattern. 'UNRRA did splendid work: its magnitude can be judged from the fact that its expenditure amounted to $3,900,000,000'.[49] UNRRA curbed epidemics, averted economic collapse, prevented famine in Austria, Yugoslavia and Greece.[50] In a single month of its operation, UNRRA distributed more supplies than the entire import programme to the UK throughout the war.[51]

This stress on statistics is indicative of the planning-orientated, technocratic approach that often dominated UNRRA. UNRRA's publicity highlighted the quality and the professionalism of its personnel.

> First consideration must be given to technical competence. Whether the task is to care for orphaned or other disadvantaged children; to provide for aged or disabled persons; to feed masses of men, women, and children; or to render any of the wide variety of services likely to be needed, the primary requisite should be knowledge of the work to be done and skill in its performance.[52]

Experienced welfare workers often welcomed this new tone. Francesca Wilson, a Quaker who had worked in Friends' voluntary relief movements since the First World War, initially applauded this 'planning-minded' approach and was pleased that relief organizations could divest themselves of the 'Lady Bountifuls'.[53]

Curiously, however, alongside these surging torrents of statistics, UNRRA's publicity also stressed some practical, down-to-earth qualities: Morgan's criticisms, cited above, miss this point. One of the earliest of UNRRA's publications caught this tone: 'There were few wasted words in the UNRRA [founding document]: its spirit, devoid of frills and formalities, was one of honest realism'; its meetings 'were characterized by an avoidance of high-flown oratory and idealistic generalities; realism was the keynote of the Council meeting'.[54] Its first history returned to this point.

> [UNRRA's] job was to act, rather than to deliberate or study ... Since it was a pioneering organisation doing a job of a scope and significance new to history, UNRRA had no background of tradition, system, language or currency. There were no sign posts along the way. It had to learn by doing ... UNRRA's approach was to put first things first.[55]

To some extent, this stress on practical realism may have been dictated to UNRRA: as an international body which – initially – hoped to gain the cooperation of all the countries of the world, it could not afford to advertise any specific political commitment. If not 'neutral' in the sense understood by the ICRC, UNRRA still defined itself as apolitical. 'Politics did not come into the scope of UNRRA' noted one of its publications.[56] UNRRA had no political ulterior motives, just the charitable aim of binding the wounds of war, commented a Swiss government report.[57] This apparently apolitical, humanist agenda may well have seemed attractive after the fierce ideological battles of the 1930s.

Yet it is clear that political ideals of a sort shaped important aspects of UNRRA's role. These related to its internationalist, egalitarian and cooperative values. Its defenders were extremely optimistic about its working methods. 'The success of UNRRA may point the way to a realistic blueprint for future unity among the free peoples of the world' one UNRRA publication noted.[58] Jan Masaryk, the deputy Czech Prime Minister was impressed by this argument. He reported that his participation in UNRRA 'proved to everyone ... that a cooperation which combines practical efficiency with great ideals is possible'.[59] UNRRA also presented itself as what we might now see as an 'equal opportunities' employer, working to a meritocratic remit. It sought to recruit an international staff, selected by qualifications, 'without discrimination on the grounds of sex, race, nationality or creed, and recruited upon as wide a geographic basis as is compatible with efficient administration'.[60] Similar principles were to shape the institutions it ran. 'Just and equal treatment to all persons and the tangible evidence of personal respect and consideration for the individual persons should permeate all administrative plans and activities in the Assembly Center' noted one pamphlet for UNRRA employees.[61] Such statements, of course, served to differentiate UNRRA from the racial policies of the Nazis, but they also suggested the extent to which UNRRA set out to embody a different ethic, even a new ideal, sharply distinct from the prejudices of the pre-war world.

Lastly, alongside its technocratic planning and global remit, there was a nurturing, participatory dimension to UNRRA's work. One of its earliest pamphlets was entitled *Helping the People to Help Themselves*, and it is noticeable that this phrase was frequently repeated by UNRRA's own field workers. To an extent, this was forced on its teams: always under-equipped and under-staffed, they depended on the active cooperation of the DPs themselves (a point to be explored in the next chapters). But it was also in this field that – just occasionally – UNRRA workers could justifiably consider that they really were helping to construct a new world.

CRITICIZING UNRRA, DEFENDING UNRRA

Even before UNRRA began operations among DPs in Germany, criticisms circulated. As early as 1941, the Friends' Service Council had argued that any post-war humanitarian organization would be unsuccessful if it appeared to be 'Anglo-Saxon'.[62] While willing to accept deliveries of supplies, the Soviet leaders became sceptical of the new organisation. *War and the Working Class,* a Soviet-backed publication, acknowledged UNRRA's humanitarian motives, but also insisted that 'one cannot ignore the fact that considerations of a more prosaic nature, reflecting the interests of some political and business circles in the US and Britain, also exist'.[63] The early history of UNRRA prefigures the later diplomatic divisions of the Cold War world.

It is, however, the early criticisms which circulated among British government officials that are the most revealing. Some, such as Viscount Halifax, predictably expressed preferences for the private charities which had worked at the end of First World War.[64] A debate in the House of Lords returned to similar themes: the Marquess of Reading observed that 'there is, undoubtedly, a feeling of disquiet in this country and outside of it, a suspicion that in the huge UNRRA organization there has been created a Colossus on so vast a scale that it has been, from the outset, muscle-bound, paralyzed by its own weight'.[65] More frequently, one finds criticisms that UNRRA was not attracting 'the right sort of people'. Internal Foreign Office minutes from June 1944 noted UNRRA's 'inability to contact sufficient first-class people to join the organization; in consequence the organization is decidedly spotty and many of them lack the right sort of experience'.[66] The British Embassy in Washington seemed to concur.

We have gained the unhappy impression of lack of purpose and of inefficiency. The reason, we are told, and we agree, is that UNRRA lacks personnel with sufficient administrative capacity and experience. Why? Because, we are told, UNRRA is 'scraping the bottom of the barrel' and can only recruit what it finds there ... More and more, one hears the rumour that UNRRA is senile before it is full-grown.[67]

More seriously, other internal records from the Foreign Office show a persistent anti-Semitism in these early criticisms. One memo complained that UNRRA had recruited too many Jews, and too many of these were Zionist-sympathizing.[68] Another noted:

> what I heard on my recent visit to the Middle East gives me the creeps. I was told that there are a very large number of American UNRRA representatives waiting out there and that these are largely American businessmen of the Jewish persuasion. It very much looks as if their main concern was the post-war prospects for American trade with Zionism as a sideline.[69]

Martha Rentsch, the ICRC delegate in Cairo, noted that many small countries perceived UNRRA as an instrument of US economic conquest, partly because many UNRRA directors had been businessmen, but also because it was believed that they were Jews.[70] This line of criticism persisted after 1945, and was repeated in the British anti-Semitic press, in which one can read the ridiculous claims that 80% of UNRRA's personnel was Jewish, and recruited from the American Jewish charitable organization, the Joint Distribution Committee.[71]

Morgan's criticisms of UNRRA raised other issues. Herbert Lehman, the Director General of UNRRA, had welcomed its 'mixed inter-organizational teams', seeing them as emblematic of post-war cooperation.[72] Conservatives did not share this optimism. Morgan came from a military background, and was frankly baffled by the cosmopolitan mix of peoples and values he encountered in UNRRA. 'What was missing in this UNRRA was any sort of community of object, of outlook, of background, of belief, of nationality, of anything'.[73] Obviously, these various strands of British-based criticism cannot be presented as a single coherent analysis of the new organization. But one can see some consistent themes emerging. UNRRA could appear to conservative British officials as an unwelcome representation of a new modernity: American, large-scale, cosmopolitan, secular and business-orientated rather than charity-based. These themes of criticism are clearly compatible with some of concerns of conservative anti-Semitism, in which Jews are presented as a force who stand outside the rooted folk of the settled nation.

Two further criticisms of UNRRA emerged extremely quickly. First, it was argued that the organization was ineffective. 'UNRRA the Unready', joked the Marquess of Reading, 'What is wanted, surely, is more sense of urgency, more contact with reality, less red tape and more white heat'.[74] In December 1944, the Earl of Huntingdon considered that the UNRRA operation in Greece was 'absolutely appalling'.[75] A visit by a French delegation to one of the first UNRRA camps in Germany, established before May 1945, was an extremely disillusioning experience. 'I merely wish to summarize the impression I had, and which all the delegates of Allied Nations must have shared, and it is this: the complete inefficiency and futility of UNRRA in the camp we have visited'.[76] The ICRC inspected DP camps in the western zones of Germany after the war. Its reports are also frequently sharply critical of UNRRA's performance, even making the shocking claim that conditions in UNRRA's DP camps were worse than those in the wartime POW camps.[77]

Secondly, it was said that the organization was corrupt. Here, the case is more difficult to debate: UNRRA's accounting was poor, and it is hard to be certain of the destiny of its funds. Some of its supplies certainly were traded on the black market. Perhaps more significant was the context in which it worked: poorly equipped relief workers often decided that in order to supply their camps, they would have to take matters into their own hands. We will return to this point in the next chapter.

The volume of public and private criticisms clearly worried UNRRA's leaders. *Fifty Facts about UNRRA*, published by UNRRA in January 1946, adopted a clearly defensive tone. It warned against the exaggerated hopes that some had of the new organization.

> Unwarranted hopes were raised that UNRRA would arrive bearing copious supplies the moment the enemy capitulated: too little attention was paid to the difficulties facing the military authorities in arranging for UNRRA to start operations, to the delays in signing Agreements with the Governments, to the world supply and shipping position and to the limited functions of UNRRA prescribed by the Allies themselves.[78]

The same publication even raised the question: 'What are the answers to criticisms about idle people on UNRRA staff, high salaries and incompetence?' The less-than-satisfactory answer was that the organization offered a reasonable salary for people embarking on a temporary career and that under these conditions 'it was impossible to pick and choose'.

Perhaps the most telling warning about the limits of UNRRA's performance, however, came from Lehman when he appeared before the House of Representatives sub-committee in October 1945.

> We have a lot of people join UNRRA because they think it is going to be a great adventure. There is a glamour to it and they expect to find conditions overseas just the same as they have known them in this country. If a person has run a boys' camp here, or a Boy Scouts' camp, or a convalescent camp, they expect to find the same conditions in Greece and in Yugoslavia and among the Displaced Persons in Europe. I have warned as strongly as I could when I spoke to people who were embarking on this work. The fact is that the conditions are completely different, just as different as they are in the case of a young soldiers leaving his home and his comforts and going to the battle front.
>
> The camps we have in Germany are not comfortable camps. They can be run only

with great resourcefulness, great improvisation, the greatest care. Obstacles confront these people day by day.

We get complaints that they are not properly cared for – that they do not have the creature comforts; that their views are not implemented immediately into our operations. Some of them are homesick. Some of them feel that progress should be made more rapidly, very much the way lots of soldiers I have talked to have felt, that things were wrong when they did not meet their own point of view…

This is a hard game. It is the toughest game. These people running the camps are out of touch with headquarters sometimes for days and days. It is difficult, when you have 350 camps, to get pay to these people promptly.[79]

Lehman's words accurately suggest some of the real difficulties that UNRRA workers would face.

RECORDING UNRRA: BEYOND BUREAUCRACY

Despite doubts and criticisms, the British government supported recruitment to UNRRA. In January 1945, the Ministry of Health noted the shortage of officials in local authorities, but still invited its permanent and temporary staff to register for service with UNRRA.[80] Alongside British recruits to UNRRA's Displaced Persons operation in Germany, many volunteers came from the USA, France, Belgium and the Netherlands. By December 1945, 16% of its Class 1 personnel were American, 18% were French and 31% were British or from the British colonies. Despite the common images of 'mother UNRRA', the majority were male: in June 1946, approximately 63.7% of its personnel were men and 36.3% of them were women.[81] In passing, one has to note that for all UNRRA's pride in a new professional approach to relief work, its statistical records were often frustratingly vague and incomplete. A document from June 1947 demonstrates this point: it enumerates UNRRA installations in the American, British and French zones of Germany. Usefully for historians, the American section lists the name of the head of each unit with the title Miss, Mrs or Mr. The British section lists unit leaders by surname and initial, but does not give them any titles: it is impossible to see from this document whether they are men or women. The French section does not give any names at all; it merely records the number of personnel in each unit.[82]

UNRRA, as a large bureaucracy, demanded form filling and regular reports. These vary in the nature and quality, but often are only of limited use to historians. In part, this is because UNRRA was clearly influenced by the ICRC, which considered it had devised robust methods by which to evaluate relief work. The ICRC documentation is usually highly technical and statistically based: its documents list the calories required by different groups, the range of nationalities in camps, the medicines and surgical instruments to be distributed, the amount of petrol used by personnel on a monthly basis, the demands for vitamins and cod liver oil. As we will see in the next chapter, UNRRA repeatedly asked Camp Directors to produce this type of documentation, but such reports reveal little about the social history of refugee experiences. On the other hand, sometimes there are other aspects to UNRRA's reports. One clear pattern was for fieldworkers to write in a more personal and expressive fashion in their last reports (usually completed in 1947), where they often surveyed their work over the past months or years. Secondly, in an almost random manner, some reports just are more descriptive: whether this was simply a means of letting off steam, or because the fieldworker in question was gripped by an experience which had to be recorded, or they enjoyed a particularly close relationship with their superiors is impossible to judge.

Because of the erratic nature of UNRRA's own records, we have often preferred to base our analyses on a collection of about 25 unofficial and autobiographical accounts that we have gathered during our research.[83] As these will feature frequently in the sections that follow, it is probably useful to give readers some clearer idea of their nature.

What motivated an UNRRA worker to go beyond form filling and keep some unofficial record of their work? One preliminary answer might be to deny any sharp distinction between informal diaries and formal records. When Harry Heath, Director of UNRRA Team 27, was arguing with Miss Deed, his administrative officer, he made her read sections of his diary so that she could understand his complaints.[84] An apparently personal account functioned here more as a log of events, aiding administration, rather than as an alternative narrative. Reading between the lines, one gathers that Team Director Donald McGonigal's *A Short History of Junkers Camp* was originally intended as a type of induction document for a new Camp Director. Others may have been considering a future publication while in service: it is noticeable that some paragraphs of General Morgan's published memoir *Peace and War* are copied, word-for-word, from his apparently private diary. In 1947, Audrey Duchesne-Cripps wrote a socio-psychological study of Displaced Persons in UNRRA camps, which was self-published in 1955. Others achieved some immediate literary success. Margaret McNeill's *By the Rivers of Babylon*, a lightly fictionalized account of her work in the Friends' Relief Service, was published in 1950. Kathryn Hulme, an American UNRRA worker, wrote the *Wild Place*, a semi-novelistic memoir based on her work in Wildflecken DP camp. The book was published in London and New York in 1954 and was awarded the Atlantic Non-Fiction award.

Some began writing for more obviously personal reasons: the works by Rhoda Dawson, Susan Pettiss and Howard Wriggins all began as letters to friends or relatives. Others were simply motivated by the recognition that their experiences would not be conveyed by the official records. Official reports left no space to record the minutia of daily life, and McNeill – a particularly self-conscious writer – wondered what future historians would make of 'all the incomplete UNRRA forms'.[85] Like so many, she was frustrated by UNRRA's form-filling exercises, considering that their main purpose was to

> convince the [Control Commission in Germany] that we were doing enough work, the British Red Cross Commission that that we were not overstepping our province, UNRRA that the work was being done in accordance with their regulations, and our Quaker office at home that we were concerned with something deeper than the alleviation of physical suffering.[86]

In response, McNeill used her diary to describe events that she could not mention in official reports, such as the visit of the 'very decent' Major who gave the Quakers a bottle of gin, 'which donation was not mentioned in the report back to Friends House!'.[87] Some fellow Quakers also wrote accounts for *The Star*, the FRS (Friends Relief Service) journal, in an attempt to convey something of their experiences, and McNeill even wrote a spoof report, 'Between the Lines'. This recorded a recent burglary, a messy dog, lost documents and general bureaucratic confusion, and at the top of the page McNeill wrote 'SECRET/ not repeat not to be transmitted by phone to Vlotho'.[88] McNeill also often used her diaries and journals as means to manage her own emotions. At a difficult point during the spring of 1947 she described her shame at having overslept and her inability to manage her own negative responses to the trials of relief work. 'Why should we *wake* with evil feelings uppermost?'.[89] she asked herself – and an unknown reader – in despair.

These more obviously private and personal documents functioned as a type of counter-narrative: these authors wanted to record what they could not say officially, and even what they could not say to their fellow team members. Because of their varied structures and content, it is not possible to treat these sources as a database which can be subjected to statistical analysis. One generalization, however, can be made. Women appear to have been significantly more likely to write these extra-official accounts: two thirds of our authors are female.

JOINING UNRRA

While the tone, nature and content of these personal manuscripts differ significantly, they do give a clear impression of what motivated people to volunteer for UNRRA. Particularly for women, who had not been conscripted to the same extent as men, joining UNRRA was an important decision, which required careful consideration. Some accounts suggest a continuity from their wartime positions. Between 1939 and 1945 Nora O'Connor worked as an ambulance driver, a bridge hostess in a hotel, the deputy commandant of a women's internment camp, a welfare officer for 1,000 female munitions workers, and then as a welfare officer for UNRRA.[90] Her CV is indicative of the sort of work carried out by middle-class women in wartime, and suggests how joining

UNRRA could be a logical next step. UNRRA also often attracted people such as pacifists, conscientious objectors and nurses who had not enlisted, and who were seeking an acceptable substitute for wartime service. Muriel Doherty, a 49-year-old Australian nurse, had applied to be posted to a war zone, but instead had spent the war in an administrative capacity in Sydney. 'The plight of millions of Displaced Persons in the former occupied countries became increasingly compelling to me. The urge to help these people was so irresistible that I decided to apply for an appointment with [UNRRA]'. She was delighted at her success. 'I was on active service at last,' she observed after her employment by UNRRA, 'even though I had been considered too old for this in Australia at the outbreak of war'.[91] While attending a meeting of the American Dietetic Association in 1944 in Washington, Frances Floore, an American Dietician, had the secular equivalent of a conversion experience.

> A former ambassador to Greece was the speaker at a banquet ... He told of the tragedies brought on that country by the occupying armies ... The famine there had taken a tremendous toll, and great numbers of adults and children had died from hunger ... As I listened, the bountiful meal I had just eaten seemed to lodge in my throat. Tears flooded my eyes. In my two years' work in Puerto Rico I had dealt with borderline cases of malnutrition and deficiency diseases ... But I have never seen a starving person, nor coped with the aftermaths of famine. Here was the brutal reality of war.[92]

She decided that she would join UNRRA. Reading Floore's and Doherty's diaries, one is struck by their concern and anger about the situation of the DPs, and by the extent to which UNRRA offered them a mission. They were convinced that their presence in the field would make a difference and that their work would be worthwhile. Looking back at her experiences, Pettiss remembered her colleagues' enthusiasm. 'Though it is seldom mentioned nowadays, UNRRA had caused quite a stir when it was established'. Driven by a 'pervasive idealism', these recruits 'hoped to see established a true world community with new social systems and international relations'.[93]

Unlike the old, voluntary associations, UNRRA also appealed directly to trained and highly skilled professionals, who admired its distinctive commitment to scientific methodology and professional approach. Aside from her humanitarian concerns, Floore was motivated by a professional interest in applying modern nutritional theories to food relief. As a highly qualified dietician, she was fascinated by UNRRA's potential.[94] By joining UNRRA, relief workers could also hope to gain a certain status and prestige. The remarkable number of articles in medical journals analysing the work of UNRRA's nurses and chronicling their medical achievements testifies to the widespread professional interest in UNRRA's work.[95] For the *British Medical Journal*, UNRRA was applying 'knowledge of recent medical progress' in war-ravaged Europe.[96] Joining UNRRA meant contributing to this endeavour. For career-minded social workers, it could provide an invaluable professional opportunity.

UNRRA launched many international careers: for example, ex-UNRRA nurses played leading roles in the subsequent development of the World Health Organization.[97] Eileen Blackey worked as a school social worker in the USA in the 1930s, as the Director of Child Search and Repatriation for UNRRA in 1944–47, and then held teaching posts in Hawaii and Jerusalem before becoming a Professor Emerita and Dean at the UCLA School of Social Welfare in the 1960s.[98] Internal records from UNRRA Team Directors often show their deep sense of commitment to humanitarian ideals as well as their passion to participate in a vanguard which would build a new world. As an internationally organized project, UNRRA was genuinely novel and raised great hopes amongst social workers.

Financial incentives also played a part, although they are mentioned less frequently in diaries and memoirs. UNRRA offered well-paid jobs at both executive and field levels. McGeachy's salary of $10,000 was more than three times what she had earned in her previous job at an embassy.[99] Pettiss observed 'for once in my life, I seem to have enough money'.[100] Jacqueline Lesdos, a French nurse in UNRRA made similar comments: 'I received what seemed to me the astronomical salary of £430 … As we received free lodgings, laundry and food, plus privileged access to cars and clubs and … as the hard times during the war had taught me how to be careful with money, I was able to save, and I even had money to spare'.[101] Generous salaries not only allowed UNRRA staff to live reasonably comfortably and to save, they also opened up new horizons, even allowing the purchase of luxury goods. Pettiss recalled the $89.50 dress that she wore to a Christmas Party. 'It is inconceivable now to conjure up what it meant for me to have a dress from Saks Fifth Avenue, that temple of fashion so worshipped from afar – Alabama – most of my life'.[102] Maurice de Cheveigné, a former French resister, was unusually blunt about his reasons for joining UNRRA.

> I had to earn some money. Could I stay a soldier? That really wasn't my cup of tea.
>
> Demobilized, I had to sort myself out. There were several possibilities: universities or professional courses. But everywhere there were long queues of ex-Resisters, all of them full of energy. For several long days I queued in vain, and then it became obvious to me that I wasn't ambitious enough to win this contest.
>
> [I learnt that UNRRA], an organisation which helped refugees, was recruiting staff. What?! Go back to Germany? After a while it seemed that this was the only option available to me. I had to get used to the idea … There weren't too many [French] volunteers for Germany. UNRRA accepted me.[103]

This disenchanted account contrasts sharply with the impassioned letters and diaries written by other relief workers. In his case, there is no sign of humanitarian concern and no taste for adventure. One senses only a resigned acceptance.

Joining UNRRA could also be a means of escape. Pettiss states explicitly that she wanted to end her marriage 'to an alcoholic and abusive husband', and that UNRRA was 'a great and socially acceptable escape'.[104] Love of travel and the desire to take part in world events often combined with humanitarian concerns. Ephraim Chase, the American Director of Team 308 explained in his last report to UNRRA: 'I felt at the time that not being a social worker I was inadequate for the tasks that lay ahead, but only the spirit of adventure, latent in most of us, lulled my doubts'.[105] Looking back at her life as a humanitarian activist, Francesca Wilson also referred to her taste for adventure.

> My urge to do relief work was not high-minded … I began without dedication or any desire (except the vaguest) to do good. I wanted foreign travel, adventure, romance, the unknown … The main force driving me … has been first of all a desire for adventure and a new experience and later on a longing for an activity that would take me out of myself, out of the all too bookish world I had lived in.[106]

Wilson's self-depreciating statement needs to be read with caution. Like many relief workers, she downplays her humanitarian commitments, presenting them as being nothing out of the ordinary.[107]

Lastly, Jacqueline Lesdos, a French nurse, had a very personal reason for joining UNRRA: her wish to find her missing brother, deported by the Germans. In January 1945, her 'absolute priority' was to be the first nurse to comfort him.[108] This personal aim was part of her broader concern for the victims of Nazism. Like Floore or Doherty, Lesdos saw her participation in UNRRA as a humanitarian and moral obligation. Painfully affected by the war and the loss of her relatives, she explained in her diary that she wanted to demonstrate [témoigner] to the unfortunate DPs that another world existed.[109] Taking care of DPs kept her mind busy while she worried about her brother's fate. When in the summer 1945 she finally learned that he had died in Neuengamme concentration camp, she tried to stay a few more months in Germany, but found that living in the country in which her brother had died was unbearable. After visiting his camp, she decided to resign. She felt that, having lost her taste of life, she could not give any 'joie de vivre' to the DPs.

In contrast, it should also be noted that some evidence points to a lack of dedication among some UNRRA personnel; perhaps de Cheveigné, cited above, was not so rare. Harry Saunders, the hard-working Director of UNRRA's mobilization Centre at Granville, complained in January 1946 about unsuitable recruits.

> Bad recruitment has been quickly reflected during the Training Course. Officers continue to appear in categories for which they have little or no qualifications. This has been explained in unconvincing ways by such remarks as 'well, that was all there was open for me' … Although it is, of course, necessary to maintain certain technical or professional standards in appropriate grades, the experiences of this operation suggest that special stress should be laid on personality, leadership and good character.[110]

UNRRA reports are not precise enough to quantify the numbers of such recruits. However, in autumn 1945, the UNRRA administration was concerned about high numbers of resignations.[111] Relief workers' dedication was severely tested by the hardship and frustration of work in the field. The administration was forced to introduce a new measure: UNRRA would not pay the transport costs of those who resigned before a year's service.[112]

These accounts suggest the variety of motivations which led people to volunteer for UNRRA. For all of them, it was an important decision; in each case, the individual applicant seems to have had a reasonably clear idea of the role that UNRRA played, and some conception of how they could participate in it. It is also striking how many speak of UNRRA as a cause. This may be a distortion due to the nature of our documentation: only the more dedicated relief workers were likely to write about their service in UNRRA and, naturally, they were more likely to see it as a cause they had to defend. Having made this qualification, it must be noted that our evidence suggests that UNRRA had been successful in attracting dedicated staff who felt some immediate sympathy for its humanitarian aims. The relative over-representation of women's voices in these sources reinforces this idea: for women who had not found a form of wartime service of which they could feel proud, UNRRA could seem a marvellous opportunity. This was, in turn, a factor which stimulated them to write of their experiences.

UNRRA AT GRANVILLE

During 1945, one experience that many UNRRA workers shared was their residence in Granville and the linked settlement of Jullouville, two small seaside towns in Normandy. Several hotels here had been previously used as quarters for German officers and then as an advanced headquarters for SHAEF. They were taken over by UNRRA in March 1945, and the first UNRRA team left from the new base for Germany on 29 March.[113] By 29 May, some 2,000 people had attended courses in Granville, and some 200 small, 'spearhead' teams had been sent out.[114] About 500 UNRRA workers were constantly present: each week some would leave, only to be replaced by new recruits from Britain, America, France and further afield. This base served two purposes: it provided training for relief workers immediately before their departure to Germany, and it also acted as a type of transit camp, allowing teams to be formed and supplied, and transport arranged, in a coordinated manner. In theory, they were to receive a six-day intensive course, and then to leave; in practice, most seem to have stayed for at least two or three weeks, sometimes longer. The base was poorly located, far from the main routes to Germany.[115] In July 1945, Harry Saunders, Granville's Director, expressed preference for a training centre in Germany, where problems could be examined 'on the spot'.[116] In September 1945, the centre was transferred to Haaren in the Netherlands.[117]

Granville was central to the history of UNRRA: its institutions embodied its ideals, and the hundreds of relief workers who passed through them took away a clear impression of the nature of the organization. The base quickly acquired a bad reputation. Military authorities noted the slowness with which its teams were mobilized for service in Germany; UNRRA's own records speak of poor management and dull lectures.[118] Marvin Klemme, an American UNRRA officer, was one of its most severe critics. He noted that 'it was the unanimous opinion of everyone, regardless of nationality, that this training centre was the most inefficiently operated undertaking they had ever seen anywhere at any time'.[119] The accounts left by other British and American relief workers, however, are more favourable. In the pages that follow we will begin by tracing the journey of the British volunteers.

The British accounts begin bureaucratically: crossing the Channel demanded no less than eight documents.

i. British passport

ii. UNRRA ID – a small green-backed booklet

iii. Allied Expeditionary Force Form Permit

iv. Personal documents passed by the Traveller Censorship Office

v. Travel tickets

vi. Three certificates by the Wellcome Trust Institution: TABC vaccine, Typhus vaccine, small pox vaccine

vii. Allotment certificate

viii. Travel authorisation certificate (in triplicate)[120]

In spring 1945, the crossing was still potentially dangerous: the last U-boats still patrolled the Channel. Frequently teams experienced delays. Sometimes this was due to U-boat activity, but more often these were just another of the 'SNAFUs' of military life: over-worked staff were using battered equipment in difficult conditions to carry out an over-ambitious task; delays were inevitable, and became a constant theme in UNRRA service. Still, crossing the Channel meant something. Writing on 11 May 1945, Dawson noted 'Here we are on the south side of the Channel; it does make it seem more possible that the war is over'.[121] Because of the wrecked condition of the northern French coast, the new recruits could not travel to Granville by train by the shortest route, westwards. Instead, they went by train to Paris, stayed overnight, and then headed out north-westwards to Normandy. The long journey allowed them to see France: many were shocked by the evidence of bombing, destruction and deprivation. 'Poor France' wrote Muriel Heath.[122] Pettiss noted that during the whole train journey from Paris she only saw one car.[123] Many were struck by the sight of French returnees from Germany, whether prisoners of war or forced labourers, and the stolid reception committees waiting for them at each station.

The sight as the people crowded from the train was worse than any word, picture or illustration. Seeing these people in the flesh made the barbarity and cruelty of the Nazi more real. All had the look of the hunted animal. They looked subhuman. Some were emaciated: not all, by any means. All wore nondescript clothes, footwear showed a wide variety. Many wore their prison clothes – a drab striped material. I saw many women with the mark of the Jew on their backs – a big X.[124]

Yet as they saw hardship, British UNRRA workers experienced something else. 'Magnificent breakfast' commented Harry Heath about the meal served to them at the Allied Officers Club in Paris.[125] Muriel Heath was even more emphatic. 'We were staggered, after the Spartan English diet, to find 2 eggs on our plates, evaporated milk in plenty, a basin full of sugar on *each* table for four, fruit juice, marmalade and butter. This we had never expected'.[126] Her reference to the sugar bowls speaks volumes: this was an extravagance that was simply unknown in wartime Britain. The luxuries continued when they arrived in Normandy. 'There are eggs and eggs' Rhoda Dawson noted excitedly.[127] Hall was delighted by their meals at Granville. 'The diet includes fruit juice for breakfast about three times per week, usually an orange each day and porridge every morning. Tinned fruits such as pears and peaches are a regular feature and so is tinned chicken; potatoes are very scarce, fresh eggs plentiful'.[128] The signs of an approximate social equality in the base also met with approval: 'There is no distinction of rank. All line up for the dining hall and all are served alike'.[129]

Granville also provided another lesson in the reality of war. The main building was still decorated in German camouflage paint, and Pettiss noted the giant murals of voluptuous nude women in the dining room, designed for the delight of the German officers. The Allies' presence was signalled only by some clothes having been painted on them.[130] German mines still lay in the fields around the base, and the days were punctuated by the sound of controlled explosions. More worryingly, on 9 March 1945 the town had been raided by one of the last German units, still holding out in the Channel Islands. UNRRA's training centre had been sprayed by machine-gun fire, and new recruits could see the broken windows and bullet holes in the walls. Muriel and Harry Heath were even woken up one night by a second German raid on the coast. 'This was, I think, my worst moment in UNRRA', commented Muriel, 'not that we weren't in uglier situations later'.[131] When they walked to the beach, past the German trenches and defences, there they saw the macabre sight of hundreds of bleached animal bones: earlier in 1945 the Germans had tried to ship out cattle from Normandy. Local French people had sabotaged the German boat, and the cows had been left to die on the beach.[132] Other features reminded the new recruits of wartime conditions in France. The local people still wore wooden-soled shoes that clattered on the cobblestones. The staff at Granville looked ill and exhausted: 'These people had starvation written all over their faces'.[133] The black market was thriving, and thefts were frequent: even in the base, the cooks stole money and the maids stole soap, and UNRRA supplies were often sold on the black market.[134]

Some of the new recruits were sent to the Hotel du Casino at Jullouville. Conditions were primitive there: Hall noted it was 'a hotel with little or no furniture and no beds'.[135] Three of them shared a room, and Hall felt glad that he had a camp bed and some blankets. Muriel Heath was placed in a bare fifth-floor room with no lights or bed. 'Actually we were rather pleased, we felt this was a challenge. This was what we had expected – to lead a hard life'.[136] Pettiss adapted less easily.

> This time the accommodation was a little worse – three in a room, sleeping on canvas cots, window panes out, no furniture, no water most of the time. Rugged!
> No water at all – no toilet facilities functioning – cold, no sheets, my jacket still serving as pillow. My hands got so cold and blue I had to go walking to get warm.[137]

Others were quartered in an old wooden barracks: Klemme resented its cold, damp rooms. He recalled that 'the local citizens had swiped all the electric light bulbs, torn out the wiring and lifted all the furnishings. The windows had mostly been stolen or blown out by concussion … the stoves had been taken away … To make matters worse, the roofs of most of the barracks leaked'.[138]

During the enforced inactivity at the base, however, many could not help feeling that this was like a holiday. Granville was 'an interesting, old-fashioned French town situated on a lovely bit of coastline' noted Harry Heath, sounding more like an enthusiastic tourist than a trainee relief worker.[139] Pettiss adopted the same tone. While Granville was never as fashionable as Deauville and Trouville, she observed, 'it was beautiful and quiet, a simple and harmonious collection of white plaster houses and small cafés threaded along cobblestone streets'.[140] For much of 1945, there were no papers delivered and no access to the radio, leaving the new recruits feeling unexpectedly out of contact. 'The next two weeks passed mainly in sunbathing, letter-writing, bathing and exploring Granville … an unexpected holiday'.[141] The rations included a monthly bottle of whisky for male personnel: Hall consumed this in one night. 'The next morning I had a really good hangover for the first time in my life'.[142] O'Connor attended lectures, but occupied most of her time in walks, talks and bridge.[143] American soldiers were stationed on leave near the camp. Sometimes they allowed UNRRA personnel to use their showers. They could also provide entertainment, including beer, dances and music. 'I jitterbugged for three hours without a break – no surprise, considering that the soldiers arrived in droves and there were only twenty of us American girls'.[144]

This was also the opportunity to find out more about their fellow workers. One obvious point was the astonishing mixture of nationalities. Many seemed delighted by this. 'The truly international character of the organization began to be apparent as recruits from other European countries and from America met together' Duchesne-Cripps noted happily.[145] Pettiss attended a meeting of welfare officers: there were 32 present, and only 2 were men. They included 12 Americans, 1 Canadian, 1 Czech, 4 Belgians, 9 English and 8 French people. She expressed some doubts about the English.

> My first impression of UNRRA's personnel was something of a shock – a lot of elderly British colonels, some still carrying their swagger sticks or tottering on canes. There were a few Belgian doctors and Dutchmen. Americans were in the minority. As time went on the image changed.
>
> Mostly men, mostly young (except the English), vital and energetic. Most of the Continentals have been in the armed services, in prison or concentration camps. Their true life stories beat all the fiction I have ever read.[146]

O'Connor was interested in the varied rates of pay: she found that Americans were paid more than her, continental Europeans less.[147]

In general, the new recruits seemed to have welcomed the cosmopolitan mixture of nationalities. The teachers encouraged them to talk to each other, and this activity was a good example of a point where the base's pedagogic practice and the recruits' informal culture interacted in a successful and memorable manner. Even the largely critical Klemme conceded that

> it was of real importance that the different nationalities learn as much as possible about each other … [Granville] did serve a very useful purpose. It was here that the different nationalities were thrown together into one large group … Through this method of personal contact our American personnel soon learned a lot of things that we could never have found in text books.[148]

Hall was struck by the tales that the continental Europeans told. 'One man told he escaped across the Rhine into Switzerland accompanied by a young boy. A woman of 35 told of her life in a German concentration camp – she had been a member of the French Maquis and had been imprisoned by the Germans'.[149] The general impression that one gains is that the recruits were both impressed and re-assured by learning of this mixture of experiences. 'It was my first real exposure to the international camaraderie which developed quickly over wine or Calvados … Sharing jokes, singing French, Belgian, Canadian songs with my new companions, I could feel my world expanding'.[150]

The purpose of the base was to complete the recruits' training, and turn this cosmopolitan, heterogeneous mixture into unified and capable teams with a relatively uniform approach to the provision of medical and social services. Differences in patterns of recruitment posed potential problems. The North American recruits often had a social work background and were generally older than continental recruits. They had undergone a rigorous selection process. Trained in the Depression Era, they were often former employees of US Federal agencies. Their professional perspectives contrasted with European social workers' views, which were shaped by their wartime experiences, while the British recruits' main relevant experience was feeding and sheltering people during the Blitz. French relief workers were often not chosen for their social work experience, but as a reward for their resistance activities.[151]

Granville courses covered administrative procedures (the registration scheme and the different Welfare services in UNRRA), practical information (the Army and its organization) and sanitation and hygiene measures.[152] According to Harry Saunders, after June 1945, the programme was the following:

1) UNRRA. One lecture only dealing with the background and leading up to the Field Work.
2) The Armies and their organization
3) 'Pictures' of centres
4) UNRRA in the Field – organization and channels
5) Registration and an exercise
6) Welfare including Recreation and Information centres and discussion of various problems
7) Feeding – including outdoor cooking by demonstration
8) Road discipline
9) Health including sanitation and hygiene from a Field point of view
10) Exercises including discussions of problems presented by members
11) Supplies.[153]

Doctors and nurses also received instructions on the specific health conditions of the DPs, including the effects of malnutrition, infectious diseases, immunisation and children's and women's special needs.[154] There were also some staged reconstructions of DP interviews (both sympathetic and unsympathetic) and counselling.[155] Sometimes courses were divided into French-speaking and English-speaking sections; for the more practical topics, instructors became adept at teaching through demonstration rather than by speech.[156] Students were challenged to consider and discuss possible problems.

> There are some disturbances, indicating a likely serious situation in your camp. There are several main causes, such as inactivity of an influential group of young men; uncertainty about repatriation; and alleged (but untrue) inequalities of feeding as between groups. The camp has 4,000 Polish with comparatively few other nationalities.
>   What steps would you take to gain confidence and cooperative action by the DPs? From whom would you seek advice if your first efforts are not successful?[157]

Aside from strengthening UNRRA workers' technical knowledge, instructors also aimed to inspire them with the 'UNRRA spirit'.[158] Laveissiere, a French instructor, explained this point in some detail:

> I quickly realized that it was not sufficient to instil into my listeners the principles of the

SHAEF guide, to explain a Flow Chart to them or to initiate them into the mysteries of registration: I had to light in their hearts that spark of enthusiasm without which they would not contribute anything to the great work of repatriation, that 'act of faith which needs a great deal of love'.

I understood that [the] aim ... was to show that UNRRA did not employ officials, but apostles.[159]

While most of the new recruits record attending lectures, they say little about their content: it is hard to judge whether they considered them useful or not. The atypical Klemme despised the impassioned lectures, describing some as 'idealistic chatter', but believed that the discussions of problems were useful. 'This was a good idea and everyone got some very good experience from the exercises' he conceded. 'It was here that some of the difficulties to be encountered through mixed nationalities working together first appeared'.[160] He recalled his first experience as a hypothetical team director. The exercise assumed that he was in charge of a large assembly centre and had to make arrangements for the reception of 1,000 additional refugees. Hall's notes also include some interesting premonitions concerning UNRRA, recording his shock when he learned that Supply Officers had to resort to 'scrounging', and his concern about the violent acts and thefts carried out by Russians and others: 'Discipline is a big task. DPs are looting, burning, stealing and murdering. Problems created in many cases are due to lack of understanding. Take action at once. Prevent looting by putting on guards'.[161]

As their wait in Granville lengthened, some began to grumble. Curiously, few speak with great bitterness about their 'rugged' accommodation: perhaps Muriel Heath's comment that this was what they expected was typical. But they do complain about 'muddles and inefficiency'.[162] The Student Council, created to represent the recruits at Granville, complained about the absence of competent and well-informed officials.

> A considerable percentage of the personnel ... has in one form or another an individual problem & one can spend many a "weary hour" wandering from one room to another trying to find someone who has the necessary knowledge & authority to give a satisfactory reply.[163]

Recruits also protested against unfair measures, in particular against the downgrading and upgrading of some students. These measures 'destroyed confidence in the administration'.[164] One American protested about the thefts by the French staff: his letter raised some wider issues about how American recruits understood their position.

> We are all supposed to be high grade people. We, from the American continent, as no doubt those from other parts, were carefully screened. For everyone accepted I understand hundreds were rejected. Our fellows at home looked with envy on our good

fortune in being complimented by UNRRA's acceptance of our credentials. Surely being the type of organization we are and the type of people we are, we should not only expect – but should be governed by and served by a high grade type of administration.[165]

While British recruits were generally delighted by the food, others complained.[166] Klemme insisted that 'we almost starved'.[167] Harry Heath also grew unhappy. He talked about his concerns with Muriel, and then wrote:

> We both agree that we don't want to stay here – the atmosphere at the base is uncomfortable and the chief seems to have gone out of his way to select the worst possible types for his staff. Ex-army officers of the "pukka sahib" type are flagrantly wangling jobs for each other and are strutting about shouting orders, presumably to hide their incompetence. The confusion and incompetence is too awful for anything. We shall be glad to leave.
>   UNRRA is being very badly served indeed.[168]

These complaints vary in their content and their gravity. One generalization which can be made, however, is that few recruits came away from Granville with a clear sense of disillusion about UNRRA's purpose. Granville's inability to organize and mobilize teams quickly was disappointing, but UNRRA's defenders are probably correct in arguing that these delays were caused by external factors, principally the failure of the military authorities to cooperate effectively.[169] The training Granville offered seems to have been unremarkable: the relief workers tend only to refer to it negatively once they started work, but here it is possible to argue that nobody could have properly prepared relief workers for what lay ahead. More encouraging was the manner in which these earnest volunteers related to each other: they really did seem to enjoy each other's company, and were genuinely impatient to leave together for Germany. The enforced leisure of Granville may have been an administrative error, but it provided time and space for the volunteers to take stock of their teams and their abilities.

ZONES AND ORGANIZATIONS

Following the creation of UNRRA in November 1943, many thought that this new, professional, international organization would monopolize relief work in post-war Europe. As early as 1945, governments began to realize that this would not be the case. The British War Cabinet noted in January 1945 that 'There are a number of societies which are eager to help Allied Displaced Persons being repatriated from Germany and neither SHAEF nor UNRRA have so much man-power to spare as to be able to afford to turn down their offers'.[170] Consequently, a variety of relief agencies operated in the British, American and French zones. (The Russians bluntly stated that there were no DPs in their zone and refused to allow the creation of DP camps.) In the British and American zones, all voluntary relief organizations were brought under the jurisdiction of UNRRA, while in the French zone, the Military Government was the primary responsible power. Sometimes voluntary relief agencies were active in all three zones; sometimes not. Sometimes they were responsible only for displaced people, sometimes also for civilians and prisoners of war.[171]

Rather than streamlined planning-mindedness, relief work was therefore a patchwork, stretching over the British, French and American zones. This mixture of military, civilian and charitable organizations can seem like an impenetrable, labyrinthine structure. Our aim in the next three chapters is not to describe the totality of this chaos, but to analyse the relationship between relief workers and refugees during these years, starting by considering the organizations which were designed to care for them. We will concentrate on UNRRA, and compare this with two other prestigious and experienced agencies: the ICRC and Quaker-linked FRS. (One important qualification needs to be made about the FRS: not everyone who worked in it was a Quaker. Margaret McNeill, one of its most dedicated workers, was an Irish-Presbyterian, who was nonetheless impressed by the Quakers' methods.) We will also make passing reference to the French MMLA (Mission Militaire de Liaison Administrative), whose first teams entered Germany in February 1945.[172] In the chapters that follow, while we will certainly note some important differences, we will concentrate on the points which the zones, nationalities and organizations shared.

CONCLUSION

In a curious way, the end of the war was like the beginning. In 1939 and 1940 the French social services were overwhelmed by the numbers of homeless people moving west to avoid the German threat. 1945 was similarly marked by massive movements of homeless people. Military authorities were conscious of these similarities, arguing that while 'swarms of refugees' may have hindered Allied attempts to fight in 1940, they would be more effectively managed in 1945.[173] There were some important administrative changes. In 1940, the state-run French social services had been complemented by the three different French branches of the Red Cross and numerous other voluntary organizations, with each tiny group maintaining its autonomy. By 1945 relief services had a far clearer management structure; they were more effectively coordinated and there were more fully established lines of control.

The history of post-war relief has been dominated by the themes of unity, professionalization, and co-ordination, in short the growth of 'planning-mindedness' during the war. 'Relief' meant the massive transportation of food and medical supplies around the world, a task which would have been impossible without managerial expertise as well as money and technological ability. Assessing UNRRA's work is complex: it is always difficult to prove a negative case, yet it may well be true that the *absence* of any severe epidemic after 1945, similar to the deadly flu pandemic that raged in Europe after the First World War, was due to UNRRA's work. In comparison with previous relief efforts the sums of money involved were both phenomenal and unprecedented.

For relief workers themselves, this sense of professionalization was important but it was not the most crucial aspect of the work. Reflecting on UNRRA in 1946, Director General Fiorella LaGuardia commented that:

> We have carried out the plan drawn up by economists and drafted by lawyers, but we did it in the spirit of the Sermon on the Mount … We have demonstrated to the world that 48 nations can work in harmony and carry out a great mission; let us see that the job is not lost to history.[174]

This seems like a glossy, romanticized vision of UNRRA: what about the careerists, adventurers and drunkards? Nevertheless, this early idealism did exist and did motivate many thousands of men and women. Without such a vision, relief workers may not have been able to deal with what they encountered in newly liberated and newly occupied Europe.

Into Darkest Germany

'No superlative is too strong to describe Berlin in 1945', noted Lieutenant Richard Brett-Smith, 'it was extraordinary'.[1] Other commentators entering Germany echoed Brett-Smith's sense of amazement. In a phrase which has become notorious, a booklet issued to British soldiers warned them that they would meet 'a strange people in a strange, enemy country'.[2] This was 'Darkest Germany' observed the publisher and polemicist Victor Gollancz in 1947.[3] His term suggests multiple meanings: Germany was dark because – like darkest Africa – it had become an unknown country, waiting for explorers and colonists; because it was the sinister site of some dreadful secrets; because it was difficult to comprehend.

In this chapter we follow relief workers' journeys into this extraordinary Germany and into other areas of liberated and occupied Europe. These people were often organized by UNRRA, but other organizations – including the Quakers, the Red Cross, the YMCA and YWCA, the American-Jewish Joint Distribution Committee, the British-based Jewish Relief Unit and even the Boy Scouts and Girl Guides – were also present. Each of these organizations brought their own concerns and policies: they ranged from old-fashioned voluntary, often religious, charities to the apparently more modern, trained professional units that UNRRA aimed to encourage. Relationships between these groups were sometimes tense: UNRRA struggled to overcome the distrust of well-established voluntary agencies, who only reluctantly accepted UNRRA's supervision.[4] These organizations recruited from different nations: while the USA and UK are certainly most prominently represented among their members, one can also find workers from France, the Netherlands, Italy, Czechoslovakia, the Baltic states and, less frequently, from South America and Australia. Yet despite this cacophony of organizations and acronyms, one can identify common strands of experience, as these generally well-meaning, middle-class, people threw themselves into unprecedented situations.

These relief workers travelled alongside military convoys: sometimes they pursued parallel routes, but more often they drew apart, following different agendas and moving at different paces. The Allied armies, now firmly under American leadership, fought from Normandy in July 1944 to central Germany in May 1945. Eisenhower, the Supreme Allied Commander, only reluctantly agreed to UNRRA's participation in November 1944, and this example of poor coordination between the two organizations is indicative of how they interacted in the following months.[5] Having been shunned by the military leadership for almost a year, in early 1945, UNRRA rushed to organize its members for relief work. Military priorities often conflicted with UNRRA's humanitarianism: one SHAEF publication, advising on the manner in which to treat Displaced Persons, noted that 'the objective of personal counselling from the point of view of Military Government is to minimize the hindrances to orderly repatriation which may be encountered'.[6] For military leaders, relief workers were only to play a strictly limited, instrumental role, assisting and completing the conquest of this strange enemy country by keeping the DPs out of their way; relief agencies tended to think in more ambitious terms of rehabilitation and even liberation.

In this chapter, we will examine the experience of UNRRA workers, setting their work within the wider context of post-1945 relief work. These people usually started their extraordinary journeys eastwards from Granville and other French bases into newly occupied Germany. Their voyage took them out of the world of largely democratic nation states into a different, uncertain polity, whose future was being shaped before their eyes, and also out of the world of largely settled citizens, into the largest collection of the long-term homeless in the history of the world. Their journey was also a voyage across history, though often the now-prestigious landmark dates seemed strangely irrelevant to our earnest humanitarians. 'Today we heard that Germany capitulated yesterday at Rheims' noted Harry Heath, Director of the UNRRA team at Hanau, in his diary. 'It is amazing how little difference it makes to our lives. The job is still there to be done. Tonight the US soldiers fired a few shots in the air by way of celebration but that is all'.[7] 'While the shooting had stopped and the war was officially over, the task of picking up the pieces had barely begun' commented Pettiss.[8] Some UNRRA workers worried that this was only a temporary period of stasis, a mere absence of conflict, before the beginning of the next war.[9] Lastly, this was also a difficult voyage into knowledge of the Holocaust, which began to feature in newsreels and soldiers' letters. For the British public, the discovery of Bergen-Belsen in April 1945, and the subsequent radio broadcasts and newsreels came as a dreadful shock: they were forced to consider that the rumours concerning mass murder on an industrial scale were not examples of government-sponsored atrocity propaganda, nor the expressions of exaggerated panic by Zionist fanatics.[10]

The sense of a continuity stretching from before 8 May 1945 to long afterwards was shared by a surprisingly large number of those present at the end of the war. Julie Summers, considering the experience of soldier's wives, makes a similar point with reference to the women taking care of mentally or physically damaged ex-soldiers. 'For these women the war did not end in 1945. For some of them it only ended with the death of the man in their care'.[11] These challenges to established chronological common sense suggest the importance of our story: the refugee's history of the war is not some strange side route, outside of the normal course of history, but something more akin to a moment of illumination, showing an alternative narrative that sometimes meets the established military chronology but – like the UNRRA workers scrambling to find their places on the bomb-shattered roads of occupied Germany – more often runs counter to it.

Forty-seven year-old UNRRA Welfare Officer Rhoda Dawson kept one of the most interesting records of UNRRA's work. Partly because of her age, she felt isolated from her younger fellow workers and at times she was sceptical, even cynical, about their work. Looking at her camp in Rosenheim in July 1945, she noted that 'Cars, drink and girls are the staples of bright interchange'.[12] This is a surprising, even revelatory observation, which contrasts with the standard perceptions of UNRRA as sober social work in practice. Her remarks are one of those rare cases in which a single sentence makes one wish to re-read and re-evaluate almost every other source, for they suggest a type of deep structure existing within the camps, beneath or beyond any established policy, shaping the actions of UNRRA teams. In this chapter we will explore the implications of her observations, concentrating of the interchange between and among the teams.

TRAVELLING INTO GERMANY

Travelling meant trouble. This was the first major test on UNRRA's organizational ability: how fast could it get its teams into newly liberated Germany? Its leadership recognized the difficulties they faced.

> The basic problem affecting our ability to turn our teams to the Army was the lack of trucks. No one should underestimate the serious effect of our inability to procure trucks. Without these trucks the teams are useless. Our ability to live up to our present recruitment and mobilisation schedules hinges entirely on the provision of first-class trucks in adequate numbers. A large proportion of the reconditioned trucks which have been already procured and are now in the field, have broken down.[13]

Before June 1945, the only trucks available to UNRRA were reconditioned vehicles from the British Ministry of Supply. These trucks had undergone at least two or three years of service and had been rejected by the Army as 'likely to require uneconomic amounts of maintenance'.[14]

Relief workers waiting in Granville found that travel arrangements rarely ran on time. For weeks teams in training would hear confusing rumours concerning their departure and then suddenly, even with only an hour's notice, they would be told it was their turn to leave.[15] Frequently they remained unclear about exactly where they were heading.[16] Many sensed the lack of preparation: 'The whole process of creating and organizing the teams seemed very disorganized and unplanned, as did our training and preparation … I had been rushed through, with very little of the training we were supposed to get'.[17] They finally left in improvised, straggling convoys of battered, pre-Dunkirk, army trucks, 'old ones which have only had first aid repairs' according to Harry Heath.[18] Muriel Heath remembered the shame she felt when her convoy of eight decrepit trucks spluttered along the Champs-Elysées.[19] Many UNRRA workers had not driven any sort of vehicle before: very few had any experience of driving these shabby two- and three-ton monsters. Some had benefitted from practice runs to Cherbourg and back, and one can sense their pride in their new accomplishments, exemplified in Harry Heath's note that he drove his own truck over the Rhine at Mainz.[20] Many also found reading maps difficult, and the more professional medical officers, welfare officers and team directors would often complain about their drivers, who seemed undisciplined and dangerous.[21] One team Director reported that his French driver 'drank six bottles of wine' on the first day, attempted to abandon his lorry in Paris, flirted with the young Welfare Officer and finally deserted the team, after having completely emptied the petrol tank.[22]

Teams found that their trucks were uncomfortable – 'infernally bumpy', according to Muriel Heath – and dangerous. As most teams travelled in spring and summer, they left the backs of their trucks open, allowing air to circulate, but also picking up dust and fumes. At the start of her journey, Pettiss applied lipstick and powder each morning, but 'by the third day on the road, it was all I could do to tie a red bandana around my head and wipe the dust and sweat off my face'.[23] Nora O'Connor's truck collapsed after 35 miles, leaving the three UNRRA workers sitting in the back 'bruised, shaken and smothered in dust'.[24] Lieutenant Colonel Woods' journey through the Netherlands and Germany was even more nerve-wracking. One of his team's trucks broke down before Nijmegen, causing severe delays. After a failed attempt to repair the truck, Woods decided to leave it behind and to drive on, following scrupulously the road sketch that they had been given. A couple of hours later, the team was stuck near the Rhine. The bridge to Wesel was being repaired and the next bridge was closed. Woods was dismayed: these bridges had been closed for three months and UNRRA's instructors should have been aware of this. The team was forced to retrace their route and make a 65-mile detour in pouring rain. The cover of one truck leaked, and so their luggage was soaked. When the team finally arrived in Spenge, their stopping point, there were no billeting arrangements. 'At two a.m. after a mighty hard day of trouble with trucks that should be scrapped, delays of hours with breakdowns and a detour, cold, wet and very hungry as well as some members feeling far from well we were given dry bread and cheese amounting to no more than one sandwich apiece and some tea'. By chance, the journey went off smoothly the next day and a good hot meal awaited them at their arrival: 'This was very fortunate as some of the personnel were set on resigning immediately on arrival as they had had enough of such treatment'.[25] Dawson's truck picked up two French MMLA girls who joyfully shouted 'at every American, black or white, who passed'. In the afternoon, the truck crashed and fell over; one of the French girls was injured and died the next day in a German hospital.[26] Dawson summed up the teams' transport problems when she noted that most convoys seemed to lose something on their journey: a truck, a wheel, a driver or the baggage.[27]

Given Germany's devastated condition, UNRRA convoys had to take their own supplies with them. But even when the UNRRA organization at Granville had provided equipment, it often proved unsuitable. Muriel Heath remembered taking a huge field kitchen that took up half their truck, and which no one ever used.[28] Harry Heath recorded that within their five days' worth of rations, the bread at the bottom of the containers was mouldy and unfit to eat.[29] Teams also took tents and camp beds, for they could not be certain of finding accommodation along the route. When they did find shelter, this was not always a blessing: Muriel Heath was initially happy to learn that they would be staying in a hotel in Château-Thierry, but then noted 'it was here that I encountered my first flea'.[30] Dawson could – just about – laugh at the memory of herself and seven other women attempting to wash themselves and their clothes in one shared bathroom.[31]

At times, however, there was almost a holiday atmosphere. For a start, the war really was over. Margaret McNeill, part of the Friends' Relief Service, thoroughly enjoyed 'the clanging and clanking' and the sheer adventure of loading the relief lorry onto the ship at Tilbury. 'I couldn't help thinking what it must have been like in wartime with bombs and black-out and sickening apprehension,' she noted, 'with us there was lovely sunshine and much fraternizing'.[32] Muriel Heath's team spotted a flower stall soon after they started: they bought up masses of lilac, and decorated their truck with it. 'We were happy – it was spring and sunny and we were on the road. We sang'. Hall remembered their stop at the Enlisted Men's Club in Chartres, where they were given free beer, iced coffee, sandwiches and chocolate éclairs. Dancing followed, and Hall's records strike an uncharacteristically flirtatious note: 'I had a very good partner but she did not speak English. However, our feet spoke the same language'.[33] The teams ate improvised picnics of bread, butter and cheese: at Metz, Harry Heath noted 'Team now on its own resources and meal prepared by the ladies. Excellent'.[34]

At first, Rosolek's team seemed to enjoy a similarly easy journey. They had good food on their way and arrived on time in Stuttgart. Once there, Rosolek invited the team for dinner and paid for it himself. 'The girls and gentlemen were very happy. They got a nice dinner with wine and cognac. Soon afterwards they started to dance with different people including French officers'. But this flirtatious atmosphere soon bothered Rosolek. 'Here began my worry because I noticed that some of them were very "jealous", and by this opportunity I was aware of the beginning of "romance" in my team'. This conscientious director felt progressively alienated from his team. 'I must express that Stuttgart was the worst [day] of my life … the whole team from 9th June until to 15th June had nothing to do except to pay visits … eating and dancing until midnight'. He was unable to relate to them and despised their shallowness. 'Their thoughts are only about good food, comfortable life and to do as little as they possibly can, because they don't have the slightest idea of responsibility'.[35] Rosolek's report provides another insight into UNRRA: tensions could develop between earnest, dedicated relief workers and those seen as pleasure-seekers and idlers. Teams – and particularly Team Directors – had to distinguish between reasonable forms of relaxation and unacceptable indulgence.

All the teams were struck by the sights on the road. Once again, we must remember that most members of UNRRA teams had not travelled widely: for the Americans, this was usually their first journey in Europe; for the Britons, it was certainly their first journey in continental Europe for at least five years. They were fascinated by what they saw, for France was still foreign to them. Hall visited Chartres Cathedral and saw people kissing the pillar on which a statue of the Virgin Mary was mounted. 'Idolatry', he noted curtly.[36] They noted the sombre French, strangely downbeat in the days following VE day, still worried about their missing soldiers, held in PoW camps. They observed the wild variations in the countryside: the pretty villages, the trees in blossom, the sunny fields, but also the bomb craters, the wrecked vehicles alongside the road, the notices warning of mines, and the replacement Bailey bridges along the rivers and canals. As they travelled east, the roads grew busier. They met streams of people walking westwards: refugees and PoWs returning from Germany. Some carried improvised flags to indicate their final destination.[37] There were also great waves of soldiers heading eastwards. Here, once again, we get another reminder of the un-travelled, inexperienced nature of our relief workers: the Europeans were fascinated by the black American soldiers. It is clear that, for many, this was the first time they had seen black people: Hall's brief reference to 'nigger Americans' is clearly not intended to be racist, but merely an indication of his surprise.[38] Harry Heath manages to sound a more positive note, praising their 'very good' contribution to a concert, 'especially with their negro spirituals'.[39]

The teams of relief workers journeyed through countries that had formed Nazi-occupied Western Europe: Belgium, Luxembourg and the Netherlands. British and American aid workers had expected to see bomb damage, but here they encountered a different form of destruction. The years of occupation, collaboration and resistance had produced long-lasting social and cultural problems. In July 1945 a COBSRA team landed at Ostende. This was a mixed team which included the British Red Cross, the International Guides and the Friends' Relief Service. They passed through Bruges, Ghent, Antwerp, Breda,

Nymegem, Arnhem to the Hague, a journey of about 250 miles. Elizabeth Bayley saw damaged buildings and mined beaches; some shops and cafés were open but they were all mainly empty. Fruit, vegetables and bread were on sale, but there were no grocers, butchers or dairies, luxury goods such as make-up, pipes or lace were not available, and bicycles were extremely expensive. The few civilian cars were powered by charcoal burners attached to their roofs, due to the petrol shortage.[40] It was also here that they saw the devastation that bombing and shelling produced. At Arnhem, Margaret McNeill noted: 'it was a desolate chilly summer evening and never to the end of my days shall I forget what that place looked like. I suppose in size it would be as big as Derry or Drogheda and as we passed through I did not see one living soul, not one single building that was habitable'.[41] In fact, these relief workers were travelling through one of the most dreadfully deprived areas of Europe. Allied troops lost the battle of Arnhem in September 1944 and the area was not liberated until April 1945. During the intervening seven months – the winter of 1944–45 – the country was cut off from both Allied and Nazi supplies. This was the legendary 'hongerperiode', when the Dutch lived on sugar beet and tulip bulbs, and had to survive a bitter winter on 300–400 calories a day.

Teams sent to the Netherlands also encountered one of the ethical dilemmas that were to dog them later. UNRRA's policy was clear: relief workers were to help the victims of German and Japanese aggression. The Quakers, however, considered they were to help all victims of war. Their policy resembled the classic principles of the Red Cross, which argued that one should not ask someone in distress about their nationality or their religion: one should simply help them.[42] Yet in post-war Europe it was not always possible to avoid asking questions or making political decisions. Amongst the starving people in the Netherlands, there were those who had supported the NSB (the Dutch Nazi party); members of the NSB who had been imprisoned as collaborationists; and children of NSB members who needed care because they were being shunned by the population at large. Those who had chosen to work in the Reich during the war were returning: they were placed in homes alongside returning evacuees. According to McNeill, it all made an 'unspeakable tangle' as human relations became fraught with suspicion, blame and hostility.[43] Relief teams met difficult dilemmas, as the following example illustrates. In June 1945 a representative from the Netherlands resistance group, 'Oranje', approached Bayley's FRS team and asked for petrol so that they could 'round up traitors'.[44] The Quaker team refused, because of their commitment to non-violence. The resistance members, however, understood the FRS's choice as a political decision, amounting to a refusal to support the resistance. Such decisions created resentment amongst the Dutch, many of whom thought that the post-war authorities were neglecting the loyal citizens of the Netherlands – the real war victims – and favouring traitors. This was further complicated by the emotional condition of the children who had known nothing but war and occupation.

For the military authorities, the immediate priority was to keep soldiers and relief workers moving eastwards: signals along the highways urged drivers to keep up speed. This wave of motorbikes, jeeps, bren-gun carriers and trucks often appeared to the defeated Germans as some form of counter-Blitzkrieg, the definitive incarnation of Allied victory. Christine Bielenberg saw them in her Black Forest village. 'They were armed to the teeth, but seemed content to rattle through the village by jeep and truckload at breakneck speed, yelling "Sale boche" at anyone who did not leap for the ditches and doorways with sufficient alacrity'.[45] Klemperer watched them in Munich, and even felt a brief, odd moment of sympathy for the Germans.

> The cars of the Americans were continually racing through the dust, the ruins, [creating] the sound of the storm. It was these cars which made the picture of hell complete; they are the angels of judgement … or something of the kind; they are the triumphant and cheerful victors and masters. They drive quickly and nonchalantly, and the Germans run along humbly on foot, the victors spit out the abundance of their cigarette stubs everywhere and the Germans pick up the stubs.[46]

To German observers, UNRRA teams might appear as a small part of this great wave of vehicles, but the teams themselves had different feelings. First, by the time they reached Germany, they were well aware of the real fragility of their trucks. It was hard for UNRRA workers to consider themselves as 'angels of judgement' while they sat in trucks that might collapse at any moment. The teams noted the strange contrasts in the German landscape: the often calm, beautiful countryside, the prosperous farms and the straight, modern *autobahn*: the first motorway system in Europe. Driving along these highways was not always easy: stretches of clear track alternated with more difficult sections, in which bomb craters and improvised detours held up progress. Most striking of all, however, was the sight of the bombed cities. While each observer had some expectation of what they would see, they were all moved by the sight of these vast heaps of urban rubble, which stretched on, empty street after empty street, in which not a single building remained standing and not a single person was to be seen. Here, our relief workers – particularly the Britons – really could claim to be experts. Hall commented 'We had seen destruction in France and I have seen the effects of Bombing in London, Clydebank, etc, and in the last war but I have never seen nothing so terrible so complete as at Saarbrücken'.[47]

How did our teams react to these sights? For many Britons the devastation of post-war Europe was the fulfilment of a long-held dread. Throughout the interwar years there had been a widespread belief that any future war would be one of unimaginable horror, unprecedented destruction and, very possibly, the complete end of human civilization.[48] A few – a clear minority – felt almost vindicated. Red Cross worker Robert Collis looked at the devastation of Osnabrück and recalled the German bombing of Rotterdam in 1940: '*they* started it'.[49] In particular, French relief workers sometimes felt a deep personal hatred of German people. Jacqueline Lesdos, mourning the death of her brother, was overwhelmed by revulsion. 'I hate them, I hate them ferociously! … No civilised people would ever have accepted the effects of such a dreadful dictatorship'.[50] Others felt more troubled, conflicting emotions. Muriel Heath noted a change in her team: while heading towards Germany, their French driver had decorated their truck with various – unspecified – postcards showing German soldiers in positions of humiliation. Once they saw devastated Germany, the postcards disappeared. Her own emotions were confused: 'one felt an overpowering surge of hatred not only against the Germans but against the whole crass idiocy of mankind which goes on permitting wars, which goes on harbouring institutions, rings and cartels that fester war and to whose advantage it is to have wars'.[51] This rather vague, reformist, humanitarian pacifism was quite common among UNRRA workers.

Even once they were established in their camps, UNRRA kept thinking about cars: first, because they needed transport but also, secondly, because cars had symbolic value. One afternoon in August 1945, Harry Heath happened to meet an American captain. He asked Heath if he wanted a car, and when Heath answered yes: 'he handed me the switch keys and pointed to a magnificent Ford V.8, saying "It's yours!" – yes, just like that!'.[52] Harry promptly celebrated VJ day by taking Muriel for a ride in the country. 'It was our first day off since we came here and we revelled in it'.[53] Pettiss was equally lucky: an American captain took her out for a ride in a new BMW, and then just gave her the car. 'I was the absolute envy of everyone in UNRRA as there was no provision for transport for teams'.[54] In addition, there was plenty of petrol, which – according to Bayley – flowed 'like milk and honey' throughout the British occupation zone.[55] Most teams managed to acquire some form of transport because camp administrations had the right to seize cars and lorries left by the Nazis.[56] In September 1945, 'Junkers' Camp' possessed one three-quarter ton Opel Truck, one Ford Truck, one ambulance, three Opel sedans, one Mercedes sedan, one Fiat sedan, all listed as 'captured'.[57]

These staples of bright interchange had an ambiguous meaning. First, we have to note the symbolic status of the motor vehicle in 1945: most British middle-class families did not possess their own cars, although they were becoming more common in the USA. To acquire the personal use of a car was an apparently impressive assertion of status, comparable to the household servants employed by minor British administrators in Palestine and India. But cars could also be good fun. Klemme observed that many

> Continentals … were much like children with a new pushmobile in their eagerness to get in and try one out. Some of the women had an insane desire to drive. At one camp we had a Belgian girl that would steal one of the team vehicles every chance she got, just to drive around the block two or three times.[58]

On the other hand, UNRRA officials later realized that these vehicles were often less useful than they appeared. A report concerning the American zone, written in June 1947 as UNRRA was being wound down, gives a more measured, accurate account of the transport used in DP camps.

> UNRRA commenced its operations with old trucks which had served their useful life in the War. Private cars were requisitioned and picked up by various methods. They varied in make, size and type, but all had one thing in common: they were old. Repairs to German passenger cars could not be undertaken by the Military authorities, and the problem of keeping this type of transport was one of major importance, usually based on a cigarette currency. For two years the Field has had to carry out its arduous duties with poor and unsuitable equipment and at the present time, the vehicles are unreliable and practically useless. They are unable to make long runs to Zone HQ for meetings and frequent delays occur. Wasted time means money and the operation becomes expensive because of the time lost on the roadside. On my last trip to the Zone I have witnessed high grade officers wasting complete days because of unserviceable cars.[59]

The International Red Cross recognized the problem, and attempted to establish repair and communication networks, but these were not comprehensive or effective services.[60] Possessing a BMW without having access to spare parts or trained repair staff amounted to a rather empty, ineffective assertion of status. Alongside Heath's and Pettiss's pleasure in acquiring impressive cars, we should also consider a couple of less flamboyant examples. Muriel Doherty, working at Belsen in the immediate aftermath of the liberation, was plagued by transport difficulties. She complained that 'Life with UNRRA is not so easy! The author-ities have provided no cars for the [Senior Medical Officer] and myself; and as the Glyn Hughes hospital is at one end of the camp, the Maternity Block the other, and the various departments scattered between, the problem of transport is great'.[61] Dr Yzerman set out from Hanau camp for Heilbrun in an impressive-looking Mercedes. He had two punctures on the way, which he managed to repair, but the third proved too difficult. He left his car on the autobahn and walked back to the camp for help: when he returned to the autobahn, he found his Mercedes had been stolen.[62]

These vehicles also illuminate a more serious, general problem which was to plague UNRRA throughout its operation: as the problems they faced in Germany grew more serious, they required more intensive, more specialist aid. Yet the UNRRA teams were making such requests during the period when the various Allied governments were attempting to scale back their operations in Germany. The superfluity of cars, trucks and other resources was often illusory; in the midst of apparent plenty, UNRRA was constantly poorly equipped and under-resourced.

FINDING THE CAMPS

During the collapse of Nazi power, most authority structures just melted away. No one was immediately prepared to take responsibility for the diverse population of migrant workers, conscript labourers, prisoners of war and concentration camp survivors who made up the 'Displaced Persons'. Improvisation was the norm. Donald McGonigal tells a revealing story from this period. Near Bettenhausen, some 900 slave labourers had worked in the Junkers aircraft factory. They were housed in relatively good conditions: the firm put them in a camp built prior to 1939 for German workers. Among the workers was Anni Shepe, an Englishwoman employed as a nurse, and married to a Pole. American soldiers liberated the camp on 4 April 1945, but would not take responsibility for the remaining DPs. On her own initiative, Shepe assumed command of the camp, which for months afterwards was then known as 'Anni's Camp'.[63] On 3 May 1945, an American captain confirmed Shepe as camp commandant, and she was finally accepted as an UNRRA employee in November 1945. Shepe uncovered German food supplies and also ensured that the camp received American rations. For a few weeks, Anni's Camp had

> much the appearance of a mining camp in the early gold rush days on a holiday. Practically no one wanted to work, DP and German schnapps was plentiful and consumed in large quantities with the usual results, many DPs slept most of the day and spent the nights dancing, drinking, fighting and frolicking, especially the latter.[64]

UNRRA finally arrived on 1 July 1945. They were represented by nine women organized into two teams: seven were French, one Belgian and one Swiss. They were astonishingly young. Tabard, the main leader of the two teams, was only 22 when she took control of a camp of some 700 people; her principal assistant was 19. The main qualification of most of these women was their Resistance record. Even after their arrival, there was little formal organization of camp activities. The camp's historian, an UNRRA team Director himself, was struck by how they obtained firewood.

> When one considers the fearful fanfare of reports, district-wide meetings, graphs, orders and the full-time assignment of field officers, which now surrounds the process of supplying the camps with firewood, it is interesting to note that John Hetrick solved the problem in Junkers Camp by typing out an authorization which he signed himself and presenting it to the Head Forester at St. Otilien. [He] was allotted his wood lots near Oberkaufungen and Waldau where he proceeded to cut about sixteen cubic meters a day with a detail of Latvian wood cutters.[65]

Elsewhere, improvised structures worked less well. When Watson's UNRRA Team entered the Ingolstadt Camp on 24 May 1945, they found that a Polish woman and three Polish men running it. Although these DPs had worked hard, the conditions were worrying.

> I made a very careful inspection of the various camps and, to say that I was frightened by what I saw is stating the case very mildly. Sanitation as understood by civilised people simply did not exist ... Every camp was bad, [or] very bad ... in the Russian camp the amount of refuse, decaying food and human excreta lying around had to be seen to be believed.[66]

In a few days, Watson's team, helped by the DPs and by some German PoWs, got the camp clean. But other problems awaited them: none of the local American forces knew anything of UNRRA, and at first they were uncooperative.

DPs were often housed in unsuitable premises that had been used for a variety of purposes during the war. Landsberg camp was located in a former Wehrmacht artillery caserne. It contained some 6,000 men, women and children. 'The dwellings, known as blocks, are three-storey brick barracks typical of any permanent Army dwellings. The rooms are very large and afford no privacy ... From a military viewpoint, the barracks are modern and well designed. For housing families, they could not be worse' commented US officer Heymont.[67] Not only were many sites unsuitable for housing DPs, but they were also in very poor repair. In Munich, the DP camp was located in the much-bombed Deutsche Museum. In the summer of 1945, there was still 'a huge hole in the wall where the door once was'. Yet, behind this bombed-out front, one could find a large lobby 'dominated by a huge painting of all the allied flags around the UNRRA insignia'. Pettiss provides a vivid description of this strange place. Although the lobby's windows had no panes, 'the kitchen is the envy of the city – all electric, complete with refrigeration room'.[68] Many buildings had been bomb-damaged, looted or deliberately vandalized, and even as late as 1947 and 1948 some DPs were living in makeshift conditions with broken windows, insufficient sanitation and severe overcrowding.[69]

DOCUMENTS AND DPS

Few relief workers travelling to Germany in 1945 knew what they would encounter. The confidence encouraged by lectures at Granville or other forms of training was usually misleading. Experienced American soldiers reckoned that the new arrivals had about six weeks to learn that all they had been taught was wrong: if they understood this, they might survive.[70] UNRRA workers had to do something similar. Their teams were understaffed. The original programme had anticipated teams of twelve or thirteen people. These were then replaced by the smaller 'spearhead' teams in spring 1945. By June 1945, UNRRA had 204 teams deployed throughout the Western zones in Germany with on average seven people each, and by August it had 349 teams with on average eight people.[71] How could these small teams translate UNRRA's idealistic rhetoric into practical measures?

Uncertainty and poor communication were the norms. DPs had often lost their identity papers, and they possessed long, complex names in foreign languages that UNRRA could not understand. The ICRC had predicted this problem, and had trained specialized staff to be familiar with different European cultures so that they were able to 'identify names and addresses written even by comparatively illiterate persons'. It also recommended that DPs should always be encouraged to write their own names on forms.[72] UNRRA failed to heed these warnings and their desperate attempts to render foreign names and terms into English created distorted records.[73] UNRRA field workers were also often puzzled about who they should accept or reject. For example:

> Quite a confusion exists in the Field on the significance of the word 'stateless', in spite of what has been written in SHAEF guide to clarify the meaning of that particular expression. Many Americans have often asked me how it was possible for a man or a woman to become stateless ... None, of course, has ever heard of a [League of Nations] 'Nansen passport'. We need in the field Legal Advisers.[74]

Statistics were at best approximations. Even the more experienced national Red Cross organizations and the ICRC were overwhelmed by the task of counting numbers of DPs. For example, in October 1945 Selby-Bigge, the British Red Cross Commissioner in Austria, wrote to the ICRC to explain that his previous statistics were outdated and that he probably needed to add another 45,000 to the final total.[75] In a similar vein, the Military Government in Austria broke down all DPs into the categories of Allied and enemy, and then into separate national categories. Having completed this exercise for a total of over 26,000 people, the final sentence of the report simply notes '+ LATER ARRIVAL OF 6,000'.[76]

UNRRA's leaders were aware of these problems, and issued increasingly strict warnings to Team Directors.

> Incorrectly filled-in reports continue to reach this HQ from some teams, and while it is fully realized that occasionally circumstances make it difficult to render an accurate report, it should be stressed that this return is becoming increasingly important as the main source of all detailed information and statistical matter required from teams by Regional and Zone HQ.[77]

On the other hand, relief workers constantly complained that they were unable to do their jobs properly because they were constantly grappling with meaningless red tape. Such frustration is well-illustrated by a file from the FRS. In one section there is a copy of an UNRRA form from 1947, detailing statistics, nationalities, numbers of arrivals, numbers of departures and so forth. Alongside this form there is an account of a relief worker's day, written by Tim

Evens, a 24-year-old Quaker from Bristol and one of the youngest in FRS Team 124. His description is entitled 'In no sense official' and was obviously written to provide a glimpse into one of his days and into his emotional responses to relief work. He begins by discussing his upset tummy – a common complaint amongst relief workers due to insanitary conditions – and then describes several small but irritating incidents. Where are his cigarettes? What about his chocolate? Does he have enough petrol? What about soap and DDT? He is bad-tempered with his colleagues and he doesn't like his spam. As the day goes on his mood rapidly improves: he interviews DPs, he likes his colleagues and he is amused by army bureaucracy.[78]

Other exceptional records illustrate how the lives of relief workers were dominated by short-term issues rather than detailed documentation. In the French zone of Austria, one Red Cross worker kept a list of the requests put to him on 9 July 1945. He listed 24 direct demands, including:

- A Lithuanian man wanted fortified food for his family
- Twelve Russian émigrés presented themselves in person and demanded help
- An Austrian Jew wanted two shirts
- Greek DPs were complaining that they had not received their food parcels. And they had no cigarettes.
- A sick Dutchman who had been forced into service by the SS was demanding a suit and all his identity papers because he wanted to marry
- A Ukrainian man wanted a smallpox vaccine and a Red Cross parcel
- A woman wanted to make contact with her husband in Palestine
- A Polish orphan who had been naturalized as French demanded an International Red Cross identity card
- A Ukrainian man wanted food for his mother, wife and daughter. And he wanted a dictionary.[79]

Welfare and medical workers were bombarded with such seemingly simply but actually difficult requests: clothes were in terribly short supply, as were basic medicines, and who knew where to find a Ukrainian dictionary?

The issue of form filling and documentation raises another point concerning UNRRA's practices. FRS members recognized the value of UNRRA's work, and on some occasions found the organization genuinely inspiring.[80] But the Quakers kept raising one criticism: they disliked UNRRA's bureaucratic professionalism. For McNeill, UNRRA procedures meant 'a huge indescribable muddle' of forms, meetings, and conferences.[81] The FRS were not alone in disliking forms. Miss Crosbie from the British Red Cross delegation sent a breezy message to the ICRC in February 1946: 'We can't be bothered with reports … we haven't the staff to do it'.[82] UNRRA team members shared this frustration. Charley del Marmol angrily commented 'No use to present any statistics. We are not interested in figures, but in human beings'.[83] Dawson joked bitterly in her account that she had finally realized 'what this work requires: a careful study of directives because each one may contradict the last; four copies of every letter, margins to begin fifteen spaces from the left-hand edge and subdivisions of subdivisions numbered (a), (b) and (c)'.[84]

This was perhaps something more than another complaint about form filling. The Quakers in particular believed that UNRRA's bureaucratic professionalism placed a barrier between themselves and the DPs, and that such a technocratic approach to relief work would inevitably erode human compassion. McNeill cited an UNRRA Area Nursing Advisor as an example of this supposedly efficient but inhuman approach. When visiting the camp nursery the Advisor was so concerned with routines, feeding schedules and the regular distribution of cod liver oil, that she simply failed to notice the 'happy and picturesque' babies and toddlers.[85] Similarly, the UNRRA concern with calorie counts struck McNeill as unfeeling. 'The DPs don't care a tuppenny stamp how many calories they get, what they want is something to fill their insides'.[86]

THE STATUS OF THE RELIEF WORKER

Curiously, however, this demanding situation provided relief workers with certain advantages. Alongside the possibility of an attractive car, there were also generous rations. According to Bayley, a typical day's rations for a relief worker were:

> Fresh meat – almost 1.2lb per person
> Tinned meat – ½ tin per person
> Potatoes – ½ tin per person or ration of dried peas, beans – ½ a tin
> Bread – ½ a loaf
> Milk – no fresh – 1/6 of a tin condensed, plus dried
> Egg – some dried
> Cheese – 1oz per day
> Fruit – some dried – sultanas, dates or apples
> Tea – a lot + oatmeal, flour, jam etc.[87]

FRS workers commented frequently on the unaccustomed quantities of meat they were eating. Dawson's description of the American rations she received as she travelled through the American Zone clearly reflect her grim memories of five long years of mean British rations. 'Two days' lunch on the perfect US Emergency pack containing cheese, biscuit, fudge, chocolate, chewing gum, cigarettes, matches, and tinned rice pudding and peaches and orangeade power, and I could scream. I eat it but I could scream. It's too perfect, too luxurious, too rich and far too sweet'.[88] Not everyone approved. Quaker teams in particular were annoyed at constant drinking around them, and Bayley insisted that 'the British army is fast drugging whatever intelligence it had with liquor'.[89]

Yet few complained about the amount of tobacco available, and when given 200 cigarettes a week as part of her rations, the Danish nurse Christiansen commented 'never did I feel so rich from a cigarette point of view'.[90] (Given the common use of cigarettes as a type of international currency in post-war Germany, her use of the term 'rich' should not be read as a metaphor.)

Alongside cars, cigarettes and sweets, there were other symbols of status. UNRRA teams usually had servants and often even chauffeurs. One Polish man and three Polish women were appointed as cooks, maids and cleaners for the UNRRA staff in Harry Heath's camp. When the male servant got drunk, Heath noted in his diary 'Must sack him tomorrow when he is sober'.[91] He was replaced by 'Ginger', a Belgian woman who could prepare both French and Polish dishes. These details show that relief workers were expecting a certain standard of comfort and – in turn – it was usually understood that their lifestyles would contribute to keeping them separate and distinct from the DPs. Their quarters were outside the main DP camps; they were not expected to mix with the DPs. UNRRA workers normally expected to wear a military-style uniform and were upset when they did not receive one.[92] When thick sheepskin jackets were issued in Wildflecken camp, the DPs wore white ones, while the UNRRA workers had theirs dyed brown: it was important that one should be able to recognize immediately who was who.[93] Dawson was formally criticized when it was learned that she had slept in the DP camp: she was not suspected of any sexual impropriety, but of breaking the unwritten rule that relief workers and DPs were not to mix as equals. Thinking the point over in her memoir, Dawson wondered what her superior would have said if he had learned that she also sometimes shared the DPs' meals.[94] These codes of behaviour resembled those recommended to Allied soldiers. 'It is important that you should *be smart and soldierly* in appearance and behaviour,' British soldiers were instructed, 'The Germans think nothing of a slovenly soldier'.[95] Their uniforms, their cigarettes, their sweets, their rations and their cars were all marks of the UNRRA workers' relatively superior status, distinguishing them from the people they were to help, and demonstrating a type of continuity in British power and prestige.[96]

There is an uncomfortable question here. While most accounts of relief agencies stress their self-sacrificing labours, noting how they confront conditions of dreadful hardship and brutality, another perspective is possible. Linda Polman has produced a vigorous critique of recent projects by international aid agencies. In the peculiar no-man's land territories in which they operate, 'the restaurants, squash courts and golf and tennis facilities are often back up and running before bombed-out schools and clinics'. Local people are only employed as interpreters, nannies and drivers, while 'the humanitarian aid community that travels to war-torn, crisis-ridden countries feels no embarrassment about looking like an international jet set on holiday'. Finally, prostitution soars.[97] Should such critical points also be applied to the relief workers of 1945? Victor Gollancz noted that in autumn 1946 German children were still living on 'biscuit soup', yet, as we have seen, relief workers had grown accustomed to hearty rations.[98]

There are two types of answer to this criticism. One is an indirect response, which would argue that while relief workers were certainly living in significantly better conditions than the DPs, this was hardly luxury (a point to which we will return) and, anyway, these relative privileges were more than justified by the dedication which the relief workers brought to their tasks. None of the UNRRA autobiographies we have found actually rehearse such an argument, but one could easily read this into them. To their credit, the Quakers answered this uncomfortable question more directly.

How were they to deal with these inequalities? Both the FRS leadership and individual Quaker relief workers worried about this point. Roger Wilson, the FRS Travelling Commissioner in Europe, urged relief teams to consider the repercussions of 'living in reasonable comfort in a country, the majority of whose citizens are suffering in body and mind'. Wilson identified three key issues – smoking, drinking and excessive heating – and urged FRS members to consider how they behaved. Should they stop smoking, as many did after the last war? Given that UNRRA workers and Allied soldiers habitually drank to excess, should FRS teams be satisfied with their own moderate drinking, or should they become teetotal? Finally, Wilson insisted that 'we need not be over-warm when many displaced persons and many Germans are always cold'.[99] FRS teams usually decided not to smoke or eat in front of the DPs, although it was obvious that they had access to plenty of food in private.[100]

Here, however, the Quakers are the exception that proves the rule. Rather than feeling guilty about their relative comfort, many relief workers were appalled by the dreadful conditions in which they were to live and work. They complained about the lack of heating, about over-crowded, dirty, under-equipped rooms which had been thoroughly looted and vandalized by previous soldiers.[101] They had to look after all their possession carefully: anything could be stolen. Dawson lost a shirt and a pair of shoes, Harry Heath saw his quarters' entire coal supply stolen.[102] The conditions in which they worked were primitive. Margrethe Langdon trained nurses to work for UNRRA. She recalled that 'my office was a desk and a chair, and then there was a telephone and a stove. I got one piece of wood a day'.[103] Dawson estimated that most of her team worked between 12 and 20 hours every day.[104] A new nurse arrived at the Belsen hospital and began work at 9 a.m. Having worked constantly for eight hours, at 5 p.m. she asked 'When do they bring round tea?' Her more experienced colleagues had to disappoint her: 'There isn't any "they"'.[105] Harry Heath suffered from repeated bouts of dysentery in Hanau Camp, and lost two stone in nine months.[106] In his diary he complained frequently about feeling very tired, very weak, 'off the hooks' and even noticed that his uniform had become far too big for him. 'I must not let this go too far' he warned himself.[107] The idea that these conditions constituted a form of extravagant luxury would have seemed a self-evident absurdity to most relief workers.

Even the more socially conscious Quakers could find themselves caught out in this strange situation. Bayley had thought that her initial training had prepared her well for establishing a camp in rough and ready conditions. Her FRS team moved into billets without furniture, electric light, cooking facilities or hot water, but they made themselves comfortable and bedded down for the night. They were prepared to cope with such physical deprivation – certainly in the short-term – and even to deal with people who were ill, hungry or maimed. But after congratulating themselves on making the best of their primitive – but clean and tidy – billets, her team were then shocked to learn that their house was only in such a good condition because it had been cleaned by a group of collaborators under armed guard. In Bayley's words, this 'spoilt the first fine Quaker Rapture'.[108]

FRAULEINS, GIRLS AND LADIES: WOMEN RELIEF WORKERS

There was a wider context to UNRRA's work. In September 1944, Eisenhower had issued a nine-page directive forbidding all friendliness, familiarity or intimacy between the conquering armies and the German population. His instructions were almost immediately flouted, and were formally withdrawn in October 1945.[109] In 1945 Berlin was 'a moral melting pot', ' its air containing more particles of eroticism per cubic centimetre than any other city's', a place with three women to every man, where over 150,000 prostitutes catered for every vice.[110] Military government meant government by mistresses, joked the German civilians.[111] LaGuardia's special representative Ira Hirschmann shuddered when he saw American soldiers and German women in a Munich nightclub, horrified by 'shameful conduct of our soldiers and German fräuleins ... The American was the conqueror, and no Roman of old ever received more flattering adulation and attention from the opposite sex ... I don't like prostitutes, in Germany or elsewhere'.[112] He left after 20 minutes: how many other men stayed? Isa Hoffmann, a Berliner, thought that the Americans were just as bad as the Russians, although they were less likely to shoot the woman afterwards. The local people called the Americans 'Russians with creases', she said, making reference to the only thing which distinguished them from each other: the GI's dapper trousers.[113] This was 'The Big Rape', in James Burke's horribly accurate phrase, referring not only to the mass rapes committed by the victorious soldiers of the Red Army, but also to the more subtle and widespread processes of humiliation, prostitution and intimidation initiated by all the Allied armies, through which German women could feel that they had been reduced to the status of 'a piece of female flesh'.[114]

Willingly or not, UNRRA was part of this process. Some German women made themselves sexually available to relief workers because good relations with UNRRA and the military could guarantee access to food and essential supplies.[115] There were also less cynical explanations. Many German women were lonely and the German war bride – especially if she married a GI – both embodied a romantic ideal and popularized the American dream.[116] DP women were under similar pressures. At the '41 Club' near Goslar, a Scots Lieutenant employed Baltic and Jewish DPs – referred to as 'his girls' – to act as hostesses for the troops. As well as payment they were given their own flats, lengths of cloth and extra rations. It is tempting to see these women simply as prostitutes but Bayley was convinced that this was not the case and that the officer could be trusted 'to keep a fatherly and kindly eye on their welfare'.[117] Romances flourished between male UNRRA workers and German frauleins. Like British or American officers, Team Directors and Deputy Directors often employed their DP or German girlfriends as maids and housekeepers, and then allowed them to occupy the same quarters.

At first sight it seems almost unbelievable that decent, well-mannered women such as Margaret McNeill and Rhoda Dawson could be living in this world: one's first instinct is to insist on the separation of the two narratives, and to see the DP camp as somehow sharply different from the Munich nightclub, the official's mistress, the soldier's 'frat' and the Berlin prostitute. This would be a mistake: McNeill and Dawson watched the behaviour of soldiers and male UNRRA workers, and then had to act accordingly.

Female participation in UNRRA raised many questions. Alongside the organization's avowed refusal of gender prejudice, there was the obvious reality of a gendered hierarchy and division of labour. Pettiss noted that only two of the 32 Welfare Officers at Granville were men: why was this? While we have not found any convincing data estimating the proportion of male and female Team Directors, it seems likely that only about one in ten were female. In general, in UNRRA women were directed away from leadership roles, and towards stereotypically feminine occupations: working with children, nursing or caring in the widest sense of the word. They very rarely protested about this. Barbara McDouall, a YWCA worker, notes that women relief workers felt outnumbered at most of the local conferences held in Germany, and therefore there was good reason to hold a specific women's conference, which finally took place in April 1947.[118] But beyond a few similar low-key grumbles, none of our autobiographical sources raise the issue of male–female equality. One reason for this is the common circulation within UNRRA of 'equal-but-different' arguments: when prominent women such as Francesca Wilson based their argument for female participation in relief work on a belief in certain native nurturing qualities shared by all women, it was then difficult to argue that women should also aspire to more formal administrative posts such as Team Directors.[119]

Male UNRRA workers welcomed female colleagues, but often for some odd reasons. 'There are still those … who object to mixed staffs,' wrote Morgan, 'but I am quite certain that if I had a male staff here, I should be both hungry, thirsty and most uncomfortable.'[120] At first glance Morgan's comments sound like simple old-fashioned sexism, yet they reflect the fact that women were largely in charge of housekeeping duties and – most crucially – that these tasks were important. Mid-twentieth century feminists were largely committed to 'relational feminism' and believed that men and women had different innate capacities. They argued that women should not adopt male roles, and that established women's roles – cooking, cleaning, caring, nursing – should become properly valued.[121] Male UNRRA workers considered other arguments in favour of female participation. Harry Heath argued that his wife Muriel should be appointed to his team, and his comments in his diary concerning her suggest both affection and respect for the work she performed. In the generally over-worked conditions on the DP camp, male relief workers were usually grateful for the contributions made by their female colleagues. Klemme thought that 'the Continentals generally had a lot of respect for the older American women', and observed 'a number of teams where an American woman Welfare Officer just about ran the show'.[122] McGonigal includes some strange, but definitely positive-sounding, notes concerning the strengths of the young MMLA women who took over 'Anni's Camp'.

> Miss Tabard could be glacially polite in the manner of the most cosmopolitan grande dame, and she could be the gum-chewing officer on active service speaking pure, or at least expurgated, GI English, as the occasion demanded. No military inspecting officer … ever failed to succumb to their charm and their technique in handling visitors of all kinds … The relations of the MMLA team with the military were excellent. They were all young, some of them were attractive, and the Director and Acting Deputy were especially charming.[123]

While women could be valued as fellow workers, they could also be valued for specifically feminine qualities.

At its best, UNRRA can be seen as offering women a certain empowerment, real but limited. In what other situation could a 22 year-old woman be made responsible for a camp of 700 people, or a young nurse like Jacqueline Lesdos take responsibility for approximately 12,000 people?[124] While women's posts were usually classified as nurses, deputy directors and other auxiliary posts, their actual duties frequently provided leadership and supervisory oppor-tunities. Women were generally appointed to lower grades than men, but their abilities could be recognized, and many progressed rapidly through the UNRRA career structure.[125] Pettiss began at Grade 7 with a salary of $3,050 and finished at Grade 11 with $5,750. It was not just the money that she appreciated: 'I was most gratified to see my rating stated as "Superior"' she observed.[126] Compared with other organizations, UNRRA really did seem to offer ambitious women a new start. But there were some serious limitations to their status.

From the moment they joined UNRRA, women were made to feel different from men. Pettiss joined 23 other women to sail over the Atlantic in a Dutch freighter: while they waited in the harbour at Baltimore, crews from other ships would yell out 'appropriate remarks' about this female cargo.[127] While working in Munich, she found that

> as soon as Yvonne and I turned the corner the whistles began. It was like a chain reaction, with grinning faces popping out of windows in turn as we moved along. Nowadays, such behaviour no doubt would be considered offensive, but at the time it seemed like a game, entertainment for all of us in a situation where entertainment was hard to come by.[128]

Muriel Heath remembered that 'there were only a handful of women of the Allies in Germany ... As for the few of us in uniform – wherever we went we were subject to wolf whistles, etc, and we were all extremely relieved when American wives were allowed into Germany'.[129] Pettiss's notes on this point are observant: in Britain, France and Germany she talked to the soldiers who shouted at her, trying to understand what motivated them, and considering how she should respond. 'I had expected our soldiers to have the need to unburden their tales of battle. Quite the opposite. They wanted to talk about everything but the war ... They wanted to flirt with women, and dance, and drink wine, and laugh with them. We were happy to oblige'.[130] In London she met 'two nice American boys', both married, both lonely for nice girls. 'It was encouraging to see that they were still normal, natural American boys even after their experiences'. In such passages, she almost sounds like a Welfare Officer considering an unexpected new task: perhaps she really did think that this was part of her role as a healer. She devised her own ground rules: 'Start out with the premise that all guys are married and learn to say "no" in all languages. A serious affair wasn't on the cards ... No relationship could be more than a light flirtation, which suited me fine'.[131]

Yet even Pettiss's careful manoeuvres carried their own dangers. The Allies' use of the word 'fraulein' changed its meaning, implying a sexually available woman, even a prostitute. American women would therefore sometimes refuse to participate in events at which 'frauleins' were present, for this implied that they were no better than the disgraced Germans.[132] Dawson faced similar dilemmas to Pettiss, but showed herself markedly less tolerant and patient. American soldiers were constantly trying to get into their quarters. The military authorities responded by blocking the holes in the fence, but Dawson commented wearily 'We ought to have barracks. It's the girls. There are lots of Army here and they all think the Camp exists to provide them with girls'.[133] After having to sit through an unhappy conversation with an American lieutenant posted to their camp who was getting divorced, she noted 'I am bored with his constant talk about girls; I know some of it is partly his unhappy state and some of it's Army, but a lot of it is sheer vulgarity'.[134] One notes the difference between Dawson and Pettiss: while Pettiss was happy to be one of the girls, Dawson always separated herself from them. These points suggest an additional dimension to female participation in UNRRA: not only did they have to face demanding work in

DP Camps, but they also had to negotiate a sexual minefield, striving to act as commendable colleagues, to appear like ladies, occasionally to enjoy themselves like girls, but *never* to resemble 'frauleins'.

REQUISITIONING, SCROUNGING AND THE BLACK MARKET

Relief workers met immense challenges almost on arrival. On the first day that she arrived in Munich, Pettiss was told that there were 2,000 DPs camping out in what had been an enormous Nazi supply depot, another 1,000 were expected the next day, the army team was moving out and all the DPs would need to be fed. 'Just like that! I was completely floored!' she commented.[135] Within ten days of her arrival at Wildflecken, Hulme was informed that 4,000 Polish DPs were arriving the next day – and, worse still, they would arrive at the nearest functioning rail station, some 60 miles away.[136] When Harry Heath's UNRRA team of eight people entered Hanau camp for the first time, they found over 10,000 DPs without water, food, cleaning materials, toilets, clothes, beds or blankets.[137] Often the military authorities who had been temporarily in control were keen to leave, and so teams belonging to UNRRA or one of the other relief agencies had to take charge almost on their arrival.

In most cases they were able to find rations for themselves and the DPs. However, almost everything else seemed to be missing. Duchesne-Cripps writes of searching for toothbrushes and prams.[138] 'You just couldn't get a saucepan' recalled Langdon.[139] Dawson was frustrated at being asked to create a school when she could not find a blackboard. She saw the limitations of UNRRA's access to supplies. 'The things we ask for that are extra special just do not come'.[140] Even some very basic commodities were in short supply: Gollancz insisted that babies' nappies simply did not exist in Germany, and McNeill found it impossible to obtain regular supplies of sanitary towels.[141] Pettiss wondered how they were going to create a medical service for the DPs when their UNRRA teams possessed 'not a pencil, no medicines, no transportation, nothing'.[142] She considered the options: none of these items were available for purchase in the shops of Munich. The Army possessed some supplies, but their resources in these areas were very limited. Requisitioning was permitted, but the bureaucratic procedure it needed seemed daunting.

Pettiss herself was given responsibility, with a male colleague, for the reception of DPs. They had to register new arrivals, dust them down with the new wonder drug, DDT, and then issue them with meal tickets, which needed to be stamped to show that each had been 'DDT'd'. How were they to do this? They found pieces of cardboard from a basement across the street, and cut them into pieces: these were the meal tickets. But how were they to be stamped? Pettiss and her colleague found an old tyre, cut a piece out of it, and carved out the words 'official' on it. Thankfully, they managed to find some German ink pads in a stock room.[143] Such heroic improvisations continued throughout

UNRRA's existence. In December 1946 Christiansen was still attempting to provide better facilities for mothers and young children, and in particular wanted to establish a kitchen and bathroom for them. 'But believe me – it is not easy to procure even the simplest things – you cannot ring a shop in Neustadt ordering a certain amount of baby bottles, teats, etc. One must possess a sixth sense to be able to procure something!'.[144] In a nearby barracks she spotted an unused horse trough: this could be the bath she'd been looking for! But it was too big to fit into her ambulance, so she had to ask the nearby Transport Office to lend her their 50-ton truck.

Most relief workers referred to these types of creative improvisation as 'scrounging'. 'We scrounged medical equipment and clothing, paper, pencils, even a typewriter' explained Pettiss.[145] The term covered a variety of actions. 'Scrounging' might simply mean bypassing cumbersome official channels by making a direct appeal to friendly military or administrative authorities to offload surplus supplies to the camps. It could mean the creative re-use of unwanted material, as referred to above. It rarely meant outright, blatant theft, but it could mean the 'requisitioning' of material from local Germans. This was a point where some UNRRA workers often felt uncomfortable. On her arrival in Erlangen, Dawson was provided with a pleasant lunch that included fresh lettuce and strawberries. She was horrified to learn that these items had just been requisitioned from local households. 'This is UNRRA, the United Nations. Requisitioning sewing machines is one thing, stealing strawberries is plain bad manners, it seems to me. One should remain a gentleman'.[146] Harry Heath's account of obtaining radios for his camp is astonishing.

> Went to see the Landrat [local municipal authority] to get radios for the camp. We were passed on to the Burgmeister at Hochstadt who gave us the names and addresses of 6 Nazis. The first 5 were no good: they only had cheap radios. At the sixth, however, there was a beauty. I had a man with me from the Landrat's office. He had been in a concentration camp for years and hated Nazis. There was only a woman there but she was a great strong and hefty one who came for us [illegible word] when I said that we needed her radio and the man reached for it. She fought like a wild cat and eventually the German had to hit her under the jaw. We later discovered that within five minutes she had a miscarriage of a 6 months baby. I hated it, but it had to be done.[147]

Surprisingly, even the Quakers 'scrounged'. McNeill's comments seem to justify rather than condemn the practices.

> We are also acquiring the essential art of 'picking things up', though occasionally this causes a turmoil in the Quaker breast. For myself I confess it gives me a grim pleasure to see Nazi sheets stamped with a swastika torn up to make babies' napkins and the enormous brown enamel kettle we use every day was left behind by a Panzer division's mess. We sent back a rather acid report to Friends House on the subject of equipment

in order to explode the myth that 'everything would be available from the Army'. It may be but certainly not if she seeks to obtain it through the regular channels.[148]

Heymont, who 'firmly believe[d] that the Germans deserve a slight taste of their own medicine', found requisitioning perfectly fair and justified.[149] On 4 October, he ordered the eviction of German families in order to make additional room for the DPs. A couple of days later, some Germans came to the DP camp to ask if they could get their belongings back. 'I politely explained that those items cannot be removed because of orders of higher headquarters. I further pointed out that they were not being dragged off to a concentration camp with only the clothing on their backs and that they are not going to see their families starved or gassed or otherwise killed'. Heymont was astonished by Germans' lack of guilt. Some relief workers, however, did feel qualms about these practices. When the Allies took things from the Germans, it was called 'requisitioning', noted Muriel Heath, but when the DPs did the same it was termed theft.[150]

Obviously, these haphazard improvisations were very different from UNRRA's public image of scientific, planned humanitarianism. In reality, in order to implement UNRRA's policies, relief workers had to bend UNRRA's rules.

Soldiers and relief workers were in a strong economic position in post-1945 Germany, because as well as having hard currency, they also had an apparently endless supply of cigarettes. Following the collapse of the money supply, the black market flourished, with cigarettes as the primary currency. A military order forbade using cigarettes in exchange for anything which would normally be paid for in money, but few paid any attention and the order was largely unenforced. Teams Directors often mentioned DPs' black marketing activities in their weekly reports, but certainly did not record when they obtained goods outside UNRRA's normal procurement channels or when they turned a blind eye on suspicious trades. Klemme believed that this involvement was significant. 'Comparatively high UNRRA officials were mixed up in the racket … Whole truck loads of cigarettes, chocolate and various canned goods are known to have been hauled across the frontier. The amount of stuff that was illegally taken out of UNRRA warehouses would probably run well into the millions of dollars'.[151] For those who had spent the war in occupied Europe or strictly rationed Britain, the black market had long been the norm anyway. Even scrupulous relief workers could not help being drawn into it occasionally. They turned a blind eye to missing bed linen, blankets and food, and Bayley felt that she and her colleague Tim Evens had to accept a Christmas gift from DPs of 'a wonderful pair of Russian boots each made of heaven knows what black market leather'.[152]

These issues indicate some of the more intractable problems of rehabilitation work. Organizing the transport and distribution of food and medicines was one aspect of their work, but there was also the more complex problem of organizing the right environment for peaceful re-development.

HELPING THE PEOPLE HELP THEMSELVES

At first sight, the situation which faced UNRRA teams often seems impossible. How could nine young women with no previous experience in welfare run a camp of 700 DPs? What could Harry Heath's team of eight do for 10,000 people, living in a camp without running water? Dawson provides one of the most memorable images of this challenge. 'Tonight in the Camp was somehow nice; I fitted out two women with shoes and gave one pregnant one an orange. What's that out of 2,000?'.[153] These words present an astonishing reversal of perspective: we move from super-mum UNRRA, shunting millions of items to distressed people around the world, to a tired 47 year-old woman with a single orange in her hand. How could such actions relieve or rehabilitate the millions of DPs?

There were some good reasons to think that maybe the challenge was not quite as severe as it seemed. The basic task to be carried out appeared simple: a mass of people were dis-placed; UNRRA was to assist in their 're-placement'. Muriel Heath recalled thinking that UNRRA DP operations would only last for between six and nine months.[154] For the majority of the DPs in 1945, this was largely true. Any statistical calculations of this process must always be understood only as approximate estimates, but the trend is clear. Of the approximately 7.7 million DPs in Germany in May 1945, more than four million had left by 31 July 1945.[155] During May and June 1945 the Allied military powers organized trains, boxcars, barges and lorries to send home up to 80,000 DPs a day.[156] Those from western Europe were the easiest to manage, because they were usually eager to go home. However, repatriation eastwards was also swiftly organized. In June and July 1945 alone, some 25,000 Hungarians were repatriated from areas around Linz and Liesen in Austria.[157] By mid-July 1945 about 2.75 million displaced people had been returned to the USSR.[158] SHAEF was primarily responsible for this movement. The relief workers' involvement was relatively straightforward: they needed to organize food supplies and trucks to take people to the appropriate stations. As will be seen in the next chapters, there then arose two unexpected problems: a large minority of the DPs did not want to 'return' to what had become alien countries to them and – worse still – several hundred thousand Jews, who had survived the Second World War in Soviet territory, and travelled westwards into the American zone in 1945 and 1946, had no intention of 'returning' to Poland.

How were the tiny relief teams to work with these formidable numbers of remaining DPs? Pettiss's comments on this question may seem naive: she noted that individual leaders to represent the various national groups among the DPs just came forward, without any formal organization.[159] But this is largely what happened. Just as Anni Shepe ran Anni's Camp for several months, so among the DPs there were talented, ambitious or combative individuals who positively wanted to act. Their reasons for putting themselves forward varied: some were motivated by a real sense of concern for their communities; some by a sense of national re-assertion (to be discussed in the next chapters); and some by almost a contrary desire: a wish to join UNRRA and so avoid an unwelcome 'return' to a country that they feared or despised. Such people were integral to UNRRA's practices: they formed one of three categories of UNRRA employees. They were one example of the principle of 'helping people to help themselves', but they were also cheap employees, keen to work hard to prove their worth, to build better connections with UNRRA and therefore the rest of the world.

	Class I	Class II	Class III
Germany	4,772	350	319
Austria	276	...	...
Italy	198	1,413	79
Middle East	158	364	26
Total	5404	...	...

Table 1: UNRRA Establishment for Displaced Persons Operations, September 1945[160]

The table above illustrates the composition of UNRRA's workforce. Class I were full-time, international employees, usually with some relevant experience or training: people like Susan Pettiss, Harry Heath and Rhoda Dawson. They were the best-paid of the three categories. Class II were people locally recruited from among the DPs, who might well be highly qualified and well-trained, but who were paid less than those in Class I. Their numbers increased dramatically. Class III were people working for the various non-UNRRA voluntary agencies, such as the FRS and the YMCA. Confusingly, at first some of these groups worked autonomously, with no requirement to report back to UNRRA, but finally they all had to become Class III employees within UNRRA's structures, while still paid by their own agencies.

Rather than literally carrying out activities themselves, the main role of Class I UNRRA employees was to encourage and to assist others. Sometimes DPs needed no encouragement. In Anni's Camp in May 1945, 'there was no organized welfare activity in the first phase. The DPs organized their own dances and sports. The camp swimming pool was much used, and a swimming instructor was on duty there part of the time'.[161] More normally, initiatives succeeded when both UNRRA employees and DPs cooperated. Sometimes the results were impressive. Dawson admired the endless energy of her colleague 'Erica' at Foehrenwald Camp, who found Russian émigrés to work as builders, Estonians to carry out repairs, to give concerts and arrange dances, Baltic women to unpick German uniforms and ski-covers, and use their artificial fur to make bags and bonnets.[162] Harry Heath seems to have adopted a more orthodox approach: he held regular meetings – sometimes even daily meetings – with the various chiefs representing Hanau camp's nationalities, and discussed proposals with them for improving the camp. By June 1945 he was able to boast that his camp now contained two schools, a kindergarten, hospital, dispensary, hospital stores, cookhouse and a scouts unit.[163]

Elsewhere, the results of DP activities were more mixed. The Belgian Marmol expressed some concerns.

> On the whole I am not too satisfied of the way the Transient Part of our Center is operated. [Due to] lack of adequate personnel, this section is practically run by excellent DPs. But they have not the authority to admit or to refuse a man or a woman who claims to have the right to come in and who throws at the face of our billeting DP officer a bunch of certificates of all sorts adorned by all sorts of pictures, signatures, rubber stamps and finger prints, the more so that some UNRRA teams are issuing [a] so-called 'permanent pass'!! In the future, I hope to have an UNRRA officer to supervise this particular section.[164]

In taking these initiatives, UNRRA employees rarely had any formal authority to compel compliance. However, they could make use of some powerful persuasive techniques: they were the most effective conduit for resources into the camp, and they could ensure that the most cooperative DPs were appropriately awarded. Furthermore, it must not be forgotten that many DPs urgently wanted to cooperate in programmes that would produce immediate benefits for their communities. Perhaps the most impressive of all these achievements was the UNRRA University at Munich, which ran courses from summer 1945 until September 1948 for DPs, and which included DPs among its lecturers.[165]

DEDICATION AND COMMITMENT

Under these circumstances, why did so many UNRRA workers stay? Why didn't more agree with Beryl Lewis that '1 year in Germany is enough for anyone'?[166] In part, we have already rehearsed two responses. As was seen in Chapter Five, there was high turnover of staff, and many Team Directors complain of staff simply deserting. But, secondly, no matter how tough the conditions, UNRRA posts could still appear as relatively high status positions. Dawson's description of camp life as revolving around 'cars, drink and girls' suggests how relief work could involve many pleasures and how the possibility of participation in a glamorous lifestyle could act as a compensation for constant hardship. But it is clear that these are only elements of the answer. Relief workers were also attracted by two other aspects of their work. For many, this was a cause in which they believed.[167] Even SHAEF echoed some of this rhetoric.

> The task is enormous, its political and humanitarian implications far-reaching … The individual military officer or UNRRA official who does his job successfully may well feel that he has contributed in no small way to solving one of the biggest problems of welfare and reconstruction facing the United Nations.[168]

While relief workers grew more sceptical about UNRRA as an organization, few stopped believing that the work they were performing was genuinely useful. 'The children made everything worth-while,' noted O'Connor, 'All difficulties and frustrations were reduced to size when the youngsters came dashing along, jumping into one's lap with big hugs and kisses, insisting on one's joining in whatever game they were playing'.[169] For Team Director Atkins, UNRRA was 'the Grandest Social Service the World has ever known'. In his last weekly report, he explained that he felt extremely privileged 'to have been in, on the ground floor, of such a social service'.[170] One senses similar enthusiasm and dedication in the last report of his predecessor, Marmol,

> This is the end of my Directorship.
> I have nothing to show and express but thankfulness and gratitude.
> Thanks to God who gave me such an opportunity to live amongst his creatures (I never realized how many different people he had to take care of…) and who kept me healthy and strong in spite of all.
> Thanks to UNRRA who trusted me and gave me a chance to be useful…
> UNRRA is not a perfect organization and a lot remains to be done. But, the only fact that UNRRA has existed, that it has been conceived and put into effect, means something…
> Thanks to my DP Personnel. They were the real field workers. UNRRA members could always return home in a comfortable billet and get something nice to eat or have their family life with music and entertainments. DPs had to remain in the Center…
> Thanks to my wife who understood my feeling to do some emergency relief work in Germany and fully shared my decision to come over here. She has suffered undoubtedly from me being away, but she knew that it was worthwhile, and so she has done her share for the DPs.[171]

Such ideas were reinforced by the collective nature of UNRRA work. UNRRA workers took their teams very seriously: this may have been, in part, because the official pro-formas asked Team Directors to comment on team morale, but it is clear that for many, concern for the team was not some formality, but a deep-rooted issue. Many were positively delighted by the cosmopolitan mixtures they represented, a practical demonstration of a new internationalism. An absence of team spirit worried them. Harry Heath sounded genuinely upset by the minor discourtesy shown to him by Deed. 'If she was less keen on her work I would know what to do about it, but I do not wish to discourage her. The position must however be remedied and soon'.[172] McNeill's accounts of her work in Holland and in Germany are initially amusing and light-hearted. She seemed to enjoy the chaos and the sheer unpredictable nature of DP work. By 1947, however, one of her closest companions had left to get married, the winter was dark, wet and cold and she was thoroughly fed up. She often felt 'overwhelmed' at thought of her 'ghastly commitments' and often seemed to forget basic tasks such as distributing porridge or chocolate.[173] Dawson sometimes sounded almost heartbroken.

Today I felt it really wasn't worth it. I can't do any Welfare, and with [Team Director] Biddulph refusing to come home to eat, Mina objecting to work with German doctors and the other men taking three hours off for meals, it's rather hopeless ... Other camps I've seen seem so happy, well-run and comfortable. Ours is awful ... There is a lack of warmth and cohesion amongst us which is tragic in a group of such intelligent and decent people.[174]

On the other hand, the presence of cooperative colleagues was a real delight. 'Had a good agreeable staff meeting tonight in which we all pulled our weight. I am more hopeful that we may soon become a real team.'[175] Pettiss neatly captures a sense of new-found confidence which could develop in this collective context. 'I could handle anything, or so I was beginning to believe. The team seemed to believe it too, and deferred to me constantly as a result. As a woman in a man's world, I was sensing a power hitherto unknown to me.'[176] There were also some enchanting moments when everything and everybody seemed to act in unison, where special status, service to a cause and cooperative hospitality was enlarged to include even the DPs. Hulme's records of Christmas 1945 in Wildflecken DP camp sound warm and even ecstatic. 'Not until 1945 had there been a Christmas that was six Christmases rolled into one with twelve thousand Poles celebrating it and a scant dozen United Nations caretakers recovering from their supervision of it ... There were too many parties ... No party really came alive until the UNRRA officer appeared, no food was touched, no punch was poured.'[177] Director Ephraim Chase noted similar occasions.

The life of a member of UNRRA Team is never dull, and there are times when it is positively exciting. Weddings, christenings and confirmations are some of the functions he is invited to attend. And if he does, a good time is assured ... And the price for admission, at least for the Director, is a toast or a speech couched in general terms and containing a reference to the hope that better days are coming.[178]

Alongside their tough work, there was a much-valued social aspect to relief work: a dense ritual of dances, parties, concerts and festivals. These varied in form: small, intimate meetings between fellow relief workers; more adventurous contacts with British, American and French military authorities; and finally the more large-scale events, often organized by DPs themselves, at which relief workers would attend as guests of honour. Friendships were formed, and romances sometimes followed. For some, service in UNRRA was also part of the wartime unloosening of strict sexual morality: relief workers left for Germany in the same years that Britain experienced record numbers of illegitimate births and divorces.[179] For some, this was reprehensible. Rosolek was appalled by the romance developing between his team's doctor and welfare officer.[180] Morgan fumed when he learned that many unmarried UNRRA couples lived together with no attempt 'to keep up the appearances of a decent society'.[181] Yet such relationships were part of a collective experience that gave relief workers the psychological strength to continue: they could learn from each other, support each other, befriend each other and in these ways acquire the ability to cope with the new demands.

CONCLUSION

Even before the war was over, a Swiss journalist had wondered if great wealth was simply inducing American planners to build a relief organization on an unprecedented scale so as to 'startle and amaze European observers'. He criticized an American impulse to accomplish great things in a short time, thus ignoring natural growth and local conditions. This great tree would 'fail to bear fruit' because it would quickly turn into a 'money spending bureaucracy', and he could not resist comparing UNRRA to its Swiss counterpart – the ICRC – which had alleviated so much suffering 'with such limited funds without great publicity nor any political aspirations'.[182] Critics also perceived UNRRA as 'a business' and argued that its staff were unprepared for work which demanded a sense of humanity and of tradition.[183] Francesca Wilson agreed, and described the Americans in UNRRA as distant and careerist.[184] To add to her chagrin, the UNRRA leadership in Britain employed 'an overweight of Indian and Colonial army men' and rejected many 'excellent experienced women'.[185]

UNRRA's planners may well have been motivated by triumphalism but UNRRA was not simply a commercial organization. Amongst the staff there were plenty of well-motivated men and women: Rhoda Dawson, Kathryn Hulme, Muriel and Harry Heath to name but a few. Yet Wilson's criticisms in particular raise a pertinent point: to what extent was UNRRA simply part of an occupying army? A relief worker from Luxemburg told Francesca Wilson that 'UNRRA was like a Foreign Legion for peace instead of war' but how easy is to act as an 'army of peace?'.[186] Simply looking at behaviour, one can see broad similarities between troops and relief workers. The leitmotivs of girls, cars and drink could just as easily be applied to the occupying military forces. Relief work and military occupation were closely linked, in that the uniformed UNRRA officers were attached to conquering armies and they enjoyed military privileges. More significantly, UNRRA's dominant culture was like a military culture: a bizarre mixture of stress, loss, escapism and recklessness.[187] As a result UNRRA workers, and many others, could be encouraged to ape military values. Even the anti-militaristic FRS was susceptible, and Bayley looked suspiciously at one of the team leaders who had adopted military manners and was a little over-friendly with the local officers.[188]

The tremendous resources devoted to UNRRA after the Second World War were, in one sense, a new and bold experiment in taking international responsibility for repairing the damage of war. Certainly this is how many relief workers saw themselves. The UNRRA experiment was also part of a process whereby the boundaries between relief work and military action became more blurred.

It is not just that UNRRA relied on military power but that the relationship between them was symbiotic. For example, there were widespread references to the 'UNRRA screening' process. As one frustrated relief worker pointed out, it was really 'Army Screening' but because UNRRA workers carried it out, they were held to be responsible for it.[189] Later in the twentieth and early twenty-first centuries, western armies have consistently stressed their role in relief work, sometimes in response to natural disasters, sometimes as an essential part of a specific military operation, most controversially in Afghanistan. As UNRRA workers travelled into 'Darkest Germany' they saved lives, they provided shelter, they made mistakes and they muddled through. Sometimes they showed great compassion; sometimes they displayed the best methods of modern, scientific social work, sometimes they were corrupt or inefficient. Amongst this patchy, inconsistent history there is one clear outcome, namely that UNRRA established relief work as an essential part of all future military planning.

7

In the Camps

- The Politics of Empathy
- The Politics of Critique
- A Liberation that was not a Liberation
- DPs and Nationality
- Protests, Initiatives and National Resurgence
- DPs and Relief Workers
- Conclusion

'Of course we are not nice people', a Jewish camp survivor told Clara Urquhart, a British philanthropist, 'in order to survive the [death] camps we had to resort to every form of ruse'.[1] This brief statement opens another line of enquiry: what did relief workers think of DPs? In this chapter we examine the cultures and structures of the DP camps, in which at least three forms of authority interacted. First, the military and political authorities who took on the task of occupying defeated Germany. Secondly, there was the untried presence of UNRRA. And lastly, often unrecognized, the DPs themselves developed their own forms of authority. This chapter will study how these three forces interacted. Once again, we will not approach this issue as a study of institutions, but instead focus on the day-to-day interactions within the camps. This focus leads us to consider some psychological issues.

Long before D-Day, welfare workers discussed how best to approach those who had been psychologically damaged by the war. In 1943, Arthur Koestler tried to predict the emotional aftermath of Nazi domination, noting how widespread these issues might be.

> What will be the reaction of the prisoner in Europe to the welfare worker? By prisoner is meant not only the man in the concentration camp, but to some extent, everyone who has been under the continual pressure of living in Nazi-occupied Europe.
>
> Remember that disinterested human kindness will have been forgotten, and this means that the feelings on seeing the welfare worker are likely to be 'What does he want out of me? What is he trying to sell me?' just as the first reaction on asking people in a camp for help in anything or for information would be 'he wants to use me e.g. as an informer'.[2]

Had the DPs been irrevocably damaged by their war experiences? Was their rehabilitation possible? Most UNRRA workers would have given positive answers. Just as soldiers endured terrible conditions without suffering complete mental collapse, so civilians could survive. Susan Pettiss was 'heartened by the

ability of the DPs in those early days to dance, laugh, work with joy'.[3] Her observation was largely accurate: if DPs were given the right food, and protected from
a variety of epidemics, then many could be physically cured, and show clear
signs of psychological recovery. This was the 'relief' that was promised in 'relief
and rehabilitation'. What of the second element? How were they to be 'rehabili-
tated' by relief workers?

Relief workers often presented a distinctive, humanitarian narrative to
describe the process that they wished to initiate. Hulme used two simple
phrases to evoke this: 'statistics turned into people and the people turned into
friends'.[4] Pettiss echoes her sentiments: 'The DPs were losing their anonymity
for me, becoming individuals with faces and stories, rather than just a crowd
moving past'.[5] Such ideas were also consistent with some long-held Quaker
relief principles: 'Make friends: don't be content simply with having relations
with people'.[6]

Are these generous, humane words accurate descriptions of what happened
in the camps? We will begin by considering evidence that suggests an ethic of
empathy; we then move on to consider some contrary evidence that suggests
paternalistic and even authoritarian ethics within the relief agencies. Finally, we
will reverse our perspective, and ask how the DPs experienced camp life and the
relief agencies.

Trained welfare workers began thinking about this relationship long
before 1945. In their ideas, curiously, we find an unexpected echo of
psychological discourse. The DPs often appeared like a sub-conscious
force or id: primitive, passionate, irrational and childlike, not necessarily
malignant, but certainly untrustworthy. The Allied authorities were more
like the ego: they had the power to control the situation, but their rule
was often short-sighted and even selfish. Finally, there was UNRRA, which
tended to present itself as the conscience or super-ego, far-sighted, selfless,
rational and humane.

THE POLITICS OF EMPATHY

If post-1945 Germany was an extraordinary place, then the 300 or so DP
camps administered by UNRRA seemed still stranger. Edward Bakis talks
of 'a fantastic, dreamlike world'; Hulme of 'the strange half-world of the DP
camps ... [which] turned into an Alice-in-Wonderland world in 1946'; Nora
O'Connor encountered situations which 'could have come from the pages of
Alice-in-Wonderland' and Beryl Lewis noted 'a world of unreality'.[7] In order
to work effectively within this strange environment, relief workers needed to
think carefully about how they should work with the DPs. Christiansen, the
Danish nurse who served with UNRRA, asked a simple question: was it better
to be friendly or to be firm with DPs? After 16 months of relief work, she
finally decided that friendliness was best, although 'you must make yourself

respected'.[8] Duchesne-Cripps argued in a more sophisticated manner that a good welfare officer needed to get close to the DPs, to learn about how they lived, their ideas, the rumours they heard, the forecasts they made, and the gossip they passed on.[9] These points raise the question of empathy, a complex and politically charged quality in this context.

The idea of relief workers identifying with the DPs is not as fanciful as it might seem: they lived similar lives. For example, during the long, cold winter of 1947 Margaret McNeill was demoralized. She spent a disproportionate amount of time on housekeeping and noticed that – just like the DPs – she was becoming 'obsessed' with, and 'mean' about, food.[10] UNRRA workers were housed alongside DPs, ate a similar monotonous diet, and had access to few diversions. This quality then became politicized: the first signs of this came when relief workers clashed with military authorities.

Harry Heath records at least three significant, public clashes with military officials who inspected his camp. On each occasion, he defended 'his' DPs against their criticism. In his diary, he returned to the same point:

> I wish to goodness that some of these Americans would try to put themselves into DP shoes occasionally …
>
> The major speaking in private a few minutes later said that I ought to have better discipline in this camp. I replied that I did not run the camp by blind brutal discipline but by cooperation which was far more effective …
>
> These blasted people in high places who give out orders for other people to carry out and then fail to comply themselves make me furious. If they would only realize that these people are human beings who were in the war while we were sitting pretty at home and that here in Hanau they have had their first opportunity for years to set up something like their own civilisation.[11]

In each incident, Heath is clearly aware of a power relationship, a type of triangle of forces: the DPs, himself and the military authorities. Within this power relationship he places himself squarely on the side of the DPs and then from this position forcefully criticizes the authorities.

UNRRA Team Director Georges Masset felt many of the same frustrations as Harry Heath. He also protested against military authorities' priorities in their inspection of his camp:

> This was not an inspection of a Displaced Persons Center with accent on the conditions and needs of 15,000 DPs. It was primarily a sanitation inspection such as might be expected in an Army barracks where every small scrap of garbage (carefully concealed by our Poles in the corners of their basement where they never expected a General would go) resulted in penalties and future restrictions for and on all concerned. The physical and moral condition of our 15,000 Polish DPs was completely ignored – save in one instance when General Watson saw a Polish mother with baby in arms on one of the roads and inquired how many baths she took a week.[12]

When military authorities imposed a harsh regime on the DPs in Wildflecken camp, Masset bitterly compared this to life in a concentration camp:

> Here now is a listing of the new orders put into effect in the new concentration camp at Wildflecken:
> 1 – Obligatory reveille at 8 o'clock and (under surveillance of an armed guard over each 4 houses) obligatory cleaning, washing and sweeping of the interiors and ridding streets of ordure; penalty of prison on bread and water for those who will not work or will not obey
> 2 – No people allowed to live in the localities belonging to the kitchens …
> 3 – The captain of the guard has received the order to bathe and shower all DP's <u>twice weekly</u> (most of our DP's are rigorously clean even though soap and cleaning material are rare. The captain is tearing his hair and asking how this order is to be achieved!)
> 4 – Throwing of paper on streets or stairways is penalized by immediate imprisonment…
> 6 – Sunday 'day off' is suppressed (this day is sacred to the Polish of whom at least two-thirds in the camp are practicing Catholics)
> 7 – Obligatory VD examination for <u>every inhabitant of the camp</u> …
> 8 – VD cases will be isolated (Where ? How ?…)
> 9 – 1500 Poles must be evacuated to Poland every 12 days – WHETHER BY THEIR OWN WILL OR BY FORCE.[13]

Hulme expressed similar sentiments. She found that the 35-mile trip to the nearest working train station to meet endless columns of boxcars, crammed with anxious and needy DPs, was becoming almost a daily routine. 'Not weariness but wrath had altered my teammates, a burning wordless wrath directed against nothing in sight because the population maps with the coloured pins in them and the military personages who moved those pins around, trimly "consolidating" the displaced masses, were as far away as God seemed to be just then'.[14]

The more pacifist-inspired Quakers echoed these ideas: the military authorities were not so much callous or uncaring, but they lacked any real sense of humanity. Bayley complained that a major 'just doesn't think of the Poles as human beings – just as a problem of administration – so long as they are housed, fed and kept from looting he doesn't care what happens to them'.[15] In some camps, DPs were not allowed to leave the camp without permission and were governed by strict rules. Similar issues were raised in 1947. One British Captain Collins, welcomed the new 'Westward Ho' labour scheme which enabled 15,000 DPs to work in Britain to alleviate the post-war labour shortage.[16] To his surprise, the DPs were far less enthusiastic. 'Westward Ho' was not an immigration scheme, DPs would not be allowed to settle permanently in Britain, they could not take their wives and children. While the Captain was exasperated by the DPs' attitudes, McNeill felt differently.

> Asylum in our country. Yes, it was a fair offer, but it must have been horribly reminiscent of another similar offer made by the Germans not so very long ago. I felt that Collins

would have found the other questions less irritating had he been able, as I was, to judge them against the background of the questioners' circumstances.[17]

At first sight, these exchanges may simply appear as bickering between two authorities, the relief worker and the military commander. The point we wish to stress is how relief workers constructed a specific type of legitimacy to defend their positions, based on their assertions of a sense of empathy with the DPs. This was not just a means to limit military authorities' interference in their camps: it was an important aspect of the relief worker's commitment to the DPs. Other sources demonstrate how their sense of empathy also informed their daily practices.

Team Director Marmol presents a telling example, concerning how to respond to a DP applying to migrate to the United States.

> One way to answer such a question is simple and correct: 'I am sorry, nothing to do for the time being. You've got to wait until the American consul arrives'. The other way is this: 'Well it's a damned good idea. Have you got any relatives over there? What kind of a job did you have in your country? Now, you must understand that the main problem for the Army is first to end the war. There is still a war in the Pacific. That means that transportation is still scarce ... But if you have some relatives in the States, as soon as possible, and eventually by Red Cross mail, get in touch with them ... In the meantime, we may have some more news about the activities of the Intergovernmental committee for refugees, the main agency which will take care of you in some time to come. Now come back in two weeks and if there is anything new on the subject I'll be very happy to let you know'.[18]

Marmol's word indicate the extent to which he empathized with the DPs. For him, this attitude was part of the 'rehabilitation' that UNRRA promised: he was not so much concerned about the 'measurable' achievements that Directors could proudly list in a monthly report as about the way relief workers approached the DPs. This was the best type of social work, whether it was formally recognized as such or not.

> For the Army, the problem is: get the people billeted, fed, [DDT] dusted ... We UNRRA men can do social work without telling anybody, but just doing it. Social aspects of our work are still vague and sometimes inefficient ... Yet, we are doing some bits of social work when we look for billet accommodation, for better distribution of food and of Red Cross Parcels, for cleaning, for giving information, and most of all by the way we talk to the people, understand their problem and try to encourage them. Some centers have recreational programs, canteen, schools. Social work is not necessarily pictured by visible achievements. It is more the way you approach every human being. I don't know if UNRRA is doing social work, as an organization but I am quite sure that UNRRA people, in their great majority, are real social workers.[19]

Such forms of empathy and commitment to the DPs suggest not just humanitarianism but also humanism: these concerned relief workers insist on the necessity to respect DPs as approximate equals, recognising their dignity. If not exactly an official expression of UNRRA policy, such thoughts were clearly compatible with UNRRA's broader humanitarian remit. However, as one reads further through records, there are also cases in which relief workers no longer simply defend an UNRRA style against military intrusion, but develop a critique of UNRRA itself based – once again – on their sense of empathy with the DPs.

Rhoda Dawson was provoked to consider such themes by the frequency with which she had to change teams, sometimes at very short notice. Dawson questioned whether this was consistent with UNRRA's avowed policies.

> There seemed to be no recognition of, or respect for, the emotional ties engendered by the actual work. The routine was much the same in each camp, and an Officer was supposed to be able to leave and start again elsewhere as easily as he could continue in the same place. But in Welfare of all things, the re-direction of the flow of energy involved a loss of impetus which reacted upon the work and in my case, I found my interest dwindle; in my second year I had acquired the correct, rather bored impersonal attitude and almost preferred filling out forms and sending in reports to encouraging activities among DPs which one might never to able to develop. The Ford Assembly Line was held up to us as a model of organisation to be followed, but we felt we were chessmen in the hands of our superior officers, and this was one of the causes of our endless frustration.[20]

As was seen in the previous chapter, Dawson has the striking ability to sum up urgent issues in a short passage. Here, she questions the technocratic, scientific, 'planning-minded' ethic that animated UNRRA. Was this really the best manner in which to deliver meaningful welfare? Her argument, as she recognized, was with UNRRA itself.

Muriel and Harry Heath also saw deficiencies in UNRRA's policies. At times, their problems seem almost comic. At one regional meeting they were reminded of UNRRA's policy to provide DPs with daily rations that contained 2,000 calories a day. Harry Heath clearly thought back to the piles of tins in Hanau camp, and then asked the obvious question: how exactly were they to achieve this goal? At that meeting he was told that 1½lbs of mixed food a day was probably the equivalent of 2,000 calories.[21] As the weeks wore on, Harry and Muriel grew more belligerent.

> I attended a meeting of UNRRA Directors and [Military Government] Officers at Wiesbaden today. It was a comic set-up. There was a whole collection of colonels and majors at a table on a platform and we smaller fry sat at another table below them – it was evident that we had been called together to be lectured like a bunch of novices. The result must have been startling for the colonels for we challenged them at every

[illegible word: verse?] and criticized them and then we lectured them. It was all quite amusing. The trouble with these colonels was that they did not know their subject while we had learnt it the hard way and knew it backwards.

I quoted my own case.[22]

A similar scene occurred in October 1945 at the Team Directors' meeting at Wiesbaden. The Directors present

> criticized the inefficiency of all UNRRA HQs at Heidelberg, Wiesbaden and Frankfurt. We said that although these HQs were full of highly paid people they had done nothing to provide transport, or to formulate any sort of policy regarded pay and promotion … [While it was the people in the field] who were doing the real work of UNRRA…
>
> [We] told the HQ people present that they knew nothing of the work in the field. We asked why staff at HQ was available to draw up long futile questionnaires which only added to our work while there was apparently none to issue pay books or clothes cards.
>
> After this meeting Miss Zimmerman (the Zone Welfare Officer) began to give me advice but I told her not to tell me how to run a camp as I had been running one for 6 months. I learned afterwards that she had only paid one visit to a DP camp. She soon left us.[23]

Muriel clearly felt the same as Harry. She attended 'a fool of a' welfare officers' meeting at Weisbaden the next month.

> An American who knew nothing of DP camps addressed welfare officers who had been in the field for months. It was ludicrous. Muriel apparently dropped a whole row of bricks by telling the HQ people that we did not need their fancy 'works projects' but that we did need building materials which had been on requisition for months.[24]

These issues are quite different from the gripes and grumbles at Granville. They are not raised by inexperienced UNRRA members complaining about relatively minor, temporary problems; these are experienced workers, active in the field, who are constructing a type of counter-legitimacy. Perhaps the most important words in the previous pages are Harry Heath's 'I quoted my own case'. Relief workers like Harry and Muriel Heath were dedicated to their work *because* they identified with the DPs; but this form of identification, rather than assisting their integration into UNRRA's structures, made them critical of its leadership and other authorities.

Finally, we must recognize some limits to the relief workers' cases. No DP *chose* Harry Heath or Margaret McNeill to represent them. Their sense of empathy is, in itself, a product of a hierarchical situation, in which the relief workers had the relative luxury of being able to consider and to choose how to perform their work.

THE POLITICS OF CRITIQUE

There were limits to the relief workers' empathy with DPs. McNeill realized early on that if she was 'to get through at all,' she would have to 'leave life histories severely alone'.[25] More to the point, was empathy even desirable? McNeill thought that many DPs liked the relief workers precisely because they had *not* been through the same harrowing experiences. In some ways, the relief worker's ignorance – or innocence – was a blessing.[26] Often they needed to keep some sense of distance from the DPs. UNRRA had warned relief workers that DPs 'may present many emotional and personal difficulties', and it had even forecast that there would be unanticipated problems which would need to be solved 'by the imaginativeness of the Assembly Centre Officers and their ability to improvise on the spot'.[27] The Welfare division of UNRRA's European Regional Office analysed the psychological condition of the DPs. Their report presented a sombre picture of 'broken' DPs, suffering regression to more primitive psychological states. 'Alcoholism, delinquency and promiscuity … are common; for they are usually the most easily available ways of mitigating the painful emotional tension of low morale situations, the sense of isolation from a friendly community, and the sense of futility of these circumstances'.[28] Such analyses certainly provided useful warnings to relief workers. A sense of distance was therefore necessary: and with distance, also came a sharper sense of critique.

In the introduction we cited Hulme's optimistic narrative: statistics turned into people who then became friends. In reality, the first meetings of relief workers and DPs often took a quite different form: it was hard to see any individuals within squalid, disorderly crowds. McNeill remembered her first days in a DP camp.

> All around us from the other buildings came an endless riotous clamour, shouting, screaming, singing, all helped on by several wirelesses at full blast. But it wasn't until we woke up in the morning that we saw the full squalor of the scene around us. Indeed it was with an awful kind of fascination that I gazed at the rows of windows opposite us out of which at any moment would be hurled empty tins, buckets of water, potato peelings and even old stoves and bits of furniture. Below amidst all the filth a group of people were busily engrossed in scraping a dead pig preparatory to some cooking orgy. There was an absolute babel of Polish and other lesser-known tongues and through it all walked the British Army with an expression of jaundiced endurance.[29]

Such images suggest the distance between the relief worker and the DPs, who appear as primitive, animalistic beings engaging in barbaric practices.

Hulme also records an interesting and telling outburst. In a much-cited section, she describes the arrival of thousands of Red Cross PoW rations in Wildflecken DP camp. These were substantial packages that contained sugar cubes, cheddar, sardines, coffee, tuna, spam, dried milk, cooking fat, chocolate and American cigarettes. Hulme was impressed, and noted that she herself had not been able to obtain many of these items during the war years – a rare example of an American relief worker being impressed by the food available in Europe.[30] Her team planned to use the camp's DPs to carry the thousands of boxes from the station to the warehouse. Hulme and her fellow workers recognized this posed a potential risk: it could awaken the famous DP hunger-syndrome. As they had often starved before 1945, DPs frequently became irrationally greedy to consume food, or even just to hold it, to possess it. At first, the team thought that they were safe: the boxes were quite anonymous, but they did bear the Red Cross symbol. Hulme's language grows particularly revealing at this point. Somehow, the DPs guessed what was in the parcels: Hulme comments that it was *as if* they could smell the food through the heavy parcelling and the tin. Several hundred Polish DPs crowded round her, shouting 'Pakiety!', or parcels: this is 'the language of hysteria' she thought, as she faced the mob of 'spam-maddened adults … like thwarted children'.[31] The crisis grew worse the next day, as a crowd of demonstrators gathered outside the camp warehouse.

Previous commentators have tended not to notice Hulme's reaction to this situation, which is well worth citing at length:

> I felt like somebody else walking in wrath toward the murmuring crowd. In that trans-formed moment, I hated the displaced person and every cause behind him that had made him what he was. I despised the insanity of international relief that imagined something could be done with this ruin in the human soul, so much more fearful than all the mountains of rubble strewn over the face of Europe.

With the help of her ever-faithful Polish countess as translator, she berated these 'bastards'.

> Slowly, in a voice that did not sound like mine, I spoke to the gaping crowd, pausing long between phrases and watching the Countess with white-hot anger ready for her too if I could detect her softening a single syllabus. I called them a pack of jealous lazy bums, a disgrace to the name of the displaced person whose cause UNRRA was trying to sell to a world that was not interested. 'And who would want people like you?' I cried.

A little later she regretted her actions, feeling only 'dull humiliation' for screaming at the 'poor devils … like a virago'. The worst part of the episode, she then thought, was the DPs' prompt obedience.

This episode suggests a different placing of the triangle of forces from that suggested by Harry Heath's confrontations: rather than the relief worker, inspired by empathy, representing the DPs to external authorities, Hulme suggests another aspect of super-mum UNRRA, the condemnatory super-ego, forcibly acting as the DPs' best self. Like McNeill and Bayley, Hulme explicitly presents the DPs as psychological inferiors: they act on the smell of objects, they are hysterical, they are like children.

Many, even most, DPs were psychologically damaged when liberated in 1945. The problem was that often the DP camps either perpetuated their psychological weaknesses, or did little to alleviate them. The structures of the DP life, their dependence on food distributions and confinement behind fences, encouraged infantilization. The Jewish Committee for Relief Abroad warned UNRRA about the potential disastrous consequences of this form of confinement:

> It is difficult, if not impossible, to re-instil them a full sense of responsibility for clean-liness as long as they are still horded in unattractive and in some cases, unhealthy barracks … The highly developed inferiority complex and the selfishness, which is really a mistrust in humanity and in those who desire to help them, can only be reduced by demonstrating to the DP's that they are on equal footing with their former German oppressors and with those who are helping them.[32]

Another report drew an interesting comparison between DPs living in private accommodation and those living in camps, even with good facilities.

> Landsberg [US Zone] is an excellent barrack camp one which has one of the best balanced UNRRA teams that I have come across, and the best local leadership. They have developed the best educational system, both extensive and intensive, that I have seen, with over 400 students and twelve different kinds of workshops … The camp is not overcrowded…
>
> Now you take a second camp – Lampertsheim, in which people are living in small houses. The other facilities have not been developed to anywhere near the extent that they have in Landsberg; they have not the same educational or social facilities.
>
> However, when you speak to the workers in these camps they tell you that the psychological and social outlook of the people who live in the private houses, who do their own cooking in their own way, have family units … where there is no necessity to mix the sexes and have married people living in the same room with unmarried people – they tell you that they have practically none of the social problems which arise in a camp like Landsberg which from every other point of view is better than Lampertsheim. It is the effect of people living under normal conditions.[33]

Unfortunately, the mass barracks of Landsberg were the norm.

Even the Quakers, officially committed to equality, occasionally treated the DPs as naughty children. Bayley and Evens were in despair when Polish DPs were reluctant to accept typhoid injections. Bayley solved the problem by arranging to distribute Red Cross parcels and to vaccinate Poles on the same day. To ensure compliance she insisted that medical staff issue DPs with a 'chit' to prove that they had been vaccinated; without this they could not collect a parcel.[34]

Such power relationships were likely to reinforce relations of dependency. This was a situation which became more rather than less pronounced with the passing of time. Fit, able, dynamic, skilled adults with valid documentation – or very good forged documentation – were the ones most likely to emigrate; the remaining 'hardcore' was composed of those most likely to become dependent. A survey among Lithuanian DPs in the British zone of Germany indicated that proportion of workers to non-workers was 3:2 in January 1947; by March 1948 the ratio was 1:1.[35]

Could relief workers maintain a generous sense of empathy under these difficult circumstances? DPs bombarded them with difficult and often completely unexpected problems. One astonishing issue that many had to face in mid-1945 was the mad consumption of alcohol by Russian DPs. 'Alcohol' here is not some medicalized euphemism, but the simple truth: in Harry Heath's camp, Russian DPs drank stolen industrial alcohol. The problem only became obvious when, days after consumption, they developed serious lead poisoning. Twenty died before 7 May 1945, and by 31 May 1945 800 had been diagnosed as suffering its effects, and 350 had been placed in hospital. A doctor considered that they would need nine months to recover.[36] Like the incidences of mass rape committed by the invading Red Army in the east, it is almost impossible to understand such practices. One guesses that factors such as the accumulated psychological brutalization of years of slave labour, the long years of living in close proximity to extraordinary levels of personal violence, personal experiences of suffering at home, the sudden, complete collapse of authority structures, and the near-certain knowledge that no hero's welcome was being prepared for these DPs in their homeland all came together to produce a brief moment of mad, self-destructive escapism.[37] This violence was another legacy of the war. The Nazi regime is often seen as an impersonal, highly industrialized, coldly efficient killing machine, with the concentration camp as the ultimate killing factory. Yet much of the slaughter took place outside of the camps, and hot-blooded individuals – rather than well-orchestrated machines – were responsible for unprecedented levels of brutality.[38]

The Russian DPs' near-suicidal drinking bouts represent just one issue amidst a mass of serious problems. Beryl Lewis recorded another telling example. In October 1945 the guards left Landsberg DP Camp to requisition some German civilian houses. On hearing this, some DPs concluded that all German possessions were also available to them. They 'declared a plundering afternoon and removed radios, clothing, bicycles, etc., from a number of houses *not* on the requisitioning list until a military guard restored order'. To make matters worse, a rumour then went round the local German population that legalized plundering was being allowed: 'The results were dramatic. Mothers removed children from school, banks closed, some businesses closed, even patients in hospital got out of bed and returned to their houses to protect their property'.[39] UNRRA's internal reports record DPs' involvement in raiding, looting and robbery, in the illegal distilling of liquor, in black market trading, in the formation of armed gangs, in fish lifting, in the illegal dyeing of American military uniforms, in the sale of narcotics and the illegal slaughtering of cattle.[40]

Excluding minor offenses, 2,700 DPs were accused of crimes in the single region of Bavaria from June to October 1945, including murder, robbery and looting.[41] This pattern of behaviour in part explains the hostility towards DPs voiced by the military and political authorities. In place of the expected welcome by grateful and obedient foreigners, the new authorities found that they were met with a serious and wide-ranging crime wave by aggressive delinquents.

DP crime seems to have taken two forms. The first wave, in mid-1945, was a spontaneous kicking-off of all the restrictions and limitations of the Nazi years. Slave labourers, fugitives who had been hidden for years and concentration camp inmates were now free: their first impulse was to celebrate. This could take violent and vindictive forms, whether in the form of violence against the self (as in the case of the Russians' alcoholism) or as the lynching of individuals accused of service in concentration camps or collaboration with the Nazi regime. There were outbreaks of wild vandalism. Newly free Russian DPs smashed every mirror and every cooker in Anni's Camp.[42] British war correspondent Leonard Mosley presented a memorable picture of this first wave of criminality in his *Report from Germany*, describing the 'reign of terror' that DP gangs imposed on German civilians. 'In those early days, while the genuine "displaced persons" waited for transport or trekked along the roads towards home, thousands of less genuine "slaves" indulged in a bloody reign of terror'.[43] They drank, looted and killed, terrorizing German farmers. Visiting the rich farms of Westphalia, Mosley noted:

> In most farms the [foreign] labour had risen up, stirred into action by men and women from other districts. The others came with their knapsacks filled with loot; they pushed barrows stuffed with stolen goods ... They told the others that the War was over, that there was no need to fear the Germans any longer ... The complaints we met were so numerous that we got hardened to them, and unless it was a rape or a murder that was taking place, we shrugged our shoulders and went on.[44]

While Mosley's overtly pro-German sympathies were unusual, his terrifying depictions of DP crime were not. Lieutenant Brett-Smith talked of the 'wilful and pointless damage' by DPs.[45] Visiting Germany in 1945, Stephen Spender found that DPs were viewed by British officers as 'gangs of destitute criminals unjustifiably wandering about marauding and robbing, more disliked by the authorities because more of a nuisance to them than the Germans'. Some even told him that they could sympathize with the Nazis, because at least they had stood up for their country, while the refugees had deserted theirs 'like rats'.[46]

Following the first moment of liberation, a second type of DP criminality then developed, involving the organized creation of networks and structures. Its profile was formed from several factors: the habits of subterfuge learned during the Nazi years, desires for revenge and for self-assertion, the often irrational desire to acquire food and possessions, but also – just as important – a deep frustration that real needs were not being met by UNRRA and other

Allied authorities. (We will analyse this in more detail below.) This led to some confusion among the UNRRA workers. Some spoke of such criminality as exceptional, an activity which was only undertaken by an immoral minority. But, elsewhere, UNRRA workers grew worried that this criminality was, in some way, a reflection of the fundamental nature of *all* DPs. As noted by Hulme, they feared that DPs could not be redeemed, that they were permanently warped by their wartime experiences, and that the experience of living in relief camps which provided them with free rations, accommodation and – most crucially – no real work was actually worsening their condition.[47] This point also explains Hulme's anger in the previously cited passages: she was concerned that *her* DPs were acting in the manner evoked by the hostile images that circulated. She was aware of the 'legend that would cling to the DPs for the rest of their days, that they were nothing more than a looting horde sitting pretty under the protection of UNRRA and free to make sorties on the poor frightened Germans any time that life in the camp became too dull'.[48] If this was true, then her work was pointless.

Were the DPs overwhelmingly criminal or was this simply a handy image to pin upon the dispossessed and foreign? This is a difficult question to answer. DPs certainly featured prominently in contemporary police reports. Cases of plunder, theft and black market activities usually received disproportionate attention from the German authorities and the press. But DPs were also easy scapegoats: Germans wanted to present themselves as victims of a rampant DP criminality.[49] Some allegations against DPs were clearly made to cover up Germans' black market activities.[50] Jacobmeyer has demonstrated that, in reality, if DPs' criminality rates were certainly higher in the first weeks following the liberation than those of the Germans, they rapidly dropped and soon did not differ from the overall German rates.[51]

Jewish Displaced Persons were particularly vulnerable to such accusations. They were readily perceived either as criminals or as persons with an innate propensity towards criminality.[52] Stereotypes of excessively privileged, corrupted or powerful Jewish DPs flourished in post-war Germany, reviving irrational fears. Officials were not exempt from such prejudices. One can find, for example, an IRO (International Refugee Organisation) report which clearly endorsed anti-Semitic views: an official claimed that one Jewish DP was illegally buying a seven-ton plane load of supplies every day, and that among 'these people' three-quarters of them had amassed considerable fortunes.[53]

The frequent references to DP criminality in reports can therefore be read in different ways. First, they do provide some documentary evidence of the violence and heightened emotions that marked the DPs' lives. But, secondly, they reveal of the relief workers' fears: their references to DP criminality are signs of a deeper pessimism concerning the viability of the whole 'rehabilitation' project. The thread of anti-Semitism which sometimes appears in such reports suggests a conservative antipathy to a world which appeared to have changed for the worst.

There were also some very practical explanations for the relief workers' sense of distance from the DPs. Conditions in the new DP camps were not as physically oppressive as the concentration camps, but many relief workers still found them repulsive. Elizabeth Bayley was disgusted when she had to clean out the Italian camp in August 1945. The DPs had left it 'in the most revolting dirty state,' she said, 'I've never seen anything so sordid – Mother would faint on the spot'. Like most well brought up young women, she probably had never seen a naked man before joining the FRS. Now, she was washing grown men in communal showers and spraying their clothes with DDT. She wanted to be kind, but she could not avoid a sense of horror: 'ugh, you should have seen our faces expressing revolted disgust,' she remembered.[54]

Many were struck by both the appalling sanitary conditions in some camps, and the DPs' refusal to obey the most elementary rules of hygiene. The disgusting conditions of the toilets appalled relief workers. At Landsberg, Lieutenant General Smith reported that

> Halls and vacant rooms are filled with old straw, garbage, empty cans and faecal matter. The floors of two empty rooms which I discovered were covered with faecal matter. Some residents of the camp defecate on the floors of modern toilets rather than use the toilet itself. The walls on all toilet compartments were smeared with faecal matter.[55]

Even the normally sensitive and compassionate Lieutenant Heymont found it difficult to understand the DPs.

> We had all worked so hard trying to help the people – and they even fail to keep just their own living areas and latrines tolerably clean. Even after concentration camp life … is it too demanding to ask that they use the urinal in the latrines and not the floor? When a garbage can is provided, is it unreasonable to expect them to put the garbage into the can and not on the ground next to the can?[56]

Aside from their behaviour, relief workers grew irritated by DPs' attitudes. Dawson voiced annoyance. 'One gets sick and tired of the concentration camp being used as an excuse for every kind of laziness or crime'.[57] In another entry, she cynically noted that ex-concentration camp inmates 'are not known by their original status; criminal, pervert and political ex-prisoner all bear the glory of Buchenwald, Auschwitz and Belsen'.[58] How are these dismissive attitudes to be explained? A longer passage from Dawson's memoir, relating to Jewish DPs, provides a fuller illustration.

> Individually they are rather charming, but the offices are now always crowded by short stout chattering figures, and by whispering groups. One is beset on all sides by people whisper that they alone need shoes, coats, cigarettes and better food; or a man wants to start a tailor's shop and begs for the sewing machine being used by someone else; and the least thing starts them off on their horrors.[59]

The casual reference to 'their horrors' speaks volumes. Caring, humanitarian UNRRA staff could easily grow weary, and come to see the recital of wartime experiences merely as another ploy by insistent DPs making difficult demands on UNRRA's limited resources. As was the case with Hulme, in such episodes, one hears distinct echoes of the super-ego posture here: mother knows best.

The great fear was that the DPs might be incurable. Some relief workers studied their psychology. At Landsberg, UNRRA's team director found many to be 'very psychologically delicate'.[60] They also showed aggressiveness and defiance of authority. They refused to work and were uncooperative. When, for example, the military authorities suggested installing bunks to solve the problem of overcrowding, the DPs refused, retorting that they had slept in bunks in the concentration camps.[61] Other relief workers encountered similar problems. The British Quaker Bertha Bracey cites a revealing example of the problems of rehabilitation.

> I'm trying to deal with the psychological readjustment of a man who has spent years in concentration camps, Esterwegen, Dachau, Buchenwald, followed by years of forced labour … Our greatest problem now is to help that man to become a man in the full sense. When we first took him to a police station, in order to obtain leave to send him into the country to recover, and to have an operation on his shot elbow, he broke into a cold sweat when he saw a policeman, because he is not familiar with the friendly reception that people get from the Metropolitan Police; he associates an uniform with something very different. He is childishly interested in a new pair of shoes, in a shirt, in a coat; he is inordinately proud because someone has given him a pocket wallet.[62]

Profoundly afraid of loneliness, many DPs refused to be separated from their families, even when hospitalized.[63] They were reluctant to be transferred from one camp to another.

Faced with uncooperative DPs, relief workers voiced annoyance or discouragement. Specialists described the DPs' symptoms as 'regressive':

> The most characteristic personality change of people under circumstances of severe emotional straining is regression … The acquired forms of civilisation easily vanish and the loss of cultural decorum is one of the first symptoms one can observe in displaced persons. They do not restrain themselves anymore; the brakes have been taken off. An additional factor in this process is the fact that various hygienic amenities and customs of civilization are no longer possible since the physical means are lacking. The means of cleanliness decline; people do not take any interest in hygiene. They wash themselves less; they do not look after their own clothes … the sense of shame disappears. Finally, their behaviour becomes both rougher and more childish.[64]

Relief workers were particularly concerned that the DPs' sexual behaviour and attitudes might be evidence of some form of permanent trauma.[65] One aspect of the horrors of the concentration camps was the common nakedness or near-nakedness of the inmates: Collis was actually directed to 'the place wiv naked corpses' on his way to Bergen-Belsen.[66] The first horrified observers accurately interpreted this as a sign of profound demoralization: the normal boundaries between the public and private self had been crushed by the concentration camp regime. However, some liberated DPs, supposedly undergoing a process of rehabilitation, continued to ignore or flout normal moral conventions. But, for the DPs, what was normal? 'Many strange activities that could have been regarded as "abnormal" in a "normal" situation were sensible adjustments to the peculiar living conditions' observed Bakis in his perceptive analysis.[67] So: should the clergy's activities in the camps therefore be welcomed, or would their rigid sexual standards only make women who had suffered sexual abuse feel guilty?[68] Colliss records an interesting example of this dilemma at Belsen.

> We went out behind the block and saw seven mothers sitting there, nursing their babies in the sun, close to a working party of British soldiers who were putting up a barbed-wire fence to keep themselves out. Sister, folding her powerful arms across her bosom, assumed a ferocious stance, every inch of her emitting disapproval. 'Disgusting!' she said. 'Those girls half naked and *those* men!' The British soldiers understood quite well. They went on hammering and smiling in a male sort of way. The girls smiled back. It was a friendly, sexy scene. Sister made an angry noise within and marched back into her block like a hurricane.[69]

Who was doing more to rehabilitate the concentration camp survivors: the censorious sister or the flirtatious soldiers?

Standards of 'normality' varied from country to country, and even from generation to generation. Duchesne-Cripps attempted to take account of such factors, explaining the premarital sexuality was normal in Poland, and therefore should not be a cause for alarm for relief workers caring for Polish DPs. But she welcomed the contribution of Catholic priests to raise their moral standards.[70] Among Jewish DPs, the desire to have children and to found families was an integral part of their post-Holocaust rehabilitation: while birth rates increased significantly in all DP camps, it was the all-Jewish DP camps which demonstrated the highest birth rates and levels of marriage.[71] Nazis had not allowed prisoners or forced labourers to marry; young people felt that they had to make up for lost time. Others, who had lost their families in the war, wanted to start new lives. In 1946–47, on average, 120 DPs' babies were born every month in the French Zone of Occupation. A record was reached in July 1946, when 169 babies were born out of a total population of 44,695 DPs.[72] Such fertility did not alarm relief workers; they did, however, grow worried by the evidence of abortions being carried out in their camps.[73]

Finally, the simple apathy of DPs remained a serious and widespread concern, for it was another indication that UNRRA was failing to work effectively. When LaGuardia spoke at the fifth session of the UNRRA Council in

1946, he made reference to the 830,000 still in UNRRA camps 'discouraged, confused, unhappy, demoralized and depressed'.[74] Hulme was worried that she was observing 'the first small rents in the tough fabric of DP morale, the inevitable result of penning up a sturdy people who loved the earth and wanted to put a plough into it'.[75] General Morgan also noted this issue, but characteristically blamed UNRRA itself. Visiting what he termed 'the so-called camp' at Weisbaden, he noted the apathy of the Polish DPs. 'Down at this level one can see very clearly the sickening, demoralizing effect on the individual and on the family group of the complete absence of any coherent, positive policy up above'.[76] He enthusiastically backed a 'no work, no eat' policy.[77]

The relief workers' sense of empathy with the DPs certainly did not prevent them from also criticizing them. Their criticisms are comprehensible, and reveal another aspect of relief work: it was exhausting and demanding, and DPs could seem irritating, destructive and aggressive. Whichever attitude they expressed, however, relief workers usually positioned themselves as the DPs' intellectual and moral superiors. While there are many examples of relief workers using DPs as convenient assistants, there are few of them accepting DPs as equal partners.

A LIBERATION THAT WAS NOT A LIBERATION

This failure to construct egalitarian relations marked the first meetings of relief workers and DPs. Ruth Kluger and her mother were Austrian Jews who survived incarceration in Auschwitz. Her robust, unromanticized memoirs record a brief moment of happiness in 1945. After the collapse of the Nazi regime, they were able to live in the luxurious house of a Nazi functionary in Straubing. She swam in the river, she met boys and went to dances. For a few weeks she was intensely happy. 'That summer in the early peace of 1945 was an enchanted time, like floating on air, beyond calendar and clock'.[78] Such moments, however, were surprisingly rare. More paradoxically still, those who one might expect had the greatest reason to celebrate the fall of Nazism were often those who complained most. Victor Frankl's classic memoir explains:

> When, on his return, a man found that in many places he was met only with a shrug of the shoulders and with hackneyed phrases, he tended to become bitter and to ask himself why he had gone through all he had. When he heard the same phrases nearly everywhere – 'We did not know about it', and 'We, too, have suffered', then he asked himself, have they really nothing better to say to me?[79]

Kluger makes almost exactly the same point about her reception.

> I used to think that after the war I would have something of interest and significance to tell. A contribution. But people didn't want to hear about it, or if they did listen, it was in

a certain pose, an attitude assumed for this special occasion; it was not as partners in a conversation, but as if I had imposed on them and they were graciously indulging me.[80]

Representing a quite different form of Jewish memory, the young pioneers of the Kibbutz Buchenwald record a similar point.

> The world, we had thought, would welcome our few survivors with open arms! We, the first victims of the Nazis. They would love us!
>
> Quickly enough, we saw that the world had other things on its mind than Jewish suffering.[81]

Other victims of the Nazis felt similarly ignored, or even discredited, after their Liberation. The insecurity of the war was simply replaced by the threat of repatriation and the insecurity of camp life. Polish, Balt and Ukrainian DPs were subjected to psychological pressures and intimidation to accept repatriation. They were torn between homesickness and fears of compulsory repatriation, and were often extraordinarily sensitive.[82] Poles were furious at the lifting of the 'non-frat' order because British soldiers immediately seemed to become very friendly with the Germans. 'We thought the British were *our* friends,' the Polish Camp Commandant told Elizabeth Bayley, 'we see their soldiers shaking Germans by the hands, walking out with German girls'.[83]

What went wrong?

First, 'planning-mindedness' could easily lead to rigid forms of over-confidence. In fact, the advice given to UNRRA and other relief agencies included some fairly accurate predictions of conditions in post-1945, but nearly always two points were ignored: the sheer quantity of homeless peoples, and the horrific nature of the death camps. Both points required a demanding and rapid re-thinking of conceptual categories, and the over-confident, under-resourced agencies of 1945 were simply incapable of enacting this mental transformation. Instead, there was a slow, difficult and often reluctant awakening to the realities of the Nazi destructiveness. This took place within a curiously competitive environment, in which almost all sections of European society felt that they had a right to special recognition for their suffering. There was therefore a common annoyance that Displaced Persons in general, and death camp survivors in particular, produced such powerful presentations of their cases. Like Dawson, many would have preferred to not to hear such 'horror stories'.

Secondly, an important aspect of this competitive re-alignment was the re-assertion of nationalism in post-war identity politics. In France, this occurred through the magical Gaullist synthesis of resistance, republicanism and patriotism, which created a new, strangely unified and firmly progressive national identity. In Britain, an equally surprising synthesis managed to combine imperial presence, patriotic solidarity, and political continuity to produce the Labour Party victory in 1945. Americans, in a sense, had an easier task: their obvious economic well-being and their military strength produced an easy confidence in their own capacities, and often also a frustration with the bloody, vindictive and just simply outdated ideologies that festered in Europe. Such discourses set the tone for the 'hardcore' DPs who remained in the camps after the summer of 1945: in order to present their cases, in order to win, one had to belong to a successful nationalism.

DPS AND NATIONALITY

To aid agencies and relief workers, national identity initially seemed straight-forward. UNRRA and the ICRC categorized DPs according to their nationality, and the subsequent structures of DP life encouraged self-definition by nation-ality, as privileges and resources were distributed to specific national groups. Red Cross parcels, initially destined for all Prisoners of War, were given to UNRRA at the end of the hostilities and were then passed on to UN nationals only, a category which automatically excluded Germans. Quite simply, a Pole was entitled to more food than a German; a German could expect their posses-sions to be requisitioned to supply Balts with the goods they lacked.

But concepts of nationality raised complex questions. Red Cross lists which classify people as Estonians, Latvians, Lithuanians, Yugoslavs and so forth mask a more complicated situation. For example, Paul Raesch wrote to the ICRC for help in 1947. As a German who had been a political prisoner of the Nazis he saw himself as a victim of both the Gestapo and the Allied bombs.[84] Should he really have been categorized as a German and denied the privileges given to other anti-Nazis? Louis Medjeschi put forward a similar argument. He was a Yugoslav, but as a royalist he did not feel that he belonged in Tito's socialist Yugoslavia. He wanted to renounce his Yugoslav nationality and claimed an ICRC passport to enable him to create a new identity.[85] Like many DPs, he wrongly thought that the ICRC had the power to issue passports. The *Volksdeutsch* constituted another slippery category. These were German-speaking peoples from the east who had initially been welcomed into the Reich. After the war, how could one tell the difference between – for example – a Pole who had been brought into the Reich as a forced labourer and one who had come voluntarily – even willingly – to join a resurgent and prosperous Germany? In practice, young, single, Polish men were more likely to have been conscripted as forced labour by the Nazis; families were more likely to have come in voluntarily.

These categories and experiences created deep divisions between groups of DPs. In the Polish camp at Goslar, FRS workers were perplexed when DPs refused to co-operate with plans to split and re-distribute the contents of the Red Cross parcels. To the relief workers it seemed to make senses: grown men did not want dried milk powder, surely the contents of each parcel should be re-distributed according to need? But Polish men who had been forced labourers were not prepared to give anything to the children of the *Volksdeutsch* who had supported the Reich. Bayley described the scene as she outlined her plans to the assembled DPs: 'There was a deathly silence, then suddenly one man, shouted out "Polish children! We see no Polish children – only children who speak German. We will not give up anything." '.[86] Should these children be categorized as Polish? According to the regulations they were Polish but their parents had acted as Germans.

Even within national or ethnic groups, DPs had very different wartime experiences. Among Jewish DPs, some had survived the concentration camps, others had got into hiding, some had fought in underground organizations, while the largest number had survived in the Soviet Union. Among Ukrainians, members of the intelligentsia who had fled the Soviet Union during the war rubbed shoulders with those who had fought on the Soviet side, combatants who had joined German armies, collaborators with the German occupation forces and conscripted labourers who chose to stay in Germany in 1945.[87] Relief workers soon realized that defining DPs was more difficult than they had originally imagined. McNeill wondered: who were the real DPs? Was it the elderly Frenchman who had been in hospital when the west-bound transports left, and was now stranded? The French government had declared that anyone who had failed to return by August 1945 would be considered as a traitor – what should be done with this man? What about the Polish woman whose divorced husband was a Hungarian and whose original home was now in Russian territory? And what should be done with an industrious and energetic White Ruthenian? He had found work which necessitated him living in rooms outside the camp. As a result he was deprived of his Red Cross parcel while his 'bone-lazy fellow countryman idling in a camp' received one regularly.[88]

PROTESTS, INITIATIVES AND NATIONAL RESURGENCE

DPs were in a poor position to articulate a political case. For many, the war years had been marked by subterfuge and silence. Aharon Appelfeld, who escaped from a ghetto to live underground in the Ukraine, was quite explicit about this point.

> We didn't speak much during the war. It was as though every disaster defied utterance: there was nothing to say. Anyone who was in the ghetto, in the camp, or hiding in the forests knows silence in his body. In time of war you don't argue, you don't sharpen differences of opinion. War is a hothouse for listening and for keeping silent. The hunger for bread, the thirst for water, the fear of death – all these make words superfluous. There's really no need for them. In the ghetto and in the camp, only people who had lost their minds talked, explained, or tried to explain. Those who were sane didn't speak…
>
> During the war, words had less currency than faces and hands … Words did not help you understand. The senses were what provided you with correct information…. The greater the suffering and the more intense the feelings of despair, the more superfluous words become.[89]

His thoughts are echoed in many other accounts. An obvious point emerges here: the simple difference between DP wartime experiences and those of the relief workers. British and American relief workers had been able to hear debate and discussion, and shared the sense of national revival, even before the defeat of Nazi Germany in May 1945. DPs were emerging from a long period of enforced silence.

Zionism – and other similar nationalist movements – could counteract some of this silencing. Leo Schwarz, an American Jewish relief worker, threw himself into collecting documents and recording the experiences of concentration camp survivors almost within days of their liberation. He was motivated by the working assumption that 'the stories of these survivors are a clue to the ultimate hidden resources in humankind'.[90] But, in a sense, their words contain their own contradictions. If Germany was the horrific past, and Palestine the glorious future, then why linger on that past? Zionists based in Palestine-Israel often showing little sympathy towards Holocaust survivors, arguing that their experiences merely confirmed the older lesson that all Jews should leave Europe. (We will return to these points in the next chapter.)

However, DPs from all national and ethnic backgrounds proved to be unexpectedly articulate. Their first actions and assertions were often provoked by the divisions among their ranks, and were expressed in their letters to international bodies. For many displaced people, it simply made no sense to be categorized by an outdated nationality. Medjeschi, the Yugoslav royalist, was one of many displaced people who wrote to the ICRC to demand stateless status and associated travel papers. Yet there was no ICRC passport and travel was impossible without the right documents. Given the importance of nationality and official papers, this was a subject which provoked much anxiety and complaint amongst DPs. This was the basis of their hatred for UNRRA screening. Initially designed to weed out 'criminals, quislings and traitors', DPs understood the process as a means to deny them both their desired nationality and basic rights, primarily the right to freedom of movement.

In other cases, DP complaints and protests were focused on more basic issues. Food was often the focus: DPs frequently complained about its quality, quantity and distribution.[91] They protested about communal dining-rooms, for they wanted to cook meals in their own space with their own families. This was partly cultural – it reinforced the family group over the wider camp identity – and also partly about trust. In particular DPs wanted to feed their own children and not leave them to the vagaries of any communal plan. In McNeill's words, they all had an 'insane suspicion' of communal feeding.[92] It was also a question of individual liberty. McNeill criticized Polish DPs for using all their rations to make 'one delicious meal a week'. Once they had eaten that they had to manage on pea soup until the next supply of rations arrived.[93] Similarly Bayley complained that when the Poles received their Red Cross parcels they were likely to make themselves ill 'by gobbling the lot at once!'.[94] Yet why not eat all the best food at once? What seemed irrational may have been a way of making a treat, of creating a brief moment of abundance.

The most striking protests were when DPs refused food. Some who were cutting timber in the British zones refused to take the hot soup UNRRA workers had prepared for them. The ingredients for the soup had been taken from their general rations and they were worried that all the deducted food had not made its way into the soup. In addition, they just wanted soup cooked by their own wives in their own quarters.[95] For UNRRA workers it was inconceivable that hungry men labouring in the cold would refuse food; the men's refusal suggested the DPs' over-riding sense of their own dignity and autonomy. Even more striking was the Baltic DPs' hunger strike, held during the conference of Foreign Ministers in Moscow on 11 March 1947. Representatives of the Baltic States – Estonia, Latvia and Lithuania – wanted to assert their rights to independence at this conference, but had been denied the opportunity to do so. In response, Baltic DPs declared a hunger strike in protest.[96] In some ways the gesture was a futile one as the Baltic States remained under Soviet control, yet the determination to make a political point was striking.

Officially DPs were better fed than the local German population – many of whom had to exist on less than 2,000 calories a day in the years immediately after the war – but DPs were not easily able to supplement their rations. Urban Germans with friends and family in the countryside could barter for extra milk, meat, vegetables or eggs. DPs did not have these contacts and so slaughtered any cows, pigs, or sheep that they could find.[97] This was clearly criminal, but even some military authorities were surprisingly sympathetic to the DPs' plight. 'Have you ever seen a DP's daily rations set out on a plate?' asked Alexander Gemmel, Head of the Military Police in the Goslar area, 'If so, you wouldn't blame them for stealing a pig or two'.[98]

Most DPs also traded on the black market, and used the cigarettes from their rations as a common currency for such deals. Observing their activities, American Zionist sympathizer Marie Syrkin concluded that they were 'about as nefarious as the housewifely expeditions of my neighbourhood'. She saw one DP selling a bottle of wine, and talked to her. The woman explained 'My child doesn't need wine. She needs milk'.[99] Such black market transactions were usually driven by need, as DP camps often lacked vegetables, sugar, footwear, clothing and soap.[100] This also explains why DPs so valued Red Cross parcels: they contained the cigarettes and coffee which could be traded for vegetables or goods. In Landeck, Camp Director Maltby faced this awkward issue.

> The father of a family seeing his children in need of shoes – and they nearly all are – will use his cigarettes to get them if he can. I don't blame him, I would shake him by the hand and blame myself for putting him in such a position where he had to make a 'shady' transaction'.[101]

DPs also used the black market to buy luxuries. Aino, a young Estonian DP swapped all her Red Cross coffee for evening shoes.[102] Was she being frivolous? On the other hand, owning something special was good for morale: it indicated that life was no longer just about bare survival. These sorts of purchases also stimulated the development of a market economy. There was a vibrant market in the UNRRA camp at Wildflecken, and some DPs made a very good living as black marketeers.[103]

DPs and relief workers both lived in a world in which survival by irregular means was applauded. McNeill – a strictly law-abiding citizen – thought of Polish looting as an expression of 'the dash and the courage that won them such glory in the RAF and in the army'.[104] Harry Heath similarly reported on the celebration of 45 Polish DP marriages.

> On the following Saturday an American R.C. priest performed the ceremonies for 45 marriages within two hours. The fact that probably everything in the church including the altar and the bridal gowns (but excepting the parson's surplice) had been acquired illegally, did not affect the pleasure of any concerned or the legality of the proceedings.[105]

Even the Quakers were amused by some tales of DP criminality. Relaying some DP gossip from Vienenburg Polish camp, McNeill recounted that 'The best story of the whole evening was that of the German doctor Eckhardt being asked to a christening during which all the petrol was drained out of his car and re-sold to him at a black market price!'.[106]

In reality, much DP 'criminality' was simply the most visible sign of their surprising drive and initiative, sometimes in the most unpromising of environments. This is best illustrated by some quite minor episodes. At Vienenburg Camp the Polish women – who had previously been 'too lazy to put a stitch in the second-hand clothing' given to them, embroidered beautiful Red Shields on DPs' football shirts.[107] More significantly, a DP building team in the same camp achieved a genuinely impressive set of results, developing skills and improving DP living conditions at the same time.[108] Ukrainian DPs at Feldkirch, frustrated by the lack of medical facilities, established their own dispensary, which could hospitalize up to six patients. Between April and November 1946 they provided medical and dental care for 3,757 patients, 507 of whom had major surgical interventions such as appendectomies.[109] In Hanau, the Lithuanian doctor, a child specialist, produced his own booklet on infant care and feeding. It was translated into four languages (Lithuanian, Latvian, Estonian and German) and given to all mothers of the camp.[110] In Spittal, in the British zone of Austria, DPs created an 'Agricultural and Gardening Committee' in November 1945 in order to grow their own vegetables. By June 1946, the total acreage under cultivation was approximately 10 acres.[111] During the latter half of 1945, about 1,200 Armenians living near Stuttgart petitioned for the creation of their own camp. Once successful, they created their own educational and work programmes.

Nine Armenian professors have organized a complete educational program for the 150 children, and a full set of cultural activities for the adults. All the children are learning English. Under the guidance of the elected leader there are health, recreation, welfare, cultural and educational committees functioning ... There is a security force of 32 men.

Their leader has realised the importance of each person's having something to do and has laid down the rule that every able-bodied person in the center must do a minimum of 10 hours work a week, apart from the individual work he must do to keep his own part of the barracks clean and tidy ... When the Armenians originally arrived, they found the barracks were badly damaged but repair squads were organized and the necessary work was put in hand at once.[112]

In other camps, DPs' priority was to recreate places of worship. On 3 May 1945, a group of Polish DPs organized a ceremony to unveil a church in the Hanau camp. The UNRRA Director noted:

In the Polish Camp a large disused stable was fitted out as a church. Young fir trees were cut and placed in order of size against the end wall. A low platform was covered with red imitation leather on which a table, completely covered with white material trimmed with red, served as an altar. Flowers in pots were lined along the back of the altar and along the back of the platform while seven white opaque electric lamps were suspended like large white moons over the altar. The effect was extraordinarily beautiful and on the 3rd May the Poles in the camp attended their first free religious ceremony since their country was overrun in 1939. The church was packed with men and women who, overcome with emotion, sang their own Polish hymns with the tears streaming down their faces.[113]

May 3 was Constitution Day, a significant date in Polish history commemorating the 1791 constitution and the creation of a liberal state. In many camps, Polish DPs celebrated this national event.[114] It became central in their 'war of symbols' with Soviet power, for it represented both their rejection of foreign repression and a commitment to democracy.

Other patriotic festivals and national celebrations punctuated DP life. In Landeck, the Polish theatre group prepared a performance for Soldiers' Day (15 August).[115] Numerous demonstrations and public meetings were also organized by Jewish DPs to express their wish to emigrate in Palestine (a point we will discuss in the next chapter). Most national celebrations incorporated religious and spiritual elements. Throughout the war, the Nazis and the Soviets had persecuted Catholic clergy and Jewish rabbis. Religious rituals recreated social bonds among DPs and enabled them to continue the traditions that the Nazis or Soviets had tried to eradicate. For most eastern Europeans, affirming their Christianity or Jewishness was also a way to affirm their difference with Communist States, thus asserting an ethnic identity and maintaining their heritage and traditional values.[116] At Spittal, in Austria, DPs produced a book describing in details their daily life, drawing attention to their religious devotion and patriotic loyalty. It praised the DPs' moral standards:

There are three Slovene choirs in the camp ... They cultivate their national and traditional songs ... Slovenes are very pious catholic people ... The Slovene priests are
endeavouring to keep the DPs on the same moral standard as they used to have in
their native country ... All these people worship the holy picture of the Virgin Mary
of Bewzje.[117]

The book was equally positive about the Croats and Serbs. The Croats had
their own priest who looked after the 'spiritual life of his people'.[118] They are
portrayed as fervent patriots. 'Serbs ... are preserving their traditional, religious
and national customs. They are worshipping their patron saint ... The Serbian
National Committee has erected a war memorial for the Serbian war prisoners
who died 1941–1945 at the cemetery of Spittal'.[119]

Commemoration of the dead and memorial services became important
occasions. They provided an opportunity for those who had lost loved ones to
join together and to share their grief. Such occasions also enabled DPs to celebrate
a common historical experience and to create a sense of continuity with their
former life. Some were obsessed with their traumatic past.[120] Despite the difficult
material conditions, almost every Jewish DP camp in Germany and Austria had
an historical commission. Jewish DPs were eager to recount their experiences
and express their loss, but were more reluctant to submit their testimonies to
a rigorous and methodological examination. Historical commissions collected
questionnaires among survivors but also among Germans and assembled an
extensive collection of thousands of photographs, folklore songs and poetry, anti-
Semitic writings and museum objects. In the American zone of Germany a total of
2,540 testimonies were collected between December 1945 and December 1948.[121]

DPs showed amazing energy in the cultural sphere. After the wartime extermination of the eastern European intelligentsia and the suppression of national
culture by the Soviets or the Nazis, the preservation of a distinct cultural
identity was seen as vital by many camp activists. DPs set up camp libraries and
reading rooms. After so many years of cultural and educational deprivation,
they were hungry for news and knowledge. Almost every camp published its
own independent DP newspaper. Given the limited resources – paper was
rationed and typewriters and other equipment were extremely difficult to find –
these achievements were quite astounding. Some newspapers were established
even before the Liberation.[122] In Munich, the DP Express was launched in July
1945.[123] It was written in seven languages and featured international news,
cartoons, poetry, chronicles about life in the camp and articles about the work
of DPs artists. While celebrating the first anniversary of the newspaper, editors
alluded to the difficulties in working with German printers.

We were compelled to have the printing job done by Germans and their willingness to
'collaborate' ... was in direct relation to American cigarettes ... We managed somehow
to appear forty-seven times, with special eight-page issues on many occasions, such as
Christmas, New Year, Easter.[124]

In Bergen-Belsen the first issue of *Unzer Sztyme* [Our Voice] appeared on 12 July 1945.[125] The editors had no typewriter with Hebrew letters and no adequate paper. The first four issues were therefore written down in longhand and duplicated.[126] Printing facilities were then quickly developed. Survivors were helped by the American Joint (JDC), which established a publishing house and printed newspapers, brochures, books, Talmud-folios and religious books. They received books from the Rothschild collection and established a library that was inaugurated officially on 8 September 1946.[127]

DPs established theatre groups and orchestras, revived traditional plays, folk songs and dances. These production often promoted an idealized vision of their country's past. In Landeck, Ukrainian DPs performed Hulak-Artemovsky's comic opera *Zaporozhets za Dunayem* describing the journey of Cossack families over the Danube after a defeat by the Russian Army in the eighteenth century. The drama showed the Cossacks seeking refuge in the Ottoman Empire, and experiencing great difficulties in adjusting to their new homes. There was, however, a happy ending: the Russians allowed the refugees to resettle in Ukraine, on Imperial Russian land. The connection between the Cossacks' experience and the DPs' lives is obvious; the opera's leaflet explained: 'The composer shows the valiant Ukrainian heroes who, gathered in a foreign country, are homesick and sing about old exploits'.[128]

DPs' nationalism was a difficult and demanding construction. They often could not identify with the existing regimes that dominated their nations, so they built an imaginary and idealized vision of their country, celebrating 'their old exploits'. 'Liberation itself had no more than clothed the nakedness of the survivors in garments of nationalities that no longer fitted' noted Leo Schwarz: he went on to propose Zionism as a solution but, of course, this option was not available to the majority of non-Jewish DPs.[129] They, instead, tried to create various forms of exile nationalisms. In the bleak context of camp life, this new national identity had a therapeutic function: it gave the DPs a sense of belonging and continuity after the disruption of their wartime experience.[130] National drama and music was a form of catharsis. DPs expressed their rage, anger and fears through these narratives. Pinson noted:

> Some of the dramatic groups have attempted to do classic pieces of the dramatic reper-
> toire … In most cases, however, the performances are more in the nature of revues
> dealing with ghetto … enabling the spectators to relive their gruesome experiences all
> over again. Even where a classic story is taken, as in Peretz's *Drei Matones,* it is freely
> adapted and 'made actual' by resetting it in the stage of ghetto and *kotzet*.[131]

Ukrainian folk songs and dances brightened up each national holiday.[132] At Christmas, they sang Kolyadki, traditional up-beat songs. In July 1946, the Landeck's Ukrainian committee reported on their accomplishments in the previous year. Alongside the establishment of schools and vocational training, they had successfully run a daily newspaper. Their theatre group had staged

123 performances (of which 35 were for the American and French troops), the camp orchestra had presented 14 large-scale concerts, Ukrainian authors and poets had organized 4 literary evenings, 4 exhibitions of Ukrainian art had been set up (including embroidery, sewing, children's pictures and sculpture), 22 popular or scientific lectures had been given and the camp had hosted the Ukrainian Scientific Congress in December 1945.[133] Preserving their traditions and folklore was a major task for the communities in exile. This quantity and diversity of publications and cultural products is impressive, and provoked George G. Grabowicz to speak of a 'small renaissance' of Ukrainian literary life in DP camps, with over 1,200 books and pamphlets published by DPs in less than 3 years.[134] Similar observations could be made about Polish DPs: by 1947, they had published approximately 360 books.[135]

DPs' Committees were also highly active in developing recreational facilities. Sporting events attracted much attention and were firmly encouraged by camp leaders and UNRRA welfare officers. They presented a major opportunity in the process of rehabilitation, enabling DPs to regain their physical strength, providing an outlet for the energy of people forced to spend their days in idleness and allowing them to overcome the stigma of their 'alleged' weakness. In Hanau, each nationality had its own sport committees. International games were held regularly. DPs played basketball, volleyball, football, boxing, table tennis, tennis and chess.[136] Scouting organizations were also revived. In Hanau, 55 tents were set up in the neighbouring forests, accommodating 143 girls and 180 boys.[137]

DPs focused much of their attention on the children in the camps. Although there was a near-total lack of teaching equipment, DPs still created schools very soon after the liberation. These gradually developed into an effective educational system. Schools were an important priority for the DPs because children had often received no systematic schooling during the war, and because they served to transmit national values, enabling DPs to recreate their identity. Children were expected to know their national language, history, traditions and to adopt patriotic attitudes toward the homeland of their parents. In Polish DPs' school, programmes replicated pre-war Polish syllabuses. Teachers paid special attention to patriotic messages.[138] Their curriculum included the Polish language, Polish literature, Polish history and geography, and tried to awaken their pupils' love for their country. DP committees also provided vocational training for adults and sponsored workshops, offering a wide range of topics, including mechanics, technical drawing, commerce, dressmaking, carpentry, lock-making and agriculture.[139] DPs organized exhibitions to present their work to local communities. At Lienz, in Austria, the UNRRA director reported proudly that 'some thousands of people visited the camp exhibition which was held in the town of Lienz'. In this exhibition were presented different kinds of goods manufactured by the DPs: lace, embroidery, clothing, leather goods, toys and carpets.[140]

UNRRA had mixed views about such initiatives. On the one hand, they facilitated the moral rehabilitation of DPs, providing a sense of belonging and of purpose, and creating a continuity with their destroyed communities and former ways of life.[141] On the other hand, such activities could become an obstacle to the orderly process of repatriation. UNRRA tightly controlled newspapers published within the camps, and on several occasions threatened to ban them. There is no doubt that many DP initiatives were aimed at avoiding forced repatriation. The Soviet repatriation campaign was a forceful operation and DPs were subjected to intimidation and pressures. Forming Committees, distributing pamphlets and illegal leaflets and creating political parties were the only means for them to gain some protection and recognition.[142]

DPS AND RELIEF WORKERS

Josef Betari, a convinced Zionist who reluctantly returned to Poland early in 1948, lived in the Freimann DP camp, near Munich, in 1947. He observed the 'motley crowd of strange people' around him: 'Chinese dance with Rumanians. A Pole flirts with a Hungarian, a Turk has a date with a Ukrainian'.[143] Among a population as varied as the multi-ethnic, pluri-linguistic, rapidly national-ising and variously traumatized DPs, there was no single, unified cultural community. The single point which held them together was, in reality, not their experiences, attitudes or hopes, but the administration which attempted to organize their camps.

Their first meetings with UNRRA and other relief agencies, occurring weeks after the first wild hopes of liberation, usually lacked passion.[144] Betari's downbeat cynicism is probably quite typical. 'An institution identified by five letters feeds us and cares for our needs. They have ascertained the number of calories that will make us feel good and the quantity of vitamins that will enable us to maintain our physical condition'.[145] Many grew irritated with Aunty UNRRA and the endless disputes over food, clothes and shelter.[146] This common irritation could form one of the few bonds between the various DP nationalities and ethnicities: Hungarian Jewish exile Magda Denes smiled when she observed the registration process on her arrival in Austria. They were inter-viewed by small teams of three or four people, representing the American Army and UNRRA. The interviewers would try to trick the interviewees by their use of Hungarian phrases, in an attempt to prove that they were not genuine DPs. On the other hand, 'DPs of all nationalities exchanged stories of these tricks, because at last and yet again, we had a common enemy: our rescuers'.[147] Later, in Paris, Denes waited in a distribution centre run by the JDC, and asked herself how it was that she could so easily identify who were the DPs and who the relief workers.

> I watched the officials and marvelled with envy at how easily they could be picked out even when they stood at the centre of the crowd. What made them so different, so unmistakably non-DP? Their clothes, yes, but that was the lesser factor. Some of

the DPs were already wearing American used clothes and were, therefore, not all that differently attired. What then? The lack of despair on their faces. Their carriage. The knowledge they emanated that they belonged in the world. DPs, in contrast, were furtive as mice, wary as beaten dogs, watchful and savage as hungry wolves, sly as foxes. Yes, that was the difference. DPs had been hammered and diminished to an in-between species on the kingdom. They didn't even speak a common language other than tears.[148]

These simple, almost emotionless phrases suggest the deep failure of UNRRA's project. Relief workers might command respect, and – as their records testify – they were often lobbied by countless desperate DPs looking for contacts and channels that could take them out of the miserable camps to the more prosperous countries of the western world. But one hears few expressions of friendship towards them.

Given the choice, DPs preferred to avoid the camps. When Yugoslavian Jew Irene Grünbaum managed to wangle her way into Italy in 1945, she worried that she might be sent to a DP camp.

> It was something I was afraid of – I knew that my physical well-being would be attended to there, but that wasn't what worried me. I could endure hunger and bad living conditions but not the restrictions of my freedom. I feared stagnation and the decline of my energy and vitality. The war was over. I didn't want to go back. I wanted to go forward, I wanted to work, I wanted to make up for all the years I had missed. I couldn't just stay idle again and wait around for what would happen to me.[149]

These criticisms are frustrating. UNRRA's field workers were well aware of the shortcomings of their organization's relief policies. They worked hard to alleviate them: they encouraged the creation of schools, recreation facilities, construction projects and work schemes to bring hope and energy into the DPs' lives. Relief workers certainly could console themselves with specific examples of particular individuals, families or groups with whom they had build up meaningful contact and even friendship. The UNRRA leadership itself showed some sensitivity to such questions, and even its ambiguous slogan 'helping the people to help themselves' suggested a respect for democratic and participatory values. But the camps remained miserable, meaningless and hopeless places, for the criteria for success was being set elsewhere: only viable nationhoods could guarantee triumph in the post-war world, and UNRRA's ersatz internationalism was no substitute for this prize.

CONCLUSION

There are clearly two means by which one could judge the success or failure of the DP camps. On the one hand, one can find images which suggest that they were buzzing with energy, from carpenters' shops to operatic concerts, from religious instruction to needlework classes: these are testimony to the abilities of both relief workers and DP activists. They show that 'DP apathy' was not inevitable, and that even among the most traumatized there was still a potential to revive and re-organize lives.

On the other hand, the camps had been set two goals: relief and rehabilitation. From the evidence surveyed in this chapter, we are drawn to conclude that while UNRRA and agencies organized relief reasonably successfully, rehabilitation was too difficult a goal, and – worse still – the technocratic, planning-minded structures that were so admired by UNRRA's organizers may well have actually obstructed relief workers in fulfilling these goals. Certainly, the unmistakable note of frustration that one finds repeatedly in its most dedicated workers' records suggest some form of internal failure. The emotional and psychological demands on them were intense and it is no surprise that these ill-prepared relief workers were unable to transform UNRRA's ideals into reality.

8

Other Paths: Returning to Nationhood

- Returning to Poland
- 'Returning' to Israel
- Conclusion

On 9 May 1945 the right-leaning Independent MP Austin Hopkinson asked a question in the House of Commons. 'In view of the defeat of Germany, is there any earthly reason why all German Jews should not now live in Germany?'.[1] It was a revealing comment, indicating the extent to which a strand of polite, orderly anti-Semitism survived in Britain during the Second World War: Hopkinson was certain that German Jewish refugees should not stay. But this is also an intervention in which Hopkinson's naive question illustrated the true nature of Allied policy. The rationale beneath the concept of the 'displaced person' was that their homelessness could be simply and neatly solved by their 're-placement' in their nations. As we have seen, for many this was true: the majority of DPs were shunted back to their places in 1945. Why was this so difficult for a minority? And what does this minority experience tell us about the manner in which refugees were treated after the Second World War?

In this chapter we will be examining a strange political consensus. Liberal patriots, progressive Zionists and Nazi sympathizers all accepted one basic principle: Jews should leave Europe. The slogan which briefly circulated among a confused but still vigorous French far right – 'France for the French, Jews to Palestine!' – is typical of this moment.[2] Indeed, this thesis seemed so obvious, that the only prominent source of opposition to it came from defenders of the British colonial presence in Palestine who – in a cautious, partial and opportunistic manner – rehearsed concepts of ethnically blind societies, in which one's sense of origin was of no political importance. Paradoxically, at times their ideas even echoed some of the most idealistic examples of UNRRA's internationalism. Yet such arguments were rare: Christopher Caldwell's recent polemical work, *Reflections of the Revolution in Europe*, turns history on its head by proposing 1945 as the beginning of the cultural hegemony of a guilt-stricken liberal multiculturalism.[3] Pieter Lagrou's analysis of the years after 1945 is clearly closer to reality: this was a period dominated by the 'imposition of a mono-cultural society', creating 'an exceptional period of frightening ethnic homogeneity'.[4] By 1945, world public opinion condemned the violence inherent in Nazism, but still retained a clear sympathy for the 'boundary-keeping urge' that was its basis.[5] 'Nationalism is the air which we breathe' observed the newly elected Richard Crossman.[6] In this period, 'internationalism' was not normally a contrary to nationalism, but rather understood as a structure through which established nation states could inter-relate to each other. UNRRA's priorities reflected such principles. Once the immediate need for relief had been satisfied, UNRRA aimed to encourage the 're-placement' of the displaced through their repatriation. 'Our first aim remains to encourage as many as possible of the Displaced Persons to accept repatriation' noted the Foreign Office in 1946;[7] 'Repatriation is the best solution', repeated an IRO report in 1947.[8] It was certainly the priority for UNRRA in 1946–47.

These easy assumptions concerning homogeneous nations as the basic building blocks of a future society caused problems for the DPs we studied in the previous chapter. If these people were to have a viable future in the emerging global structure, then they had to belong to a nation. Their wartime experiences, however, had largely taught them that they belonged to no nation. The new, swiftly constructed national narratives of European states centred on 'an exclusive patriotic interpretation of the veteran'.[9] The fugitives, forced labourers, refugees and concentration camp survivors were generally judged to be inglorious: where was their heroism? They had not fought. The response of people like DPs, rather than challenging the conceptual basis of this new heroic patriotism, was to attempt to re-position themselves through the creation of their own patriotism. Their efforts only achieved a partial success. Morgan's anger at the 'artificial' movement of Jews out of Poland in 1945–46, and Dawson's irritation at 'their horrors' are both echoes of the same argument: that the DPs' patriotism was not an authentic culture.

The chapter will discuss the experiences of post-Holocaust Jews. In citing them, we cross another boundary, for our intention is not to write Jewish history, but rather to cite a Jewish experience as illuminating a more general European – even global – experience. We place this Jewish experience next to the similar experience of Polish patriots, who faced an agonizing decision about the location of their nation. Both groups presented UNRRA and other relief agencies with unexpected dilemmas.

RETURNING TO POLAND

In 1945, Poland was a nation with an identity crisis. To some extent, this was a long-standing debate, which continues to this day. Was Poland part of the 'East' or the 'West'? Several factors in the months after the war made this debate more agonizing and acute. First, particularly for British and French commentators, Poland had a type of 'special status': it has been in order to save Poland from Nazi invasion that Britain and France had gone to war in September 1939, and for three weeks, as Warsaw was besieged, Poland had grabbed international attention in the same manner as 'plucky little Belgium' had during 1914. Following the collapse of Poland, about 100,000 Poles escaped to French-controlled Syria, and about 80,000 managed to reach Britain.[10] Some 23,000 enrolled in British military units, and henceforth were of immense symbolic importance, providing a clear and newsworthy representation of the survival of a non-Nazi Europe after 1939.[11] Those who stayed in Poland faced brutality almost immediately: Nazi policy was to use exclusion, mass terror and executions to ensure that Poles would be replaced by Germans.[12] In May 1945, nearly 1.9 million citizens of pre-war Poland were in Germany. About 1.2 million were in the western zones and some 700,000 in the Soviet Zone; 90% of them had been slave labourers.[13] If the fate of Poland had provided the spark that began the war for Britain and France, then it seemed vital in 1945 that this country should not just be restored to its former condition, but that it should provide an unequivocal and successful example of liberal and democratic values.

A second reason for Poland's special status, less prominently acknowledged by British and French commentators, was that Warsaw had been site of Europe's largest Jewish community in 1939, housing about 400,000.[14] Nazi policies of ghetto-ization increased the numbers of Jews in the city to almost half a million in 1941; numbers then fell as death camps were established. By October 1942, fewer than 60,000 remained.[15] The ghetto rising of April and May 1943 provided a brief, iridescent example of tragic heroism, but did not stop the murderous progress of the Holocaust. Ruth Kluger's brief musings on the fate of her father sums up their deaths in the simplest and starkest possible terms: he 'was made to breathe poison in a cramped room full of people'.[16] While about 5% of Polish society was killed during the Second World War, about 95% of Poland's Jewish community did not survive.[17] If Europe was to be restored to anything resembling 'normality', then some means was needed to mark both the previous presence and the actual absence of this community.[18]

However, not all Polish Jews were killed in the Holocaust. Between 50,000 and 60,000 managed to survive in hiding in Poland during the war; another third of a million took refuge in the Soviet Union.[19] There, they were treated harshly: anti-Semitism and anti-Polish prejudice flourished during the Second World War, and there was a permanent suspicion of these unwelcome newcomers, doubly condemned as Poles and as Jews. In 1939–41, Soviet rulers cooperated with the Nazis in the dismantling of Poland.[20] Yet, for all these hardships, this substantial section of Polish Jewry survived, and looked to return to their homes in 1945.

They then faced the question hanging over Poland in 1945: where was it? Who represented it? A London-based committee of Polish patriots had created a government-in-exile in 1942; it was shunned by the advancing Red Army, and Soviet politicians assisted the creation of a second committee to represent a future Poland. Henceforth, there was a bitter rivalry between the 'London Poles' and the 'Warsaw Poles'. Furthermore, Poland's borders changed after the international conference at Yalta in February 1945. The Soviet priority at this moment was not so much the implementation of Communist rule in Poland, as a guarantee of Soviet military security. One result of this policy was a re-drawing of Poland's borders. While the Soviet Union kept much of the land it had seized in the east of the pre-1939 Poland, the post-1945 Poland was extended into ex-German land: in effect, the nation had been pushed westwards.

UNRRA workers became aware of the importance of European politics in their camps. New American recruits, in particular, had tended to think of 'Europe' as forming a single mass. They soon had to come with terms with a more complex reality. On her first day in Munich Susan Pettiss learned that there were 1,322 DPs in her camp. These were then sub-divided into separate national groups.

> Yugoslav – 75, Polish – 188, Russian – 210, Greek – 13, French – 347, Ukrainian – 60, Belgian – 27, Austrian – 3, Hungarian – 66, Czech – 32, Turkish – 42, Danish – 3, Spanish – 3, Lithuanian – 3, Roumanian – 14, Italian – 4, Latvian – 11, Miscellaneous – 57.[21]

Pettiss was honest enough to record her confusion: she knew little of European geography or history. She therefore failed to see the political considerations that played a part even in the formation of these apparently simple lists. One notices, for example, that no one was categorized as 'Jewish'. Was this because there were no Jews in Pettiss's camp? Or were Jewish DPs subsumed within existing national categories? Other difficult questions were suggested by such lists: who was really Polish? One British Ministry of Labour official complained that Poles had been 'getting through' the screening system for the Westward Ho work placement scheme by pretending to be Ukrainian and so fraudulently entering Britain. As Margaret McNeill acknowledged, it was 'extremely hard' to distinguish between Poles and Polish Ukrainians.[22]

Poles quickly attracted the attention of relief workers. By 1946, after the relatively rapid departure of west Europeans and Russians, they formed the largest national category among the remaining DPs. One official estimate calculated that there were 639,684 DPs in UNRRA care in Germany in December 1946: of these 236,630 (37%) were Poles.[23] UNRRA workers noted their intense religiosity. In Dawson's camp in July 1945, once an altar had been constructed in an open-air area previously used for dances, Polish DPs gathered flowers and candles with which to decorate it, and then held a simple service. Dawson was moved by this spectacle.[24] McNeill observed something similar:

> A scene which provided ample evidence of Polish piety and Polish industry. Many hours of work must have been put into those decorations. The open walls were entirely filled in with young silver birch saplings … the altar was covered with a spotless white cloth; and before it, above it, and on every side of it, were flowers: flowers crammed into vases, flowers tucked behind the picture of the Virgin of Czestichowa, flowers framing the shield bearing the white eagle of Poland.[25]

Duchesne-Cripps was struck by the Poles' national feelings, which she hesitated to categorize as 'patriotism'. 'I was conscious rather in them of a personal love for their country, together with the wish to renew as soon as possible their life there'.[26] Muriel Heath noted something else about the Poles which she pointed out to her husband: Polish forced labourers in Germany had been made to wear a large 'P' during the Nazi regime, similar to the infamous yellow star forced upon Jews. In the DP camps, they continued to wear this sign, now seen as a 'badge of honour'.[27] For UNRRA workers, these were all signs of hope: they suggested that rehabilitation was possible, and that even after the hardship of the war and the Nazi regime, there still existed a substantial and vigorous sense of Polish nationhood among the DPs, which would be expressed in dignified and peaceful forms. Protestant relief workers were therefore swift to admire the Catholic ceremonies improvised by Polish DPs.

At first sight, it seemed obvious that these patriotic, religious people would wish to return to their home. There was a labour shortage in Poland: this was another pressing reason to encourage repatriation. Indeed, the labour shortage was so acute that the all men and women were expected to work in Poland, and a welfare state was being constructed to aid them.[28] UNRRA circulated calls for Poles to return to their nation. Jessica Reinisch's observations are pertinent: 'The message in these instructions was clear: DPs owed it to their country to leave the relative comfort and security of the refugee camps, and to contribute, even at personal cost, to the reconstruction of the Polish state'.[29] Some responded almost immediately, but even these people felt anguish and mixed motives. They knew that there would be 'no happy confident returning'; they were simply motivated by 'a despairing urge to get home, no matter what they find there'.[30]

UNRRA workers were then puzzled and concerned to see that many Polish DPs seemed unwilling to go. McNeill considered this 'the most tragic paradox of all – the paradox of a people who could never be happy in any country but their own, yet who stayed away'.[31] For some of the harsher critics, the answer to this conundrum was to be found in the policies which UNRRA had introduced into the camps. Morgan, visiting the DP camp at Hersfeld, expressed his frustration with the moral condition of the Poles. 'One saw how almost hopeless the Pole is. These people are just sitting about and had been sitting about for months without doing anything at all, and they all made trivial complaints with regard to the food, which I thought was ample and very good'.[32] When she grew exasperated, Dawson would repeat similar sentiments. 'One would not mind if these people here were really politically inspired, but 95% of them could go home without any trouble but they are just lazy, or demoralized, or afraid of a hard life'.[33] For such critics, it seemed obvious that the DPs had become lazy and apathetic; camp life was too easy for them, and they preferred living off free handouts to hard but honest work in Poland itself.

Relief workers were, however, usually more perceptive. Dawson and Kathryn Hulme both worked in Wildflecken camp which – as Dawson noted – had the reputation of being the 'capital of Poland outside Poland'.[34] In some ways, it seemed a model camp. Arriving in March 1946, Dawson was impressed by the camp's post office, bakery, carpenters' and engineers' shops, court, gaol, kindergarten, primary and secondary schools, technical schools and adult classes, sewing room, and 600 scouts and guides.[35] To some extent, this impressive range of facilities was due to the Polish DPs' capacity for self-organization. 'Working with Poles was something like working with Jews', noted Dawson, 'their own organisation was exceedingly active'.[36] Her comment is double-edged: the organization that could support the creation of a carpenter's shop could also present UNRRA with problems. Dawson observed that the Poles were always 'busy with irresponsible but alarming rumours'.[37] McNeill observed something similar. 'No matter how wretched their present lives, the uncertainty of the future in Poland seemed to produce a kind of mental paralysis which was conveniently covered by political catchwords'.[38] How were these to be countered? Dawson noted one means: the arrival of 'a terrible Hollywood musical, all drums, girls and noise' which at least did some good for the Poles: it stopped 'them fussing about their own politics for an hour or so'.[39]

Allied authorities grew worried about DPs' apparent reluctance to return to Poland, and reports from 1946 note the disappointing levels of repatriation.[40] Some attempts were made to investigate the reasons for their reluctance: an enquiry at Wildflecken in May 1946 found that 95% of those who refused repatriation cited a political reason: Poland was 'under communism and not free'.[41] The same enquiry found little evidence that such opinions were the result of anti-repatriation propaganda from groups such as the London Poles. Wildflecken camp's Polish Committee issued a statement in January 1947: its first line read 'We do not recognize any so-called Government of Warsaw which is sent from Moscow as a communistic clique'.[42] On occasion, this issue led to tension and even violence. In January 1947, Poles at Wildflecken rioted after UNRRA introduced a compulsory screening programme: it was feared that this was a preliminary to the introduction of compulsory repatriation.[43] In May 1947, Polish DPs near Heidelberg rebelled when their chosen representative, who was sometimes critical of the repatriation programme, was dismissed by UNRRA officials.[44] However, it is important to stress that Polish DPs did not refuse categorically repatriation. 'Opposition to repatriation was often tentative and temporary' notes Anna Holian.[45] Poles were certainly less resistant to repatriation than Ukrainians, Bielorussians, Balts and, to a lesser extent, Yugoslavs. Holian argues that four factors were determinant in DP's decision whether or not to return: DP wartime and pre-war experiences, political and economic conditions in their home countries, conditions of DP life in Germany and opportunities for emigration. In the case of Polish DPs, she demonstrates that fears of persecution were not as prevalent as among Baltic DPs, but economic concerns weighed more heavily.

The apparent failure of the repatriation drive represented one of the first cracks in the new world order and – furthermore – left relief agencies with the significant problem of over a quarter of a million long-term DPs. For once, it is possible that Morgan was quite prescient about this point. As early as September 1945, he noted that 'almost everything depends on the solution of

the Poland problem'.[46] UNRRA's avowed preference for avoiding politics made
it unable to deal with the obvious and deep tensions between the London Poles
and the Warsaw Poles.[47] Morgan predicted that UNRRA would soon be left with
a hardcore of stateless, criminals and political refugees who could not be repatriated: another organization would have to be formed to deal with them. An
UNRRA report from July 1946 summarizes some of the organization's debates
about DPs who refused repatriation.

> DPs are in many cases unwilling to return to their country, because it is dominated
> by a Foreign Power. This appears now to be the principal factor against repatriation.
> Some are unable to return for fear of action being taken against them. Others, mainly
> the peasant and labouring class, will not return because of stories they have heard of
> hardships, and difficulties, some of which are true and some of which are not. Action
> taken within UNRRA's scope with regard to this factor is to investigate any anti-
> repatriation propaganda, and put right any false impressions given by means of talks
> and notices in camps; any information likely to be good propaganda for repatriation is
> also circulated: eg the work done by UNRRA in Poland; DPs are also given talks and it
> is pointed out to them that their duty to their country is to return and help rebuild it.
> Films have also been shown showing the rebuilding of Warsaw.[48]

In such reports, one sees the continuity with some of arguments considered
in the last chapter: DPs are presented as childlike and irrational. The voice of
authority is automatically assumed to be correct and accurate; the dissenting
voices of the DPs are automatically assumed to be wrong and inaccurate.
The repatriation problem was understood as a communications and propaganda problem. For agencies that followed such perspectives, the solution was
therefore to reduce contacts between Polish DPs and the London-based Polish
committee, which was discouraging repatriation, and revise and improve
repatriation propaganda.[49]

> The majority of the information sent to the refugees … does more harm than good with
> respect to repatriation.
>   We who have studied the refugee – and particularly my officers in the field – are
> quite convinced that political propaganda does not encourage the refugee to decide
> on repatriation. We hold this conviction not because we or the refugees do not agree
> with the political views expressed but because we know that the refugee does not want
> propaganda – he wants facts.
>   The refugee who is deciding on his future wants to know facts stated in the simplest
> language about conditions in his own country. Remember that he is generally a peasant
> and thinking like a peasant and may not be very literate.[50]

The measures taken in Wildflecken camp illustrate such thinking: American
newspapers were banned, as their comments on the Polish elections in January
1947 appeared to only exacerbate DPs' worries. The camp's director called for

loudspeakers, documentary films and a permanent repatriation officer.[51] 'We can crack some of these problems as soon as we receive the famous *Return to Poland* documentary, and have use of UNRRA film unit exclusively for a given period of time', he stated.[52] This sort of paternalistic perspective blinded commentators to the political dimensions of the problem, which some Polish DPs had understood far more quickly than UNRRA workers: the Soviet domination of Poland was being quickly implemented.

Creating effective propaganda for repatriation was also more difficult than some UNRRA administrators imagined. Hulme saw one example of repatriation propaganda failing spectacularly: the poster in question showed the borders of the new nation.

> The Poles clustered around the bulletin boards looking at the map of the new Poland. You could tell from their faces which ones came from east of the River Bug. Some of the women wept quietly while the men stared in disbelief too keen for comment, uttering only the names of home towns in a lost litany of sorrowful sounds … 'Lwow … Rovno … Stanislav…'.[53]

Instead of encouraging optimism in a re-born Poland, this poster made many Poles more fearful of the Soviet domination of their country. Hulme observed that those from west Poland were less likely to feel strong doubts than those from the lost provinces in the east. A Warsaw-based group circulated another publication before Christmas 1947: it presented a simple contrast between the welcome for Poles in Poland, and the terrors which threatened them in the DP camps. 'Even if they have a Christmas tree it is not our Polish Christmas tree – it does not smell with our woods. It is only an artificial decoration, even increasing their nostalgia and feelings of longing'.[54] The text went to argue that in the camps, Polish DPs faced a revival of the white slave trade, as agents circulated, selecting young girls and healthy young men for migration to other countries. Here, a simple, almost physical, national spirit is proclaimed: but the publication's stress on the horrors of the DP camps obviously could not be repeated by UNRRA.

In April 1947, UNRRA implemented another policy: all who returned to Poland were offered 60 days' worth of rations. In Wildflecken camp, this prize was laid out on tables: 94 pounds worth of flour, dried peas, oats, salt, evaporated milk, canned fish and lard.[55] Hulme and the other UNRRA workers 'watched our DPs stare at the terrible fascination of the bait, thrashing, twisting and turning before they took the hook'.[56] Across the Allied zones, the 60-day ration policy seemed to persuade few DPs. Indeed, it may have caused more resentment: one Polish publication later described it as a policy which aimed to 'purchase [the DPs'] soul for a plate of food'.[57] A later report concluded that 'the offer of rations has not justified the cost, negotiation, planning and amount of work involved'.[58] If this policy of bribery by rations did not work, what could UNRRA propose?

In these months, UNRRA workers observing the Polish DPs grew worried about the effects and implications of Allied policies. Hulme noted how depressed the Poles were looking.

> The DPs we took off incoming transports began to look the same … Their universal expression was of weariness and despair. The army was moving them around, shifting groups from camp to camp, uprooting them as soon as they had tacked up a private-room partition or strung a light bulb, giving them no chance to create a temporary home, in the hopes that maybe they might begin thinking of their real home in Poland and go there, if for no other reason than for the peace of staying put. It looked like a cruel and senseless scheme to break the deadlock, but no voice outside our tight and teeming Occupation world spoke up with a better solution or, for that matter, with any mention at all of the displaced – as if, at war's end, all that dreary and embarrassing refugee business had ended too.[59]

If the Poles would not go back to Poland, then what was to become of them? Hulme was concerned when she heard rumours from her fellow relief workers that forced repatriation would be introduced soon.[60] Dawson clearly felt the same concerns. 'The policy so far was not to encourage people either to stay or to return. We had at that time, to be absolutely non-committal. UNRRA had undertaken that force would never be used in sending DPs home, and at that time, persuasion was not expected of them either.'[61] On the other hand, the stifling of contacts with the London Poles, and the circulation of pro-repatriation propaganda was starting to look like some form of political choice by UNRRA. The new priority was repatriation, which was to be given precedence over welfare. 'We've paid for you long enough, now get out' summarized Dawson.[62]

UNRRA, other relief agencies and Allied authorities understood resistance to repatriation as a communications and propaganda issue, which perhaps reflected a deeper moral malaise in the camps. Such concerns meant that they ignored other vital practical issues, and often failed to consider how the process of repatriation might appear to Polish DPs. One can better understand the DPs' concerns by examining, in detail, the manner in which they were returned to Poland. The journey was arduous and undignified. At first sight, this might puzzle twenty-first-century readers: what could be so awful about a train journey from Germany to Poland? Dawson's accounts of her August 1946 and October 1946 journeys to Poland with – respectively – 491 and 793 DPs from Wildflecken camp provide an illuminating insight into the conditions. On both occasions, she had to be ordered to go. She was apprehensive from the start, noting the possible dangers: 'terror, arrest, rheumatism, discomfort'.[63] Her 'heart sank; there is the nervous strain about box-car travel even in summer, which I felt would be intolerable in the pouring wet autumn. The dirt, the noise and shaking'.[64] The usual 'Snafus' continued: in August, when the train finally arrived, it was shorter than expected: instead of 40 carriages, there were only 28. Predictably, there were delays while they waited for the right engine to be connected, and in October the train left four hours late.

Worse still, these were not neat carriages with comfortable seats for passengers: Poles were expected to go back in bare boxcars, with only straw to cushion them from the frequent bumps. Dawson commented ironically 'were it not for the filth, smuts, grit and dust, our box-car would be quite agreeable'.[65] By October she knew exactly what she had to do: choose the most comfortable and strongest boxcars for the UNRRA personnel, rations and soldiers, and at all costs avoid wagons which had carried horses or potatoes. UNRRA personnel distributed stoves, beds, blankets, candles, lanterns, cards and games along the train. Buckets were placed in the boxcars to be used as toilets: there was only one two-seater latrine for the entire convoy. UNRRA workers attempted to repair the roofs of some of the wagons. On the second trip, two wagons were simply unusable. These were left behind: the Polish repatriants immediately stripped them for wood for their stoves. Dawson took some books with her, but 'it is almost impossible to write and difficult to read on account of the shaking'.[66] She banged nails in her wagon, so that goods could be hung from the walls. In October, she also realized too late that one mistake had been made: the children were placed in the wettest wagon of all. A Catholic Mission came with them, and Dawson was ashamed to see that these volunteer relief workers were quick to spot some vulnerable DPs that the UNRRA team had missed.[67]

The moment of leaving was perhaps the one dignified moment of the entire expedition. Carriages were decorated with chalk slogans, flowers and leaves, and even a few Polish flags. The camp orchestra played as they left, and the remaining DPs and UNRRA workers waved as the train pulled out. Dawson tried to make herself comfortable in her bed, but even with light from three candles, she was unable to read.[68] It was also impossible to sleep: the shaking, rattling and rumbles kept her awake. 'Every stop and start throughout the night was accompanied by a cataclysm of jerks and shuddering'.[69] Throughout the trip, there were long and unpredictable stops: each time, the repatriants would rush for open countryside, searching for space to use as toilets. During the longer stops, they would bake potatoes in ashes. When the train was finally about to start again, they would be warned by a long blast of its whistle, at which point the most alert DPs would hang onto something: the hospital car filled up with people who had been thrown against a wall or a stove by an unexpected jolt.[70] When the train reached Prague, there was a brief flurry of bartering. Cigarettes were swapped for schnapps, silk stockings, underwear and baby clothes. Dawson herself wanted cheese, but found she had to pay for this in cash. There was then a long delay at the Czech–Polish border, and Dawson looked round at the rubbish left from previous trains.

> The ground was covered with greasy black mud, the tracks were filthy, there was
> evidence of enormous numbers of people everywhere, in the rubbish, the trodden mud,

the crowds sitting along the tracks, the tents full of baggage, the people milling around the hutments of the camp itself, and sitting everywhere waiting for trains.[71]

The one bright spot was a shop, in which Dawson bought saucepans, account books, teapots, scissors, crêpe paper, hair pins, combs and a thimble – a list which forms an interesting commentary on the shortages in Wildflecken camp, and shows the extent to which 'scrounging' was still necessary in 1946. 'To my shop-starved eyes it seemed wonderful.'[72]

On the return journey, the train took Germans back from Poland: Dawson noted what little enthusiasm they showed for this 'return'.[73] After a 12-day round trip, she returned to Wildflecken. 'I am frightfully tired and aching all over from the trip to Poland, and am not clean yet.'[74] Dawson's experience was not exceptional, and in December 1946 new UNRRA regulations attempted to lessen the over-crowding and discomfort of such journeys. But it is hard not to agree with Dawson's conclusion about the process. 'I am constantly surprised how badly people do things. They did not send the train in time, they made mistakes in the travel orders, they make absurd rules at the last minute.'[75] One could say that this was just one uncomfortable journey for one middle-aged woman but, on the other hand, there are aspects of this experience which say something more general about the nature of UNRRA, about all the relief agencies and the Allied occupation. The 'human touch' was missing: even the basic point about expecting vulnerable people to travel in wagons designed for the transportation of horses or potatoes seems to have been ignored. Polish workers had been taken out of Poland by the Nazis in boxcars, and they were returned to their country in the same manner. Predictably, the remaining Polish DPs felt frustrated by UNRRA's perfor-mance. One Polish publication from June 1947, reviewing the end of UNRRA and its replacement by IRO, spoke of their 'mixed sentiments of gratitude for the help it has rendered, as well as of disillusionment and deep disappointment which has been ours in dealing with the general policy of the organisation'.[76] While UNRRA had certainly fed them, it had not given them freedom.

The case of the Polish DPs presents a paradox. At first sight, they presented many signs of a successful rehabilitation: they were quick to organize religious services, national ceremonies, and camp facilities, and often keen to cooperate with UNRRA. But it was precisely this reviving spirit of national self-assertion which then conflicted radically with the policies which the Allied authorities set for UNRRA. Relief agencies seemed singularly incompetent in appreciating the quite understandable worries and fears of the DPs, and far too quick to rely on technocratic solutions for human problems.

'RETURNING' TO ISRAEL

In the strict sense of the word, there were very few Jewish Holocaust survivors in Europe in 1945. Some belated changes in Nazi policy enabled a few to survive the Holocaust's violence: in some cases, Jews were valued as specialist workers (as happened to Primo Levi), in others, Nazis calculated that they could be valuable as hostages or bargaining chips in end-of-war negotiations (as happened at Bergen-Belsen). The overall picture, nevertheless, is clear: the Holocaust killed millions of people with an industrial efficiency previously unseen in world history. While any statistics on this question can only be understood as approximations, no serious scholar would dispute the picture cited in Barbara Engelking's research: in May 1945 there were some 300,000 Polish Jews in the Soviet Union, 50–60,000 Jews in Poland itself, of which only about 800 were actual survivors from the death camps.[77] Gerard Cohen suggests that 50–60,000 Jews were found alive in all the concentration camps liberated by the Allies.[78] The numbers of Jews present in Germany then rose in the succeeding months: by October 1946 156,705 Jews were registered in Germany, and about 71 per cent of them lived in organized DP camps.[79]

In a looser, more metaphorical sense, the Jews who remained in Europe after 1945 could all be considered as Holocaust survivors. They had lived through six years, sometimes even twelve years, of dreadful fear and devastating hardship; they could each cite the tragic fate of close family members, friends and neighbours. This experience changed their lives. Tracing that process of identity change is difficult, and is often occluded in historical narratives. The independent, Zionist-sympathizing American journalist I. F. Stone cites an apparently clear example of a 22-year-old woman he interviewed in 1946. 'I was never a Jew before the war. But now that six million Jews have been killed, I will be a Jew too'.[80] French Jew Jacqueline Mesnil-Amar talks more obliquely about the mysterious process by which 'they made us into Jews, slowly, externally ... we, who had so firmly forgotten this'.[81] Like the political cultures of the dissident, anti-Warsaw Poles, post-war European Jewishness was a new identity, created rapidly, under the pressures of the immediate context. To the militants of the transformation, the Zionist activists who arrived in Europe in 1945 and 1946, it was a natural, inevitable process, akin to a necessary and belated coming of age of a naive diasporic generation. To the process's most ardent critics, the defenders of the British presence in Palestine, this was, on the contrary, an artificial, politically manipulated movement, which distorted the natural contours of European identity. We will debate these issues in the pages below.

The presence of post-Holocaust Jews in Europe became a serious issue as the months went by. While other groups left DP camps in Germany, Jews fled from eastern Europe *into* German DP camps. In December 1945, approximately 10% of the DPs were Jewish; by December 1947 the proportion had risen to 25%.[82] An UNRRA survey of 127,000 Jews in the American zone of Germany in November 1946 found that 71% were Polish, 6% Hungarian, 4% Czech, 2.5% German, 2.5% Romanian, 2% Austrian and the others were largely classified as 'stateless'.[83] The Poles had made a difficult journey: most had left the Soviet Union for Poland in 1945, but were then confronted with the reality of a vigorous and violent anti-Semitism in Poland. Between 1,500 and 2,000 Jews were murdered in Poland between 1945 and 1947, while the post-war political parties popularized an image of wartime Poland as a solid, united 'community of heroes and martyrs'.[84] Under these circumstances there was no opportunity for a discussion of a specific Jewish experience, nor for an assertion of the place of a Jewish community within a newly reconstructed Poland. Many Jews therefore left Poland for the DP camps of the Allied zones in Germany. A new term was coined for them, 'infiltrees', as often they had to evade border controls. In general, British authorities were unsympathetic, and refused to accept them as genuine DPs, while American authorities not only accepted them, but also accorded them a specific status as Jews.

One can distinguish between three encounters between Jews and Allied representatives, whether soldiers or relief workers. The first was the contact in the liberated concentration camps, when unprepared soldiers, overwhelmed by the babel of incomprehensible languages and dreadful sights, often failed to register that the majority of people they met were Jewish. Descriptions of this moment often contain references to the indescribable and the un-sayable. Entering Dachau, American Medical Officer Marcus Smith found

An incredible sight, a stench that is beyond experience. Horror-stricken, outraged, we react with disbelief. 'Oh God!' says Rosenbloom. Ferris is silent, and so is Howcroft, his vocabulary inadequate to describe this circle of evil. I hear Hollis … say that even primitive, savage people give a decent burial to their own dead and the dead of their enemies. I shut my eyes. This cannot be the twentieth century, I think.[85]

One could also cite the placard placed by British forces outside Bergen-Belsen.

This is the site of the infamous Belsen concentration camp, liberated by the British on 15 April 1945.
  10,000 unburied dead were found here, another 13,000 have since died. All of them victims of the German New Order in Europe, and an example of Nazi Kultur.[86]

Reading this statement, one has to think for a moment or two before one spots the missing word: 'Jew'. 'Reports and soldiers described an undifferentiated mass of human refuse', observes Hitchcock, 'Even the living were reduced to inanimate, nonhuman objects of pity and almost contempt'.[87] The cameramen of the British Army's Film and Photographic Unit, sent with almost no preparation to film Bergen-Belsen, slowly noticed one astonishing point: unlike almost any other war-damaged people, including those imprisoned in the Nazi ghettoes, the survivors did not react at all to the presence of their cameras.[88] The idea of assigning ethnic or national identities to these walking corpses must have seemed absurd, and British and American authorities simply did not consider the creation of all-Jewish camps.[89]

Because of the delays in the formation and transport of UNRRA teams, most relief workers did not confront these dreadful sights. They tended to meet surviving Jews a few weeks later, and then were faced with the awkward problem of how to categorize them. Just as American relief workers knew little of European politics, so most relief workers had inaccurate or – worse still – romanticized ideas about politics and identities in Palestine and the Middle East. Dawson confessed that she was 'brought up on T. E. Lawrence' – hardly a good beginning point for a perceptive understanding of the post-war Middle Eastern identities.[90] Pettiss had a more traditional source of knowledge.

> In 1945, when I first encountered the surge of Jewish DPs' desperate quest for a haven in Palestine, my knowledge of Palestine and its history was almost non-existent. The name conjured up Sunday School stories from the Bible with images of palm trees, camels, villages with cream-coloured block-like houses, and people in long flowing robes, the men wearing strangely draped headgear. It was the 'Holy Land', with names like Bethlehem and Jerusalem scrambled in my consciousness.[91]

How were these Jewish DPs to be classified? One British private contacted a Jewish philanthropic organization in May 1945 to alert them of the fate of Hungarian and Romanian Jews in the DP camp at Haffkrug. 'Every nationality has got a representative there except the Jews,' he complained.[92] His argument was clear: Jews formed a distinct group, therefore they deserved the right to be recognized as a nationality as much as all the other groups in the camps. The British government firmly and consistently adopted a quite different policy. In September 1945, the Cabinet Office put forward the following statement.

> We entirely disapprove of attempts to segregate Jews or 'non-repatriables' as such, since a) we refuse to recognise Nazi attempts to deprive Jews of their German (or other) nationality, or Jewish attempts to regard Jews as possessing separate and overriding Jewish nationality as distinct from their political nationality, and b) it is our policy to regard all Displaced Persons and refugees as ultimately repatriable until their non-repatriability has been finally and irrefutably established beyond all doubt or question.[93]

Their ideas were repeated in a Foreign Office report from April 1947. 'We do not recognize that the Jews form a separate nationality but rather a cultural community within each nation'. While various representative committees were founded by Jewish DPs, these were rarely given any official recognition by British officials. The same report recognized that the Jewish infiltrees who were heading towards the DP camp near Belsen 'undoubtedly show that they have suffered from persecution', and so 'this is not an agreeable policy to administer'.[94] Nonetheless, the policy was not to be changed. When required to consider Polish Jews fleeing to Germany, the same arguments were repeated by British officials. 'The Jews may not feel comfortable in Poland, but this mass migration is not the cure of the disease. They are exposing themselves and all bona fide refugees and Displaced Persons, Jew and non-Jew, to avoidable misery and suffering by magnifying by their unnecessary movement the already immense problem of resettlement'. Their movement out of Poland was an artificial movement, encouraged and organized by Zionists, argued British officials, rather than a comprehensible reaction to the unchecked anti-Semitism.[95] Accepting them into the British zone in Germany would merely be 'adopting the Nazi view that there was no place for the Jews in Central and Eastern Europe'.[96]

Within such arguments, there was also a more strictly political dimension relating to the unfolding crisis in Palestine, as militant Jewish groups adopted more radical and often more violent forms of protest. Any acceptance by the British government of concepts of separate Jewish identity would – it was argued – be seized on by the Zionist groups in Palestine as another justification for the immediate creation of an independent Jewish state. Furthermore, as stated in previous chapters, anti-Semitic ideas continued to circulate within British government circles. Reviewing the exodus of Jews from eastern and central Europe, one Foreign Office official commented: 'As most of the Jews are not engaged in productive work, their departure will mean a loss of consumers without a corresponding loss of producers'.[97]

British imperialists and Zionists presented two contrasting views of the nationalism and identity, one based on an established nation state, the other invoking ethnic, experiential and religious concepts. In the abstract, each case has its merits. However, it is striking how the British government's arguments were not accompanied by any recognition that post-Holocaust Jews deserved some specific aid, or even that they had suffered a particular hardship. Instead, British politicians often seemed to go out of their way to deny or to minimize Jewish suffering: one recalls Bevin's notorious comment that the Jews should not try to push their way to front of the queue.[98]

It is interesting that even British politicians who accepted Zionist arguments still tended to use the same political concepts as the anti-Zionists. Richard Crossman, who became a Labour MP in 1945, was also a member of 1946 Anglo-American Committee of Enquiry into the Problems of European Jewry and Palestine. He eventually became convinced that the Zionist case was correct. Early in 1946, he still considered that arguments for a separate Jewish identity were merely an extension of anti-Semitism.

> I argued yesterday that in this world of 1945 Zionist assertions that the Jews *are a nation* are really a reflex of anti-Semitism. Whereas the few survivors of European Jewry should be liberated from that awful *separateness* which Hitler imposed and reconstituted Europeans with full rights and duties, Zionism actually strengthens the walls of the spiritual concentration camp.[99]

The shift in Crossman's attitudes came when he began to consider the position of the militant Jew in the established European nation states. 'I could not understand ... the attitude of Jews who call themselves and feel themselves Zionists, yet remain in their home countries'. The concept of a 'double loyalty' was 'exasperating' to Crossman, as it was to 'every Gentile'.[100] Crossman explained his anger by referring back to Britain's wartime experience: if a new Israel was there as a refuge in times of crisis for all Jews, then British Jews would be like the cowards who left Britain in 1940. 'To think that a fellow-citizen of mine is contemplating escape, in case things go wrong, arouses my basest emotions'.[101] Yet when he realized how many of Europe's Jews seem to feel precisely this form of 'double loyalty', Crossman came to accept Zionism and the creation of the state of Israel as the least bad solution to a serious problem. 'The Jew who wanted to be a Jew, separate from the rest of the nation, must leave Europe; those who remained must accept assimilation'.[102]

What one notes in both the arguments presented by the British government and the counter-arguments by Crossman is the absolute priority given to the singular status of the nation and nationhood. Plural identities are simply impossible: in the case of the British government, they are simply denied as 'artificial'; for Crossman, they are reluctantly accepted, but are then to be accompanied by the departure of the insufficiently patriotic.

Such policies led to administrative chaos. British officials tried to deny or ignore the presence of organized Jewish groups. One group around Belsen did achieve some limited recognition, but this was the exception.[103] American policy shifted during 1945: in August 1945, all-Jewish camps were created, and by November 1945 Jews were to be counted in the American zone as a separate group.[104] This change in attitudes was partly as a result of the Harrison Report, commissioned by Eisenhower in June 1945 and published in September 1945, which exposed some cruelty and much carelessness in the treatment of Jews in the American zone. A consequence of this incoherence is that accurate statistics concerning the number of Jews in Europe are simply impossible to calculate.

So far we have reviewed two images of Jewishness encountered by UNRRA workers: the terrible sights in the liberated concentration camps, and the rather more perplexing debate concerning the status of Jews in DP camps. After 1945, however, a third image developed.

Hulme first met Jewish DPs at Wildflecken Camp early in 1948. She was initially resentful. She had noted how this minority among the DPs – she calculated that they only constituted a fifth of the DPs in the American zone – had become so successful in monopolizing attention, due to their 'apocryphal publicity'.[105] They were certainly different from the other groups she was familiar with: 'They didn't seem like DPs at all'. Hulme was struck by their intensity and force.

> They were not the ashes of a people at all. They were charged with the intensest life force I had ever experienced. From the moment of my first encounter with their contrary, critical and demanding leaders, I had the feeling that I was dealing not with people but

with phoenixes ... I had been arguing, not with ordinary people, but with something almost abstract and transcendental ... The superbly organized Jews ran their own show the way they wanted it – fast, efficient and tumultuous as an incoming tide ... The driving spirit that animated them all, a passionate nationalism for a country that had just been born was still a bitter background.[106]

As with the dissident Poles, one notes the same uncertain tone in these external valuations of the Jewish presence: were relief workers witnessing a model rehabilitation? Or was this something unwelcome, even sinister?

British relief workers in particular tend to record incidents of tension and conflict involving Jews. Lieutenant Colonel Kerr ran a transit camp for refugees in Bari, northern Italy. He was amazed at the arrival of several thousand 'Palestine-minded' young male Jews early in 1946. As they got off the train, one of them knocked Kerr's hat off his head! 'They were to become the most difficult Displaced Persons I had yet met'.[107] Lively demonstrations in the large Jewish camps in the American zone, in Zeilsheim in particular, surprised and worried the British authorities: the protestors demanded greater access to Palestine.[108] A mass hunger strike was organized at Fohrenwald on 15 November 1945.

> The strike was in protest of the British announcement that they will not permit 100,000 Jews to enter Palestine as had been requested by President Truman. The strike was held today to coincide with a national protest strike being held in Palestine. This afternoon, the DPs held a big meeting at the camp. The meeting was climaxed by a parade into town to the office of the military government where a letter of protest was presented to be forwarded to Attlee ... They marched in well-ordered ranks. As they marched, they sang various songs including 'Hatikvah', which they consider as the Jewish National anthem.[109]

Such initiatives were effective in drawing the attention of the media and politicians to Jews and gaining the sympathy of most Western public opinion and governments. In the DP camps which organized such protests, a creative cultural dynamic developed, in which Zionist ideals and DPs' needs created new forms. One UNRRA worker reported that

> It is impossible to organize this camp along any line without accepting that fact ... If you organize a boys' club to read, to talk, to debate, to conduct dances, at the second meeting it turns out to be reading Zionist books, debating Zionist politics, and dancing the *Hora*.[110]

Morgan was puzzled by these Jewish DPs: his notes concerning his visit to the Jewish camp at Wolfratshausen in March 1946 give a good indication of his feelings, and also show the impression made by the small groups of kibbutzim that sprang up across Germany.

I was pleasantly surprised with this party. The whole atmosphere seemed to be good, with the exception of that engineered by the Camp Committee. These miserable creatures rehearsed all the usual Jewish grievances and were determined to radiate gloom. For the rest, the children were grand, the hospital, staffed largely by Hungarian doctors, was quite first-rate, and there is a very definite feel of uplift about these Kibbutzim. I was given a pretty fast one in one of the Kibbutzim dining halls by being suddenly confronted with a large caricature representing Jerusalem with an armed British sentry at the gate, excluding a party of Jewish immigrants. It took a bit of laughing off, but it was done.[111]

Dawson also recorded some striking images of the kibbutzim.

The kibbutheim [sic] however are different; groups of big boys and girls who live all together a completely communal life, preparing themselves most earnestly for Palestine and the life there. They work well, either in the roads or in technical classes here in the camp, marching to and fro in companies, singing songs and beating a drum, to set a good example and encourage the others to do the same. They go to school half-time, 8am to 12 noon, or 2pm until 6pm, and are very independent. Several of them are very fine indeed and they all big; there are usually one or two girls in overalls marching and singing on their way to heavy work with the boys.

I do not understand how they can be so finely grown when from twelve to eighteen or longer, they have been in [concentration camps] doing heavy labour on poor food. But they have been well fed for the last six months and had a good rest, and they have the hope of forth-coming life in Palestine. I fear they will not all get there. But almost all of these so-called children are promising. The elder people are naturally more hopeless.[112]

On the other hand, some more old-fashioned prejudices circulated. Dawson described a Talmud class as 'dark, narrow, and backward-looking'.[113] Marching activities were another obvious point for criticism: 'far too military and like Nazi Youth, singing their songs ... They stick up their blue and white double star everywhere – it is very dull – and their heavy startling Hebrew lettering – it always makes me jump'.[114]

Relief workers saw Jewish DPs as objects of pity, as illegitimate petitioners for special privileges or as militant patriots. Within this spectrum of images, there was little room for ideas of equality or participation: Jewishness was almost always conceived of as 'other' to the relief worker's culture.

These simple images, based on external observation, ignore some important points. First, it has to be stressed that we are examining a fluid identity, under-going rapid transformation during a moment of deep and traumatic crisis. In reality, it was not an identity which was as fixed as either anti-Semites or Zionists argued. Prior to the Second World War, western European Jews had shown little interest in the Zionist project. According to Ehud Avriel, only 0.5%

of Vienna's pre-1938 Jewish population joined Zionist organizations – and even this tiny minority was split into competing factions.[115] For many, assimilation was the obvious model. One could cite Primo Levi's memories at this point: he recalled a time in pre-war Italy when 'within myself, and in my contacts with my Christian friends, I had always considered my origin as an almost negligible but curious fact, a small amusing anomaly, like having a crooked nose or freckles'.[116] During the terror of the Holocaust, there were many examples of liberal, assimilated Jews, like Levi, who were astonished when the Nazis defined them as Jewish.[117] There was nothing automatic or natural about the massive shift by such people to re-define themselves as Jewish after 1945. Some Jews drew different lessons from their wartime experiences: it is noticeable that some French Jews chose to change their Jewish surnames after 1945, to make themselves appear more French. '[French] Jews aspired above all to return to a normal life,' explains Renée Poznanski, 'Hence Jewish militancy was out of the question'.[118] Annette Wieviorka concurs: some French Jews saw themselves as French patriots first. 'To be a Jew had no national significance for them'.[119]

The idea that the Holocaust united all European Jews by giving them a common trauma can also be questioned. First – as Hannah Arendt pointed out – there was no single European anti-Semitism, but different national anti-Semitisms.[120] Certainly, the experience of the Holocaust and terror divided Jews from the existing nation states. Frank Stern gives a single telling example: the different attitudes by Germans and Jews to the Allied bombing raids. To Germans, these constituted a 'great catastrophe', to the surviving German Jews, they were a 'ray of hope'.[121] Magda Denes, a Hungarian Jew, no longer felt at home in her native Budapest.

> I felt that overnight the city had changed. As in a fairy tale turned wicked, the world had revealed its layers of menace. The well-known streets through which we travelled had turned alien. There was no more Budapest. We were in a city of evil populated by hidden monsters. One accusing word, one pointing finger, could get us instantly killed.[122]

This sharp sense of separation from the rest of society did not, in itself, lead to a construction of a solid, united Jewish identity. One obvious point here is that many Jews wanted to avoid looking like Jews or sounding like Jews. Polish Jew Helena Szereszewska remembered being told: 'Careful, that's the most important thing. Look like everybody, move like everybody, don't stand out in the grey crowd by the way we behave or dress'.[123] Some survived in disguise underground, usually in small groups, taking steps to hide their Jewishness. Joseph Joffo, a French–Jewish boy, was told by his father 'You are Jews, but never admit it. Do you understand? *Never*'.[124] Hiding in Belgium, Alexandra Brodsky was aware of how uncertain was her knowledge of the outside world. 'It was extremely difficult to form an accurate assessment even of our situation, let alone of things that happened far away'.[125] She was also instructed: 'Do not write, do not telephone, do not travel to [Brussels] for any reason'.[126] In Auschwitz, Elie Cohen learned that the golden rule was 'be inconspicuous'.[127] Denes speaks eloquently about how difficult she found thinking and even dreaming during these years.

> I wanted to think of other things, but I had noticed lately that my mind had become a country of mines, of trenches, of barbed-wire checkpoints. I started out in a direction and I was almost immediately stopped by signs of No Entry, Verboten für Juden, Proceed at Your Own Risk, and suchlike. I turned back, and turned to the side, and turned again, and always encountered the same obstacles.[128]

Such evidence suggests that the various strategies devised for survival during the Holocaust worked as much as forms of identity-denial as they did as identity-formation.

Some Jews were pushed together, first into ghettos, then into work camps and death camps. Such institutions could inculcate a sense of common destiny and identity, but their overall effects were mixed. Ruth Kluger's aggressively de-romanticized account of her life during the Holocaust presents two contrasting images of her experience. On the one hand, despite her personal lack of faith, she learned an important lesson in the ghetto at Theresienstadt. 'I learnt for the first time who we were, what we could be, this people to whom I belonged, or had to belong, according to our oppressors, and now wanted to belong'.[129] In a later passage, however, she suggests almost the contrary: 'Auschwitz was no instructional institution … You learned absolutely nothing there'.[130] Thomas Rahe's careful analysis of Jewish religious life in Bergen-Belsen makes an important point concerning Jewish unity during the Holocaust.

> Bergen-Belsen … represented a heterogeneous forced community with all its resulting social and psychological conflicts … Prussian civil servants and Greek fishermen, Polish rabbis and Hungarian students, Yugoslavian communists and Dutch Zionists – apart from their Jewish origin, which had been the reason for their deportation into the concentration camp – mostly they had hardly anything in common.[131]

Nazi authorities themselves were aware of sub-groups among Jews, and were willing to stimulate and exploit rivalries between them.[132] These cultural, social and political divisions existed during the Holocaust and were still present at Liberation. The surviving minority of highly acculturated German Jews still looked down on the less well-educated, Yiddish-speaking Jews from eastern Europe.[133] Many Jews from western European countries, rather than adopting the separatist language of Zionism in 1945, were tempted by the heroic myths of unified, generous, tolerant, progressive national communities, represented by the Gaullist drama of the Resistance, the Italian *resistenza* or even, for some, by the briefly resurgent Communist parties.[134]

There remained, however, serious obstacles to the integration of post-Holocaust Jews into European society. Some of these were discussed in the previous chapter: as noted, Liberation was rarely a collective experience. Attitudes such as those current among British government officials and military authorities existed in other countries: what might be presented as a praise-worthy political neutrality, refusing to recognize special interest groups or to accept racist arguments, often also functioned as means to deny the true tragedy of the Holocaust. Here, we encounter one of the constant paradoxes of apparently unprejudiced state policies: by refusing to extend formal recognition to different cultures, it can then be *more* difficult for such groups to integrate and assimilate. In the Netherlands, an impeccably liberal tradition created a situation in which Jewish survivors were assimilated with all others, as if they 'no longer existed'.[135] Jewish survivors found that they faced a deaf society, with little interest in their story.[136] Primo Levi, returning from Auschwitz to Italy, recorded a bizarrely typical experience. 'Nobody was much concerned with me: colleagues, the director, and workers had other things to think about'.[137] Thus no publisher could be found for Anne Frank's diary in years immediately after 1945.[138]

Frankl gave a brief speech to his fellow inmates after the liberation of Auschwitz in March 1945. He told them that 'They must not lose hope but should keep their courage in the certainty that the hopelessness of our struggle did not detract from its dignity and its meaning'.[139] These are brave words, but it is by no means certain that they are true. Did their struggle have a meaning? Those who sought to record their experiences as concentration camp survivors faced multiple obstacles. Their first struggle was with themselves: psycho-logically, did they want to remember? Was it not better to try to forget? If they wished to write, could they do so? How was one to conceptualize, to register, an experience which appeared inhuman or meaningless? Being Jewish was not easy in this context. Denes' mother cursed their bad luck when she found that the newly victorious Russian troops were no friendlier than the Hungarians. 'According to the Hungarians, we are Jews. According to the Russians, we are Hungarians. Whichever, we are always shuffled to the losing side'.[140]

Yet many surviving Jews turned to Jewishness as a source of identity. Why? In some cases, even the survivors themselves could not explain it. Thirteen-year-old Aharon Appelfeld, stuck in a miserable, violent, corrupt transit camp in southern Italy, suddenly felt a need to pray: something that his Ukrainian Jewish parents had never taught him. A black market dealer spent two months teaching him how.[141] The espousal of radical expressions of Jewishness could also function as a means of defining the individual in this confusing situation: they could articulate a sense of hatred against Germany and Germans.[142] Examples from Jewish religious culture could provide apparent analogies between the oppression of the Holocaust and past Jewish experiences.[143] The old Hebrew word *galut*, meaning exile or diaspora – or, more simply, 'to be in the wrong place' – could acquire a new resonance among post-Holocaust Jews.[144] By studying Jewish culture, one could even gain a type of linguistically orientated historical lesson: Yiddish represented the past of the European Jews, Hebrew their future.[145] The Zionist slogan which circulated in the camps – 'Speak Yiddish, learn Hebrew' – is indicative of this awkward, transitional moment.[146]

In these circumstances, 'identity' was not some abstract, psychological issue, to be treated separately from apparently more practical issues such as food and accommodation. Defining one's identity was also a practical decision about where to go and where to belong.

> The Jews suddenly faced themselves. Where now? Where to? They saw that they were different from all the other inmates of the camps. For them things were not quite so simple. To go back to Poland? To Hungary? To streets empty of Jews, towns empty of Jews, a world without Jews.[147]

Jews were left with the question of what Jewishness meant. American–Jewish relief worker Leo Schwarz provides one answer. He describes a touching scene at a meeting of some 400 Jews in Saint-Ottilien monastery in Bavaria on 27 May 1945, one of the first public meetings of Jews in Germany after the end of the war. Their strongest emotion was a sense of surprise and disappointment that no Jewish representatives had been sent to help them. Their meeting ended with the collective singing of the national anthems of the United States, Britain, France and Soviet Union, folksongs of the ghetto and Palestine, and finally 'the collective singing of the Zionist anthem, Hatikvah, the Song of Hope'. This represented

> a new spirit aborning [sic]. A feeling of brotherhood fed by shared sorrow and hope was slowly emerging. The concert was a symbol, an act of faith; a weathervane indicating that the instinct to live was stronger than any anguish or remorse.[148]

For such people, Jewishness suddenly made sense. The experience of Nazi terror could be reduced to a single, brutally simple lesson. 'Of all the peoples participating in this war, the Jews were the hardest hit', argued a Rumanian Jewish group. Following this experience, they would now present 'complete unity' to the rest of the world.[149] Such arguments could be reduced to simple, hard-hitting slogans. Facing British opposition to the extension of Jewish migration to Palestine, an American-Jewish chaplain replied: 'You mean that we Jews had a right to die as Jews but we have no right to live as Jews?'.[150]

Jewishness could articulate resentments concerning wartime oppression: it created an immediate sense of solidarity, it provided a critical perspective by which to judge events, it formed an effective lobby with which to campaign for better treatment, and it gave hope. But with such developments, also came political considerations. These could be expressed in the most basic forms. An orphan at Bergen-Belsen camp told one Zionist sympathizer. 'Everybody has a home ... The British have a home. The Americans. The Russians. The French. Only we don't have a home. Don't ask us. Ask the world'.[151] 'We want a home!' shouted Zionist demonstrators to Bartley Crum.[152]

The confused, often despairing, Jewish DPs came into contact with Jewish activists, including army chaplains, British and American philanthropists, and Zionist militants from Palestine. Such people represented a broad spectrum of views.

The philanthropic groups often seemed to represent some sort of alternative to UNRRA. British Jewry worked to create the Jewish Relief Unit (JRU), because they considered the existing relief agencies were not able to address the specific problems of post-Holocaust Jews.[153] British Jews noted the incomplete nature of the Liberation. 'Peace in Europe has increased rather than lessened the need among the surviving populations. Only now can we see the full extent of their misery and we must reach the sufferers and help them'.[154] The JRU was formed in February 1944. It started work in Italy in October 1944, but found it considerably more difficult to gain access to the DP camps in Germany.[155] In January 1947, 56 JRU relief workers were active in Germany, and there were also some smaller teams in Greece and Italy.[156] The political implications of their activities were ambiguous. On the one, the JRU was essentially philanthropic in nature: their first aim was to 'clothe the naked'.[157] JRU workers seemed willing to work alongside UNRRA: they showed no spirit of particularism.[158] When they learned of the activities of Zionist militants to organize illegal immigration from Europe to British-controlled Palestine, the JRU's leadership issued a swift, clear condemnation.

> We need not discuss whether the illegal immigration is justified or not, because it is crystal clear to me as head of this organisation, and it should be to all of us that we cannot, we must not take any active part in it.
>
> If people come to us hungry or in need of shelter who have entered the zone illegally, then we must, as welfare workers, give them what help we can. Whence they depart or how they travel is not our duty to enquire into – but equally we have no right to break military government regulations by helping them to move…
>
> To sum up my views and instructions as official head of this organization. None of our workers must take an active part in the organization of illegal immigration. If any do, he or she must be dismissed.[159]

On the other hand, the JRU demanded that the specific experience of Jews during the years of Nazi terror be acknowledged. Discussing UNRRA's initial proposal to ignore issues of ethnicity and religion when distributing aid, the JRU leadership responded:

> The chief criterion in the distribution of relief is the relative needs of the population. There is to be no discrimination because of race, creed or political belief, but it is recognised that in determining the relative needs of the population the diverse needs caused by discriminatory treatment by the enemy must be taken into account. Jews have been the chief sufferers and the enemy has not hesitated to starve those whom it has allowed to escape wholesale slaughter.[160]

In other words, the JRU's policies were premised on what Crossman would have termed a 'double loyalty': they remained British *and* Jewish, and refused to give one identity precedence over the other.

Groups like the British JRU and the American JDC were important in presenting Jewish DPs with another form of relief work. Their workers were swift to recognize that there had been a specific Jewish experience; that Jews had a claim to special treatment; and Jewish organizations and cultures should be recognized by the Allied authorities. However, they could not provide any real solution to the Jewish DPs' sense of homelessness, nor alleviate their sense that they had been deserted.[161]

Avowedly Zionist militants represented a different type of Jewishness. At one extreme, one could cite the Jewish Brigade, slowly and reluctantly created by the British authorities in Palestine in September 1944.[162] They entered German-occupied territory in Europe in the last weeks of the war. The slogans 'Kein Reich, kein volk, kein Führer!' decorated their trucks: many of these soldiers were looking for revenge. Some of them thought in terms of an exemplary violence, 24 hours of murder and rape which would teach the German people a lesson about Jews which they would never forget.[163] They represented a different type of Jewishness: forceful, active and confident of their ability to change the world. Schwarz records a memorable account of his meeting with them. On 20 June 1945

> trim bronzed men in khaki, waving emblems with blue-and-white Stars of David, were quickly surrounded and all but overwhelmed … As the crowd surged around the soldiers and clung to them, a current of mutual discovery and sympathy was generated. For these emissaries, unlike the Allied liberators, had come to seek out their families and their people, to instil courage and hope, to organize and lead an exodus to the land of Israel.[164]

David Ben-Gurion (1886–1973) was the rising star in Zionism. He represented the Jewish community established in Palestine, and led their campaign to establish a Jewish state, even in the face of British resistance. He toured Europe five time between 1944 and 1946, on occasion giving fiery speeches to Jewish DPs. He himself drove home this message in his speeches to Jewish DPs.

> The Brigade soldiers you see here are living proof that there are not only slain Jews, but that there are fighting Jews among us … You can accomplish a great deal. You, the direct emissaries of the suffering of our people, are the driving force. You must be strong, and from what I have seen, I know you will be strong.[165]

Alongside them, a network of Zionist activists and sympathetic volunteers worked to create an underground network which would aid Jews to leave central Europe, to reach ports along the Mediterranean coast, and then to leave in specially hired boats to reach Palestine. While the JRU retained a strong sense of loyalty to the British state, these new Zionists were often flamboyantly and provocatively anti-British. They represented a recent shift within Zionism itself, from the more conciliatory and pragmatic policies of Chaim Weizmann, always respectful of the British presence, to the more confrontational attitudes of Ben-Gurion, based among Jews living in Palestine. For such Zionists, this was a political confrontation.

> In peacetime, we were again fighting a political battle. We had to bring Jews to Palestine not only because they had nowhere else to turn, but to increase the Jewish population of Palestine and prove to the British that the right of Jews to return to their one land was not negotiable ... We now faced one single enemy: His Majesty's government.[166]

This network also taught another lesson: alongside the rhetoric of toughness and strength, it also valued cunning. Jon and David Kimche document the creation of illegal and underground transport, and include a single, revealing phrase about its working methods. 'It was astonishing what one could do in those days with a bottle of Scotch and a few packets of Camels and Chesterfields'.[167] Here, there was open delight in being able to turn the tables, to outwit a better-equipped but clumsy and demoralized British force.

There were corresponding signs of Jewish self-assertion among the DPs, particularly in reaction to moves from German authorities. Joined by Polish Jews fleeing anti-Semitic persecution, their camps became the base for a strange, unexpected, late flowering of Yiddish culture, as schools, theatres, publishing houses and libraries promoted a culture which was banned in Soviet-controlled area, superseded by assimilation in the USA and which was to be rejected in Israel.[168] There was also a religious revival, often led by Orthodox Jews from eastern Europe, whose forms of faith were quite different from those of the liberal, assimilated, German Jews.[169] In many Jewish camps, DPs were proud of the creation of their own police force. Observing Bergen-Belsen camp, Norman Bentwich noticed this: 'thoroughly trained and disciplined ... a smart Force whenever there is a celebration or event in the camp, while it is their daily business to maintain order'.[170] Such developments could transform camps from centres of apathy to centres of activity and assertion. For example, in March 1946 German police, concerned about the spread of black market practices, staged an armed raid on the Stuttgart DP camp, using 230 police with dogs: to their surprise, the camp's Jewish DPs fought back. In the ensuing violence, one was shot dead, and hundreds wounded.[171]

What did Zionism mean to such people? First: hope. Zionism seemed to provide answers that the Allies, UNRRA and even the Jewish philanthropic agencies could not provide. It offered a home. Ben-Gurion had offered them the chance to become 'free people in their own land amongst their brethren'.[172] However, it should be remembered that many Jews who attempted to travel illegally to Palestine did so not because they were Zionists, but simply because they wanted a safe and secure home.[173] Zionism offered still more: it promised the cultural and almost spiritual transformation of these marginalized strands of Europe's nations into a single, powerful body. It would turn 'weary, leaden-footed wanderers into well-organized spiritual communities'.[174] 'Unite! Be organized and disciplined!' was the slogan recorded by Schwarz.[175] The idealists of Buchenwald *kibbutz* were proud that their different approaches to politics and religion did not prevent them from proclaiming 'we are all Zionists ... [for] we had a unity that was beyond politics'.[176] Alongside this was a type of cult of force. Those who wished to migrate to the new land needed to give up the decadent, effete habits of the diaspora.

> Self-confidence and egotism ... are essential for surviving the fight against climate, desert and hostile people ... We have two alternatives: to remain as we were in Europe, passively waiting for the new Spanish Inquisition, Nazi extermination, Czarist pogrom, or what-have-you; or, to sacrifice politeness and sentimentality for strength and toughness.[177]

It is easy to laugh today at the romanticized images that Zionists circulated: young pioneers, bursting with health, working in idyllic rural conditions, protected by the calm, determined warriors of the Haganah.[178] But many Jews responded to this promise. One immigrant recorded that 'In Israel, every newcomer is cordially welcomed ... A Jew is never a stranger in Israel. Collective memories are awakened, and the holy places and biblical history seem familiar. Jewish immigrants from all over the world have the same feeling when they first set foot on Israel's soil'.[179] Another illegal immigrant to Israel leaves an eloquently utopian image of the essential unity of her fellow voyagers: 'All of them, old and young, believers and free thinkers, socialists and bourgeois, easterners or westerners, all have come with the same aim: to return to the land that was promised them by the Lord! They all wanted to "see again" a land that they had never seen!'.[180] Age-old national and ethnic rivalries were set aside, for this effort had created 'one people'.[181] In the best traditions of the *aliyah*, the spiritual ascent, this was also a journey which would transform its voyagers from remnants of humanity, brutalized by a dictatorial machine, into full human beings. 'I have no name. All these years I have had a number. I still have a number. Now I am going to Eretz Israel, to the Land of Israel, where I shall live as a Jew and a human being. Then I shall have a name'.[182] As was seen above, the determination and resilience of these people impressed many observers: amid the despair of the DPs, their pride and force marked them out.

Yet this was often a strange form of rallying: the experienced Jewish commentator Norman Bentwich observed that this sense of brotherhood with Israel was not a result of some mass nationalist conversion, but the consequence of persecution.[183] Pinson noted the spread of religious practices among Jewish survivors, but considered 'while there may be formal observances and official symbols there is little true piety' and no true Sabbath in the camps.[184] He was even sceptical of the desperate clinging to Palestine: for Pinson, this 'burning conviction in their own possession of the truth' among these recent Zionist converts was more like a totalitarian creed than an authentic form of political belief.[185] 'They had no faith in humanity and were suspicious of everything and everyone. They had one desire – to get to Israel'.[186] Bentwich also noted the decay of the fervent Jewish unity of 1945, to be replaced by a more normal spectrum of political parties in 1946. National difference among Jews continued: relief worker Zippy Orlin noticed that Polish Jews wanted to eat herrings and potatoes, Hungarians preferred goulash, while Russian Jews wanted cabbage soup.[187] The activism of the Zionists was not necessarily welcome to all Jews. Accustomed to the enforced silence of the years of Terror, this launch into ardent speech could appear frightening and unfamiliar. Appelfeld recalled 'The years 1946 to 1950 were years of verbiage; when life [was] full of ideology, words and clichés abound. Everyone talked'.[188] In this context, he longed for solitude, not community. Finally, the effects of a mass Jewish migration to Palestine / Israel on the Arab population were barely mentioned in debates, beyond a few cursory references by British colonial officials. This was, once again, one of the unwritten rules of the debate: Arabs had no right to nationhood, and therefore did not need to be considered.

When Zionist militant finally met Holocaust survivor, the encounter was not necessarily as anticipated in the idealized accounts of Zionist militancy. Records from the soldiers of the Jewish Brigade suggest something else: they were dismayed when they finally saw the 'dull faces' of the survivors, who seemed so 'different' from them that it was as if an 'electric wire' separated survivor from soldier.[189] Did they really want to take in these remnants of Europe's disasters? As recently as 1938, when Zionist militants from Palestine attempted to negotiate with German politicians, their aim was to recruit active, healthy militants.

> They were looking for young men and women who wanted to go to Palestine because they wanted a national home of their own and were prepared to pioneer, struggle and, if necessary, fight for it. Their interest in those German Jews who turned to Palestine as a haven of refuge, as the next best after the United States or the United Kingdom, was secondary to their main purpose.[190]

The survivors of the concentration camps and the fugitives who hidden during the war, looked different from the idealized pioneers.

> The people – their people – whom they were supposed to help to Palestine presented a frightening picture. Before any kind of disciplined movement was practical, the poison had to be expelled, and it could only be done with the strongest emetic. Education was too weak in its impact, too slow in taking effect to meet the pressing urgency of

counteracting the disastrous effects of their gnawing demoralisation. Another means had to be found, and soon enough was in operation, the propaganda of hatred.[191]

Finally, it was accepted that the new state would need all the settlers it could find, and the Zionist leadership decided to assist the survivors travel to Palestine / Israel, whether illegally or legally.[192] In 1948, about 25,000 Jews left Germany for Israel; in 1949, 50,000.[193] It seems likely that greater numbers migrated to United States, which remained, for many, the more attractive destination.

Those who travelled to Israel often found that they took their problems with them. 'For many, their first impression of Israel was that of a deprived country in which life was depressing and difficult'.[194] Sometimes the same rules of memory seemed to apply in Israel as in Europe: Appelfeld found his first manuscript was rejected because editors wanted a story which celebrated heroism, rather than dwelling on the victims' weakness.[195] The young idealists of the Buchenwald *kibbutz* were dismayed to find that once they arrived in Palestine, their proud statements of unity were treated as expressions of naivety by the native Jews. 'Things seem a little different with the various parties and factions in Palestine. They have welcomed us with warmth and respect, but they seem sceptical of how long our plan will live'.[196] Rather than being welcomed as surviving heroes, survivors met with frequent criticisms. 'Why didn't you resist? Why did you let yourselves be led like lambs to the slaughter?'.[197] Amos Oz recalls the contempt felt in his household for the 'effeminate, Diaspora-born worms' who arrived after 1945.[198] At the same time, established Israelis noted that few of the newcomers seemed to be genuinely committed to Zionist principles.[199] Established Israeli Jews worried that the new migrants showed few signs of integrating.

	Recent Migrants	*Established Natives*
Reading a daily paper	19%	81%
Listening to radio everyday	18%	74%
Going to cinema at least once a month	21%	31%
Going to a Hebrew play	6%	79%

Table 1: Cultural Practices of Recent Migrants and Natives in Israel, c.1950

In a sense, the new immigrants faced the same problem in Israel that they had faced in Europe: the new state aspired to be a mono-ethnic, monocultural entity, and demonstrated surprisingly little tolerance for dissidence.[201] In particular, Yiddish was discouraged. 'It had become a symbol of sloppiness, weakness and the Diaspora. Everyone disparaged it'.[202]

CONCLUSION

This chapter has analysed two difficult examples of 'return', in which the displaced could not simply be re-placed in their homes. In each case, the minority group then lobbies for recognition: whether for the right to recreate the true Poland outside of the current nation-state, or for the right to 'return' to a land that they had never seen. One notes the constant recurrence of themes such as home and nation in such debates, which point to an unspoken consensus. The new world that was to be created by the United Nations was a world of united nations: ethnically, culturally, politically united. Post-war anti-Semitism provoked an understandable reaction among Holocaust survivors, which resulted in their own nationalism. While this initiative changed the shape of the board, it did not challenge the rules of the game.

The generous idealism of our relief workers was of little permanent importance. Eventually, as UNRRA was replaced by IRO, the ethic of 'helping the people help themselves' was replaced by a more calculating, instrumental, problem-solving perspective, and repatriation was superseded by resettlement as the desired solution. Refugee rights were reduced to a minimum: the new organization worked on the assumption that the refugee must be persuaded to accept the organization's priorities.

Yet, curiously, the refugees retained a formidable power. The Great Journey to Israel was instrumental in the creation of three national identities – Israeli, German and Palestinian. The old joke asks what is the difference between nationalism and regionalism, and replies that nationalism is regionalism with an army. Jewishness became a nationalism. Frankl had drawn the following lesson from his concentration camp experience.

> There were always choices to make. Every day, every hour, offered the opportunity to make a decision, a decision which determined whether you would or would not submit to those powers which threatened to rob you of your very self, your inner freedom; which determined whether or not you would become the plaything of circumstance, renouncing freedom and dignity to become moulded into the form of the typical inmate.[203]

In 1945, this decision-making capacity was interpreted as the possession of a nation-state and a national army. One can question whether this is the best interpretation of Frankl's lesson.

Conclusion

[I wished] 'to make people in the land I was coming to understand the suferings of Europe, and realize that by their own apathy and blindness they had contributed much to that suffering.[1]

Flavia Kingscote, 1942

Now let the poets come forth to write their epitaphs, let the historians browse in the dog-eared files, let the statisticians loose on the uncompleted UNRRA forms.[2]

Margaret McNeill, 1948[2]

Radical journalist I. F. Stone produced a memorable image of the effects of the Second World War: it was like a hurricane which had scattered and dispersed peoples across the globe.[3] The substance of this book has argued against the logic of his image: our key argument is that where there is movement, there is meaning. The scattering of peoples across Europe in the 1930s and 1940s was not the result of some arbitrary, blind catastrophe, but a consequence of planning, rationality and design. Our book has been structured around the lines of many journeys, ranging from pleasant excursions to tragic odysseys. Significantly, even the relief workers' programmes were often premised on their journeys, echoing and imitating the movements of the refugees. In the first part of this work, we demonstrated that even the most apparently 'panic-stricken' refugee was also motivated by a rational decision-making process. In the second part, we showed that the 'chaos' of post-1945 Europe was not produced by the DPs, but by inept authorities who attempted to direct, relieve and rehabilitate outcast people. In making these critical comments, we are not seeking to deny the heroism and humanitarian ideals that motivated so many to contribute to the war effort against Nazi power, but to place these qualities into a wider context. Rather than the 'good war' of popular mythology, we have portrayed a flawed war, in which bungling, bigotry and the victors' over-confidence wrecked many promising initiatives. The post-war authorities – whether armies, national governments or international relief agencies – failed to respond adequately to the deep thirst for a humane social order.[4]

In the accounts by refugees and relief workers one finds some memorable images concerning the end of the war. One of the most striking comes in Ruth

Kluger's autobiography. In February 1945, with her mother and her newly adopted sister, she was made to go on one of the infamous death marches from a forced labour camp into central Germany. Then they made 'a real, a free, decision' to walk out.[5] On the one hand, they realized that the forced march would eventually end in their own deaths but, on the other hand, they had little clear idea about what they were escaping into. In place of the settled, *völkisch*, communities that had sustained Nazi rule, they found something quite different: a shifting, itinerant society, in which everyone seemed to be on the roads, fleeing the Russian advance. Most striking of all was the sudden evaporation of all barriers. Ruth and her mother had been taught for over a decade that Jews were radically different from the rest of society. Their experiences among the refugee Germans suggested something else. 'We followed the train of the newly homeless who were choking on their own misery and hadn't the stomach to ask suspiciously where we came from … Most of the people in that area didn't care anymore who was who and who was on the road. They were themselves about to be uprooted'.[6] There remained some points of concern: did Ruth look 'too Jewish' to be accepted by the Germans? Would people notice that they had no luggage? While all three spoke German, would they accidently slip Yiddish expressions or forms into their speech? In practice, by begging, stealing and dressing themselves in second-hand clothes, they passed without arousing any suspicion.

A rather more romantic and idealised version of the same lesson was produced by the Quakers. Disobeying just about every written and unwritten rule concerning DP camps, the FRS produced multi-national, multi-ethnic, multi-lingual, ecumenical nativity plays, open to Protestants, Catholics and Orthodox Christians, deliberately involving DPs, relief workers and Germans in an approximately equal fashion.[7] At the Marketkirche in Goslar, six children, all dressed as angels, sat around a Christmas tree and recited a little speech: 'I remember, before our homes were destroyed, before our parents were killed or taken away, before the war made everything so unhappy – I remember that we used to have trees like this little tree and we sang and were happy'.[8] Each child spoke in turn, so the words were heard in Ukrainian, Polish, German, Lithuanian, Estonian and Latvian. This may well have been the first occasion on which German and Polish DP children talked to each other. One can see the limits to this initiative: the Virgin Mary had to be played by a Quaker, for the rival Poles and Germans could never have found a mutually acceptable candidate from among their own ranks. And, lastly, what about the Jews and other non-Christians? There was no place for them in this ceremony. Nonetheless, the Quaker achievement is a striking one, pointing to a different ethic.

These examples suggest not so much compassion for those who had suffered, as a sense of trans-national, trans-ethnic empathy or solidarity: they echo François Lafitte's resolute call, made in 1940, for 'a people's war of liberation in which there are no "aliens" except the destroyers of freedom and the preservers of privilege and social injustice in every country, including our own'.[9] Few institutions responded to such urges after 1945. As previously noted, the new United Nations actually reinforced the structures and cultures of nationalism and nation states. The great social and political advances of the period – the final widening of political suffrage to all adults, the development of universal welfare provision, the attempts to plan economies – were all predicated on the existence of viable nation states. Refugees – however they are defined – were but one small element in a bigger contest, in which all players were 'equal believers in national identities'.[10] In the decades that followed, refugee law became immigration law, stressing protection of national borders, not the welfare of persons.[11] The new structures of the Cold War were still more resistant to any thinking beyond nation states. Zionism did not challenge this context: on the contrary, it contributed to it, by proposing that Jewishness should form one further nationality among a host of competing nations. Orwell's cynical, ugly conclusion about the politics of identity which developed in this context is probably as accurate a summing-up as one could wish for. 'Because two days ago a fat Jewess grabbed your place on the bus, you switch off the wireless when the announcer begins talking about the ghettoes of Warsaw; that is how people's minds work nowadays'.[12]

The refugee and the relief worker were constituent elements in the creation of this post-war order. As id and super-ego, amateur and professional, subordinate and superior, ethnic minority and patriot, other and self, this couple confronted some of the key issues that would plague European societies in later decades. The relief workers represented all the qualities of the post-war social settlement: they were benevolent, professionalized, scientific, bureaucratic, far-sighted and planning-minded. UNRRA even initially suggested a type of internationalist idealism to some. An optimistic Quaker in 1943 argued that 'the provision of relief provides an excellent starting-point from which to apply the principle of dealing rather with human-beings or with "Europeans" than with nationals of particular countries'.[13] But this brief flowering of a humanist internationalism was swiftly curtailed by material circumstances: relief workers dealt with nation states, while refugees tried to join – or, if necessary, form – nation states. At first sight, one would almost automatically conclude that the relief workers were the winners in the contest. Even in the 12-year period that we have analysed, their methods and procedures improved, and the creation of UNRRA marked an important step in the politics of relief: rather than reacting to each crisis as a singular, exceptional event, the most important nation states of the world were accepting a permanent (or at least long-term) commitment to the welfare of refugees. Much of the rather ineffective, rather patronising ethos of the old religious charities was rejected. The new relief agencies were largely successful in their attempts to re-place the displaced; they prevented famine and mass epidemics in the post-1945 world; they created permanent legal and practical structures for the reception of refugees.

On the other hand, in the early twenty-first century, the relief worker's position looks less secure. The still untested nature of globalization suggests a different world culture from the secure national cultures which UNRRA took for granted. The refugee camp is in decline, now often seen by international powers as potentially a dangerous and costly institution, capable as acting as a base for contestation and challenge.[14] 'Relief' may still feature as a necessary minimum provision, but one hears fewer proposals for 'rehabilitation'; super-powers prefer to declare that 'they don't do nation-building'. And, correspondingly, some elements of the refugees' practices and cultures are now looking disturbingly familiar. Zygmunt Bauman – a writer with personal experience of exile – has coined the phrase 'liquid modernity' to identify the features of today's society. He writes that 'being modern came to mean, as it means today, being unable to stop and even unable to stand still'.[15] This sounds more like the life of the refugees that we have been studying than the life of the relief workers. Here, one has to distinguish between the first reaction by many refugees (belong to a nation state) and a deeper lesson that one can take from their experience (can nation states solve refugees' problems?).[16] Despite initial appearances, refugees' actions probably had a greater long-term impact on the post-war world than relief workers' programmes. The great, transformative journeys undertaken by the displaced and homeless were not unthinking, sheep-like rituals, to be resolved by intelligent social workers, but acts which permanently changed the face of political power. Since 1945, some of the great political issues which have concerned global opinion were those initiated by refugees' journeys: the fate of Franco's Spain, the creation of the state of Israel, the struggle of Palestinian nationalism, the relationship between the two Germanys ... However, rather than constantly proposing viable nationhoods as the obligatory solutions to these problems, it is time to start considering other proposals: the recurring debates in Israel / Palestine concerning dual-state and single-state schemas is perhaps an example of this. More significantly, the refugee's inherent, sometimes even unwilling, questioning of the nation state makes more sense in the twenty-first century. How often have we heard that all identities are multiple, not singular?[17]

In place of a study of big institutions, this work has presented a history of little peoples. E.F. Schumacher subtitled his *Small is Beautiful* 'economics as if people mattered'. A similar ethic has guided our study. We have refused to follow the dividing lines set up by different bureaucracies, and have instead stressed the common history shared by the Catholic volunteer, the Quaker humanitarian, the ICRC specialist and the UNRRA relief worker, by the Spanish republican, the French *exodien*, the Pole, the Jew, the Lithuanian, the Russian and the stateless DP. We understand why some scholars might prefer a more strictly focused study that differentiated sharply between – for example fugitives, slave labourers, ex-collaborators, concentration camp survivors and political exiles, but we insist that such forms of study run the risk of accepting arbitrary bureaucratic parameters as constituting 'real' social categories. When François Lafitte considered the political errors of the 1930s, he warned that 'thinking in terms of nations … prevented a full appreciation of the changing character of European reaction'.[18] Seventy years later, his words are echoed by Ned Thomas. 'We should seek to write a common European history which is more than a collection of nation state histories, and that we should do this while there is a surviving sense of the true complexity of what happened, suppressing nothing, and celebrating acts of human generosity and courage wherever they are found'.[19] The 'chaos' of the post-1945 world was largely the creation of ill-adapted bureaucracies: beneath and beyond the rival acronyms, there was a common outcast condition which can only be perceived by stepping outside of those parameters.

This condition was not a tragic exception to European history. Just as Zygmunt Bauman has placed the Holocaust in the mainstream of the development of European history, so we argue that the 'outcast' experience was emblematic of this era.[20] Many of the movements we have studied were the largest movements of people in their time; within them, there were people with some legitimate claim to represent the entirety of their societies; but, more importantly, their experiences represent, in concentrated form, the dilemmas faced by the majority population. At this moment, the settled patriot and the outcast rebel were not so much opposing forces as phases within the same movement: today's settled patriot might well be on the road tomorrow, while the outcast could be forming the government. Moreover, even the most settled of patriots found it difficult to maintain a consistent loyalty to government and nation during this period, marked by so many bewildering and unexpected political changes. One could, for example, consider the inhabitants of Berlin in 1945, who might be in houses in which their families had lived for generations, yet who could well consider that they were 'like refugees', for around them there was no government with which they could identify and which could aid them. Bauman recommends that, in place of singular nations, 'the trick is to be at home in many homes'.[21] Our study has shown the ability of little people to found many homes.

Notes

Notes to Introduction

1   George Orwell, 'Not Counting Niggers', in *Collected Essays, Journalism and Letters, Vol I* (London: Secker & Warburg, 1969), pp. 394–98 (p. 397).
2   See George Orwell, 'My Country Right or Left' in *Collected Essays, Journalism and Letters, Vol I* (London: Secker & Warburg, 1969), pp. 535–40. On this change of heart, see Bernard Crick, *George Orwell: A Life* (Harmondsworth: Penguin, 1980), pp. 380–96.
3   Victor Klemperer, *I Shall Bear Witness: the Diaries of Victor Klemperer, 1933–41,* abridged and translated by Martin Chalmers (London: Phoenix, 1999), pp. 157, 388.
4   *I Shall Bear Witness*, pp. 286, 293.
5   *To the Bitter End*, p. 62.
6   *I Shall Bear Witness*, p. 164.
7   Victor Klemperer, *To the Bitter End: The Diaries of Victor Klemperer, 1942–45,* abridged and translated by Martin Chalmers (London: Phoenix, 2000), pp. 13–14.
8   *I Shall Bear Witness*, p. 227.
9   *I Shall Bear Witness*, p. 374.
10 *To the Bitter End*, p. 34.
11 *To the Bitter End*, pp. 78 and 105.
12 *To the Bitter End*, p. 218.
13 *I Shall Bear Witness*, pp. 249, 306, 431; *To the Bitter End*, p. 110.
14 Richard J. Evans, *The Third Reich at War, 1939–1945* (London: Allen Lane, 2008), pp. 71–72.
15 Ana Delso, *Trescientos hombres y yo; estampa de una revolución,* translated by Antonia Ruiz Cabezas (Madrid: Anselmo Lorenzo, 1998), pp. 29, 53.
16 Jean-Paul Sartre, 'Paris sous l'Occupation' in Sartre, Jean-Paul, *Situations III: Lendemains de la guerre* (Paris, 1976), pp. 16–42 (p. 41).
17 François Lafitte, *The Internment of Aliens* (London: Penguin, 1988 [1940]), p. 21.
18 Pépita Carpeña, *Mémoires* (Paris: Editions du Monde Libertaire, 2000), pp. 41–5.
19 Rebecca Manley, 'The Perils of Displacement: the Soviet Evacuee between Refugee and Deportee', *Contemporary European History* 16:4 (2007), pp. 495–509.
20 *To the Bitter End*, pp. 508–9.
21 *To the Bitter End*, p. 601.
22 *Le Grand Robert, Dictionnaire alphabétique et analogique de la Langue Française,* Deuxième Edition entièrement revue et enrichie par Alain Rey, Vol VIII (Paris: Le Robert, 1992).
23 *Le Littré, Dictionnaire de la Langue Française,* Vol IV (Paris: Hachette, 1883).
24 Cited in Janine Ponty, 'Réfugiés, exilés, des catégories problématiques', *Matériaux pour l'histoire de notre temps* 44:1 (1996), pp. 9–13 (p. 9).
25 Saskia Sassen, *Guests and Aliens* (New York: New Press, 1999), pp. 35–7.
26 Geoffrey Best, *Humanity in Warfare* (London, Weidenfeld and Nicolson, 1980), p. 31.
27 J. Hutchinson, *Champions of Charity: War and the Rise of the Red Cross* (Boulder, Colorado; Oxford: Westview Press, 1995), p. 19.

28 F. M. Wilson, *They Came as Strangers: The Story of Refugees to Great Britain* (London: Hamish Hamilton, 1959), p. xv.

29 On the Ottoman case, see: Peter Loizos, 'Ottoman Half-lives: long-term Perspectives on Particular Forced Migrations', *Journal of Refugee Studies* 12:3 (1999), pp. 237–63

30 For a useful study of European refugees in the interwar period see C. M. Skran, *Refugees in inter-war Europe: the emergence of a regime* (Oxford: Clarendon, 1995).

31 Francesca M. Wilson, *Advice to Relief Workers* (London: John Murray and Friends Relief Service, 1944), p. 4.

32 Frank Caestecker, 'Les réfugiés et l'Etat en Europe occidentale pendant les XIXe et XX siècles', *Mouvement social* 225 (2008), pp. 9–26.

33 Julie Peteet, 'Unsettling the Categories of Displacement', *Merip* 244 (2007), http://www.merip.org/mer/mer244; accessed 7 March 2008

34 E. Valentine Daniel and John Chr. Knudsen, 'Introduction' to their *Mistrusting Refugees* (Berkeley: University of California Press, 1995), pp. 1–12.

35 When DPs from Eastern Europe and the Baltic states returned to their former homes after the collapse of Germany, they were often treated with suspicion or hostility. See Mark Wyman, *DPs: Europe's Displaced Persons, 1945–51* (Ithaca and London: Cornell University Press, 1998), pp. 9–10.

36 Jacques and Mona Ozouf, ' "Le Tour de France par deux enfants" ' in Pierre Nora (ed.), *Les Lieux de Mémoire* Vol I (Paris: Quarto / Gallimard, 1997) pp. 277–303.

37 We would like to acknowledge the assistance of our colleague, Professor Gavin Edwards, in the elaboration of this paragraph.

38 Wilson, *Advice to Relief Workers*, p. 19.

39 Jacques Vernant, *The Refugee in the Post-War World* (London: Allen & Unwin, 1953), p. 3.

40 *Mémoires d'un révolutionnaire* (Paris: Stock, 1951), p. 379.

41 Janine di Giovanni, *The Place at the End of the World; Essays from the Edge* (London: Bloomsbury, 2006), p. 8.

42 John Chr. Knudsen, 'When Trust in on Trial: Negotiating Refugee Narratives' in E. V. Daniel and J. C. Knudsen (eds), *Mistrusting Refugees* (Berkeley: University of California Press, 1995), pp. 13–35 (p. 22).

43 Jean-Paul Sartre, *Carnets de la drôle de guerre* (Paris: Gallimard, 1995); Georges Sadoul, *Journal de Guerre* (Paris: Français Réunis, 1977).

44 Mariano Constante, *Les années rouges, de Guernica à Mauthausen* (Vienne: Mercure de France, 1971), p. 7.

45 Nicole Dombrowski, `Beyond the Battlefield: the French civilian exodus of May–June, 1940', Unpublished PhD, New York University (1995); Antony Beevor, *Berlin: The Downfall 1945* (London: Penguin, 2002).

46 Gustave Folcher, *Les carnets de guerre de Gustave Folcher, paysan languedocien* (1939–1945) (Paris: Maspero, 1981), p. 70.

47 AMR, 6.H.10, dated 31 July 1940.

48 These have been carefully evaluated in Jean-Claude Pruja, *Premiers Camps de l'exil espagnol: Prats-de-Mollo, 1939* (Saint-Cyr-sur-Loire: Alan Sutton, 2003).

49 For example, ADBRhône, 174 W 34 and 148 W 185.

50 Francesca M. Wilson, *In the Margins of Chaos* (London: William Clowes and Sons, 1944). Appendix p. 269.

51 InternetArchive.org at http://www.archive.org/details/SeedsofDestiny accessed 25 March 2010.

52 Michel-Acatl Monnier, 'The Hidden Part of Asylum Seekers' Interviews in Geneva, Switzerland: Some Observations about the Socio-Political Construction of Interviews between Gatekeepers and Powerless', *Journal of Refugee Studies* 8:3 (1995), pp. 305–25 (p. 320).

53 Paul Burmetz, *Our Share of Morning* (London: Alvin Redman, 1961), pp. 89–90.

54 Jorge Semprun, *Literature or Life*, translated by Linda Coverdale (Harmondsworth: Penguin, 1998).

55 Scott Soo, 'Ambiguities at work: Spanish republican exiles and the organisation Todt in occupied Bordeaux', *Modern and Contemporary France* (2007), 15:4, pp. 456–77.

56 Pierre Miquel, *Histoires vraies de la Seconde guerre mondiale* (Paris, Fayard, 1988).

57 T. Néilas, *Des Français Face à L'invasion: Mai–Septembre* 1940 (Paris: Pygmalion, 2008).

58 Eduardo Pons Prades, *Las guerras de los niños republicanos (1936–1955)* (Madrid: Compañía Literaria, 1997); Neus Català, *Ces Femmes Espagnoles: de la Résistance à la Déportation; témoignages vivants de Barcelone à Ravensbrück*, translated by Caroline Langlois (Paris: Tirésias, 1994); Gabrielle Garcia and Isabelle Matas, *La mémoire retrouvée des Républicains espagnols: Paroles d'exilés en Ille-et-Vilaine* (Rennes: Editions Ouest-France, 2005); Natalia Benjamin, *Recuerdos: The Basque Children Refugees in Great Britain* (Norwich: Mousehold Press, 2007).

59 Kibbutz Buchenwald, 'Homecoming in Israel' in Leo W. Schwarz (ed.), *The Root and the Bough: the Epic of an Enduring People* (New York: Rinehard, 1949), pp. 308–45.

60 Manuela Consonni, 'The Written Memoir: Italy, 1945–1947', in D. Bankier (ed.), *The Jews are Coming Back* (New York: Berghahn, 2005 & Jerusalem: Yad Vashem, 2005), pp. 169–85 (p. 170).

61 On the simple, almost technical, problem of remembering, see the useful work by Karl Sabbagh, *Remembering Our Childhood: How Memory Betrays Us* (OUP, 2009).

62 Karl Marx, 'The Eighteenth Brumaire of Louis Napoleon' in Karl Marx and Frederick Engels, *Selected Works in Three Volumes: I* (Moscow: Progress, 1977), pp. 478–79.

63 ADHG, W, 2054/143, document dated 19 July 1940.

64 AMR, 6.H.17, undated document [July 1940?].

65 Luisa Passerini, 'Introduction' to her *Memory and Totalitarianism* (Oxford: OUP, 1992), pp. 1–21 (p. 3).

66 Juan Goytisolo, *Señas de identidad* (Madrid: Alianza Editorial, 1999 [1966]); Jorge Semprun, *Le Grand Voyage* (Paris: Gallimard, 1963).

67 Knudsen, 'When Trust in on Trial', p. 29.

68 John Beverly, 'The Margin at the Centre', in S. Smith and J. Watson (eds), *Decolonizing the Subject* (Minneapolis: University of Minnesota Press, 1992), pp. 91–114.

69 Beevor, *Berlin*, p. 75.

70 Beevor, *Berlin*, p. 53.

71 On the development of studies in this area, see the useful analysis by Claudena Skran and Carla N. Daughtry, 'The Study of Refugees before "Refugee Studies"', *Refugee Survey Quarterly* 26:3 (2007), pp. 15–35.

72 Wyman, *DPs: Europe's Displaced Persons*, p. 12.

73 See special issue of *Journal of Contemporary History*, 43:3 (July 2008); see also Sharif Gemie and Laure Humbert, 'Writing History in the Aftermath of "Relief": Some Comments on "Relief in the Aftermath of War", a reply to a special issue of the *Journal of Contemporary History', Journal of Contemporary History* 44:2 (2009) pp. 309–18.

74 Catherine Gousseff, *L'Exil Russe: La Fabrique du Réfugié Apatride (1920–1939)* (Paris: CNRS éditions, 2008).

75 *Life between Memory and Hope: The Survivors of the Holocaust in Occupied Germany* (Cambridge: Cambridge University Press, 2002).

76 Atina Grossmann, *Jews, Germans, and Allies: Close Encounters in Occupied Germany,* (Princeton: Princeton University Press, 2007).

77 Ben Wicks, *No Time to Wave Goodbye* (London: Bloomsbury, 1988).

78 Wicks, *No Time to Wave Goodbye*, p. 38.

Notes to Chapter 1

1 Hugh Thomas, *The Spanish Civil War* third edition (Harmondsworth: Penguin, 1986), p. 863.

2 Alicia Alted, *La voz de los vencidos: el exilio republicano de 1939* (Madrid: Santillana Ediciones Generales, 2005), pp. 31–4; Alicia Alted Vigil, 'Le retour en Espagne des enfants évacués pendant la guerre civile espagnole: la Délégation extraordinaire au rapatriement des mineurs (1938–1954)' translated by H. Poutet in [no editor], *Enfants de la guerre civile* (Paris: l'Harmattan, 1999), pp. 47–59.

3   Solano Polacio, 'El éxodo', *Cultura Proletariana* 581 (17 June 1939).
4   Geneviève Dreyfus-Armand, *L'exil des républicains espagnols en France* (Paris: Albin Michel, 1999), p. 32.
5   Hywel Frances, *Miners against Fascism: Wales and the Spanish Civil War* (London: Lawrence and Wishart, 1984), pp. 97–103.
6   Silvio Pons, 'La diplomatie soviétique, l'antifascisme et la guerre civile espagnole' in S. Wolikov and A. Bleton-Ruget (eds), *Antifascisme et nation* (Dijon: Editions Universitaires de Dijon, 1998), pp. 59–66.
7   David Berry, 'French Anarchists in Spain', *French History* 3:4 (1989), pp. 427–65.
8   Farah Mendelsohn, 'Denominational Difference in Quaker Relief Work During the Spanish Civil War: the Operation of Corporate Concern and Liberal Theologies', *Journal of Religious History* 24:2 (2000), pp. 180–95.
9   On the propaganda circulating among the Francoist authorities, see Francisco Sevillano, *Rojos: la representación del enemigo en la guerra civil* (Madrid: Alianza Editorial, 2007).
10 Francisco Espinosa Maestre, 'Julio de 1936: golpe militar y plan de exterminio' in Julián Casanova (ed.), *Morir, Matar, Sobrevivir* (Barcelona: Critica, 2004), pp. 51–119 (pp. 69–72).
11 Espinosa, 'Julio de 1936', p. 85.
12 Mariano Constante, *Les années rouges, de Guernica à Mauthausen* (Vienne: Mercure de France, 1971), pp. 101–2, 123.
13 Abel Paz, *Viaje al Pasado (1936–1939)* (Madrid: Anselmo Lorenzo, 2002), p. 282–3.
14 Andrés Capdevila, *Un episodio de nuestra evacuación a Francia* (Perpignan: privately published, 1970), p. 5.
15 Pépita Carpeña, *Mémoires* (Paris: Editions du Monde Libertaire, 2000), p. 35.
16 Jean-Claude Pruja, *Premiers Camps de l'exil espagnol: Prats-de-Mollo, 1939* (Saint-Cyr-sur-Loire: Alan Sutton, 2003), p. 12.
17 Federico Gargello Edo, *La Raison douleureuse* (Madrid: Anselmo Lorenzo, 1999), pp. 76, 83.
18 Dreyfus-Armand, *L'exil républicaine*, pp. 20–2.
19 'El Campesino' with Maurice Padiou, *Jusqu'à la mort* (Paris: Albin Michel, 1978), p. 46.
20 Ramon Moral i Querol, *Journal d'Exil, 1938–1945,* translated by N. Besset and M. Prudon (Paris: Eole, 1982), p. 26.
21 Isabel de Palencia, *Smouldering Freedom: the Story of the Spanish Republicans in Exile* (London: Gollancz, 1946), p. 37.
22 Neus Català, *Ces Femmes Espagnoles: de la Résistance à la Déportation; témoignages vivants de Barcelone à Ravensbrück,* translated by Caroline Langlois (Paris: Tirésias, 1994), p. 162.
23 Dolores Torres, *Chronique d'une femme rebelle* (Paris: Wern, 1997), p. 166.
24 Vicente Marti, *La Saveur des patates douces; histoire de ma vie, 1926–76* (Lyon: Atelier de Création Libertaire, 1998), p. 49.
25 Isabelle Alonso, *L'exil est mon pays* (Paris: Héloïse d'Ormesson, 2006), pp. 25, 173.
26 Carmen Martínez Ten and Purificación Gutiérrez López, 'Prólogo' in Carmen Martínez Ten, Purificación Gutiérrez López and Pilar González Ruiz (eds), *El movimiento feminista en España en los años 70* (Madrid: Fundación Pablo Iglesias, 2009), pp. 7–15 (p. 8).
27 Julio Martin Casas and Pedro Carvajal Urquijo, *El exilio español (1936–1978)* (Barcelona: Planeta, 2002), p. 25.
28 Abel Paz, *Entre la Niebla (1939–42)* (Barcelona: EA, 1993), pp. 16–17.
29 Torres, *Chroniques*, p. 139.
30 Capdevila, *Un episodio*, p. 14.
31 Vicente Llorens, *Estudios y Ensayos sobre el exilio republicano de 1939* (Sevilla: Renacimiento, 2006), p. 131.
32 Alted, *La voz*, p. 72.
33 Jordi Gracia, *La resistencia silenciosa: fascismo y cultura en España* (Barcelona: Anagrama, 2004), pp. 50–1.
34 Conxita Mir, 'El sino de los vencidos: la represión franquista en la Cataluña rural de posguerra' in J. Casanova (ed.), *Morir, Mater, Sobrevivir* (Barcelona: Crítica, 2004), pp. 123–95 (p. 154).
35 Carpeña, *Mémoires*, p. 36.

36 Federica Montseny, *Pasión y muerte de los españoles en Francia* (NP: Espoir, 1969 [originally published 1945–50]), p. 6.
37 Cited in Antonio Soriano (ed.), *Éxodos; historia oral del exilio republicana en Francia, 1939–1945* (Barcelona: Crítica, 1989), p. 88.
38 Constante, *Années rouges*, p. 140.
39 Delso, *Trescientos hombres y yo*, p. 73.
40 Carpeña, *Mémoires*, p. 35.
41 Capdevila, *Un episodio*, p. 8.
42 Solano Polacio, 'El Éxodo', *Cultura Proletaria* 579, 3 June 1939; Paz, *Entre la Niebla*, p. 19; Carpeña, *Mémoires*, p. 35.
43 Marti, *La Saveur*, p. 27.
44 Palencia, *Smouldering Freedom*, p. 38.
45 Solano Polacio, 'El éxodo', *Cultura Proletaria* 580 (10 June 1939).
46 Carpeña, *Mémoires*, p. 35.
47 Montseny, *Pasión y muerte*, p. 10.
48 Torres, *Chroniques*, p. 161.
49 Capdevila, *Un episodio*, p. 19.
50 Montseny, *Pasión y muerte*, p. 9.
51 Sara Berenguer, 'Éxodo' in Antonina Rodrigo (ed.), *Mujeres Libres: luchadoras libertarias* (Madrid: Anselmo Lorenzo, 1999), pp. 155–7.
52 Capdevila, *Un episodio*, p. 12.
53 Moral, *Journal*, p. 26.
54 Paz, *Viaje al Pasado*, pp. 289–90.
55 Torres, *Chroniques*, p. 160.
56 Capdevila, *Un episodio*, p. 13.
57 Paz, *Entre la Niebla*, p. 19.
58 Moral, *Journal*, p. 30.
59 Solano Polacio, 'El éxodo', *Cultura Proletaria* 582 (24 June 1939).
60 Solano Polacio, 'El éxodo', *Cultura Proletaria* 583 (1 July 1939).
61 Palencia, *Smouldering Freedom*, p. 35.
62 Carpeña, *Mémoires*, p. 35.
63 Paz, *Entra la niebla*, pp. 25–9
64 Capdevila, *Un episodio*, p. 26.
65 Polacio, 'El éxodo', *Cultura Proletaria* 579, 3 June 1939.
66 Delso, *Trescientes hombres*, p. 52.
67 Cited in Neus Català (ed.) *Ces Femmes Espagnoles: de la Résistance à la Déportation; témoignages vivants de Barcelone à Ravensbrück,* translated by Caroline Langlois (Paris: Tirésias, 1994), pp. 162–4 (p. 162).
68 Neil MacMaster, *Spanish Fighters; An Oral History of Civil War and Exile* (London: MacMillan, 1990), pp. 106–7.
69 Arturo Barea, *The Clash,* translated by Ilsa Barea (London: Faber and Faber, 1946), p. 308.
70 Paz, *Entre la Niebla*, p. 25.
71 Moral, *Journal*, pp. 27–8.
72 Palencia, *Smouldering Freedom*, p. 35.
73 Torres, *Chroniques*, pp. 163–5.
74 Maria Seco Mateo, 'Mi maletín, mi vida', *El País*, 12 January 2003.
75 Moral, *Journal*, p. 26.
76 MacMaster, *Spanish Fighters*, pp. 107–8.
77 Capdevila, *Un episodio*, p. 16.
78 Delso, *Trescientos hombres*, p. 52.
79 Capdevila, *Un episodio*, p. 17.
80 Paz, *Entre la Niebla*, p. 27.
81 Capdevila, *Un episodio*, p. 14.
82 Delso, *Trescientos hombres*, p. 53.
83 Montseny, *Pasión y muerte*, p. 10.

84 Delso, *Trescientos hombres*, p. 53.
85 Carpeña, *Mémoires*, p. 36.
86 Montseny, *Pasión y muerte*, p. 10.
87 Capdevila, *Un episodio*, p. 22.
88 Solano Polacio, 'El éxodo', *Cultura Proletaria* 581 (17 June 1939).
89 Paz, *Entre la Niebla*, pp. 25–7.
90 Constante, *Années rouges*, p. 132.
91 Solano Polacio, 'El éxodo', *Cultura Proletaria* 581 (17 June 1939).
92 Solano Polacio, 'El éxodo', *Cultura Proletaria* 579 (3 June 1939).
93 Capdevila, *Un episodio*, p. 14.
94 Delso, *Trescientos hombres*, p. 53.
95 Interview cited in Nancy MacDonald, *Homage to the Spanish Exiles: voices from the Spanish Civil War* (New York: Insight Books, 1987), p. 187.
96 Paz, *Entre la Niebla*, p. 27.
97 Paz, *Entre la Niebla*, p. 29.
98 Capdevila, *Un episodio*, p. 18.
99 Solano Polacio, 'El éxodo', *Cultura Proletaria*, 581 (17 June 1939).
100 Torres, *Chroniques*, p. 159.
101 Capdevila, *Un episodio*, p. 25.
102 Pierre Laborie, *Les Français des années troubles: de la guerre d'Espagne à la Libération* (Paris: Seuil, 2003), p. 108.
103 *La Dépêche*, 8 January 1939.
104 *La Dépêche*, 15 January 1939.
105 *Le Journal des Débats,* 6 and 7 February 1939.
106 *Gringoire*, 9 February 1939.
107 Copy in ADI&V, 4/M/414 dated 27 September1937.
108 Copy in ADI&V, 4/M/414 dated 18 October 1937.
109 Copy in ADI&V, 4/M/414 dated 10 June 1938.
110 Georges Bernanos, 'Les grands cimetières sous la lune' in *Essais et écrits de combat* (Paris: Gallimard, 1971), p. 427.
111 Dreyfus-Armand, *L'exil républicaine*, p. 31.
112 For example, André Chamson, 'Retour d'Espagne: rien qu'un témoignage' in his *Les Livres de la guerre* (Paris: Omnibus, 2005), pp. 139–42.
113 Greg Burgess, *Refuge in the Land of Liberty* (London: Palgrave Macmillan, 2008), p. 217.
114 Arturo Barea, *The Clash* translated by Ilsa Barea (London: Faber & Faber, 1946), p. 321.
115 *La Dépêche*, 28 January1939.
116 *L'Humanité*, 30 January 1939.
117 *L'Oeuvre,* 29 January 1939.
118 *L'Humanité,* 30 January 1939.
119 *Ouest-Eclair*, 26 January 1939.
120 *The Times*, 30 January 1939.
121 *Ouest-Eclair*, 29 January 1939.
122 *Ouest-Eclair*, 30 January 1939.
123 *The Times*, 31 January 1939.
124 *L'Oeuvre,* 29 January 1939.
125 *La Dépêche*, 29 January 1939.
126 *La Croix*, 7 February 1939.
127 *L'Oeuvre,* 31 January 1939.
128 *La Dépêche*, 30 January 1939.
129 *Ouest-Eclair*, 1 February 1939.
130 *La Croix*, 28 August 1939.
131 *Ouest-Eclair*, 9 February 1939.
132 *La Dépêche* 29 January 1939.
133 *La Croix,* 8 February 1939.
134 *Ouest-Eclair*, 2 February 1939.

135 *La Dépêche*, 31 January 1939.
136 *La Dépêche*, 1 February 1939.
137 ADPO, W/31/274, reported dated 17 March 1939.
138 Palencia, *Smouldering Freedom*, p. 37.
139 Capdevila, *Un episodio*, p. 28.
140 Constante, *Années rouges*, pp. 136–7.
141 Moral, *Journal*, p. 29.
142 Delso, *Trescientos hombres*, p. 55.
143 Torres, *Chronique*, pp. 166–7.
144 Eduardo Pons Prades, *Las guerras de los niños republicanos (1936–1955)* (Madrid: Compañía Literaria, 1977), p. 165.
145 Cited in Nancy MacDonald, *Homage to the Spanish Exiles; voices from the Spanish Civil War* (New York: Insight Books, 1987), p. 103
146 MacMaster, *Spanish Fighters*, pp. 109–11.
147 MacMaster, *Spanish Fighters*, pp. 113–14.
148 Capdevila, *Un episodio*, p. 28.
149 Carpeña, *Mémoires*, pp. 37–8.
150 Cited in Català, *Ces femmes espagnoles*, p. 206.
151 Carpeña, *Mémoires*, p. 39.
152 Montseny, *Pasión y muerte*, p. 50.
153 Capdevila, *Un episodio*, p. 29.
154 Constante, *Années rouges*, p. 138.
155 Carpeña, *Mémoires*, p. 39.
156 Palencia, *Smouldering Freedom*, p. 68.
157 *La Dépêche*, 2 February 1939.
158 *Gringoire*, 9 February 1939.
159 *La Dépêche*, 29 January 1939.
160 *Journal des débats,* 1 February 1939.
161 *Ouest-Eclair*, 2 February 1939.
162 *Ouest-Eclair*, 31 January 1939.
163 *La Dépêche*, 30 January 1939.
164 *Ouest-Eclair*, 7 February 1939.
165 *La Dépêche*, 4 February 1939.
166 *Ouest-Eclair*, 8 February 1939.
167 *L'Action Française*, 18 February 1939.
168 *Ouest-Eclair*, 8 February 1939.
169 *La Dépêche*, 2 February 1939.
170 *Journal des Débats*, 3 February 1939.
171 *La Dépêche*, 5 February 1939.
172 *L'Intransigeant,* 8 February 1939.
173 *L'Intransigeant,* 1 February 1939.
174 *La Dépêche*, 1 February 1939.
175 Cited in Català, *Ces femmes espagnoles*, p. 162.
176 *La Dépêche*, 4 February 1939.
177 *La Dépêche*, 1 February 1939.
178 *Ouest-Eclair*, 10 Febuary 1939.
179 *L'Action Française*, 10 February 1939.
180 *Le Journal des débats*, 10 February 1939.
181 *Le Figaro,* 1 February 1939; see also *Le Figaro,* 4 February 1939.
182 *Ouest-Eclair*, 8 February 1939.
183 *Le Figaro,* 1 February 1939; *Le Figaro,* 2 February 1939.
184 *La Dépêche*, 5 February 1939.
185 *La Dépêche*, 6 February 1939.
186 *Gringoire,* 2 March 1939.
187 *L'Action Française,* 3 February 1939.

188   *L'Action Française,* 10 and 27 February 1939.
189   *La Croix,* 24 February 1939.
190   *L'Oeuvre,* 31 January 1939; *La Dépêche,* 1 February 1939; *Le Figaro,* 3 February 1939; *Le Figaro,* 2 February 1939; *L'Action Française,* 18 February 1939.
191   *Gringoire,* 9 February 1939.
192   Montseny, *Pasión y muerte,* p. 18.
193   Prujo, *Premiers camps,* pp. 93–7.
194   'A Woman', *Report on Spanish refugee camps near Perpignan,* NA, FO 371/24154. Some left-wing French papers also published criticisms: for example, *Le Canard Enchaîné,* 1 February 1939; *L'Humanité,* 12 and 13 February 1939.
195   Montseny, *Pasión y muerte,* p. 13.

Notes to Chapter 2

1   W. Somerset Maugham, *France at War* (London: William Heinemann, 1940), p. 27.
2   *Marianne in Chains: in search of the German occupation of France 1940–45* (London, MacMillan, 2002), p. 514.
3   *The Times,* 1 February 1881.
4   On French attitudes to war, see the perceptive analysis of Daniel Hucker, 'French public attitudes towards the prospect of war in 1938–9: "pacifism" or "war anxiety"?', *French History* 21:4 (2007), pp. 431–9. The reception of images of war is also discussed in: Jean-Pierre Azéma, *1940 L'année terrible* (Paris: Seuil, 1990), p. 21. Ben Wicks stresses the importance of these images in justifying the need for mass evacuation in Britain: *No Time to Wave Goodbye* (London: Bloomsbury, 1988), p. 43.
5   In reality, more civilians died in the Second World War than in previous conflicts: they counted for approximately two-third of all war victims: Ian Kershaw, 'War and political violence in twentieth century Europe', *Contemporary European History* 14:1 (2005), pp. 107–23 (p. 109).
6   For attitudes to war among French teachers see Mona Siegel, '"To the Unknown Mother of the Unknown Soldier": Pacifism, Feminism and the Politics of Sexual Difference among French Institutrices between the Wars', *French Historical Studies* 22:3 (1999), pp. 421–51; for attitudes to war among French war veterans see Antoine Prost, *Les anciens combattants et la société française 1914–1939,* 3 volumes (Paris: Presses de la Fondation Nationale des Sciences Politiques, 1977); on intellectuals and war see Jean-François Sirinelli, *Génération intellectuelle. Khâgneux et normaliens dans l'entre deux guerres* (Paris: Fayard, 1988).
7   Philippe Garraud, 'The Politics of Fortification of the Borders, 1925–40: logic, constraint, and the use of the *Maginot Line*', *Guerres Mondiales et Conflits Contemporains* 57 (2007), pp. 3–22.
8   See the references to Daladier's speech in H. Shamir, 'The drôle de guerre and French public opinion', *Journal of Contemporary History,* 11:1 (1976), pp. 129–43, (p. 136).
9   Samuel Goodfellow, 'From Germany to France? Interwar Alsatian national Identity', *French History,* 7:4 (1993), pp. 450–71 (p. 455). On the complex problem of the eastern regions and French identity, see also Stephen L. Harp, *Learning to Be Loyal: Primary Schooling as Nation Building in Alsace and Lorraine, 1850–1940* (Dekalb: Northern Illinois University Press, 1998).
10   Personal communication to the authors, 2008.
11   ADBRhin, 98/AL/923, circular dated 12 August 1933.
12   Garraud, 'The politics of fortification of the borders'; Philippe Garraud, 'French rearmament policy, 1936–40: priorities and constraints', *Guerres Mondiales et Conflits Contemporains* 55 (2005), pp. 87–102; Roxanne Panchasi, '"Fortress France": Protecting the Nation and its Bodies, 1918–1940', *Historical Reflections* 33:3 (2007), pp. 475–504; Robert Doughty, 'The Maginot Line', *Military History Quarterly* 9:2 (1997), pp. 48–59; J.-M. Marrill, 'French Military Doctrine between the two wars', *Revue Historique des Armées* 3 (1991), pp. 24–34.

13   Philippe Nivet 'Les réfugiés de guerre dans la société française (1914–1946)', *Histoire, Economie et société*, 23:2 (2004), pp. 247–59 (p. 248).

14   For the impact of Great War memories see: Antoine Prost, *Republican Identities in War and Peace: Representations of France in the Nineteenth and Twentieth Centuries*, translated by J. Winter and H. McPhail (Oxford: Berg, 2002), pp. 93–106; Julian Jackson, *The Fall of France: the Nazi invasion of 1940* (Oxford: Oxford University Press, 2003) p. 177; Jean Vidalenc, *L'Exode de mai–juin 1940* (Paris: Presses Universitaires de France, 1957) p. 64.

15   On planning for evacuation, see Marcel Neu, *L'évacuation en Lorraine, 1939–40* (Sarreguemines: Pierron, 1989), pp. 15, 43 and 57. For an example of a French study of another country, see Ministère de l'Air, *La Défense passive en Allemagne* (Paris: Imprimerie Nationale, 1938).

16   AMR, 6/H/1, noted dated 20 April 1939; ADM, 127/W/49, dated 7 July 1939.

17   AMM, H [unclassified], report dated 21 June 1939.

18   Vidalenc, *L'Exode*, p. 34.

19   P. Schaeffer, *Moselle et Mosellans dans la Seconde Guerre Mondiale* (Metz: Editions Serpenoise, Société d'Histoire et d'Archéologie de la Lorraine, 1983), p. 21.

20   AN, F/23/233, minutes dated 25 February 1940.

21   Schaeffer, *Moselle et Mosellans*, p. 23.

22   'Une initiative de M. Burrus. Considérations en faveur de la non-évacuation', *Le Messin*, 6 March 1939.

23   Paul Burmetz, *Our Share of Morning* (London: Alvin Redman, 1961), p. 128.

24   ADBRhin, 98/AL/275, undated circular (September 1939?).

25   ADM, 2/J/1521, undated notes for public lectures, 1939.

26   AMM, H [unclassified], 31 Jan 1939.

27   J.-Y. Besselievre, 'La défense passive en France, 1930–44: l'exemple de Brest', Revue Historique des Armées 4 (1998), pp. 97–103; *Bulletin de la Société de Secours aux Blessés Militaires* July 1935, pp. 59–60.

28   A collection of *Défense passive* literature is held at the Institut d'histoire du temps présent. ARC 074–01.

29   *Ce qu'est la Défense passive* (Paris: Publicité et Progande, nd [1939/40?]), p. 16.

30   Observations by: Janet Flanner, 'Letter from Paris' and A. J. Liebling, 'Letter from Paris' in *The New Yorker Book of War Pieces: London, 1939 to Hiroshima, 1945* (New York: Schocken Books, 1988), pp. 6–8, 9–10; Simone de Beauvoir, *La force de l'âge* Vol II (Paris: Gallimard, 1960), pp. 436–40.

31   AMR, 6/H/1, circular dated 9 October 1939.

32   ADHG, W/2024/142, circular dated 26 September 1939.

33   AMR, 6/H/1, dated 4 September 1939; AMR, 6/H/22, 5 September 1939.

34   ADHG, W/2024/102, circular dated 14 September 1939.

35   D. Weiller, *Les Morts en Moi*, held at Institut d'histoire du temps présent ARC 061 (s.d.), p. 84.

36   ADHG, W/2024/102: see, for example, the letter dated 13 September 1939 by the mayor of Arbas.

37   ADR, 4/M/236, Police report, 18 September 1939.

38   Julian Jackson, *France: the Dark Years, 1940–44* (Oxford: Oxford University Press, 2003) p. 113; see also Vicky Caron, *Uneasy Asylum: France and the Jewish Refugee Crisis 1933–1942* (Stanford: California, 1999). For France as the last asylum, see Victor Serge, *Les Derniers Temps* (Paris: Bernard Grasset, 1951), p. 130; on changing immigration policies, see Rahma Harouni, 'Le débat autour du status des étrangers dans les années 1930', *Mouvement social* 188 (1999), pp. 61–75 and, more generally, Gérard Noiriel, *Réfugiés et Sans-Papiers; la République face au droit d'asile, XIX–XXe siècle* (Paris: Calman-Levy, 1998).

39   'Volontaires Etrangers', *Revue des Deux Mondes* 51 (1 May 1939), p. 53.

40   See, for example, ADR, 3958/W/118, report dated 6 February 1940. The lack of a 'Union Sacrée' may well have exacerbated conflicts during the *drôle de guerre* but Nivet has argued that even during the First World War there was hostility between the northern refugees and their southern hosts. See Philippe Nivet, 'Les réfugiés de guerre dans la société française (1914–1946)', *Histoire, Economie & Société* 23:2 (2004), pp. 247–59 (p. 250).

41   The atmosphere of these years is analysed in Talbot Imlay, 'Mind the Gap: the Perception and Reality of Communist Sabotage of French War Production during the Phoney War, 1939–40', *Past and Present* 89 (2005), pp. 179–204. These fears became even more acute after the invasion: see, for example, *Le Temps*, 14 May 1940; *L'Oeuvre*, 29 May 1940.

42   Christian Delporte, 'The Image and Myth of the "Fifth Column" during the Two World Wars' in Valerie Holman and Debra Kelly (eds), *France at War in the Twentieth Century* (Oxford: Berghahn, 2000), pp. 49–64.

43   Paul Lawrence, ' "Un flot d'agitateurs politiques, de fauteurs de désordre et de criminels"; adverse perceptions of immigrants in France between the wars', *French History* 14:2 (2000), pp. 201–21; Mary Dewhurst Lewis, *The Boundaries of the Republic: Migrant Rights and the Limits of Universalism in France, 1918–1940* (Stanford, California: Stanford University Press, 2007).

44   Serge, *Les Derniers Temps,* p. 30.

45   Nicole Ollier, *L'Exode sur les routes de l'an 40* (Paris: Culture, Art, Loisirs, 1969), p. 44.

46   Denis Peschanski, *La France des camps: l'internement, 1938–1946* (Paris: Gallimard, 2002), p. 77. See also: Sabine Meunier, 'Les Juifs de Belgique dans les camps du Sud-Ouest de la France' in Max Lagarrigue (ed.), *1940: La France du repli; l'Europe de la défaite* (Toulouse: Privat, 2001), pp. 33–49; Regina Delacor, 'From Potential Friends to Potential Enemies: the internment of "Hostile Foreigners" at the Beginning of the Second World War', *Journal of Contemporary History* 35:3 (2000), pp. 361–8.

47   Arthur Koestler, *The Scum of the Earth* (London: Jonathan Cape, 1941), pp. 89–90, 97.

48   SHAT, DA 53083–53075/ F: 20.438–20.475, 26 May 1940.

49   J.-P. Sartre, *Carnets de la drôle de guerre Septembre 1939–1940* (Paris: Gallimard, 1995), pp. 231–3.

50   A. Sarraut, *Instruction générale à l'usage de messieurs les préfets sur les mouvements et transports de sauvegarde* (Melun: no publisher, 1938), p. 57.

51   ADHG, 2054/W/142, 5 October 1939.

52   ADHG, 2054/W/142, 14 September 1939.

53   AMR, 6/H/10, undated [September 1939?].

54   AMR, 6/H/10, circular dated 1 September 1939.

55   The information given in the following paragraphs comes from ADHG, W/2024/102; most of the mayors' letters were written in September and October 1939. On local preparation for evacuation, see also the useful study by Pascal Plas, 'L'encadrement administratif des réfugiés. L'exemple de la Haute-Vienne' in Max Lagarrigue (ed.), *1940: La France du repli; l'Europe de la défaite* (Toulouse: Privat, 2001), pp. 175–86. Plas stresses the need for local, private initiatives to supplement the inadequately organized official bodies.

56   One can find similar attitudes expressed by the mayors of the Pyrénées-Orientales: see ADPO, W/38/63, letters from September and October 1939. See also the letters from Prefects to the Home Minister in AN, F/23/229.

57   Weiller, *Les Morts en Moi,* p. 90.

58   See Prefect's circulars to mayors, AMR, 6/H/10, dated 2, 9 and 13 September 1939.

59   Neu, *Evacuation*, p. 151. AN, F/23/229, Rapport Fredault sur les évacuations de septembre 1939, 15 October 1939, p. 4.

60   ADBRhin, 99/AL/281, report dated 25 October 1939.

61   *The Times*, 15 May 1940.

62   AN, F/23/229, Rapports de préfets fragmentaires et en désordre septembre 39 février 1940.

63   ADBRhin, 98/AL/282, 2 September 1939.

64   Juliette Droz, 'Les Evacués de Paris dans les départements-refuge', *Service Social Familial* 34:1 (November 1939), pp. 14–20.

65   Gustave Folcher, *Les Carnets de Guerre de Gustave Folcher, Paysan Langeudocien 1939–1945* (Paris: François Maspero, 1981), pp. 21–2.

66   AN, F/23/333, Conférence interdépartementale, 25 February 1940.

67   AN, F/23/233, letter from Léon Lagrange to C. Chautemps, 2 April 1940.

68   AN, F/23/229, Rapport Fredault sur les évacuations de septembre 1939, 15 October 1939, p. 8; Rapport suisse sur la Défense passive de Paris et le problème de l'évacuation Rapport

Secret, no.3009, Institut d'Etudes Européennes de Strasbourg (Moutaines-le-Haut, le 12 mars 1940), p. 7. See also Neu, *Evacuation*, p. 126.

69 IHTP Fonds Vallotton ARC101–1, 8 September 1939.
70 IHTP Fonds Vallotton ARC101–1, letter from Pierre Vallotton to his parents, 15 September 1939.
71 IHTP Fonds Vallotton ARC 101–1, A. Vallotton to her parents, 20 December 1939.
72 IHTP Fonds Vallotton ARC 101–1, A. Vallotton to her parents, 20 December 1939.
73 ADBR, 98/AL/282, 10 September 1939.
74 IHTP Fonds Vallotton ARC101–1, A. Vallotton to her parents, 20 December 1939.
75 AMN, (6b) H4–5. Lettre de Madame Lafleur, 18 May 1940.
76 ADBRhin, 98/AL/280, report dated 17 October 1939.
77 Droz, 'Les évacués de Paris', p. 15.
78 IHTP ARC 100 (3–4) Fonds documentaires J.-L. Cremieux-Brillhac, E. Muller, Sénat Séance 27 December 1939.
79 ADMM, W/18/28, Mayor of Ancerviller, 25 September 1939; Mayor of Roville, 23 September 1939.
80 ADMM, W/18/218, 14 September 1939.
81 ADMM, W/18/218, 12 September 1939.
82 ADMM, W/18/28, 11 September 1939.
83 ADBRhin, 98/AL/218, 3 November 1939.
84 IHTP Fonds Vallotton Annie Vallotton to her parents, 1 February 1940.
85 IHTP Fonds documentaires J-L Cremieux-Brillhac ARC 100 (3–4) Fonds Crem-Bril Letter from G. Cros to Mme Ganne, 12 October 1939.
86 IHTP Fonds Vallotton ARC101–1 A. Vallotton to her parents, 18 November 1939.
87 AN Série F/23/229. Lettre d'un rédacteur aux « Dernières nouvelles de Colmar » à Monsieur le Directeur Général des Services d'Alsace et de Lorraine, 21 November 1939.
88 *The Times*, 28 February 1940.
89 AN, F/23/229. Dordogne Prefect, letter dated 9 October 1939.
90 AN, F/23/233, 'Brève étude des Fonctionnaires évacués du Bas Rhin', February 1940.
91 AN, F/23/229, Maurice Breton 'Compte-rendu d'une seconde mission effectuée en Dordogne concernant les populations abandonnées du Bas Rhin', 1939, p. 1. See also AMM, H [unclassified], Copie d'un rapport à Monsieur le maire concernant le voyage de mission auprès des évacués messins en Charente-Inférieure, Metz, le 24 novembre 1939.
92 AMM, H [unclassified], account dated 12 October 1939.
93 Folcher, *Les Carnets de Guerre,* pp. 22–4.
94 AN F/23/229, Letter from the Calvados Prefect dated 10 September 1939.
95 Tereska Torres, *Une française libre; Journal 1939–1945* (Paris: France-Loisirs, 2000), p. 24.
96 Laird Boswell, 'Franco-Alsatian Conflict and the Crisis of National sentiment during the Phoney War', *Journal of Modern History* 71:3 (1999), pp. 552–84. We have found this article extremely useful.
97 F. Le Gros Clark and Richard W. Toms, *Evacuation: Failure or Reform* (London: The Fabian Society, 1940), pp. 2–3.
98 ADBRhin, 98/AL/288, police reports, dated 4 January and 3 February 1940.
99 ADBRhin, 98/AL/288, police report, dated 29 January 1940.
100 ADBRhin, 98/AL/287, undated report by the Fédération française des éclaireuses [November 1939?].
101 IHTP Fonds Vallotton ARC101–1 A. Vallotton to her parents, 20 December 1939. Similar sentiments were recorded by the Prefect of Bas-Rhin: ADBR, 98/AL/288, 9 December 1939.
102 Sartre, *Carnets*, p 247.
103 IHTP Fonds documentaires J.-L. Crémieux-Brillhac ARC 100 (3–4), Letter from British Consulate General of Strasbourg to The Right Honourable Sir R. Campell, 29 December 1939.
104 AN Série F/23/229 Rapport Fredault and Lettre d'un rédacteur aux 'Dernières nouvelles de Colmar' à Monsieur le Directeur Général des Services d'Alsace et de Lorraine, 21 November 1939.

105 *Journal du Loiret*, 14 April 1940.
106 AN, F/23/233, M. Ott, 'Les fonctionnaires evacués du Bas-Rhin', February 1940 p. 13.
107 ADBRhin, 98/AL/288, reports dated 15 February and 7 March 1940.
108 Somerset Maugham, *France at War*, pp. 29–31.
109 AN Série F/23/233, M. Ott, 'Les fonctionnaires evacués du Bas-Rhin', February 1940 p. 3.
110 H. Bordeaux, 'La jeunesse féminine dans la guerre', *Revue des Deux Mondes* (55), 15 February 1940, pp. 595–618; P. Lesourd, 'L'Action Catholique au service de la nation', *Revue des Deux Mondes* (56), 1 April 1940, pp. 634–58.
111 *La Croix*, 8 October 1939.
112 See, for example, A. Lacroix, 'L'abandon de la terre', *Revue des Deux Mondes* (55), 1 February 1940 pp. 493–505.
113 ADBRhin, 98/AL/288, report by Contrôleur-Général Monnard, 7 November 1939.
114 ADBRhin, 98/AL/ 288, reports dated 11 November and 6 December 1939.
115 ADBRhin, 98/AL/288, police report for the Périgueux, dated 3 January 1940.
116 ADBRhin, 98/ AL/288, police reports concerning the Charente, 2 and 4 January 1940; police report on the Landes, 4 January 1940.
117 ADBRhin, 98/AL/288, report dated 5 May 1940.
118 ADBRhin, 98/AL/288, report dated 5 May 1940.
119 ADBRhin, 98/AL/288, 5 December 1939.
120 ADBRhin, 98/AL/288, report dated 15 January 1940.
121 ADBRhin, 98/AL/288, report by the Controleur-Général de la Sûreté National, 13 January 1940.
122 ADBRhin, 98/AL/288, report by the Controleur-Général de la Sûreté National, 15 March 1940.
123 On such suspicions, see also: ADBRhin, 98/AL/287, letter dated 15 November 1939; Somerset Maugham, *France at War*, p. 31.
124 Giraudoux, 'Messages du Continental. Allocutions radiodiffusées du Commissaire Général à l'Information', *Cahiers Jean Giraudoux* 16 (1987), pp. 81–4.
125 *Le Comité Français de Service Social Historique de son action, 1927–41* (Bergeur-Levrault, 1947) pp. 45–6.
126 IHTP Fonds Vallotton ARC101–1 A. Vallotton, 27 December 1939.
127 See, for example, ADBR, 98/AL/288, report for the Haute-Vienne, 5 January 1940; report by Contrôleur-général de la Sureté Nationale, 13 January 1940; report for the Charente-Inférieure, 12 January 1940.
128 IHTP Fonds Vallotton ARC101–1 A. Vallotton, 29 December 1939.
129 IHTP Fonds Vallotton ARC101–1 A. Vallotton, 27 December 1939.
130 IHTP Fonds Vallotton ARC101–1 A. Vallotton, 26 February 1940.
131 IHTP Fonds Vallotton ARC101–1 A. Vallotton, 29 December 1939.
132 IHTP Fonds documentaires J-L Cremieux-Brillhac ARC 100 (3–4) letter from British Consulate General of Strasbourg to the Right Honourable Sir R. Campell KCMG, 29 December 1939.
133 *The Times*, 28 February 1940.
134 IHTP Fonds Vallotton ARC101–1 E. Rupp to M. Boegner, 15 September 1939.
135 AN Série F/23/229, *Rapport suisse sur la Défense passive de Paris et le problème de l'évacuation*, no.3009, Institut d'Etudes Européennes de Strasbourg (Moutaines-le-Haut, le 12 mars 1940).
136 Weiller, *Les Morts en Moi*, p. 85.
137 D. Barlone, *A French Officer's Diary*, translated by L. V. Cass (Cambridge: CUP, 1942), p. 12.
138 Roland Dorgelès, *La drôle de guerre, 1939–40* (Paris: Albin Michel, 1957), p. 56.
139 Somerset Maugham, *France at War* pp. 23–4.
140 ADR, 4/M/236 Rapport sur les opérations de la commission de contrôle intérieur de Lyon, 16–30 novembre 1939.
141 Père Amand Boulé, *De Dunkerque à la Liberté* (Saint-Brieuc: Les Presses bretonnes, 1976), pp. 19–20.
142 Sartre, *Carnets*, p. 98.

143 Folcher, *Carnets*, pp. 40–1.
144 Raymond Guérin, *Lettres à Sonia, 1939–1943* (Paris: Gallimard, 2005), p. 24.
145 Christian Habrioux, *La Déroute (1939–1940)* (Paris: Aux Armes de France, 1941), pp. 140 and 170.
146 ADBRhin, 98/AL/283, report given in the Chamber of Deputies, 25 November 1939.
147 ADR, 4/M/236 [undated].
148 Sartre, *Carnets*, p. 217.
149 Valentin Feldman, *Journal de Guerre* (Tours: Farrago, 2006), p. 150.
150 Folcher, *Carnets*, p. 40.
151 Sartre, *Carnets*, p. 369.
152 ADBRhin, 98/AL/283, letters dated 28 October, 2 November, 7 November and 9 November 1939.
153 ADBRhin, 98/AL/283, report dated 18 October 1939.

Notes to Chapter 3

1   Georges Friedmann, *Journal de Guerre 1939–1940* (Paris: Gallimard, 1987), p. 272.
2   Jean-Pierre Azéma, *1940 L'année terrible* (Paris: Seuil, 1990), pp. 119–20.
3   Claire Chevrillon, *Une résistance ordinaire; septembre 1939 – août 1944* (Paris: Félin, 1999), pp. 14–15. For a relevant discussion see Sharif Gemie and Fiona Reid, 'Chaos, panic and the historiography of the exode (France, 1940)', *War and Society*, 26 (2007), pp. 73–97.
4   Nicole Ollier, *L'Exode* (Paris: Culture, Art, Loisirs, 1969), p. 100.
5   Pierre Miquel, *Histoires vraies de la Seconde guerre mondiale* (Paris, Fayard, 1988), p. 223.
6   Georges Sadoul, *Journal de Guerre (2 septembre 1939 – 20 juillet 1940)* (Paris: Français Réunis, 1977), p. 25.
7   René Rémond 'L'opinion française des années 1930 aux années 1940. Poids de l'évènement, permanence des mentalités', in Jean-Pierre Azéma and Bedarida (eds) *Vichy et les Français* (Paris: Fayard, 1992), pp. 481–92 (p. 483).
8   Jean Loubignac, *Sommes-nous défendus?*, 1938–39. Also see Vincent Lowy, *Guerre à la guerre ou le pacifisme dans le cinéma français, 1936–40* (Paris: L'Harmattan, 2006), p. 37.
9   Paul Allard, *La guerre du mensonge. Comment on nous a bourré le crâne* (Paris, Les Editions de France, 1940), p. 2. The poster is reproduced in Laurent Gervereau, *La propagande par l'affiche* (Paris: Syros Alternative, 1991), p. 94.
10 Roland Dorgelès, *La drôle de guerre, 1939–40* (Paris: Albin Michel, 1957), pp. 101–04. This work reproduces Dorgelès's journalism, but also includes his retrospective commentaries on his own work.
11 Friedmann, *Journal de Guerre*, p. 39.
12 Léon Werth *33 jours* (Paris: Viviane Hamy, 1992), p. 46.
13 Dorgelès, *La drôle de guerre*, p. 33.
14 D. Barlone, *A French Officer's Diary (23 August 1939 – 1 October 1940)*, translated by L. V. Cass (Cambridge: CUP, 1942), p. 35.
15 Henri Alexandre Sautreuil, *J'avais dix ans en 1940* (Luneray: Bertout, 2000), p. 106.
16 Edith Thomas, *Pages de Journal, 1939–1944* suivies de *Journal Intime de Monsieur Célestin Costedet* (Paris: Viviane Hamy, 1995), 3–8 mai 1940, pp. 58–9.
17 Pierre Laborie, *L'opinion française sous Vichy* (Paris: Seuil, 2001), p. 222.
18 Leonard V. Smith, Stéphane Audoin-Rouzeau and Annette Becker, *France and the Great War, 1914–1918* (Cambridge: Cambridge University Press, 2003), p. 181.
19 Thierry Nélias, *Des Français face à l'invasion, mai–septembre 1940* (Paris: Pygmalion, 2008), p. 40.
20 *Une jeunesse bretonne: an durzunell* (Rennes: Sareda, 1998), p. 22. See also Eric Alary, *L'Exode: un drame oublié* (Paris: Perrin, 2010), pp. 91–5.
21 For anti-war sentiment among French veterans, see Antoine Prost, *Les anciens combatants et la société française 1914–1939*, 3 volumes (Paris: Presses de la Fondation Nationale des

Sciences Politiques, 1977). See also Jean-Louis Crémieux-Brilhac, *Les Français de l'an 40 (I): La guerre oui ou non?* (Paris: Gallimard, 1990), p. 713; Julian Jackson, *The Fall of France: the Nazi invasion of 1940* (Oxford: Oxford University Press, 2003) p. 177.

22 Werth, *33 jours*, p. 130.

23 Cited in Jacques Bardoux, *Journal d'un Témoin de la Troisième; 1 septembre 1939–15 juillet 1940* (Paris: Libraire Arthème Fayard, 1957), p. 166.

24 Archives Nationales 72/AJ/2277, Georgette Guillot, *Trois semaines d'Exode,* journal dacty-lographié de Georgette Guillot, secrétaire au ministère de l'Intérieur, 9 juin – 14 juillet 1940, p. 3.

25 This topic has been the subject of an extended historical debate. See: F. Bédarida, 'Huit mois d'attente et d'illusion: la " drôle de guerre" ', in J.-P. Azéma & F. Bédarida (eds), *La France des années noires,* Tome 1 (Paris: Seuil, 1993), pp. 37–67; William Irvine 'Domestic Politics and the fall of France in 1940', in Joel Blatt (ed.) *The French Defeat of 1940: Reassessments* (Providence and Oxford: Berghahn, 1998), pp. 85–99; Peter Jackson 'Returning to the Fall of France: recent work on the causes and consequences of the "Strange defeat" of 1940', *Modern and Contemporary France* 12:4 (2004), pp. 513–6.

26 Dorgelès, *La drôle de guerre*, p. 221.

27 Luc Capdevila and Fabrice Virgili, 'Guerre, femme et Nation en France (1939–1945),' *Institut d'histoire du temps présent,* Ressources en ligne (2000). http://www.ihtp.cnrs.fr/spip.php%3Farticle511.html, accessed 4 March 2009.

28 *L'Est Républican*, 11 May 1940; *Ouest Eclair*, 11 May 1940; *La Dépêche* 12 May 1940.

29 ADM, 127/W/49, poster dated 13 May 1940.

30 ADPO, 38/W/63, circular to Prefects dated 21 May 1940.

31 AMR, 6/H/1, circular dated 16 May 1940.

32 AMR, 6/H/1, letters dated 10 May 1940, 16 May 1940.

33 *Est républicain*, 16 May 1940.

34 José Gotovitch, 'Les Belges du repli: entre pagaille et organisation' in Max Lagarrigue (ed.), *1940: La France du repli; l'Europe de la défaite* (Toulouse: Privat, 2001), pp. 51–64.

35 ADPO, W/138/5, circular dated 23 May 1940.

36 Consuelo Vanderbilt Balsan, *The Glitter and the Gold* (Melbourne and London: Heinemann, 1953), p. 244.

37 Maurice Rajsfus, *Les Français de la débâcle: juin–septembre 1940, un si bel été* (Paris: Le Cherche Midi, 1997), p. 40.

38 Damien Cousin, 'Le repli du gouvernement français à Bordeaux en juin 1940', in Max Lagarrigue (ed.), *1940: La France du repli; l'Europe de la défaite* (Toulouse: Privat, 2001), pp. 155–61 (p. 159).

39 Hélène Chaubin, 'Une micro-Europe des défaites: le refuge héraultais de 1940', in Max Lagarrigue (ed.), *1940: La France du repli; l'Europe de la défaite* (Toulouse: Privat, 2001), pp. 125–32.

40 Archives Nationales 72/AJ/2277, Georgette Guillot, *Trois semaines d'Exode, journal dacty-lographié de Georgette Guillot, secrétaire au ministère de l'Intérieur, 9 juin – 14 juillet 1940*, p. 4.

41 Françoise Meifredy, *Mission sans frontières* (Paris: Editions France Empire, 1966), p. 12.

42 Chevrillon, *Une résistance ordinaire*, p. 25.

43 Tereska Torres, *Une française libre; Journal 1939–1945* (Paris: France-Loisirs, 2000), p. 43.

44 AMN, 6(b)–H4–5, Letter of Madame Haller to Mayor, 22 May 1940.

45 AMN, 6(b)–H4–5, Letter of M. J. Keller [membre de l'A.P.P.C Rédacteur correspondant de la cinématographie Française] to Mayor, 24 May 1940.

46 *Ouest-Eclair*, 14 May 1940.

47 'Les réfugiés', *Le Temps,* 26 May 1940.

48 Denis Peschanski, *La France des camps: l'internement, 1938–46* (Paris: Gallimard, 2002), p. 152.

49 Paul Burmetz, *Our Share of Morning* (London: Alvin Redman, 1961), p. 88.

50 Lisa Fittko, *Escape Through the Pyrenees,* translated by David Koblick (Evanston, Illinois: Northwestern University Press, 1991), p. 11.

51 Soma Morgenstern, *Errance en France,* translated by Nicole Casanova (Paris: Liana Levi, 2002), pp. 15–16.
52 Peschanski, *La France des camps,* p. 152.
53 AMR, 6/H/10, 15 May 1940.
54 *La Dépêche,* 24 May 1940.
55 AMR, 6/H/20, circular dated 20 May 1940.
56 *Ouest-Eclair,* 20 May 1940.
57 ADHG, W/2054/1476, circular dated 13 June 1940.
58 Henry Bordeaux 'Sur cette belle route de France: Deux cortèges se sont croisés', *Le Jour-L'echo de Paris,* 31 May 1940.
59 Christian Habrioux, *La Déroute (1939–1940)* (Paris: Aux Armes de France, 1941), p. 103.
60 Dorgelès, *La drôle de guerre,* pp. 132, 223–7.
61 Friedmann, *Journal de Guerre,* p 265.
62 Barlone, *A French Officer's Diary,* p. 46.
63 Valentin Feldman, *Journal de Guerre, 1940–41* (Tours: Farrago, 2006), p. 144.
64 G. Freeman and D. Cooper, *The Road to Bordeaux* (The Cresset Press: London, 1940) pp. 195–9.
65 'Gun Buster', *Return via Dunkirk* (London: Hodder and Stoughton, 1940), p. 111.
66 Winston S. Churchill, *The Second World War, Volume II: Their Finest Hour* (London: The Reprint Society, 1951), p. 79.
67 Barlone, *A French Officer's Diary,* p. 48.
68 Miquel, *Histoires vraies de la Seconde guerre mondiale,* p. 221.
69 Miquel, *Histoires vraies de la Seconde guerre mondiale,* p. 215.
70 J. Vidalenc, *L'Exode de mai–juin 1940* (Paris: Presses Universitaires de France, 1957) p. 98.
71 Vidalenc, *L'Exode de mai–juin 1940,* p. 119.
72 Vidalenc, *L'Exode de mai–juin 1940,* p. 377.
73 J.-P. Rioux, 'L'Exode: un pays à la dérive', *L'Histoire* 129 (1990), pp. 64–70 (p. 66); N. Ollier, *L'Exode* (Paris: Culture, Art, Loisirs, 1969) p. 40.
74 Eric Alary *Les Français au quotidien, 1939–1949* (Paris: Perrin, 2006), p. 87.
75 Mark Wyman, *DPs: Europe's Displaced Persons, 1945–1951*(Ithaca and London: Cornell University Press, 1998) p. 40; Michael R. Marrus, *The Unwanted: European Refugees from the First World War through the Cold War* (Philadelphia: Temple University Press, 2002) p. 309.
76 Jean de Baroncelli, *Vingt-Six Hommes* (Paris: Bernard Grasset, 1941) p. 13
77 Paul Nizan, 'Correspondance de guerre', in *Intellectuel communiste, 1926–40, Vol II* (Paris: Maspero, 1979), pp. 104–41.
78 J.-P. Sartre, *Carnets de la drôle de guerre Septembre 1939–1940* (Paris, Gallimard, 1995), pp. 135 and 148.
79 Georges Sadoul, *Journal de Guerre (2 septembre 1939–20 juillet 1940)* (Paris: Français Réunis, 1977), p. 120.
80 Feldman, *Journal de Guerre,* pp. 114–115.
81 Friedmann, *Journal de Guerre,* p. 186.
82 Père Amand Boulé, *De Dunkerque à la Liberté* (Saint-Brieuc: Les Presses Bretonnes, 1976), p. 32.
83 G. Folcher, *Les carnets de guerre de Gustave Folcher, paysan languedocien 1939–1945* (Paris: François Maspero, 1981), pp. 32–4.
84 Sartre, *Carnets,* pp. 217–218, 231–3, 238–9, 247–9, 369.
85 Henry de Montherlant, *Textes sous une occupation, 1940–44* (Paris: Gallimard, 1940), pp. 17–18.
86 Montherlant, *Textes sous une occupation,* p. 28.
87 Baroncelli, *Vingt-Six Hommes,* p. 97.
88 Barlone, *A French Officer's Diary,* p. 10.
89 Feldman, *Journal,* p. 31.
90 'L'Etrange Défaite' in *L'Histoire, La Guerre, la Résistance,* A. Becker and E. Bloch (eds) (Paris: Quarto-Gallimard, 2006), pp. 519–653 (p. 534); Folcher, *Carnets de guerre,* p. 67.

91 Friedmann, *Journal de Guerre*, p. 240.
92 'Buster', *Return*, p. 135.
93 Guillot, *Trois semaines d'Exode*, p. 13.
94 For a brief background to 'Système D', see Geoffrey Best, *Humanity in Warfare* (London, Weidenfeld and Nicolson, 1980) p. 92.
95 Habrioux, *La Déroute*, p. 102.
96 Claude Jamet, *Carnets de Déroute* (Paris: Sorlot, 1942), p. 91.
97 Friedmann *Journal de Guerre*, p. 263.
98 Sautreuil, *Dix ans*, p. 160.
99 Roland de Kermadec, *1937–1946; De l'Orne au Finistère; ma drôle de guerre* (Spézet: Keltia, 1995), pp. 74–81.
100 Baroncelli, *Vingt-Six Hommes*, p. 313
101 *Assignment to Catastrophe, Vol II: the Fall of France, June 1940* (London: Heinemann, 1954), p. 236.
102 *Return via Dunkirk*, pp. 134, 141.
103 Bloch, *L'Etrange Défaite*, p. 551.
104 Dorgelès, *La drôle de guerre*, p. 229.
105 Charles de Gaulle, *Mémoires de Guerre: L'Appel* (Paris: Plon, 1994), p. 13.
106 Boulé, *Dunkerque*, p. 53.
107 Bloch, *L'Etrange Défaite*, p. 560.
108 Baroncelli, *Vingt-Six Hommes*, pp. 320–21.
109 André Chamson, 'Le dernier village' in Chamson André, *Livres de la guerre* (Paris: Omnibus, 2005), pp. 215–80 (p. 217).
110 Folcher, *Carnets de guerre*, p. 145.
111 Miquel, *Histoires vraies de la Seconde guerre mondiale*, p. 224.
112 François-Xavier Goutalier (ed.), 'L'exode de 1940', posted on http://perso.wanadoo.fr/fx.goutalier/120640.htm, accessed 27 June 2006.
113 Werth, *33 jours*, pp. 65–6.
114 *Report on France* (London: The Bodley Head, 1942), p. 14.
115 Sadoul, *Journal*, pp. 249–50.
116 Folcher, *Carnets de guerre*, p. 115.
117 Baroncelli, *Vingt-Six Hommes*, p. 167.
118 *De l'Orne de Finistère*, passim.
119 Habrioux, *La Déroute*, p. 175.
120 Montherlant, *Textes sous une occupation*, p. 68.
121 Baroncelli, *Vingt-Six Hommes*, p. 313.
122 For a consideration of women's coping mechanisms on the road see Nicole Dombrowski, `Beyond the Battlefield: the French civilian exodus of May–June, 1940', unpublished PhD, New York University (1995), pp. 202–3.
123 G. Le Bon, *The Crowd: a study of the popular mind* (np: Ernest Benn, 1896); See also Robert Nye, *The Origins of Crowd Psychology: Gustave Le Bon and the crisis of mass democracy in the Third Republic* (London and Beverley Hills: Sage, 1975).
124 Ollier, *L'Exode*, p. 139.
125 *Ouest-Eclair*, 22 May 1940.
126 André Morize, *France: Eté 1940* (New York: Editions de la Maison Française, 1941), pp. 42–43.
127 Dorgelès, *Le drôle de guerre*, p. 236.
128 Alfred Fabre-Luce, *Journal de la France, mars 1939–juillet 1940* (Trévoux: Imprimerie de Trévoux, 1940), pp. 315–16.
129 Irène Némirovsky, *Suite française* (Paris: Denoël, 2004), p. 74.
130 Friedmann, *Journal de Guerre*, p. 260.
131 Ollier, *L'Exode*, p. 157; J. Jackson, *The Fall of France: the Nazi invasion of 1940* (Oxford: Oxford University Press, 2003), p. 175; Guillot, *Trois semaines d'Exode*, p. 5.
132 Louis Mexandeau, *'Nous, nous ne verrons pas la fin': un enfant dans la guerre (1939–1945)* (Paris: Cherche-Midi, 2003), p. 73.

133   Werth, *33 Jours*, p. 37.
134   Georges Filoque, *Souvenirs de l'exode de 1940,* manuscript stored in IHTP ARC 1000 No.18.
135   G. Freeman and D. Cooper, *The Road to Bordeaux*, pp. 202–3.
136   R. Aron, *De l'armistice à l'insurrection nationale* (Paris: Gallimard, 1945), cited in Vidalenc, *L'Exode de mai–juin 1940*, p. 367. On the fate of the elderly during the exode, see Eric Alary, *L'exode: un drame oublié* (Paris: Perrin, 2010), pp. 290–4.
137   Mexandeau, 'Nous, nous ne verrons pas la fin', p. 76.
138   Arthur Koestler, *Scum of the Earth* (London: Jonathan Cape, 1941), p. 163.
139   Fabre-Luce, *Journal*, p. 86; Dorgelès, *Le drôle de guerre*, p. 285.
140   Document in ADI&V, 1/Z/8.
141   Ollier, *L'Exode*, p. 43.
142   Victor Serge, *Les Derniers Temps* (Bernard Grasset, Paris, 1951) p. 44.
143   Miquel, *Histoires vraies,* pp. 217–20.
144   Miquel, *Histoires vraies,* pp. 191–6.
145   Morize, *France Eté 1940,* pp. 42–4.
146   Sautreuil, *Dix Ans,* p. 147.
147   Dorgelès, *La drôle de guerre,* pp. 275–6.
148   Edmond Delage, 'Au jour le jour: Sur la route', *le Temps*, Lundi 27 mai 1940, p. 2.
149   Sautreuil, *Dix ans,* p. 159.
150   Werth, *33 jours,* p. 57.
151   Werth, *33 jours,* p. 108.
152   Vidalenc, *L'Exode de mai–juin 1940,* pp. 415–6.
153   Thomas, *Pages de Journal*; Mary-Jayne Gold, *Crossroads at Marseilles 1940* (New York: Doubleday and Company, 1980).
154   Miquel, *Histoires vraies de la Seconde guerre mondiale* p. 222.
155   Werth, *33 jours,* p. 86.
156   Thomas, *Pages de Journal,* 14 juin 1940, p. 72.
157   Sautreuil, *Dix Ans,* p. 163.
158   Sadoul, *Journal,* p. 352.
159   Guillot, *Trois semaines d'Exode,* p. 5.
160   Morize, *France: Eté 1940,* p. 51.
161   Fittko, *Escape through the Pyrenees,* p. 72.
162   Werth, *33 jours,* pp. 12, 119, 128–9; Baroncelli, *Vingt-Six Hommes,* p. 41; Christian Habrioux, *La Déroute (1939–1940)* (Paris: Aux Armes de France, 1941), p. 54. On the "mirage" of the Loire, see Eric Alary, *L'exode: un drame oublié* (Paris: Perrin, 2010), pp. 158–9.
163   Werth, *33 jours,* p. 13.
164   Dorgelès, *La drôle de guerre,* p. 275; Guillot, *Trois semaines* p. 6.
165   Kermadec, p. 78.
166   Guillot, *Trois semaines* p. 5; Fittko, *Escape through the Pyrenees,* p. 93.
167   Fittko, *Escape through the Pyrenees*, p. 93.
168   Serge, *Les derniers temps,* p. 121.
169   Morgenstern, *Errance en France,* p. 122.
170   Jose Antonio de Aguirre, *Escape via Berlin; Eluding Franco in Hitler's Europe* (Reno and Las Vegas: University of Nevada Press, 1991), pp. 29–31.
171   Mariano Constant, *Les années rouges, de Guernica à Mauthausen* (Vienne: Mercure de France, 1971), p. 146; Abel Paz, *Entre la Niebla (1939–1942)* (Barcelona: EA, 1993), p. 132; Dolores Torres, *Chronique d'une femme rebelle* (Paris: Wern, 1997), p. 181.
172   *L'Est Républicain,* 13 mai 1940; *Ouest-Eclair,* 18 May 1940; *La Dépêche,* 20 mai 1940.
173   *Journal du Loiret,* 22 May 1940.
174   For example, *Ouest-Eclair,* 19 May 1940.
175   See, for example, the partly censored article in *Ouest-Eclair,* 20 May 1940.
176   Guillot, *Trois semaines d'Exode,* p. 3.
177   *Ouest-Eclair,* 1 June 1940.
178   Stanley Hoffman, 'Témoignage' in Max Lagarrigue (ed.), *1940: La France du repli; l'Europe de la défaite* (Toulouse: Privat, 2001), pp. 15–19 (p. 18).

179   Sautreuil, *Dix ans*, p. 183.
180   *De l'Orne au Finistère*, p. 90.
181   Rupert Downing, *If I laugh: The Chronicle of my Strange Adventures in the Great Paris Exodus
      – June 1940* (London, George G. Harrap & Co, 1940), pp. 66–7.
182   Werth, *33 Jours*, p. 103.
183   Churchill, *Their Finest Hour*, p. 158.
184   Montherlant, *Textes sous une occupation*, p. 68.
185   Montherlant, *Textes sous une occupation*, p. 71.
186   On how Petain tried to depict *exodiens* as guilty, see Alary, *L'exode*, p. 13.
187   Dienke Hondius, 'Bitter Homecoming: the Return and Redemption of Dutch and Stateless
      Jews in the Netherlands', in D. Bankier (ed.), *The Jews are Coming Back* (New York:
      Berghahn, 2005 and Jerusalem: Yad Vashem, 2005), pp. 108–35 (p. 124).

Notes to Chapter 4

1   ADR, 45 W 118, anonymous letter, dated 2 July 1940.
2   'Le retour des réfugiés', *Le Figaro*, 4 July 1940.
3   Alfred Fabre-Luce, *Journal de la France, 1939–1944* (Paris: Fayard, 1969), p. 235.
4   Charles Rist, *Une saison gâtée. Journal de la guerre et de l'occupation (1939–1945)* (Paris:
     Fayard, 1983), p. 79.
5   Alexandre Arnoux, 'L'école des nomades', *Le Figaro*, 14 July 1940.
6   George W. Kyte, 'War damage and problems of reconstruction in France, 1940–1945' *The
     Pacific Historical Review* 15:4 (1946), pp. 417–26 (p. 417); N. Ollier, *L'Exode* (Paris, 1969),
     pp. 243–44.
7   AD I&V, 4 W 5, Letter to the Prefect dated 2 September 1940.
8   Archives Nationales 72/AJ/2277, Georgette Guillot, *Trois semaines d'Exode, journal dacty-
     lographié de Georgette Guillot, secrétaire au ministère de l'Intérieur, 9 juin – 14 juillet 1940*, p. 59.
9   AML, 132 II 48, letter dated 9 July 1940.
10   'Un litre d'avoine est aussi rare qu'un litre d'essence', *Le Figaro*, 16 July 1940.
11   'Le ravitaillement de la population', *Le Figaro*, 3 July 1940; 'Candidats à l'essence: Enquête de
     L. Gabriel-Robinet', *Le Figaro*, 11 July 1940.
12   Eric Alary, *Les Français au quotidien, 1939–1949* (Paris: Perrin, 2006) pp. 171–2.
13   ADMM, WM 399, undated note (September 1940?).
14   N. Ollier, *L'Exode*, p. 255.
15   ADI&V, 4 W 5, undated chart.
16   ADR, 45 W 35, police report dated 15 September 1940; ADR, 4 M 422, Chart dated 13
     September 1940.
17   Pierre Miquel, *L'Exode, 10 mai – 20 juin 1940* (Paris: Plon, 2003), p. 427; Hanna Diamond,
     Fleeing Hitler: France 1940 (Oxford: OUP, 2007), p. 142.
18   *Le Figaro* published a daily column, 'Trait d'Union des réfugiés' in this period.
19   Louis Chauvet, 'On recherche parmi beaucoup d'autres sept cent quarante enfants perdus au
     cours de l'Exode de juin', *Le Figaro*, 13 August 1940.
20   'J'ai recueilli et sauvé un tout jeune enfant', *Le Figaro*, 20 August 1940.
21   Alary, *Les Français au quotidien*, p. 90.
22   ADPO, 38 W 63, letter dated 28 June 1940.
23   ADPO, 38 W 63, letter dated 4 July 1940.
24   ADPO, 38 W 63, letter dated 5 July 1940.
25   AMR, 6 H 17, letter dated 10 July 1940.
26   AMR, 6 H 17, undated.
27   Stanley Hoffmann, 'Le trauma de 1940', *La France des années noires* (Paris: Seuil, 1993), pp.
     131–50 (p. 137). On French fears, see also Talbot Imlay, 'Mind the Gap: the Perception and
     Reality of Communist Sabotage of French War Production during the Phoney War, 1939–40',
     Past and Present 189 (2005), pp. 179–224.

28 Jean-Pierre Rioux, 'L'exode: un pays à la dérive', *L'histoire* (1990) pp. 64–70 (p. 70).
29 Charles Rist, *Une saison gâtée. Journal de la guerre et de l'occupation (1939–1945)* (Paris: Fayard, 1983), p. 79.
30 Arthur Koestler, *Scum of the Earth* (London: Jonathan Cape, 1941), pp. 208–9.
31 Paul Burmetz, *Our Share of Morning* (London: Alvin Redman, 1961), p. 104.
32 Burmetz, *Our Share*, p. 129.
33 Léon Werth, *33 jours* (Paris: Viviane Hamy, 1992).
34 Guillot, *3 semaines d'exode*, p. 72.
35 *Bulletin d'Informations de l'Ille-et-Vilaine*, 28 June 1940.
36 All the following brief quotations are from letters written by refugees to the Prefect of the Ille-et-Vilaine, usually in July 1940, contained in ADI&V, 4 W 7.
37 ADPO, 38 W 63, letter to the Prefect dated 3 July 1940.
38 AMR, 6 H 17, letter dated 26 June 1940.
39 AMR, 6 H 17, undated letter.
40 AMR, 6 H 17, letter dated 25 June 1940.
41 Hoffmann, 'The Trauma of 1940', *The French defeat of 1940: reassessments*, p. 356.
42 Quoted in Jackson, *The Fall of France*, p. 229.
43 Georges Friedmann, *Journal de guerre 1939–1940* (Paris: Gallimard, 1987), p. 307.
44 Pierre Miquel, *Histoires vraies de la Seconde guerre mondiale* (Paris, Fayard, 1988), p. 171.
45 Werth, *33 jours*, p. 149.
46 Jean Guehenno, *Journal des années noires* (Paris: Gallimard, 1973), pp. 39–40.
47 Marc Bloch, *Strange defeat: A statement of evidence written in 1940* (New York: Octagon Books, 1986), p. 132.
48 Marshall Petain's speech, 20 June 1940. [reproduced in http://ww3.ac–poitiers.fr/hist_geo/lp/bep1/sommdocs/pagedoc/guerrmond/tpeta20ju.htm].
49 M. Leblond, cited in Jean Vidalenc, *L'Exode de mai–juin 1940* (Paris: Presses Universitaires de France, 1957), p. 364.
50 Eric Alary, *La ligne de démarcation 1940–1944* (Paris: Perrin, 2003), p. 9.
51 Agnès Humbert, *Notre guerre: Souvenirs de résistance* (Paris: Emile-Paul Frères, 1946), pp. 18–20.
52 ADI, 13/R/824/5, Lettre de Camille Hanilis au Maréchal Pétain, 4 April 1941.
53 Renée Poznanski, *Etre juif en France pendant la Seconde Guerre mondiale* (Paris: Hachette, 1994), p. 56.
54 Poznanski, *Etre juif en France*, p. 61.
55 Shannon L. Fogg, 'Refugees and Indifference: the effects of shortages on Attitudes towards Jews in France's Limousin Region during World War II', *Holocaust and Genocide Studies*, 21:1 (2007), pp. 31–54 (p. 34).
56 ADHG, 2054 W 142, circular dated 11 September 1940.
57 Christine Morrow, *Abominable Epoch* (privately published, no date [1972?]), p. 46.
58 Morrow, *Abominable Epoch*, p. 69.
59 Guillot, *Trois semaines d'Exode*, p. 49.
60 Mary Jayne Gold, *Crossroads at Marseilles, 1940* (Doubleday and Co., New York 1980), pp. 74–81.
61 AML, 1127 WP 30, report dated 8 July 1940.
62 Gritou et Annie Vallotton, *C'était au jour le jour. Carnets (1939–1944)* (Paris: Payot, 1995), p. 96.
63 ADI&V, 4 W 7, letter dated 5 July 1940.
64 Jacques Bardoux *Journal d'un témoin de la Troisième. 1 Septembre 1939 – 15 juillet 1940* (Paris: Fayard, 1957), p. 388.
65 Guillot, *3 semaines d'Exode*, p. 70.
66 ADHG, 2054 W 1476, circular dated 4 July 1940.
67 ADHG, 2054 W 346, circular dated 13 July 1940.
68 ADHG, 2054 W 1476, circular dated 6 August 1940.
69 Ollier, *L'Exode* pp. 247–9.
70 Alary, *Les Français au quotidien*, p. 136.
71 'Pour se rendre en zone occupée: Nouveaux itinéraires', *Le Figaro*, 2 August 1940.

72   L. Gabriel-Robinet, 'Candidats à l'essence', *Le Figaro*, 11 July 1940.

73   ADI, 13R824/4 telegram dated 21 August 1940.

74   'Un premier contingent d'agriculteurs est rendu à la terre', *Le Figaro*, 9 July 1940.

75   IHTP ARC 1000 No.18, G. Filoque, *Souvenirs de l'exode de 1940* (sl; sd).

76   Ollier, *L'Exode*, p. 247.

77   P. Miquel, *Histoires vraies de la Seconde guerre mondiale* (Paris, Fayard, 1988), p. 171.

78   R. de F., 'Leur retour', *Le Nouvelliste*, 5 July 1940.

79   AML, 132 II 48, Fiche de documentation sur les Jeunes réfugiés (no 3), juillet, août, septembre, octobre 1942.

80   AML, 132 II 48, letter dated 9 July 1940.

81   ADR, 45 W 118, police report dated 3 July 1940.

82   ADR, 45 W 52, police report, 3 July 1940.

83   Eric Alary, *La ligne de démarcation 1940-1944* (Paris: Perrin, 2003), p. 41.

84   Lucien Rebatet, *Les décombres* (Paris: Denoel, 1942), pp. 281-2.

85   Barbara Vormeier 'La pratique du droit d'asile à l'égard des réfugiés en provenance d'Allemagne et d'Autriche en France (de septembre 1939 à octobre 1940)', Max Lagarrique (ed.) *1940 La France du repli*, (Toulouse: Privat, 2001), pp. 105–12 (p. 112).

86   José-Alain Fralon, *A Good Man in Evil Times: the story of Aristides de Sousa Mendes – the unknown hero who saved countless lives in World War II,* translated by Peter Graham (London: Viking, 2000), p. 46.

87   Marcel Junod, *Warrior without Weapons,* translated by Edward Fitzgerald (London: Non-Fiction Book Club, nd), p. 175.

88   Fralon, *A Good Man*, p. 59.

89   Howard Wriggins, *Picking up the Pieces from Portugal to Palestine: Quaker Refugee Relief in World War II: A Memoir* (Lanham: University Press of America, 2004), p. 18.

90   Erich Maria Remarque, *The Night in Lisbon,* translated by Ralph Manheim (London: Hutchinson, 1964), p. 11.

91   Wriggins, *Picking up the Pieces*, p. 21.

92   Remarque, *Night*, p. 6.

93   Remarque, *Night*, p. 6.

94   Emilienne Eychenne, *Pyrénées de la Liberté: les évasions par l'Espagne, 1939–45* (Toulouse: Privat, 1998).

95   On this valley's history as refugee crossing-place, see Sharif Gemie, 'France and the Val d'Aran; Politics and Nationhood on the Pyrenean Border, 1800–25', *European History Quarterly*, 28:3 (1998), pp. 311–46.

96   ADHG 1M 1906 00132, minutes dated 29 November 1939.

97   ADHG 1M 1906 00132, minutes dated 29 November 1939.

98   Information drawn from various documents in ADHG 1M 1906 00132.

99   ADHG 1M 1906 00132, interview dated 3 March 1941.

100   Soma Morgenstern, *Errance en France* (Paris: Liana Levi, 2002), p. 201.

101   Morgenstern, *Errance*, p. 287.

102   Morgenstern, *Errance*, pp. 193 and 342.

103   Jean-Marie Guillon notes the Marseille's Consulates attracted refugees. See his 'La Provence refuge et piège. Autour de Varian Fry et de la filière américaine', in Max Lagarrigue (ed.), *1940: La France du repli; l'Europe de la défaite* (Toulouse: Privat, 2001), pp. 269–85 (p. 272).

104   Morgenstern, *Errance*, p. 393.

105   Morgenstern, *Errance*, p. 394.

106   Burmetz, *Our Share*, p. 154.

107   Burmetz, *Our Share*, p. 159.

108   Burmetz, *Our Share*, p. 153.

109   Morrow, *Abominable Epoch*, pp. 22–3.

110   Morrow, *Abominable Epoch*, p. 24.

111   Morrow, *Abominable Epoch*, p. 36.

112   Lisa Fittko, *Escape Through the Pyrenees* translated by David Koblick (Evanston, Illinois: Northwestern University Press, 1991), pp. 84–9.

113 Morrow, *Abominable Epoch*, p. 40.
114 Burmetz, *Our Share*, pp. 181–2.
115 Lisa Fittko, *Escape Through the Pyrenees*, translated by David Koblick (Evanston, Illinois: Northwestern University Press, 1991), p. 72.
116 Morrow, *Abominable Epoch*, p. 27.
117 Emmanuelle Loyer 'La débâcle, les universitaires et la fondation Rockfeller: France / Etats-Unis, 1940–41,' *Revue d'histoire moderne et contemporaine* 2001–1, pp. 138–59 (p. 143).
118 Guillon, 'La Provence refuge et piège', p. 283.
119 Loyer, 'La débâcle', p. 157.
120 Gustave Cohen, *Lettres aux Américains*, quoted in Loyer, 'La débâcle, les universitaires et la fondation Rockfeller', p. 154.
121 Anna Seghers, *Transit*, translated by Jeanne Stern (Paris: Autrement, 1995), p. 184.
122 Morrow, *Abominable Epoch*, p. 28.
123 Morrow, *Abominable Epoch*, p. 44.
124 Morrow, *Abominable Epoch*, p. 38.
125 Morrow, *Abominable Epoch*, p. 49.
126 Morrow, *Abominable Epoch*, p. 64.
127 Pertti Ahonen, Gustavo Corni, Jerzy Kochanowski, Rainer Schulze, Tamás Stark and Barbara Stelzl-Marx, *People on the Move: Forced Population Movements in Europe in the Second World War and Its Aftermath* (Oxford and New York: Berg, 2008), p. 15.
128 Christopher R. Browning, *The Origins of the Final Solution: The Evolution of Nazi Jewish Policy, September 1939–March 1942* (Nebraska: University of Nebraska Press, 2007), p. 90.
129 Guenter Lewy, *The Nazi Persecution of the Gypsies* (Oxford: Oxford University Press, 2000), p. 81.
130 ADMM, WM 399, document, 7 November 1940.
131 ADMM, WM 389, police report, 28 November 1940.
132 Léon Strauss, 'Les associations de PRAF (Patriotes Réfractaires à l'Annexion de Fait) d'Alsace et de Moselle', *Cahiers du centre d'études d'histoire de la Défense* 31 (2007), pp. 109–118 (p. 109).
133 ADI, 13R824/5, police report, 3 September 1940.
134 Similar conditions were imposed on the Poles expelled by the Nazis see: Ahonen, *People on the Move*, p. 115.
135 ADR, 45 W 40, police reports, 13 May 1941 and 7 Oct 1941.
136 See, for example, ADR, 45 W 39, police report, 22 Feb 1941.
137 ADR, 4 M 422, police report, 7 August 1940.
138 ADR, 4 M 422, police report, l7 August 1940.
139 ADR, 45W40, police report, 13 mai 1941.
140 ADR, 45 W 40, police report, 4 December 1940.
141 ADR, 45 W 40, police report, 18 December 1940.
142 ADR, 31 J B 156, police report, 9 September 1940.
143 ADR, 45 W 40, police report, 21 November 1940.
144 ADR, 45 W 40, police report, 16 November 1940.
145 ADR, 45 W 39, confidential memo from Général Commandant militaire du Département du Rhône, 28 December 1940.
146 ADR, 45 W 42, police report, 10 March 1942.
147 ADR, 31 J B 156, police report, 9 September 1940.
148 ADI, 13/R/824/4, circular, 17 August 1940.
149 Vicky Caron, *Uneasy Asylum: France and the Jewish refugee crisis, 1933 – 1942* (Stanford University Press, 2002), p. 333.
150 Renée Poznanski, *Jews in France during World War II* (University Press of New England, 2001), pp. 130–31.
151 ADI, 13 R824/4, René Mer 'Le problème des réfugiés', extrait de *La France de ce mois*, 10 December 1940, p. 5.
152 ADI, 13 R824/4, 'Aspect de la propagande en faveur des réfugiés', December 1940, p. 1.
153 'Aspect de la propagande en faveur des réfugiés', December 1940, p. 2.

154 ADI, 13R824/5, Circulaire N. 3 du GERAL (Groupement d'Entr'aide des Réfugiés d'Alsace et de Lorraine), Périgueux, 30 November 1940, p. 3.
155 ADI, 13R824/5, letter, dated 29 January 1941.
156 ADI, 13R824/4, René Mer, 'Le problème des réfugiés', p. 4.
157 H. Frenay, *La nuit finira*, quoted in Hanna Diamond, *Fleeing Hitler; France 1940* (Oxford: Oxford University Press, 2007), p. 194.
158 ADR, 45 W 41, letter dated 30 May 1941.
159 ADR, 45 W 40, police report, 18 April 1941.
160 ADR, 45 W 40, police report, 3 April 1941.
161 ADR, 45 W 39, circular, 13 March 1941.
162 Shannon L. Fogg, 'Refugees and Indifference: the Effects of Shortages on Attitudes towards Jews in France's Limousin Region During World War II', *Holocaust and Genocide Studies* 21:1 (2007), pp. 31–57.
163 ADR, 45 W 40, police report, 29 July 1941.
164 ADI, 13R824/3, Réunion du comité du Groupement des expulsés et réfugiés de Lorraine, 30 novembre 1941, p. 2.
165 ADI, 13R824/3, Réunion du comité du Groupement des expulsés et réfugiés de Lorraine, 30 novembre 1941, pp. 3–4.
166 ADR, 45 W 42, police report, 29 mai 1941.
167 Alf Lüdtke, 'Explaining forced migration' in R. Bessel and C. Haake (eds), *Removing peoples: Forced Removal in the Modern World* (Oxford: Oxford University Press, 2009), pp. 13–32 (p. 19).

Notes to Chapter 5

1 *Hansard*, House of Commons debate, 25 January 1944, pp. 569–63 (p. 582).
2 UNRRA, *Helping the People to Help Themselves: The Story of the United Nations Relief and Rehabilitation Administration* (London: His Majesty's Stationery Office, 1944), p. 20.
3 Susan T. Pettiss and Lynne Taylor, *After the Shooting Stopped: the Story of an UNRRA Welfare Worker in Germany 1945–1947* (Crewe: Trafford, 2004), p. 18.
4 William Blake, 'The Marriage of Heaven and Hell', *The Poetry and Prose of William Blake* (London: Nonesuch, 1956), p. 181.
5 Available at http://gamma.onf.ca/film/now_the_peace.
6 See *Hansard*, 25 January 1944, pp. 569–632 (p. 575).
7 *The Times*, 29 March 1944.
8 William B. Ziff, *The Coming Battle of Germany* (London: Hamish Hamilton, 1942), pp. 7 and 173.
9 *The Times*, 18 April 1944.
10 Lieutenant General Sir Frederick Morgan, KCB, *Peace and War: A Soldier's Life* (London: Hodder and Stoughton, 1961), p. 139.
11 Norman Lewis, *Naples '44: An Intelligence Officer in the Italian Labyrinth* (London: Eland, 2002 [1978]), pp. 11–15.
12 Grigor McClelland, *Embers of War: Letters from a Quaker Relief Worker in War-torn Germany* (London and New York: I. B. Tauris, 1997), p. 19.
13 See Noel Annan, *Changing Enemies: The Defeat and Regeneration of Germany* (London: Harper Collins, 1995), p. 128.
14 Winston S. Churchill, *The Second World War, Vol III: The Grand Alliance* (London: Reprint Society, 1952), p. 300.
15 Political Warfare Executive, *Instructions*, p. 17.
16 Susan Cohen suggests that a report in *Daily Telegraph* on 25 June 1942, concerning the massacre of 700,000 Polish Jews, should have been sufficient to alert the British public about the real nature of the disaster. See her *Rescue the Perishing: Eleanor Rathbone and the Refugees* (London: Vallentine Mitchell, 2010), p. 167.

17   Tony Kushner, 'From "This Belsen Business" to "Shoah Business": History, Memory and Heritage, 1945–2005', in Suzanne Bardgett and David Cesarani (eds), *Belsen 1945: New Historical Perspectives* (London: Vallentine Mitchell, 2006), pp. 189–216

18   Brian Stone, *Prisoner from Alamein* (London: Witherby, 1944), p. 39.

19   Jennifer Carson, *The Friends Relief Service – Faith into Action: Humanitarian Assistance to Displaced Persons Camps in Germany, 1945–1948*, unpublished PhD thesis, University of Manchester, (2009) p. 85.

20   Examples cited in Tony Kushner, *The Persistence of Prejudice: Antisemitism in British Society during the Second World War* (Manchester: MUP, 1989).

21   Tony Kushner, 'The Memory of Belsen', in Tony Kushner, David Cesarani, Jo Reilly and Colin Richmond (eds), *Belsen in History and Memory* (London: Frank Cass, 1997), pp. 181–205.

22   See, for example, Winston S. Churchill, *The Second World War, Volume II: Their Finest Hour* (London: The Reprint Society, 1951), p. 495.

23   Joan Rice, *Sand in My Shoes; Coming of Age in the Second World War: A WAAF's Diary* (London: Harper Perennial, 2006), p. 180.

24   *The Times*, 31 January 1944.

25   Mary Kinnear, *Woman of the World; Mary McGeachy and International Cooperation* (Toronto: Toronto University Press, 2004), p. 151.

26   Susan Armstrong-Reid and David Murray, *Armies of Peace: Canada and the UNRRA years* (Toronto: University of Toronto Press, 2008), p. 113.

27   Kinnear, *Woman of the World*, p. 173.

28   Tessa Stone, 'Creating a (gendered?) military identity: the Women's Auxiliary Air Force in Great Britain in the Second World War', *Women's History Review* 8:4 (1999), pp. 605–24 (p. 609).

29   Even in the twenty-first century Britain, after the obvious achievements of second-wave feminism, there remains deep discomfort at the thought of female troops on the front line. For example, on the contested role of female British soldiers currently serving in Afghanistan see *The Times* 19 June 2008; http://webarchive.nationalarchives.gov.uk/tna/+/http://www.mod.uk/DefenceInternet/DefenceNews/MilitaryOperations/FemaleSoldierFightsItOutWithMarinesInHelmand.htm

30   Gerard J. De Groot, '"I Love the Scent of Cordite in Your Hair": Gender Dynamics in Mixed Anti-Aircraft Batteries during the Second World War', *History* 82 (1997), pp. 73–92. Penny Summerfield, *Women Workers in the Second World War: Production and Patriarchy in Conflict* (London: Routledge, 1989) arrives at similar conclusions.

31   John Guest, *Broken Images: A Journal* (London: Leo Cooper, 1970 [1949]), pp. 35–42.

32   Barbara Euphan Todd, *Miss Ranskill Comes Home* (London: Persephone Press, 2003 [1946]), p. 234.

33   Marilyn Lake has suggested a different interpretation of such developments: she argues that the 'new' femininity of the late 1940s and 1950s was quite distinct from the cultures of the pre-war era, and therefore they should not be seen as a retreat. 'Female Desires: the meaning of World War II' in Gordon Martel (ed.), *The World War Two Reader* (New York and London: Routledge, 2004), pp. 359–76 [originally published in 1990].

34   Geoffrey Best, *Humanity in Warfare* (London, Weidenfeld and Nicolson, 1980) p. 4; ICRC, Geneva G68 1132 International Migration Service, 21 February 1946.

35   *The Times*, 30 December 1944.

36   *The Times*, 30 December 1944.

37   Roger Wilson, *Quaker Relief: An Account of the Relief Work of the Society of Friends, 1940–1948* (London: George Allen & Unwin, 1952). In particular, see chapter 7.

38   Archives of the International Committee of the Red Cross, Geneva (hereafter) ICRC G86 1132 Département Politique Fédérale, Berne, 14 February 1944, pp. 3–4.

39   ICRC G86 1132, Note of meeting between the Director General and Mr A. Zollinger, 2 August 1944; Marconigram, Zollinger to InterCroixRouge, Geneva, 24 August 1944.

40   ICRC G68 936, Draft Memorandum, 7 May 1945.

41   Richard Ford, *UNRRA in Europe, 1945–1947* (London: UNRRA European Regional Office, June 1947), p. 14.

42 *The Story of UNRRA* (Washington: Office of Public Information, UNRRA, February 1948), p. 1.
43 Morgan, *Peace and War*, pp. 222–3.
44 Gene Fowler Jr, *Seeds of Destiny* (US War Department: 1946), available at http://www.archive.org/details/SeedsofDestiny
45 Ford, *UNRRA in Europe*, p. 9.
46 Wilbur A. Sawyer, 'Achievements of UNRRA as an International Health Organization', *American Journal of Public Health* 37 (January 1947), pp. 41–58 (p. 41).
47 UNRRA, *Helping the People to Help Themselves: The Story of the United Nations Relief and Rehabilitation Administration* (London: His Majesty's Stationery Office, 1944), p. 3.
48 *Story of UNRRA*, p. 7.
49 Gunnar Jahn, 'Presentation Speech', Nobel Peace Prize 1945, http://nobelprize.org/cgi-bin; accessed 5 November 2009.
50 *Story of UNRRA*, pp. 4 and 18.
51 Sawyer, 'Achievements of UNRRA', p. 41.
52 Cited in Donald S. Howard 'UNRRA: A new venture in international relief and welfare services', *The Social Service Review*, 18:1 (March 1944), pp. 1–11 (p. 6).
53 F. Wilson, *In the Margins of Chaos* (London: William Clowes and Sons, 1944) p. 123.
54 UNRRA, *Helping the People*, pp. 4 and 8.
55 *The Story of UNRRA*, pp. 4–8.
56 UNRRA, *Helping the People*, p. 12.
57 ICRC G86 1132 Département Politique Fédérale, Berne, 14 February 1944, p. 1.
58 UNRRA, *Helping the People*, p. 20.
59 Article in *Free World*, undated [March 1944?], copy held in National Archives, FO 371/38956.
60 UNRRA, *Helping the People*, p. 19.
61 UNRRA, *Welfare Guide to United Nations Nationals Displaced in Germany* (London: European Regional Office, February 1945), p. 16.
62 FL Box FRS 1992/30 Friends Service Council Post-War Relief Meeting, 21 February 1941.
63 *The Times*, 21 January 1944.
64 NA, FO 371/40522, note to the Foreign Office, 25 January 1944.
65 *Hansard*, 'House of Lords Debate on Relief Problems', 14 December 1944, pp. 326–44 (p. 333).
66 NA, FO 371/41163, memo dated 22 June 1944.
67 NA, FO 371/41163, memo dated 15 June 1944.
68 NA, FO 371/41163, minute dated 9 October 1944.
69 NA, FO 371/41163, letter dated 11 September 1944.
70 CICR Geneva, G.68 1132 *Resumé d'entretien avec Mlle Marthe Rentsch, Déléguée du CICR au Caire,* 10 January 1945.
71 W. L. Richardson, *Know Your Enemy: The UNRRA Infiltra(i)tors* (Aberfeldy: McKinlay, 1947).
72 *The Times*, 8 March 1944.
73 Morgan, *Peace and War*, p. 226.
74 *Hansard*, 'House of Lords Debate on Relief Problems', 14 December 1944, pp. 326–44 (p. 337).
75 *Hansard*, 'House of Lords Debate on Relief Problems', 14 December 1944, pp. 326–44 (p. 327).
76 NA, T188/259, statement to the Standing Technical sub-Committee on Displaced Persons in Europe, 8 May 1945.
77 See, for example, ICRC G68 936 Jósef Kwaciszewski, Camp Commandant, to ICRC 17 December 1946
78 UNRRA, *Fifty Facts about UNRRA* (London: European Regional Office of UNRRA, January 1946), unpaginated publication.
79 'Hearing Before the Sub-committee', p. 40.
80 NA, F0 371/41165, Ministry of Health Circular, dated 3 January 1945.
81 G. Woodbridge, *UNRRA: the History of the United Nations Relief and Rehabilitation*

Administration (New York: Colombia University Press, 1950), Volume III, pp. 415–18. For a reference to 'mother UNRRA' see F. Wilson, *Aftermath: France, Germany, Austria, Yugoslavia 1945 and 1946* (London: Penguin, 1947) p. 174; Kathryn Hulme refers to 'aunty UNRRA': *The Wild Place*, (London and New York: Shakespeare Head, 1954) p. 136.

82   AN, AJ/43/578, document dated June 1947.

83   The vagueness of our figure is due to the looseness of the category with which we are concerned: for example, Lieutenant Colonel Kerr's private papers certainly provide useful information about UNRRA and relief work, but they largely concern his experiences in Italy; the Quakers in the Friends Relief Service were ultimately responsible to UNRRA, and certainly could write about UNRRA – but were they, strictly speaking, UNRRA employees?

84   Mr H. [Harry] Heath, IWM, 98/25/1, diary entry for 7 May 1945.

85   Margaret McNeill, FL MSS Temp H, June 1947.

86   McNeill, *Rivers*, p. 189.

87   Temp MMS 981-A McNeill, 17 June 1945 p. 9.

88   FL TEMP MSS 981/F McNeill, undated, but probably May 1947; COBSRA Headquarters were located in Vlotho, Westphalia close to the military HQ of the British zone.

89   Margaret McNeill, FL MSS Temp D, 18 May 1947.

90   Miss Nora O'Connor, IWM 87/14/1, untitled typed manuscript, undated [1986?].

91   Muriel Doherty, *Letters from Belsen 1945: an Australian nurse's experience with the survivors of war*, edited by J. Cornell and R. Lynette Russell, (Sydney, Allen and Unwin, 2000), pp.xv, 18 and 210–11.

92   Frances Berkeley Floore, *The Bread of the Oppressed* (New York: Exposition Press, 1975), pp. 11–12.

93   Pettiss, *After the Shooting Stopped*, pp. 4–7.

94   Floore, *The Bread of the Oppressed*, pp. 11, 27–8.

95   See among others, Margaret G. Arnstein, 'Nursing in UNRRA Middle East Refugee Camps', *The American Journal of Nursing*, 45:5 (May 1945), pp. 378–81; Olive Baggallay, S.R.N., 'UNRRA Nurses in Athens Hospitals', *American Journal of Nursing*, 45:8 (August 1945) pp. 635–6; Lorraine Setzler, 'Nursing and Nursing Education in Germany', *The American Journal of Nursing* 45:12 (December 1945), pp. 993–95; *The Journal of the American Medical Association* also devoted a series of articles to UNRRA's field practice. See for example their articles 'Medicine and the War'. Their foreign correspondent from London described the wonderful job that UNRRA was accomplishing in Germany in 'Foreign Letter, The Health Conditions of European Countries', *The Journal of the American Medical Association*, 130:1 (January 1946), p. 45. Lyle Creelman wrote a series of articles for the *Canadian Nurse* including 'Letters to the Editor, With UNRRA in Germany', *Canadian Nurse* 41:12 (1945), pp. 986–7; 'With UNRRA in Germany', *Canadian Nurse* 43:7 (1947), pp. 532–6; 'With UNRRA in Germany', *Canadian Nurse* 43:8 (1947), pp. 605–10; 'With UNRRA in Germany', *Canadian Nurse* 43:9 (1947), pp. 710–12. In Britain, the work of UNRRA in the field was also widely covered. See for example, 'The Task of UNRRA. Medical services in Liberated Countries', *The British Medical Journal*, 9 June 1945, p. 816; 'Belsen Camp: a preliminary report', *The British Medical Journal*, 9 June 1945, p. 814; 'Report of an UNRRA conference on famine relief'; *The British Medical Journal* 20 July 1946, p. 96; 'UNRRA Activities, Czech Psychiatrist's Study Tour', *The British Medical Journal*, 24 August 1946, p. 271; Agnes C. Clark 'Tuberculosis in a DP Camp in Austria', *The British Medical Journal*, 9 August 1947, p. 226; Martha Branscombe, 'The Children of the United Nations: U.N.R.R.A's Responsibility for Social Welfare', *Social Service Review* 19:3 (September 1945), pp. 310–23.

96   'UNRRA Activities, Czech Psychiatrist's Study Tour', *The British Medical Journal*, 24 August 1946, p. 271.

97   Lynne M. Healy, *International Social Work: Professional Action in an Interdependent World* (New York: Oxford University Press, 2001), p. 69. Also see for example the careers of Lyle Creelman, Muriel Graham and Helena Reimer, detailed in Susan Armstrong-Reid and David Murray, *Armies of Peace: Canada and the UNRRA years* (Toronto: University of Toronto Press, 2008), pp. 354–5.

98   http://content.cdlib.org/xtf/view?docId=hb1j49n6pv&doc.view=frames&chunk.
     id=div00013&toc.depth=1&toc.id=; accessed 29 July 2010.
99   Kinnear, *Woman of the World,* p. 151.
100 Pettiss, *After the Shooting Stopped,* p. 26.
101 AN 72/AJ/1968, Jacqueline Lesdos, *Souvenirs,* p. 15.
102 Pettiss, *After the Shooting Stopped,* p. 154.
103 Maurice de Cheveigné, *Radio Libre* (unpublished memoir put online by a member of his
     family: http://www.alyon.org/litterature/livres/lyonnais/radio_libre/lug10.html; accessed 15
     May 2009.)
104 Pettiss *After the Shooting Stopped,* p. 8.
105 UN Archives, S-0436-0055, Team 308, Report of Activities, 18 November 1945, Mr. Ephraim
     Chase, Director, USA, p. 1.
106 Quoted in Siân Lliwen Roberts, 'Place, Life Histories and the Politics of Relief: episodes in
     the life of Francesca Wilson, Humanitarian Educator Activist', PhD thesis, University of
     Birmingham, April 2010, p. 271.
107 Sybil Oldfield, *Women Humanitarians: A Biographical Dictionary of British Women active
     between 1900 and 1950* (London: Continuum, 2001), p.xii; Roberts 'Place, Life histories and
     the Politics of Relief', pp. 271–2.
108 AN 72/AJ/1968, Jacqueline Lesdos, *Souvenirs,* p. 1.
109 AN 72/AJ/1968, Jacqueline Lesdos, *Souvenirs,* p. 28.
110 UN Archives, S – 0527 – 0505, Final report by Director of Training, UNRRA administrative
     base, 28 January 1946, Holland.
111 UN Archives, S – 0527 – 0505, Statement regarding coordinated training to combat excessive
     turnover of field personnel, 9 October 1945.
112 W. H. Wickwar, 'Relief supplies and Welfare distribution UNRRA in retrospect', *Social
     Service Review* 21:3 (1947), pp. 363–74 (p. 369).
113 M. Proudfoot, *European Refugees, 1939–1952* (London: Faber and Faber, 1957), p. 143; NA
     T/188/259, minutes dated 19 April 1945.
114 NA, T/188/260, document dated 14 June 1945.
115 AN F/9/3286, UNRRA, Standing Technical Sub-Committee on Displaced Persons for
     Europe, 23rd meeting, 5 July 1945.
116 UN Archives, S-0527-0505, Memo from H. Saunders, 29 July 1945; Report by Harry
     Saunders, Director of Training, period June – October 1945, p. 3.
117 UN Archives, S-0527-0505, 'UNRRA Mobilization and Training Base', Daily bulletin
     number 7, 11 September 1945.
118 G. Woodbridge, *UNRRA: the History of the United Nations Relief and Rehabilitation
     Administration* (New York: Colombia University Press, 1950), volume II, p. 484. See also
     UN Archives, S-0527-0505, Report by Harry Saunders, Director of Training, period June –
     October 1945, p. 2.
119 Marvin Klemme, *The Inside Story of UNRRA; An Experience in Internationalism* (New York:
     Lifetime editions, 1949), p 22.
120 IWM, 67/106/1, Hall, entry for 30 April 1945.
121 *The Stagnant Pool: Work among Displaced Persons in Germany, 1945–1947* (undated typed
     manuscript, contained in Imperial War Museum, UNRRA, catalogued under the name Mrs
     R. N. Bickerdike, but signed as Rhoda Dawson 95/26/1) p. 1.
122 Mrs N. Heath, IWM, 98/25/1; untitled, undated [1948?], unpaginated manuscript.
123 *After the Shooting Stopped,* p. 30.
124 IWM, 67/106/1, Hall, entry for 30 April 1945.
125 IWM, 98/25/1, Heath, entry for 25 March 1945.
126 IWM, 98/25/1, unpaginated manuscript.
127 Dawson, 95/26/1, p. 2.
128 IWM, 67/106/1, Diary entry for 6 May 1945.
129 IWM, 67/106/1, Hall, Diary entry for 7 May 1945.
130 *After the Shooting Stopped,* p. 32.
131 IWM, 98/25/1, unpaginated manuscript.

132 IWM, 98/25/1, Heath, diary entry for 31 March 1945.
133 Klemme, *Inside Story,* p. 31.
134 UN Archives, S–0527–0505, Letter from K. M. Barr to Mr Patterson, Director UNRRA mobilisation Centre, Jullouville, France, July 19 1945 and Report on Meal prepared with outdoor facilities at the Training school on 20 July 1945; IWM 95/26/1, Dawson, *Stagnant Pool,* p. 1.
135 IWM, 67/106/1, Diary entry for 6 May 1945.
136 IWM, 98/25/1, Manuscript.
137 *After the Shooting Stopped,* p. 33.
138 Klemme, *Inside Story,* p. 28.
139 IWM, 98/25/1, Diary entry for 30 March 1945.
140 *After the Shooting Stopped,* p. 32.
141 IWM, 98/25/1, Muriel Heath, manuscript.
142 IWM, 67/106/1, Diary entry for 17 May 1945.
143 Chapter on UNRRA, p. 3.
144 Pettiss, *After the Shooting Stopped,* p. 34.
145 *Mental Outlook,* p. 8.
146 Pettiss, *After the Shooting Stopped,* p. 34.
147 IWM, 87/14/1, O'Connor, chapter on UNRRA, p. 3.
148 Klemme, *Inside Story,* p. 32.
149 IWM, 67/106/1, Hall, diary entry for 14 May 1945.
150 Pettiss, *After the Shooting Stopped,* p. 37.
151 Woodbridge, *UNRRA,* vol 1, pp. 251–2.
152 UN Archives, S–0527–0505, Report by Harry Saunders, Director of Training, period June – October 1945, p. 1.
153 UN Archives, S–0527–0505, Report by Harry Saunders, Director of Training, period June – October 1945.
154 UN Archives, S–0527–0505, Lectures used in the training of doctors and nurses, undated.
155 IWM, 95/26/1 Dawson, *Stagnant Pool,* p. 6.
156 IWM, 67/106/1, Hall, diary entry for 12 May 1945.
157 UN Archives, S–0527–0505, UNRRA Administrative Base Training Division, 15 November 1945.
158 UN Archives, S–0527–0505, Letter from Ancia, 9 October 1945. Also see Letter from Herman H. Jungeling, Jullouville, 22 August 1945.
159 UN Archives, S–0527–0505, Adieu à Mr Anorld-Foster par F. Laveissiere, 3 juin 1945.
160 Klemme, *Inside Story,* p. 44.
161 IWM, 67/106/1, Diary entries for 12 and 17 May 1945.
162 IWM, 95/26/1, Dawson, *Stagnant Pool,* p. 1.
163 UN Archives, S-0527–0505, Letter from Mr Richardson and Mr Goldsby on behalf of the Student Council, 15 August 1945.
164 UN Archives, S-0527–0505, Letter from Mr Richardson and Mr Goldsby on behalf of the Student Council, 15 August 1945.
165 UN Archives, S-0527–0505, Letter from K. M. Barr to Mr Patterson, Director UNRRA mobilisation Centre, Jullouville, France, July 19 1945.
166 UN Archives, S-0527–0505, Menno Duerksen 'Report on Trip to Cherbourg', undated [1945?] and letter from L. C. Smith, 20 July 1945.
167 Klemme, *Inside Story,* p. 30.
168 IWM, 98/25/1, Harry Heath, diary entry for 7 April 1945.
169 On the point, see NA, T/188/259, minutes dated 19 April 1945, 8 May 1945.
170 NA, FO/371/51081, minutes dated 22 January 1945.
171 ICRC G.68 920 *Organisme de Secours,* 26 November 1945.
172 George W. Davis, 'Handling of Refugees and Displaced Persons by the French M.M.L.A. (Section Féminine)' *The Social Service Review* 22:1 (1948), pp. 34–9 (p. 38).
173 Mark Wyman, *DPs: Europe's Displaced Persons, 1945–1951*(Ithaca and London: Cornell University Press, 1998) p. 40.
174 LaGuardia, 'The Director General's Final Report', *UNRRA Review of the Month,* December 1946, p. 3.

Notes to Chapter 6

1   *Berlin '45: the Grey City* (London: MacMillan, 1966), p.ix.
2   The Political Warfare Executive, *Instructions for British Servicemen in Germany* (Oxford: Bodleian Library, 2007 [1944]), p. 8.
3   Victor Gollancz, *In Darkest Germany* (London: Gollancz, 1947).
4   W. Jacobmeyer, *Vom Zwangsarbeiter zum heimatlosen Ausländer: Die Displaced Persons in Westdeutschland, 1945–1951* (Gottingen: Vandenhoeck & Ruprecht, 1985), p. 34.
5   On Allied planning and the relations between the military authorities and UNRRA, see Jacobmeyer, *Vom Zwangsarbeiter*, pp. 23–35.
6   Supreme Headquarters Allied Expeditionary Force, *Guide to the Care of Displaced Persons in Germany* (SHAEF, May 1945).
7   Unpublished, unpaginated diary, Mr H. Heath, IWM, 98/25/1, entry for 8 May 1945.
8   Susan T. Pettiss and Lynne Taylor, *After the Shooting Stopped: the story of an UNRRA welfare worker in Germany 1945–1947* (Crewe: Trafford, 2004), p. 47.
9   Audrey M. Duchesne-Cripps, *The Mental Outlook of the Displaced Person as Seen through Welfare Work in Displaced Persons Camps* (Cambridge: self-published, 1955), p. 32.
10 On the discovery of the camp, see Toby Haggith, 'The Filming of the Liberation of Bergen-Belsen and Its Impact on the Understanding of the Holocaust' in Suzanne Bardgett and David Cesarani (eds), *Belsen 1945: New Historical Perspectives* (London: Vallentine Mitchell, 2006), pp. 89–122.
11 Julie Summers, *Stranger in the House: Women's Stories of Men Returning from the Second World War* (London: Simon & Schuster, 2008), p. 141.
12 Rhoda Dawson, *The Stagnant Pool: Work among Displaced Persons in Germany, 1945–1947* (undated typed manuscript, contained in Imperial War Museum, UNRRA, Mrs R. N. Bickerdike, 95/26/1), p. 42.
13 NA, T/188/259, UNRRA: committee of Council for Europe; UNRRA Operations in Europe during March; 13th Meeting Held on 19 April 1945 in Portland Place, London.
14 M. Proudfoot, *European Refugees, 1939–1952* (London: Faber and Faber, 1957), p. 145.
15 Dawson, *The Stagnant Pool*, p. 4.
16 Duchesne-Cripps, *Mental Outlook*, p. 9.
17 Pettiss, *After the Shooting*, pp. 37–8.
18 IWM, 98/25/1, Heath, entry for 3 April 1945; see also Pettiss, *After the Shooting*, p. 39.
19 IWM, 98/25/1, Mrs N. Heath, untitled, unpaginated manuscript.
20 IWM, 98/25/1, Harry Heath, entry for 18 April.
21 UN Archives, S-0527-0503, Letter from UNRRA Mobilization and Training Base to Flechter C. Kettle, UNRRA ERO, 24 June 1945.
22 UN Archives, S-0527-0503, First report by L. Rosolek sent to Mr Patterson, UNRRA Mobilisation Centre, 5 July 1945, p. 1.
23 Pettiss, *After the Shooting Stopped*, p. 42.
24 IWM, 87/14/1, Miss Nora O'Connor, UNRRA chapter, p. 4.
25 UN Archives, S-0527-0503, Letter from Lt. Col. P.A. Woods to Capt. Carpenter, Wunsdorf, Germany, 27 October [1945?].
26 IWM, 95/26/1, Dawson, *Stagnant Pool*, pp. 19–21.
27 IWM, 95/26/1, Dawson, *Stagnant Pool*, p. 13.
28 IWM, 98/25/1, Muriel Heath, unpaginated manuscript.
29 IWM, 98/25/1, entry for 13 April 1945.
30 IWM, 98/25/1, unpaginated manuscript.
31 IWM, 95/26/1 Dawson, *Stagnant Pool*, p. 14.
32 FL M. McNeill, Temp MSS 981-A 17 June 1945.
33 IWM, 67/106/1, Hall, entry for 1 June 1945.
34 IWM, 98/25/1, entry for 18 April 1945.
35 UN Archives, S-0527-0503, First report by L. Rosolek to Mr. Patterson, UNRRA Mobilisation Centre, 5 July 1945.
36 IWM, 67/106/1, Hall, entry for 1 June 1945.

37   Duchesne-Cripps, *Mental Outlook*, p. 9.

38   IWM, 67/106/1, Hall, entry for 1 June 1945.

39   IWM, 98/25/1, Heath, entry for 1 April 1945.

40   FL Temp MSS 981-F Elizabeth Bayley, 14 June 1945.

41   FL Temp MSS 981-A 17 June 1945.

42   Institut d'histoire de temps présent, ARC 074 French Red Cross pamphlet (undated [1940–41 ?]).

43   FL, MSS Temp 981-A, McNeill, 1 July 1945.

44   FL, Temp MSS 981-F, Bayley, 22 June 1945.

45   Christabel Bielenberg, *The Road Ahead* (London: Bantam Press, 1992), p. 6.

46   Victor Klemperer, *To the Bitter End: The Diaries of Victor Klemperer, 1942–45*, abridged and translated by Martin Chalmers (London: Phoenix, 2000), p. 596.

47   IWM, 67/106/1, entry for 1 June 1945.

48   For inter-war fears see Richard Overy, *The Morbid Age: Britain and the Crisis of Civilisation, 1919–1939* (London: Penguin, 2009).

49   Robert Collis and Han Hogerzeil, *Straight On* (London: Methuen, 1947), p. 28.

50   AN 72/AJ/1968, Jacqueline Lesdos, letter dated 19 April 1946.

51   IWM, 98/25/1, manuscript; Kathryn Hulme later expressed similar feelings: *The Wild Place* (London and New York: Shakespeare Head, 1954), p. 22.

52   IWM, 98/25/1, Harry Heath, entry for 13 August 1945.

53   IWM, 98/25/1, entry for 16 August 1945.

54   Pettiss, *When the Shooting Stopped*, p. 66.

55   FL, Temp MSS 981-J Bayley, 29 June 1945.

56   ICRC Archives, Geneva G68 920 Activities Report, 16 July 1945.

57   Donald F. McGonigal, *A Short History of Junkers Camp, Bettenhausen, Kassel*, typed manuscript in AN, AJ 43 578, p. 19.

58   Marvin Klemme, *The Inside Story of UNRRA: An Experience in Internationalism* (New York: Lifetime Editions, 1949), p. 236.

59   AN, AJ/43/577, report dated 20 June 1947.

60   ICRC, G68 920 Activities Report, 16 July 1945.

61   Muriel Doherty, *Letters from Belsen 1945: An Australian Nurse's Experiences with the Survivors of War* edited by Judith Cornell AM and R. Lynette Russell AO (London: Allen and Unwin, 2000) p. 87.

62   IWM, 98/25/1, Heath, diary entry for 15 September 1945.

63   McGonigal, *A Short History*, p. 3.

64   McGonigal, *A Short History*, p. 6.

65   McGonigal, *A Short History*, pp. 17–18.

66   UN Archives, S-0436-0033, J. W. Watson, First report, Ingolstadt, 14 June 1945, p. 1.

67   Letter 2, 20 September 1945, *Among the Survivors*, p. 8.

68   UN Archives, S-0436-0031, Susan Pettiss, 'The story of a Museum', undated [July 1945?], p. 1.

69   See descriptions of DP camps in the Hanover area in Red Cross Archives, Moorgate, London, Acc 1977/17 British Red Cross Commission: report on work of sections in the field for the period 8 December 1947 to 7 January 1948.

70   Paul Fussell, *The Boys' Crusade: American GIs in Europe: Chaos and Fear in World War II* (London: Weidenfeld & Nicolson, 2003), p. 77.

71   Jacobmeyer, *Vom Zwangsarbeiter zum heimatlosen Ausländer*, p. 55.

72   ICRC, G68 1132 Ferrière, November 1943.

73   Daniel G. Cohen, 'Naissance d'une nation: les personnes déplacées de l'après-guerre, 1945–51', *Genèses* 38 (2000), pp. 56–78 (p. 66); Collis, *Straight On*, p. 72.

74   UN Archives, S-0436-0031, UNRRA Team report, 15 October 1945, C. del Marmol, Munich, Deutches Museum, p. 1.

75   ICRC, G68 936 Selby-Bigge, 23 October 1945.

76   ICRC, G68 936 Appendix « C » to DP Section MG Staff (Austria), monthly report for August 1945.

77 IWM, 84/47/1, Miss B. [Beryl] N. Lewis, unpublished documents, memo, 'For Inclusion in Routine Orders', undated [1946?].

78 FL, Temp MSS 981-F Tim Evens, late summer 1945.

79 ICRC, G68 920 Activities, July 1945 Bregenz.

80 Wilson, *Quaker Relief,* pp. 258, 233.

81 FL, Temp MSS 981 B, McNeill, 24 April 1946.

82 ICRC, G68 936, report from the delegation in Austria, 18 March 1946.

83 UN Archives, S-0436-0031, Report Number 7, UNRRA Team 108, August 5, 1945.

84 IWM, 95/26/1, Dawson, *Stagnant Pool,* pp. 237–8.

85 FL, Temp MSS 981 B, McNeill, 24 April 1946.

86 FL, Temp MSS 981 B, McNeill, 20 October 1946.

87 Gollancz, *In Darkest Germany*; Bayley, 23 June 1945.

88 IWM, 95/26/1, Dawson, *Stagnant Pool,* p. 14.

89 FL, Temp MSS 981-J, E. Bayley, 16 July 1945.

90 IWM, 85/31/1, Christiansen, *Work and Experience,* p. 4.

91 Heath, *diary* entry for 23 April, 20 May 1945.

92 UN Archives, S–0527–0505, confidential letter, 21 August 1945.

93 Hulme, *Wild Place,* p. 77,

94 IWM, 95/26/1, Dawson, *Stagnant Pool,* p. 59.

95 Political Warfare Executive, *Instructions,* p. 29.

96 On this point, see Matthew Frank, 'Working for the Germans: British voluntary societies and the German refugee crisis, 1945–1950,' *Historical Research* 82:215 (2009), pp. 157–75.

97 Linda Polman, *War Games: The Story of Aid and War in Modern Times,* translated by Liz Waters (London: Viking, 2010), pp. 45–6.

98 Gollancz, *Darkest Germany* p. 24.

99 FL, Temp MSS 981-F, letter from Roger Wilson (Friends House), 17 December 1945.

100 FL, Temp MSS 981-J, Bayley, 16 June 1945.

101 IWM, 98/25/1, Heath, diary entry for 23 April 1945; IWM 87/14/1, O'Connor, Chapter on UNRRA, manuscript; Pettiss, *After the Shooting,* p. 51.

102 IWM, 95/26/1, Dawson, *Stagnant Pool,* p. 38; Heath, diary entry for 3 May 1945.

103 IWM 12518, Margrethe Claudine 'Pip' Langdon, sound archive, recorded 21 March 1992.

104 IWM, 95/26/1, Dawson, *Stagnant Pool,* p. 54.

105 Collis, *Straight On,* p. 69.

106 IWM, 98/25/1, Mrs N. Heath, 'Some Afterthoughts on Hanau DP Camp', paragraph 7 [undated; paginated by paragraphs].

107 IWM, Heath, 98/25/1, diary entry for 27 July.

108 FL, Temp MSS 981-J, Bayley, 14 June 1945.

109 Petra Goedde, *GIs and Germans: Culture, Gender, and Foreign Relations, 1945–49* (New Haven and London: Yale University Press, 2003), p. 50.

110 Brett-Smith, *Grey City,* pp. 102–03 and George Clare, *Berlin Days* (London: Pan, 1990), p. 55.

111 Atina Grossmann, *Jews, Germans and Allies: Close Encounters in Occupied Germany* (Princeton & Oxford: Princeton University Press, 2007), p. 72.

112 Ira A. Hirschmann, *The Embers Still Burn; an eye-witness view of the postwar ferment in Europe and the Middle East and out disastrous get-soft-with-Germany policy* (New York: Simon and Schuster, 1949), pp. 94–95. On the prevalence of prostitution after 'liberation', see also Norman Lewis's astonishing memoir, Norman Lewis, *Naples '44: An Intelligence Officer in the Italian Labyrinth* (London: Eland, 2002 [1978]).

113 FL, Temp MAA 981-Aa McNeill, 16 December 1945.

114 Burke uses the term as the title of his sensationalistic, mildly salacious novel: *The Big Rape* (Frankfurt am Main: Friedrich Ruhl – Verleger Union, 1952). The second quote is from 'Anonymous', *A Woman in Berlin: Diary 20 April 1945 to 22 June 1945,* translated by Philip Boehm (London: Virago, 2005), p. 96.

115 Klemme, *Inside Story,* p. 229.

116 Raingard Esser, '"Language No Obstacle": War Brides in the German Press, 1945–1949,' *Women's History Review* 12:4 (2003), pp. 577–604.

117 FL, Temp MSS 981-J, Bayley, 30 August 1945.
118 IWM, 89/19/1, Miss Barbara McDouall, *Album*, p. 15.
119 Francesca M. Wilson, *Advice to Relief Workers: Based on Personal Experience in the Field* (London: John Murray and Friends Relief Service), p. 9.
120 IWM, 02/49/1; The Papers of Lieutenant General Sir Frederick Morgan, undated [Sept 1946?] entry for 4 October 1945.
121 For a discussion of relational vs. individual feminism see Karen Offen, *Signs: Journal of Women in Culture and Society* 14:1 (1988) pp. 119–57.
122 Klemme, *Inside Story*, p. 221.
123 McGonigal, *Short History*, pp. 14, 24–5.
124 AN 72/AJ/1968, Jacqueline Lesdos, 'Souvenirs', p. 20.
125 S. Armstrong-Reid, and D. Murray, *Armies of Peace: Canada and the UNRRA years* (Toronto: University of Toronto Press, 2008), pp. 357–8.
126 UN Archives, S-0436-0038, Service Memo, 16 August 1945.
127 Pettiss, *After the Shooting*, p. 3.
128 Pettiss, *After the Shooting*, pp. 55–6.
129 IWM, 98/25/1, Heath, 'Some Afterthoughts', p. 10.
130 Pettiss, *After the Shooting*, pp. 24–25.
131 Pettiss, *After the Shooting*, p. 65.
132 Pettiss, *After the Shooting*, pp. 130–1.
133 IWM, 95/26/1, Dawson, *Stagnant Pool*, p. 45.
134 IWM, 95/26/1, Dawson, *Stagnant Pool*, p. 32.
135 Pettiss, *After the Shooting*, p. 50.
136 Hulme, *Wild Place*, p. 26.
137 H. Heath, 'Two Years in UNRRA with Displaced Persons – II', *The Journal of the Association of Officers of the Ministry of Labour*, 25:10 (August 1948), pp. 10–13 (p. 10).
138 Duchesne-Cripps, *Mental Outlook*, p. 21.
139 IWM, 12518, Margrethe Claudine 'Pip' Langdon, sound archive, recorded 21 March 1992.
140 IWM, 95/26/1, Dawson, *Stagnant Pool*, p. 44.
141 Gollancz, *Darkest Germany* p. 55; FL Temp MSS 981-A McNeill, 1 July 1945.
142 *After the Shooting*, p. 17.
143 *After the Shooting*, p. 53.
144 IWM, 85/31/1, Christiansen, *Work and Experience*, p. 8.
145 *After the Shooting*, p. 76.
146 IWM, 95/26/1, *Stagnant Pool*, p. 17.
147 IWM, 98/25/1, diary entry, 17 July 1945. On requisitioning by the Allied authorities, see the useful observations by Richard Bessel, *Germany 1945: From War to Peace* (London: Simon & Schuster, 2009), pp. 180–1.
148 FL Temp McNeill, MSS 981-A. 1 July 1945.
149 Irving Heymont, *Among the Survivors of the Holocaust, 1945: The Landsberg DP Camp Letters* (np: Hebrew Union College Press, 1982), p. 71.
150 IWM, 98/25/1, Heath, 'Some Afterthoughts', p. 11.
151 Klemme, *Inside Story*, p. 231.
152 FL, Temp MSS 981-J, Bayley, 13 January 1946.
153 IWM, 95/26/1, Dawson, *Stagnant Pool*, p. 29.
154 IWM, 98/25/1, Heath, 'Some Afterthoughts', p. 2.
155 Bessel, *Germany 1945*, pp. 256–7.
156 Marrus, *The Unwanted* p. 310. See also Jacobmeyer, *Vom Zwangsarbeiter zum heimatlosen Ausländer*, p. 82.
157 ICRC Geneva G68 920 'Hungarian DP and POW', Mrs Goossens and Commdt Goossens, 28 August 1945 p. 4.
158 Marrus, *The Unwanted*, p. 310.
159 *After the Shooting*, pp. 60–1.
160 Woodbridge, *UNRRA*, Vol III, pp. 411–14.
161 McGonigal, *A Short History*, p. 8a [irregular pagination].

162 IWM, 95/26/1, Dawson, *Stagnant Pool*, p. 67.

163 IWM, 98/25/1, diary entry for 20 June 1945.

164 UN Archives, S-0436-0031, UNRRA Team Report Number 9, 12 September 1945, p. 1.

165 Anna Holian, 'Displacement and the Post-War Reconstruction of Education: Displaced Persons at the UNRRA University of Munich', *Contemporary European History* 17:2 (2008), pp. 167–95.

166 IWM, 84/47/1, Miss B. [Beryl] N. Lewis, unpublished documents; letter dated 13 July 1946.

167 See references in Hulme, *Wild Place*, p. 68; IWM, 98/25/1, Heath, diary entry for 7 April 1945.

168 Supreme Headquarters Allied Expeditionary Force, *Guide to the Care of Displaced Persons in Germany* (SHAEF, May 1945).

169 IWM, 87/14/1, O'Connor, UNRRA chapter, p. 16.

170 UN Archives S-0436-0031, final report, UNRRA Team 108, Deutsches Museum, Munich, 27 January 1946.

171 UN Archives S-0436-0031, final report, UNRRA Team 108, Deutsches Museum, Munich, 25 October 1945.

172 IWM, 98/25/1, diary entry for 26 April 1945.

173 FL Temp MSS 981 D-E (McNeill's journals for 1947 and 1948).

174 IWM, 95/26/1, Dawson, *Stagnant Pool*, pp. 29, 41–2, 110.

175 IWM, 98/25/1, Heath, diary entry 14 June 1945.

176 Pettiss, *After the Shooting Stopped*, p. 62.

177 Hulme, *Wild Place*, pp. 95–7.

178 UN Archives, S-0436-0055, Team 308, Report of Activities, 18 November 1945, Mr. Ephraim Chase, Director, USA, p. 5.

179 Summers, *Stranger in the House*, pp. 154–64.

180 UN Archives, S-0527-0503, first report by L. Rosolek sent to Mr. Patterson, UNRRA Mobilisation Centre, 5 July 1945, p. 4.

181 IWM, 02/49/1; Morgan papers, undated memo [Sept 1946?] on the 'Present Condition of the UNRRA Paris Office'.

182 ICRC, G68 936, telegram from Bosshard (Swiss journalist) to the *Gazette de Zurich*, 1 October 1944.

183 ICRC, G68 920 *Mission Médicale d'enquête Zone française*, 11 September 1945 p. 6.

184 Wilson, *Aftermath* p. 28.

185 Wilson, *Aftermath* pp. 23–6.

186 Wilson, *Aftermath*, p. 18.

187 For a brilliant tale about the absurdity of military culture, and the irrepressible buoyancy of the black market during times of desperate shortage, see Joseph Heller's *Catch 22*.

188 FL, Temp MSS 981-J Bayley, 16 July 1945.

189 ICRC, G68 927, *The Refugee: Bulletin of the Central Ukrainian Relief Bureau* 1/4 March 1947 p. 28.

Notes on Chapter 7

1 ICRC G.68 927 Clara Urquhart to the ICRC, Naples, 20 June 1946.

2 Arthur Koestler at Friends' Emergency Relief Training Centre, FL, Box FRS/199/28, circa June–September 1943.

3 Susan T. Pettiss and Lynne Taylor, *After the Shooting Stopped: the Story of an UNRRA welfare worker in Germany 1945–1947* (Crewe: Trafford, 2004), p. 63.

4 Kathryn Hulme, *The Wild Place* (London and New York: Shakespeare Head, 1954), p. 17.

5 Pettiss, *After the Shooting Stopped*, pp. 81–2.

6 FL Box FRS 1992/28, Instructions at Friends' Emergency relief Training Centre, circa September 1943.

7 Edward Bakis, 'The So-Called DP-Apathy in Germany's DP Camps', *Transactions of the*

Kansas Academy of Science 55:1 (1952), pp. 62–86; Hulme, *The Wild Place*, pp. 7 and 107; IWM 87/14/1, Miss Nora O'Connor, chapter on UNRRA, p. 11; IWM, 84/47/1, Miss B. [Beryl] N. Lewis, unpublished documents, Hannover Region's Monthly Report, August 1946.

8   IWM, 85/31/1, Mrs M. Christiansen, *The Work and Experience of an UNRRA Nurse during 16 months in Germany* (typed manuscript, pagination in pencil; 15 January 1947), p. 6.
9   Audrey M. Duchesne-Cripps, *The Mental Outlook of the Displaced Person as Seen through Welfare Work in Displaced Persons Camps* (Cambridge: self-published, 1955), p. 18.
10 FL, Temp MSS 981-B McNeill, 26 February 1947.
11 IWM 98/25/1, diary entries, 13 June 1945, 20 December 1945, 17 June 1945.
12 UN Archives, S-0436-0008, Report, dated 13 September 1945.
13 UN Archives, S-0436-0008, Report, September 17 1945.
14 *The Wild Place*, p. 33.
15 FL, Temp MSS 981-J, Bayley, 27 July 1945.
16 Similar schemes were created in France. See: Julia Maspero, 'La question des personnes déplacées polonaises dans les zones françaises d'occupation en Allemagne et en Autriche: un aspect méconnu des relations franco-polonaises (1945–1949)', *Relations internationales* 138 (2009), pp. 59–74.
17 McNeill, *Rivers of Bablyon*, p. 202.
18 UN Archives, S-0436-0031, Report, UNRRA Team 108, 11 July 1945, Charley del Marmol.
19 UN Archives, S-0436-0031, Report dated 19 June 1945, Charley del Marmol, p. 3.
20 Rhoda Dawson, *The Stagnant Pool: Work among Displaced Persons in Germany, 1945–1947* (undated typed manuscript, contained in Imperial War Museum, UNRRA, Mrs R. N. Bickerdike, 95/26/1), p. 63.
21 IWM, 98/25/1, Diary entry for 5 May 1945.
22 IWM, 98/25/1, Diary entry for 21 August 1945.
23 IWM, 98/25/1, Diary entry, 11 October 1945.
24 IWM, 98/25/1, Diary entry, 1 November 1945.
25 McNeill, *Rivers of Babylon*, p. 56.
26 McNeill, *Rivers of Babylon*, p. 159.
27 UNRRA, *Welfare Guide to United Nations Nationals Displaced in Germany* (London: European Regional Office, February1945), pp. 1 and 22.
28 WL, HA5-4/3, Psychological problems of Displaced Persons, June 1945, p. 15.
29 FL, Temp MSS 981-A, McNeill, 1 July 1945; Bayley provides a similar description in FL Temp MSS 981-J, 16 July 1945.
30 *Wild Place*, p. 52.
31 *Wild Place*, pp. 56–7.
32 AN Archives, AJ/43/78, Survey of conditions of Jews in the British Zone in March 1946.
33 AN Archives, AJ/43/78, Report of a meeting on Jewish Survey held at Bunde, 10.00 am, 2 April 1946.
34 FL Temp MSS 981-J, Bayley, 20 December 1945.
35 ICRC G68 922, Lithuanian Red Cross, 29 April 1948.
36 IWM, 98/25/1, Diary entries for 7 and 31 May 1945. Also see UN Archives, S-0436-0022, Report on working at the DP centre at Hanau, H. Heath, 7th June 1945; IWM, 87/14/1, O'Connor, UNRRA chapter, p. 12 and AN, 72/AJ/1968, Lesdos, 'Souvenirs', p. 24.
37 On the fate of Russians in Allied territory, one of the most eloquent descriptions is Norman Lewis's short sketch, 'The Cossacks Go Home' in his *A View of the World: Selected Journalism* (London: Eland, 1986), pp. 230–46.
38 Timothy Snyder, *Bloodlands: Europe between Hitler and Stalin* (London: Bodley Head, 2010).
39 IWM, 84/47/1, Miss B. [Beryl] N. Lewis, unpublished documents, memo on 'Public Safety', 27 October 1945.
40 IWM, 84/47/1, all incidents cited in 'Public Safety' reports in Miss B. [Beryl] N. Lewis, unpublished documents; reports dated 27 October 1945, 15 November 1945, 17 November 1945, 30 November 1945, 4 December 1945.

41 IWM, 84/47/1, Miss B. [Beryl] N. Lewis, unpublished documents, memo dated 17 November 1945.

42 McGonigal, *A Short History*, pp. 6–7.

43 Leonard O. Mosley, *Report from Germany* (London: Victor Gollancz, 1945), p. 57.

44 Mosley, *Report from Germany*, p. 53.

45 *Berlin '45: the Grey City* (London: MacMillan, 1966), p. 26.

46 *European Witness* (London: The Right Book Club, nd [1946?]), pp. 71–3.

47 IWM, 84/47/1, Miss B. [Beryl] N. Lewis, unpublished documents; report dated 30 November 1945.

48 Hulme, *Wild Place*, p. 83.

49 Stefan Schröder, *Displaced Persons im Lankreis und in der Stadt Münster 1945–1951* (Munster: Aschendorff Verlag, 2005), pp. 224–5.

50 AN, AJ/43/806, Report of Displaced Persons Criminal activities in Bavaria signed by Earl H. Mineau, IRO Public information officer, Bad Kissingen, 18 August 1948.

51 See for example Jacobmeyer's comparison of the rates of the DP and German criminality in the region of Bremen in the American Zone. Wolfgang Jacobmeyer, *Vom Zwangsarbeiter zum heimatlosen Ausländer: Die Displaced Persons in Westdeutschland, 1945–1951* (Gottingen: Vandenhoeck & Ruprecht, 1985), pp. 48–50.

52 Michael Berkowitz, *The Crime of My Very Existence: Nazism and the Myth of Jewish criminality* (University of California Press, 2007); Michael Berkowitz and Suzanne Brown-Fleming, 'Perceptions of Jewish Displaced Persons as Criminals in Early Postwar Germany' in Avinoam J. Patt and Michael Berkowitz (eds), *We are Here: New Approaches to Jewish Displaced Persons in Postwar Germany* (Wayne State University Press, 2010), pp. 167–93; Ruth Kluger, *Landscapes of Memory: A Holocaust Girlhood Remembered* (London: Bloomsbury, 2003), p. 185.

53 AN AJ/43/797, Rapport de M. De Soucy sur sa mission à Berlin, 29 September 1948.

54 FL Temp MSS 981-J, Bayley, 12 August 1945.

55 UN Archives, S-0425-0043, Report from W. B. Smith, Lieutenant-General, 7 December 1945, p. 1.

56 Irving Heymont, *Among the Survivors of the Holocaust, 1945: The Landsberg DP Camp Letters* (np: Hebrew Union College Press, 1982), p. 34. See also UN Archives, S-0425-0043, Report from the Assistant District Medical Officer, 6 December 1945.

57 IWM, 95/26/1, Dawson, *Stagnant Pool*, p. 227.

58 IWM, 95/26/1, Dawson, *Stagnant Pool*, p. 153.

59 IWM, 95/26/1, Dawson, *Stagnant Pool*, p. 87.

60 UN Archives, S-0425-0043, Report from the Assistant District Medical Officer, 6 December 1945.

61 UN Archives, S-0425-0043, Report from W.B. Smith, Lieutenant-General, 7 December 1945, p. 2.

62 Bertha L. Bracey, 'Practical Problems of Repatriation and Relocation', *International Affairs* 21:3 (1945), pp. 295–305 (p. 299).

63 AN, AJ/43/760, Counselling Service, rapport du mois de juillet 1948, signed by E.W.D Steel, Zone Welfare and Counselling Officer.

64 WL, HA5-4/3, Psychological Problems of Displaced Persons, June 1945, p. 18.

65 For further details see Lisa Haushofer, 'The Contaminating Agent: UNRRA, Displaced Persons and Venereal Disease in Germany 1945–1947', *American Journal of Public Health*, 100:6 (2010), pp. 993–1003.

66 Collis, *Straight On*, p. 27.

67 Bakis, 'So-Called DP Apathy', p. 64.

68 WL, HA5-4/3, Psychological problems of Displaced Persons, June 1945, p. 17.

69 Collis, *Straight On*, p. 63.

70 *Mental Outlook*, pp. 95–7.

71 Margaete Myers Feinstein, 'Jewish Women Survivors in the Displaced Persons Camps of Occupied Germany: Transmitters of the Past, Caretakers of the Present, and Builders of the Future', *Shofar* 24:4 (2006), pp. 67–89; Atina Grossmann, 'Trauma, Memory and

Motherhood: Germans and Jewish Displaced Persons in Post-Nazi Germany, 1945–1949', *Archiv für Sozialgeschichte* 38 (1998), pp. 215–39; Atina Grossmann, 'Victims, Villains and Survivors: Gendered Perceptions and Self-Perceptions of Jewish Displaced Persons in Occupied Postwar Germany', *Journal of the History of Sexuality* 11:1/2 (2002), pp. 291–318; Margarete L. Meyers 'Jewish Displaced Persons reconstructing individual and community in the US Zone of Occupied Germany', *Leo Baeck Institute Year Book* 42 (1997), pp. 303–24; Anna D. Jaroszyńska-Kirchmann, *The Exile Mission: The Polish Political Diaspora and Polish Americans, 1939–1956* (Athens: Ohio University Press, 2004), p. 76.

72 Andreas Rinke, *Le Grand retour – Die französische Displaced Person-Politik (1944–1951)* (Krankfurt: Peter Lang, 2002), p. 291.

73 IWM, 95/26/1, Dawson, *Stagnant Pool*, p. 162; Hulme, *Wild Place*, p. 73; IWM, 98/25/1, Harry Heath, diary entry, 26 July 1945.

74 AN, AJ/43/1149; *United Nations Relief and Rehabilitation Administration: Journal, fifth Session of the Council* (Geneva 1946), 4, 8 August 1946, p. 19.

75 Hulme, *Wild Place*, p. 110.

76 IWM, 02/49/1; The Papers of Lieutenant General Sir Frederick Morgan; entry for 13 September 1945.

77 IWM, 02/49/1; Morgan, Papers, entry for 27 November 1945.

78 Kluger, *Landscapes of Memory*, p. 183.

79 Viktor E. Frankl, *Man's Search for Meaning*, translated by Ilse Lasch (London: Rider, 2008 [1946]), p. 98.

80 Kluger, *Landscapes of Memory*, p. 107.

81 Kibbutz Buchenwald, 'Homecoming in Israel' in Leo W. Schwarz (ed.), *The Root and the Bough: the Epic of an Enduring People* (New York: Rinehard, 1949), pp. 308–45 (pp. 310–11).

82 Ivan Z. Holowinsky, 'DP Experience, Personality Structure and Ego Defence Mechanisms: A Psychodynamic interpretation' in Wsevolod W. Isajiw and Yury Boshyk (eds), *The Refugee Experience: Ukrainian Displaced Persons after World War II* (Edmonton: Canadian Institute of Ukrainian Studies, 1992), pp. 480–8.

83 FL, Temp MSS 981-J, Bayley, 19 July 1945.

84 ICRC G68 56 Letter, 18 March 1947.

85 ICRC G68 32 Letter, 23 January 1946.

86 FL, Temp MSS 981-J, FL Bayley, 23 September 1945.

87 Marta Dyczok, *The Grand Alliance and Ukrainian Refugees* (London: Palgrave Macmillan, 2000), pp. 15–18, p. 77.

88 FL, Temp MSS-981-A, McNeill, 26 October 1945.

89 Aharon Appelfeld, *The Story of a Life* translated by Aloma Halter (London: Hamish Hamilton, 2004), pp. 102–4.

90 Leo W. Schwarz, 'Introduction' to his edited *The Root and the Bough: the Epic of an Enduring People* (New York: Rinehard, 1949), pp.xi–xviii (p.xiii).

91 See for example UN Archives, S-0435-0014, Petitions from the National Groups [Estonian group, Latvian group, Lithuanian group, Ukrainian group], UNRRA Team 1066, Munich-Freimann, 19 May 1947.

92 McNeill, *Rivers* p. 81.

93 McNeill, *Rivers,* p. 83

94 FL, Temp MSS 981-J, Bayley, 7 September 1945.

95 McNeill, *Rivers,* pp. 193–4.

96 FL, MSS 981-F, Statement, 11 March 1947.

97 FL, Temp MSS-981-A, McNeill, 26 July 1945.

98 FL, Temp MSS 981-J, Bayley, 7 September 1945.

99 Marie Syrkin, *The State of the Jews* (Washington: New Republic, 1980), pp. 43–4.

100 ICRC, G68 920, various documents.

101 UN Archives, S-0527-0211, Payment of workers and rehabilitation, 23 February 1946, R. Maltby, Landeck.

102 *Rivers*, 124–25.

103 Hulme, *Wild Place* p. 83.

104   FL, Temp MSS 981-F, McNeill, 26 February 1946.
105   UN Archives, S-0436-0022, UNRRA Monthly report, Team 27, 7 June 1945, H. Heath, p 6.
106   FL, Temp MSS-981-E, McNeill, letter home [undated] circa 1948.
107   FL, Temp MSS 981-A, McNeill, 26 April 1946.
108   FL, Temp MSS 981-G.
109   ICRC G68 936, Note a l'attention de MP Kuhne, 11 November 1946.
110   UN Archives, S-0436-0022, UNRRA Monthly team report, 19 August 1946, p 7.
111   UN Archives, S-0527-0119, Narrative reports, 30 November 1945 and June 1946.
112   AN, AJ/43/78, Restricted Displaced persons monthly report no 5, 30 December 1945,
      UNRRA, Central headquarters for Germany, prepared by reports and analysis Division.
113   UN Archives, S-0436-0022, UNRRA Monthly report, Team 27, 7 June 1945, H. Heath, p 6.
114   Jaroszynska-Kirchmann, *The Exile Mission,* pp. 95–96; Laura Hilton, 'Cultural Nationalism
      in Exile: The case of Polish and Latvian Displaced Persons', *The Historian,* 71:2 (2009), pp.
      280–317 (p. 310).
115   UN Archives, S-0527-0121, UNRRA Weekly report, Team 148, 4 August 1945, E.S. Bankoff,
      p. 11.
116   Margarete Myers Feinstein, 'Jewish Observance in Amalek's Shadow' in Avinoam J. Patt
      and Michael Berkowitz (eds), *We are Here: New Approaches to Jewish Displaced Persons in
      Postwar Germany* (Wayne State University Press, 2010), pp. 257–288.
117   UN Archives, S-0527-0202, UNRRA DP Camp Spittal, Internal camp edition, June 1946,
      pp. 66–8.
118   UN Archives, S-0527-0202, UNRRA DP Camp Spittal, Internal camp edition, June 1946, p.
      73.
119   UN Archives, S-0527-0202, UNRRA DP Camp Spittal, Internal camp edition, June 1946, p.
      76.
120   Koppel S. Pinson, 'Jewish Life in Liberated Germany', *Jewish Social Studies* 9 (1947), pp.
      101–26 (p. 108).
121   Laura Jockusch, 'A Folk Monument to Our Destruction and Heroism', in Avinoam, J. Patt
      and Michael Berkowitz (eds), *We are Here: New Approaches to Jewish Displaced Persons in
      Postwar Germany* (Wayne State University Press, 2010), pp. 31–73 (p. 42).
122   Roman Ilnytzkyj, 'A Survey of Ukrainian Camp Periodicals, 1945–1950' in W.W. Isajiw, Y.
      Boshyk, R. Senkus (ed.) *The Refugee Experience. Ukrainian Displaced Persons after World
      War Two* (Edmonton: Canadian Institute of Ukrainian Studies Press, 1992), pp. 271–91 (p.
      272); Also see Jaroszynska-Kirchmann *The Exile Mission,* pp. 89–90.
123   UN Archives, S-0436-0031, 'The "DP Express" one year old', *The DP Express,* 6 July 1946, p.
      1.
124   UN Archives, S-0436-0031, 'The "DP Express" one year old', *The DP Express,* 6 July 1946, p.
      1.
125   Anne-Katrin Henkel, 'Bücher zum Trauern und zum Leben – Druckerei und Bibliothek im
      Displaced-Persons-Camp Bergen-Belsen (1945–1950)', *Zeitschrift für Bibliothekswesen und
      Bibliographie,* 56:1 (2009), pp. 20–9 (p. 23).
126   Henkel, 'Bücher zum Trauern und zum Leben', p. 23.
127   Henkel, 'Bücher zum Trauern und zum Leben', p. 26.
128   UN Archives, S-0527-0219, 'Saporoshetz on the Other Side of the Danube', operetta's
      programme.
129   Leo W. Schwarz, *The Redeemers: A Saga of the Years, 1945-52* (New York: Farrar, Strauss and
      Young, 1953), p. 21.
130   Bakis, 'DP Apathy', p. 73.
131   Pinson, 'Jewish life in liberated Germany', p. 125.
132   UN Archives, S-0527-0121, UNRRA Monthly report, Team 148, 15 December 1945, M.
      Segond, p. 4.
133   UN Archives, S-0527-0219, A short report, Prof Kylymnyk, 23 July 1946, pp. 2–3.
134   George G. Grabowicz, 'A Great Literature' in Wsevolod W. Isajiw and Yury Boshyk (eds), *The
      Refugee Experience: Ukrainian Displaced Persons after World War II* (Edmonton: Canadian
      Institute of Ukrainian Studies, 1992), pp. 240–68 (pp. 242–3).

135 Jaroszynska-Kirchmann, *The Exile Mission,* p. 93.
136 UN Archives, S-0436-0022, UNRRA Monthly Team, 15 July 1946.
137 UN Archives, S-0436-0022, UNRRA Monthly Team, 15 July 1946.
138 For further details on Polish DP schools see Anna D. Jaroszynska-Kirchmann, 'Patriotism, Responsibility, and the Cold War: Polish Schools in DP Camps in Germany, 1945–1951', *The Polish Review,* 47:1 (2002), pp. 35–66.
139 AN, AJ/43/594, Report on vocational training schools in the British Zone, 31 October 1947, Dorothy Marshall, Zone Welfare Officer.
140 UN Archives, S-0527-1119, Narrative report for the month of August 1946, Team 331, Ryder Young, p 2.
141 Bakis, 'DP Apathy', p. 73.
142 AN, AJ/43/760, Rapport number 4, October 1947.
143 Josef Betari, 'I Found the Answer' in Leo W. Schwarz (ed.), *The Root and the Bough: the Epic of an Enduring People* (New York: Rinehard, 1949), pp. 135–41 (p. 136).
144 Schwarz, *Redeemers*, p. 32.
145 Betari, 'I Found the Answer', p. 139.
146 Marie Syrkin, *The State of the Jews* (Washington: New Republic, 1980), p. 19.
147 Magda Denes, *Castles Burning: A child's life in war* (London: Transworld, 1997), p. 278.
148 Magda Denes, *Castles Burning*, pp. 305–6.
149 Irene Grünbaum, *Escape through the Balkans,* translated and edited by Katherine Morris (Lincoln & London: University of Nebraska Press, 1996 [1949–50]), pp. 146–7.

Notes to Chapter 8

1 NA, FO/371/51117, document dated 9 May 1945. See also the comments in Bernard Wasserstein, *Vanishing Diaspora: the Jews in Europe since 1945* (London: Hamish Hamilton, 1996), p. 13.
2 Cited in Anne Grynberg, 'Des signes de résurgence de l'antisémitisme dans la France de l'après-guerre (1945–53)?', *Les Cahiers de la Shoah* 5 (2001), pp. 171–223 (p. 176).
3 Christopher Caldwell, *Reflections on the Revolution in Europe: Immigration, Islam and the West* (London: Penguin, 2010).
4 Quotations from Pieter Lagrou, 'Victims of Genocide and National Memory: Belgium, France and the Netherlands 1945–1965', *Past and Present* 154 (1997), pp. 181–222 (p. 184) and Pieter Lagrou, 'Return to a Vanished World: European Societies and the Remnants of their Jewish Communities, 1945–47 in D. Bankier (ed.), *The Jews and Coming Back* (New York: Berghahn and Jerusalem: Yad Vashem, 2005), pp. 1–24 (p. 6).
5 On boundary-keeping, see Zygmunt Bauman, *Modernity and the Holocaust* (Cambridge: Polity, 2005), p. 34 and passim. See also Peter Gatrell and Nick Baron (eds), *Warlands: Population Resettlement and State Reconstruction in the Soviet-East European Borderlands, 1945–50* (London: Palgrave Macmillan, 2009).
6 Richard Crossman, *Palestine Mission: A Personal Mission* (London: Hamish Hamilton, 1947), p. 74.
7 NA, FO/945/708, memo dated 18 October 1946.
8 AN, AJ/43/328, IRO report dated 16 September 1947.
9 Lagrou, 'Return to a Vanished Land', p. 16.
10 Norman Davies, *Rising '44: The Battle for Warsaw* (London: MacMillan, 2003), pp. 34–6.
11 Jan E. Zamajski, 'The Social History of Polish Exile (1939–1945); the exile state and the clandestine state: Society, Problems and Reflections' in Martin Conway and José Gotovitch (eds), *Europe in Exile; European Exile Communities in Britain, 1940–1945* (New York and Oxford: Berghahn Books, 2001), pp. 183–212.
12 Pertti Ahonen, Gustavo Corni, Jerzy Kochanowski, Rainer Schulze, Tamás Stark and Barbara Stelzl-Marx, *People on the Move: Forced Population Movements in Europe in the Second World War and Its Aftermath* (Oxford and New York: Berg, 2008), pp. 21–2.

13 Anna Jaroszynska-Kirchmann, *The Exile Mission* (Athens: Ohio University Press, 2004), p. 60.
14 Davies, *Rising '44*, p. 76.
15 Barbara Engelking, *Holocaust and Memory: The Experience of the Holocaust,* translated by E. Harris (Leicester: Leicester UP, 2001), p. 91.
16 Ruth Kluger, *Landscapes of Memory: A Holocaust Girlhood Remembered* (London: Bloomsbury, 2003), p. 36.
17 Joanna Michlic, 'The Holocaust and Its Aftermath as Perceived in Poland: Voices of Polish Intellectuals, 1945–47' in D. Bankier (ed.), *The Jews are Coming Back* (New York: Berghahn, 2005 and Jerusalem: Yad Vashem, 2005), pp. 206–30 (p. 208).
18 One the problems of 'restoration' in Warsaw, see the perceptive analysis in: Jasper Goldman, 'Warsaw: Reconstruction as Propaganda' in L. J. Vale and T. J. Campanella (eds), *The Resilient City* (OUP, 2005), pp. 135–48.
19 Engelking, *Holocaust and Memory*, p. 3.
20 On Soviet policies in Poland, see Ahonen, *People on the Move*, pp. 23–6.
21 Susan T. Pettiss and Lynne Taylor, *After the Shooting Stopped: the Story of an UNRRA Welfare Worker in Germany 1945–1947* (Crewe: Trafford, 2004), p. 53.
22 FL, Temp MSS 981-C McNeill, 26 May 1947.
23 AN, AJ/43/577, estimate dated 22 March 1947.
24 IWM, 95/26/1, Rhoda Dawson, *The Stagnant Pool: Work among Displaced Persons in Germany, 1945–1947*, p. 43.
25 Margaret McNeill, *By the Rivers of Babylon; A Story of Relief Work among the Displaced Persons of Europe* (London: Bannisdale Press, 1950), p. 38.
26 Audrey M. Duchesne-Cripps, *The Mental Outlook of the Displaced Person as Seen through Welfare Work in Displaced Persons Camps* (Cambridge: self-published, 1955), p. 41.
27 IWM, 98/25/1, Harry Heath, Diary, entry for 21 June 1945.
28 Marie Dresden Lane, 'A Social Worker Behind the Iron Curtain', *New York Herald Tribune*, 13 October 1949.
29 '"We Shall Rebuild Anew a Powerful Nation": UNRRA, Internationalism and National Reconstruction in Poland', *Journal of Contemporary History* 43:3 (2008), pp. 451–76 (p. 467).
30 FL, Temp MSS 981-C, McNeill papers, 26 July 1945.
31 Margaret McNeill, *By the Rivers of Babylon; A Story of Relief Work among the Displaced Persons of Europe* (London: Bannisdale Press, 1950), p. 37.
32 IWM 02/49/1, Morgan, Papers, diary entry for 11 October 1945.
33 IWM, 95/26/1, *Stagnant Pool*, p. 251.
34 IWM, 95/26/1, *Stagnant Pool*, p. 147a [irregular pagination].
35 IWM, 95/26/1, *Stagnant Pool*, p. 147a [irregular pagination].
36 IWM, 95/26/1, *Stagnant Pool*, p. 145a [irregular pagination].
37 IWM, 95/26/1, *Stagnant Pool*, p. 155a [irregular pagination].
38 *Rivers of Babylon*, p. 161.
39 IWM, 95/26/1, *Stagnant Pool*, pp. 140–41a [irregular pagination].
40 See, for example, IWM, 84/47/1, Lewis, unpublished papers, Hannover Monthly Narrative Report, May 1946.
41 UN, S-0436-0008, Wildflecken, Analysis of Tabulation of Questionnaires on Repatriation, 14 May 1946.
42 UN, S-0436-0008, Resolution of the Polish Committee, 22 January 1947 (Wildflecken).
43 UN, S-0436-0008, Report on Nationality Screening Incident, 22 January 1947 (report signed K. Hulme).
44 AN, AJ/43/806. Report from Mr. H.A. Washington, UNRRA Area Team 1064 Mittenwald, Heidelberg, May 1947.
45 Anna Marta Holian, 'Between National Socialism and Soviet Communism: the Politics of Self-Representation among Displaced Persons in Munich, 1945–1951', (PhD, University of Chicago, 2005) p. 184.
46 IWM, 02/49/1, Papers, Diary entry for 10 September 1945.
47 Lieutenant General Sir Frederick Morgan, KCB, *Peace and War: A Soldier's Life* (London: Hodder and Stoughton, 1961), p. 231.

48 IWM, 84/47/1, Miss B. [Beryl] N. Lewis, unpublished documents; Hannover Region's Monthly Narrative, July 1946, p. 10.
49 IWM, 84/47/1, Lewis, unpublished documents, Hannover Region's Monthly Report, August 1946, p. 12.
50 AN, AJ/43/608, IRO report, dated 13 January 1948. See also AN, AJ/43/577, report dated 20 June 1947; and UN, S-0436-0033, Ingolstadt, Team 121, Report from UNRRA Field Supervisor, 22 May 1946, p. 3.
51 IWM, 95/26/1, Dawson, *Stagnant Pool*, p. 251. UN, S-0436-0008, Report from G. Masset, to Mr. E. Nordby, District Director, UNRRA Dist, No.2, Wiesbaden, 27 August 1946 (Wildflecken).
52 UN, S-0436-0008, UNRRA Monthly team report, 15 November 1946 (Wildflecken).
53 *Wild Place*, p. 45.
54 Wladyslaw Wolsk, 'Do Rodaków na Obczyznie', *Repateiant* (December 1947), translation in AN, AJ/43/608.
55 Hulme, *Wild Place*, p. 129.
56 Hulme, *Wild Place*, p. 130.
57 *The Polish Refugee*, 1 (1947), p. 4.
58 AN, AJ/33/577, report dated 20 June 1947.
59 Hulme, *Wild Place*, pp. 127–8.
60 Hulme, *Wild Place*, p. 43. See also UN, S-O527-0121, Team 148, Camp Landeck, June 30 1946.
61 IWM, 95/26/1, Dawson, *Stagnant Pool*, p. 157a [irregular pagination].
62 IWM, 95/26/1, *Stagnant Pool*, p. 229.
63 IWM, 95/26/1, Dawson, *Stagnant Pool*, p. 171.
64 IWM, 95/26/1, *Stagnant Pool*, p. 185.
65 IWM, 95/26/1, *Stagnant Pool*, p. 172.
66 IWM, 95/26/1, *Stagnant Pool*, p. 189.
67 IWM, 95/26/1, *Stagnant Pool*, p. 190.
68 IWM, 95/26/1, *Stagnant Pool*, p. 196.
69 IWM, 95/26/1, *Stagnant Pool*, p. 196.
70 IWM, 95/26/1, *Stagnant Pool*, p. 199.
71 IWM, 95/26/1, *Stagnant Pool*, p. 208.
72 IWM, 95/26/1, *Stagnant Pool*, p. 209.
73 IWM, 95/26/1, *Stagnant Pool*, p. 219.
74 IWM, 95/26/1, *Stagnant Pool*, p. 225.
75 IWM, 95/26/1, *Stagnant Pool*, p. 233.
76 'Polish Refugees Greet the International Refugee Organisation', *The Polish Refugee* 1 (1947), pp. 3–5.
77 Engelking, *Holocaust and Memory*, pp. 3–4.
78 Gerard Daniel Cohen, 'The Politics of Recognition: Jewish Refugees in Relief Policies and Human Rights Debates, 1945–1950', *Immigrants and Minorities* 24:2 (2006), pp. 125–43 (p. 126).
79 Kolinsky, *After the Holocaust*, p. 137.
80 I. F. Stone, *Underground to Palestine* (London: Hutchinson, 1979), p. 147.
81 Jacqueline Mesnil-Amar, *Ceux qui ne dormaient pas: Journal, 1944–46* (Paris: Stock, 2009 [1957]), p. 57.
82 Ariel J. Kochavi, *Post-Holocaust Politics: Britain, the United States and Jewish Refugees, 1945–48* (Chapel Hill: University of North California Press, 2001), p. 31.
83 Königseder, *Waiting for Hope*, p. 52.
84 Michlic, 'The Holocaust and Its Aftermath', pp. 211–12.
85 Marcus J. Smith, *Dachau: the Harrowing of Hell* (Albany, N.Y.: State University of New York Press, 1995 [1972]), p. 80.
86 Private photograph in the authors' possession.
87 William I. Hitchcock, *The Bitter Road to Freedom: A New History of the Liberation of Europe* (New York: Free Press, 2008), p. 299.

88 Toby Haggith, 'The Filming of the Liberation of Bergen-Belsen and Its Impact on the Understanding of the Holocaust' in Suzanne Bardgett and David Cesarani (eds), *Belsen 1945: New Historical Perspectives* (London: Vallentine Mitchell, 2006), pp. 89–122.

89 Angelika Königseder and Juliane Wetzel, *Waiting for Hope: Jewish Displaced Persons in Post-World War II Germany* translated by John A. Broadwin (Evanston: Northwestern University Press, 2001 [1994]), p. 16.

90 IWM, 95/26/1, Dawson, *Stagnant Pool*, p. 95.

91 Pettiss, *After the Shooting*, p. 143. Almost exactly the same point is made in Bartley C. Crum, *Behind the Silken Curtain: A Personal Account of Anglo-American Diplomacy in Palestine and the Middle East* (London: Gollancz, 1947), p. 8.

92 NA, FO/371/51118, letter dated May 1945.

93 NA, FO/943/759, memo dated 28 September 1945.

94 NA, FO/371/64424, report dated April 1947.

95 NA, PREM/8-384, Foreign Office memo for the Prime Minster, 4 September 1946.

96 NA, PREM/8-834, notes on a meeting between Atlee and La Guardia, 5 September 1946.

97 NA, FO/371/61956, minute dated 20 September 1947.

98 See Crossman, *Palestine Mission*, p. 85.

99 Crossman, *Palestine Mission*, p. 27.

100 Crossman, *Palestine Mission*, p. 76.

101 Crossman, *Palestine Mission*, p. 80.

102 Crossman, *Palestine Mission*, p. 103.

103 Eva Kolinsky, *After the Holocaust: Jewish Survivors in Germany after 1945* (London: Pimlico, 2004), pp. 58–9.

104 Kolinsky, *After the Holocaust*, pp. 68 and 117.

105 Hulme, *Wild Place*, pp. 179–80.

106 *Wild Place*, pp. 180–5.

107 Lieutenant Colonel W. Kerr, [Private Papers], IWM, 86/53/1, pp. 43–4.

108 See, for example, IWM, 84/47/1, Lewis, unpublished papers, Report dated 30 November 1945.

109 Irving Heymont, *Among the Survivors of the Holocaust, 1945: The Landsberg DP Camp Letters* (np: Hebrew Union College Press, 1982), p. 94.

110 Quoted in Crum, *Behind the Silken Curtain,* p. 71.

111 IWM, 02/49/1, Morgan, Papers, diary entry for 23 March 1946.

112 IWM, 95/26/1, Dawson, *Stagnant Pool*, pp. 89–90. Crossman records similar impressions: *Palestine Mission*, p. 90.

113 IWM, 95/26/1, *Stagnant Pool*, p. 95.

114 IWM, 95/26/1, *Stagnant Pool*, p. 105.

115 Ehud Avriel, *Open the Gates! – A Personal Story of 'Illegal' Immigration to Israel* (London: Weidenfeld and Nicolson, 1975), p. 8.

116 Primo Levi, *The Periodic Table* translated by Raymond Rosenthal (London: Abacus, 1995), p. 35.

117 Engelking, *Holocaust and Memory*, p. 39.

118 'French Apprehensions, Jewish Expectations: From a Social Imaginary to a Political Practice' in D. Baukier (ed.), *The Jews are Coming Back* (New York: Berghahn, 2005 and Jerusalem: Yad Vashem, 2005), pp. 25–57 (p. 56). On French Jews' French patriotism, see also Annette Wieviorka, 'Jewish Identity in the First Accounts of Extermination Camp Survivors from France', *Yale French Studies* 85 (1994), pp. 135–51.

119 Annette Wieviorka, 'Jewish Identity in the First Accounts of Extermination Camp Survivors from France', *Yale French Studies* 85 (1994), pp. 135–51 (p. 149).

120 Hannah Arendt, *Eichmann in Jerusalem: A Report on the Banality of Evil* (London: Penguin, 2006 [1964]), p. 154.

121 Frank Stern, 'Antagonistic Memories: The Post-War Survival and Alienation of Jews and Germans' in L. Passerini (ed.), *Memory and Totalitarianism* (Oxford: OUP, 1992), pp. 21–43 (p. 28).

122 Magda Denes, *Castles Burning: A child's life in war* (London: Transworld, 1997), p. 67.

123 Helena Szereszewska, *Memoirs from Occupied Warsaw,* translated by Anna Marianska (London: Valentine Mitchell, 2000), p. 399.

124 Joseph Joffo, *Un sac de billes* (Paris: Librairie Générale française, 1973), p. 33.

125 Alexandra Fanny Brodsky, *A Fragile Identity; Survival in Nazi-occupied Belgium* (London: Radcliffe, 1998), p. 206.

126 Brodsky, *A Fragile Identity,* p. 154.

127 Elie A. Cohen, *Human Behaviour in the Concentration Camp,* translated by M. H. Braaksma (London: Greenwood Press, 1984 [1954]), p. 169.

128 Denes, *Castles Burning,* p. 156.

129 Ruth Kluger, *Landscapes of Memory: A Holocaust Girlhood Remembered* (London: Bloomsbury, 2003), p. 98.

130 Kluger, *Landscapes of Memory,* p. 70.

131 Thomas Rahe, 'Jewish Religious Life in the Concentration Camp Bergen-Belsen' translated by K.-M. Meyke in Tony Kushner, David Cesarani, Jo Reilly and Colin Richmond (eds), *Belsen in History and Memory* (London: Frank Cass, 1997), pp. 85–121 (p. 106).

132 Engelking, *Holocaust and Memory,* p. 191.

133 Michael L. Meng, 'After the Holocaust: the History of Jewish Life in West Germany', *Contemporary European History* 14:3 (2005), pp. 403–13.

134 Mario Toscano, 'The Abrogation of the Racial Laws and the Reintegration of Jews in Italian Society (1943–1948)' in D. Bankier (ed.), *The Jews are Coming Back* (New York: Berghahn, 2005 & Jerusalem: Yad Vashem, 2005), pp. 148–68.

135 Frank Caesteker, 'The Reintegration of Jewish Survivors into Belgian Society, 1943–1947' in D. Bankier (ed.), *The Jews are Coming Back* (New York: Berghahn, 2005 & Jerusalem: Yad Vashem, 2005), pp. 72–107 (p. 79).

136 Manuela Consonni, 'The Written Memoir: Italy, 1945–1947' in D. Baukier (ed.), *The Jews are Coming Back* (New York: Berghahn, 2005 & Jerusalem: Yad Vashem, 2005), pp. 169–85.

137 Primo Levi, *The Periodic Table* translated by Raymond Rosenthal (London: Abacus, 1995), p. 151.

138 Ido de Haan, 'Paths of Normalisation after the Persecution of the Jews: the Netherlands, France and West Germany in the 1950s' in R. Bessel and D. Schumann (eds), *Life after Death: Approaches to a Cultural and Social History of Europe during the 1940s and 1950s* (Cambridge: CUP, 2003), pp. 65–92 (p. 74).

139 *Man's Search for Meaning,* p. 90.

140 Denes, *Castles Burning,* p. 190.

141 Aharon Appelfeld, *The Story of a Life,* translated by Aloma Halter (London: Hamish Hamilton, 2004), p. 81.

142 Jon and David Kimche, *The Secret Roads: The 'Illegal' Migration of a People* (London: Secker and Warburg, 1954), pp. 81–2.

143 Andrea Reiter, *Narrating the Holocaust,* translated by Patrick Collier (London: Continuum, 2000), p. 65.

144 Howard Wettstein, 'Introduction' to his edited, *Diasporas and Exiles: Varieties of Jewish Identity* (Berkeley, Los Angeles and London: University of California Press, 2002), pp. 1–17.

145 Victyor Jeleniewski Seidler, *Shadows of the Shoah: Jewish Identity and Belonging* (Oxford: Berg, 2000), p. 49.

146 Koppel S. Pinson, 'Jewish Life in Liberated Germany', *Jewish Social Studies* 9 (1947), pp. 101–26 (p. 112).

147 Kibbutz Buchenwald, 'Homecoming in Israel' in Leo W. Schwarz (ed.), *The Root and the Bough: the Epic of an Enduring People* (New York: Rinehard, 1949), pp. 308–45 (p. 310).

148 Leo W. Schwarz, *The Redeemers: A Saga of the Years, 1945–52* (New York: Farrar, Strauss and Young, 1949), p. 9.

149 NA, FO/371/51110, 25 November 1944.

150 George Vida, *From Doom to Dawn: A Jewish Chaplain's Story of the Displaced Persons* (New York: Jonathan David, 1967), p. 73.

151 Ruth Gruber, *Exodus 1947: the Ship that Launched a Nation* (New York and London: Union Square Press, 1999 [1948]), p. 20.

152 Bartley C. Crum, *Behind the Silken Curtain: A Personal Account of Anglo-American Diplomacy in Palestine and the Middle East* (London: Gollancz, 1947), p. 74.

153 WL, 1367/5/2, document dated 14 June 1945. Such concerns were shared by many Jewish philanthropic groups. See the surprisingly prescient: Zorach Warhaftig, *Relief and Rehabilitation: Implications of the UNRRA Program for Jewish Needs* (New York: Institute of Jewish Affairs of the American Jewish Congress and World Jewish Congress, 1944).

154 WL, Henriques Archive, 51/1, 'For Liberated Jewry', undated leaflet.

155 WL, 1367/5/2, document dated 22 June 1945. Norman Bentwich complains about this point: see his *My 77 Years; An Account of My Life and Times, 1883–1960* (London: Routledge & Kegan Paul, 1962), p. 194.

156 WL, Henriques Archive, 51/1, 'Tasks Undertaken', *The Central British Fund for Jewish Relief and Rehabilitation Annual Report 1946*, pp. 3–12.

157 WL, Henriques Archive, 51/1, 'Wanted Clothing for These Children', undated leaflet [1947?].

158 See, for example, WL, Henriques Archive, 51/1, 'Profile: Portrait of a Relief Worker', *Jews in Europe, A Review of the Work of the Jewish Relief Unit* [undated, unpaginated].

159 WL, Henriques Archive, 51/1, circular to all members of JRU, undated.

160 WL, Henriques Archive 51/1, Anonymous, 'Relief and the United Nations' in Norman Bentwich (ed.), *Aspects of Jewish Relief* (no publisher, undated), pp. 8–15 (p. 10).

161 Brenner, *After the Holocaust*, p. 37.

162 Königseder, *Waiting for Hope*, p. 20.

163 Hanoch Bartov, *The Brigade* translated by David S. Segal (New York, Chicago and San Francisco: 1968), pp. 64, 117.

164 Schwarz, *The Redeemers*, p. 15.

165 Cited in Schwarz, *The Redeemers*, p. 51.

166 Ariel, *Open the Gates*, p. 221.

167 Kimche, *The Secret Roads*, p. 80.

168 Brenner, *After the Holocaust*, pp. 18–19.

169 Angelika Königseder and Juliane Wetzel, *Waiting for Hope: Jewish Displaced Persons in Post-World War II Germany* translated by John A. Broadwin (Evanston: Northwestern University Press, 2001 [1994]), p. 5.

170 Professor Norman Bentwich, 'The Jewish Relief Units in Germany', *Jewish Monthly* (February 1948), pp. 2–8 (p. 4).

171 Kolinsky, *After the Holocaust*, p. 201.

172 Avriel, *Open the Gates*, p. 196.

173 Conny Kristel, 'Revolution and Reconstruction: Dutch Jewry after the Holocaust' in D. Bankier (ed.), *The Jews are Coming Back* (New York: Berghahn, 2005 & Jerusalem: Yad Vashem, 2005), pp. 136–47 (p. 143).

174 Leo W. Schwarz, 'Introduction' to his edited *The Root and the Bough: the Epic of an Enduring People* (New York: Rinehard, 1949), pp.xi–xviii (p.xiv).

175 Leo W. Schwarz, *The Redeemers: A Saga of the Years, 1945–52* (New York: Farrar, Strauss and Young, 1949), p. 22.

176 'Homecoming in Israel', pp. 317, 323.

177 Alexander Ramati, *Rebel Against the Light* (New York: Page, 1960), p. 60.

178 Catherine Nicault, 'L'utopie du "nouveau Juif" et la jeunesse juive dans la France de l'après-guerre. Contribution à l'histoire de l'Alyah française', *Les Cahiers de la Shoah* 5:1 (2001), pp. 105–69 (p. 138).

179 Rachel Cohn, 'Women Emigrés in Palestine' in Sibylle Quack (ed.), *Between Sorrow and Strength; Women Refugees of the Nazi Period* (Cambridge: CUP, 1995), pp. 89–95 (p. 95).

180 Account reproduced in Jacques Derogy, *La loi du retour: la secrète et véritable histoire de l'Exodus* (Paris: Fayard, 1969), p. 165.

181 Gruber, *Exodus 1947*, p. 151.

182 Gruber, *Exodus 1947*, p. 76.

183 Norman Bentwich, *My 77 Years; An Account of My Life and Times, 1883–1960* (London: Routledge & Kegan Paul, 1962), p. 123.

184 Pinson, 'Jewish Life', p. 111.

185 Pinson, 'Jewish Life', p. 114.
186 Zippy Orlin, 'What it's really like in a DP Camp: A South African Girl in Belsen' in Erik Somers and René Kok (eds), *Jewish Displaced Persons in Camp Bergen-Belsen, 1945–1950* (Seattle: University of Washington Press and Netherlands Institute for War Documentation, 2004), pp. 154–83 (p. 157).
187 'A DP Camp', p. 156.
188 *The Story*, pp. 122–3.
189 Bartov, *Brigade*, p. 148.
190 Kimche, *The Secret Roads*, p. 27.
191 Kimche, *Secret Roads*, p. 81.
192 The best analysis of this issue is Idith Zertal, *From Catastrophe to Power: Holocaust Survivors and the Emergence of Israel* (Berkeley: University of California Press, 1998). For an interesting analysis of the politics of memory in Israel, see Dan A. Porat, 'From the Scandal to the Holocaust in Israeli Education', *Journal of Contemporary History* 39:4 (2004), pp. 619–36.
193 Kolinsky, *After the Holocaust*, p. 133.
194 Judith T. Shuval, *Immigrants on the Threshold* (New York: Atherton Press, 1963), p. 20.
195 *The Story*, p. 124.
196 'Homecoming in Israel', p. 338.
197 Appelfeld, *Story*, p. 168.
198 Amos Oz, *A Tale of Love and Darkness* (London: Vintage, 2005), p. 407.
199 Shuval, *Immigrants on the Threshold*, p. 50.
200 Shuval, *Immigrants on the Threshold*, p. 14.
201 Seidler, *Shadows*, p. 73.
202 Appelfeld, *Story*, p. 148.
203 *Man's Search*, p. 75.

Notes to conclusion

1 Flavia Kingscote, *Balkan Exit* (London: Geoffrey Bles, 1942), p. 179.
2 FL, Temp MSS 981 F, Margaret McNeill, 3 March 1948.
3 I. F. Stone, *Underground to Palestine* (London: Hutchinson, 1979), p.vii.
4 On post-1945 idealism see, for example, Matthew Frank, 'The New Morality – Victor Gollancz, "Save Europe Now" and the German Refugee Crisis, 1945–46', *Twentieth Century British History* 17:2 (2006), pp. 230–56 and Michael Gehler and Wolfram Kaiser, 'Transnationalism and Early European Integration: The *Nouvelles Equipes Internationales* and the Geneva Circle, 1947–1957', *Historical Journal* 44:3 (2001), pp. 773–98.
5 Ruth Kluger, *Landscapes of Memory: A Holocaust Girlhood Remembered* (London: Bloomsbury, 2003), p. 156.
6 Kluger, *Landscapes of Memory*, pp. 164–70.
7 FL, FRS/Pics/3/Envelope 14/3147 American Friends Service Committee, Warsaw, Poland, 1 August 1948 [details of Christmas 1947].
8 FL, Temp MSS–981–F, Margaret McNeill, scrapbook [undated].
9 François Lafitte, *The Internment of Aliens* (London: Penguin, 1988 [1940]), p. 237.
10 E. Valentine Daniel and John Chr. Knudsen, 'Introduction' to their *Mistrusting Refugees* (Berkeley: University of California Press, 1995), pp. 1–12 (p. 6).
11 T. Alexander Aleinikoff, 'State-centred Refugee Law: From Resettlement to Containment' in E. V. Daniel and J. C. Knudsen (eds), *Mistrusting Refugees* (Berkeley: University of California Press, 1995), pp. 257–78.
12 'London Letter' in *Collected Essays, Journalism and Letters of George Orwell*, Vol II, edited by Sonia Orwell and Ian Angus (London: Secker and Warburg, 1968), pp. 286–92 (p. 291)
13 Friends Library, Box FRS 1992 88; A. Hewlett, 'The Prospects for Relief Service Abroad', 21 May 1943.

14   Julie Peteet, 'Unsettling the Categories of Displacement', *Merip* 244 (2007), http://www.
     merip.org/mer/mer244; accessed 7 March 2008.
15   Zygmunt Bauman, *Liquid Modernity* (Cambridge: Polity, 2000), p. 29.
16   On this point, see Sharif Gemie, 'Re-defining Refugees: Nations, Borders and Globalization',
     Eurolimes 9 (2010), pp. 28–37.
17   See, Amartya Sen, *Identity and Violence; the Illusion of Destiny* (London: Penguin, 2006).
18   Lafitte, *The Internment of Aliens*, p. 12.
19   Ned Thomas, 'Two Cataclysms', *Planet: the Welsh Internationalist* 198 (2010), pp. 93–102.
20   Zygmunt Bauman, *Modernity and the Holocaust* (Cambridge: Polity, 2005).
21   Bauman, *Liquid Modernity*, p. 207.

Bibliography

Unpublished Sources
Archives Départementales du Bas-Rhin (ADBRhin)
Series AL
98/AL/218; 98/AL/275; 98/AL/280; 98/AL/282; 98/AL/283; 98/AL/287; 98/AL/288

Archives Départementales des Bouches du Rhône (ADBRhône)
Series W
174 W 34 and 148 W 185

Archives Départementales de la Haute-Garonne
Series M
1/M/1906/00132
Series W
2024/102; 2024/142; 2054/142; 2054/143; 2054/346; 2054/1476

Archives Départmentales de l'Ille-et-Vilaine
Series M
4/M/414
Series W
4 W 5; 4/W/7
Series Z
1/Z/8

Archives départementales de l'Isère
Series R
13/R/824/4; 13/R/824/5

Archives Départementales de la Manche
Series J
2/J/1521
Series W
127/W/49

Archives Départementales du Meurthe-et-Moselle
Series W
W/18/28; W/18/218
Series WM
WM 389; WM 399

Archives Départementales des Pyrénées-Orientales
Series W
31/W/274; 38/W/63

Archives Départementales du Rhône
Series J
31/J B/156
Series M
4/M/236; 4/M/422
Series W
45/W/35; 45/W/39; 45/W/40; 45/W/41; 45/W/42; 45/W/52; 45/W/118;
3958/W/118

Archives Municipales de Lyon
132 II 48, 1127/WP/30

Archives Municipales de Metz (AMM)
Series H
Unclassified files

Archives Municipales de Nancy
Series H
H4–5

Archives Municipales de Rennes
Series H
6/H/1; 6/H/10; 6/H/17; 6/H/22; 6/H/20

Archives Nationales
Series AJ
43/AJ/78; 43/AJ/328; 43/AJ/577; 43/AJ/578; 43/AJ/594; 43/AJ/608; 43/AJ/760;
43/AJ/797; 43/AJ/806; 43/AJ/1149; 72/AJ/1968; 72/AJ/2277
Series F
F/9/3286; F/23/229; F/23/233; F/23/333

Archives of the International Committee of the Red Cross, Geneva
Series G
G68 32; G68 56; G68 920; G68 922; G68 927; G68 936; G86 1132

Friends Library
FRS/199/28; FRS 1992/28; FRS 1992/30
FRS/Pics/3/Envelope 14/3147
MSS: 981–A; 981–B; 981–D; 981–F

Imperial War Museum
Mrs M. Christiansen, 85/31/1
Rhoda Dawson, documents classified as donated by Mrs R. N. Bickerdike
95/26/1
T. S. Hall, 67/106/1
Mr H. [Harry] Heath, 98/25/1
Mrs N. Heath, 98/25/1
Lieutenant-Colonel W. Kerr, [Private Papers], 86/53/1
Margrethe Claudine 'Pip' Langdon, sound archive, 12518
Miss B. [Beryl] N. Lewis, IWM, 84/47/1
Lieutenant General Sir Frederick Morgan, 02/49/1
Miss Barbara McDouall, *Album*, 89/19/1
Miss Nora O'Connor, 87/14/1

Institut d'histoire du temps présent
Fonds Vallotton: ARC 100 (3–4); ARC 101–1
ARC 061; ARC 074; ARC 1000

National Archives
Cabinet Office
8–834; 8–384;

Foreign Office (FO)
371/24154; 371/38956; 371/41163; 371/41165; 371/51081; 371/51110; 371/51117;
371/51118; 371/61956; 371/64424; 943/759; 945/708

Series T
188/259; 188/260

Red Cross Archives (London)
1977/17

Service Historique de l'Armée de Terre
DA 53083–53075

United Nations Archives (New York)
S–0425–0043
S–0435–0014
S–0436–0008; S–0436–0022; S–0436–0031; S–0436–0038; S–0436–0055;

S–0527–0119; S–0527–0121; S–0527–0211; S–0527–0219; S–0527–0503; S–0527–0505

Weiner Library (London), (WL)
HA5–4/3
1367/5/2
Henriques Archive
51/1

Published Primary Sources
Aguirre, Jose Antonio de, *Escape via Berlin; Eluding Franco in Hitler's Europe* (Reno and Las Vegas: University of Nevada Press, 1991)
Alary, Eric, *L'Exode: un drame oublié* (Paris: Perrin, 2010)
Alonso, Isabelle, *L'exil est mon pays* (Paris: Héloïse d'Ormesson, 2006)
Annan, Noel, *Changing Enemies: The Defeat and Regeneration of Germany* (London: Harper Collins, 1995)
'Anonymous', *A Woman in Berlin: Diary 20 April 1945 to 22 June 1945* translated by Philip Boehm (London: Virago, 2005)
Appelfeld, Aharon, *The Story of a Life* translated by Aloma Halter (London: Hamish Hamilton, 2004)
Arnstein, Margaret G., 'Nursing in UNRRA Middle East Refugee Camps', *The American Journal of Nursing*, 45:5 (May 1945), pp. 378–81
Avriel, Ehud, *Open the Gates! – A Personal Story of 'Illegal' Immigration to Israel* (London: Weidenfeld and Nicolson, 1975)
Baggallay, S.R.N., Olive, 'UNRRA Nurses in Athens Hospitals', *American Journal of Nursing*, 45:8 (August 1945), pp. 635–6
Balsan, Consuelo Vanderbilt, *The Glitter and the Gold* (Melbourne and London: Heinemann, 1953)
Bardoux, Jacques, *Journal d'un Témoin de la Troisième; 1 septembre 1939–15 juillet 1940* (Paris: Libraire Arthème Fayard, 1957)
Barlone, D., *A French Officer's Diary*, translated by L. V. Cass (Cambridge: Cambridge University Press, 1942)
Baroncelli, Jean de, *Vingt-Six Hommes* (Paris: Bernard Grasset, 1941)
Bartov, Hanoch, *The Brigade*, translated by David S. Segal (New York, Chicago and San Francisco: 1968),
Bakis, Edward, 'The So-Called DP-Apathy in Germany's DP Camps', *Transactions of the Kansas Academy of Science* 55:1 (1952), pp. 62–86
Barea, Arturo, *The Clash*, translated by Ilsa Barea (London: Faber & Faber, 1946)
Beauvoir, Simone de, *La force de l'âge*, Vol II (Paris: Gallimard, 1960)
Bentwich, Professor Norman, 'The Jewish Relief Units in Germany', *Jewish Monthly* (Feb 1948), pp. 2–8
Bentwich, Norman, *My 77 Years; An Account of My Life and Times, 1883–1960* (London: Routledge & Kegan Paul, 1962)

Berenguer, Sara, 'Éxodo', in Antonina Rodrigo (ed.), *Mujeres Libres: luchadoras libertarias* (Madrid: Anselmo Lorenzo, 1999), pp. 155–7

Bernanos, Georges, *Essais et écrits de combat* (Paris: Gallimard, 1971)

Betari, Josef, 'I Found the Answer' in Leo W. Schwarz (ed.), *The Root and the Bough: the Epic of an Enduring People* (New York: Rinehard, 1949), pp. 135–41

Bielenberg, Christabel, *The Road Ahead* (London: Bantam Press, 1992)

Blake, William, 'The Marriage of Heaven and Hell', *The Poetry and Prose of William Blake* (London: Nonesuch, 1956, pp. 181–93),

Bloch, Marc, 'L'Etrange Défaite' in *L'Histoire, La Guerre, la Résistance* edited by A. Becker and E. Bloch (Paris: Quarto-Gallimard, 2006), pp. 519–653

Bloch, Marc, *Strange defeat: A statement of evidence written in 1940* (New York: Octagon Books, 1986)

Bordeaux, H., 'La jeunesse féminine dans la guerre', *Revue des Deux Mondes* (55), 15 (February 1940), pp. 595–618

Boulé, Père Amand, *De Dunkerque à la Liberté* (Saint-Brieuc: Les Presses bretonnes, 1976)

Bracey, Bertha L., 'Practical Problems of Repatriation and Relocation', *International Affairs* 21:3 (1945), pp. 295–305

Branscombe, Martha, 'The Children of the United Nations: U.N.R.R.A.'s Responsibility for Social Welfare', *Social Service Review* 19:3 (September 1945), pp. 310–23

Brett-Smith, Lieutenant Richard, *Berlin '45: the Grey City* (London: MacMillan, 1966),

Brodsky, Alexandra Fanny, *A Fragile Identity; Survival in Nazi-occupied Belgium* (London: Radcliffe, 1998)

Burke, James, *The Big Rape* (Frankfurt am Main: Friedrich Ruhl – Verleger Union, 1952).

Burmetz, Paul, *Our Share of Morning* (London: Alvin Redman, 1961)

Capdevila, Andrés, *Un episodio de nuestra evacuación a Francia* (Perpignan: privately published, 1970)

Carpeña, Pépita, *Mémoires* (Paris: Editions du Monde Libertaire, 2000)

Ce qu'est la Défense passive (Paris: Publicité et Progande, nd [1939/40?])

Chamson, André, *Les Livres de la guerre* (Paris: Omnibus, 2005), pp. 139–42

Cheveigné, Maurice de, *Radio Libre* (unpublished memoir put online by a member of his family: http://www.alyon.org/litterature/livres/lyonnais/radio_libre/lug10.html; accessed 15 May 2009)

Chevrillon, Claire, *Une résistance ordinaire; septembre 1939–août 1944* (Paris: Félin, 1999)

Churchill, Winston S., *The Second World War, Volume II: Their Finest Hour* (London: The Reprint Society, 1951)

Churchill, Winston S., *The Second World War, Vol III: The Grand Alliance* (London: Reprint Society, 1952)

Clare, George, *Berlin Days* (London: Pan, 1990)

Cohen, Elie A., *Human Behaviour in the Concentration Camp*, translated by M. H. Braaksma (London: Greenwood Press, 1984 [1954])

Cohn, Rachel, 'Women Emigrés in Palestine', in Sibylle Quack (ed.), *Between Sorrow and Strength; Women Refugees of the Nazi Period* (Cambridge: Cambridge University Press, 1995), pp. 89–95

Collis, Robert and Han Hogerzeil, *Straight On* (London: Methuen, 1947)

Constante, Mariano, *Les années rouges, de Guernica à Mauthausen* (Vienne: Mercure de France, 1971)

Creelman, Lyle, 'Letters to the Editor, With UNRRA in Germany', *Canadian Nurse* 41:12 (1945), pp. 986–7

Creelman, Lyle, 'With UNRRA in Germany', *Canadian Nurse* 43:7 (1947), pp. 532–6

Creelman, Lyle, 'With UNRRA in Germany', *Canadian Nurse* 43:8 (1947), pp. 605–10

Creelman, Lyle, 'With UNRRA in Germany', *Canadian Nurse* 43:9 (1947), pp. 710–12

Crossman, Richard, *Palestine Mission: A Personal Mission* (London: Hamish Hamilton, 1947)

Crum, Bartley C., *Behind the Silken Curtain: A Personal Account of Anglo-American Diplomacy in Palestine and the Middle East* (London: Gollancz, 1947)

Davis, George W., 'Handling of Refugees and Displaced Persons by the French M.M.L.A. (Section Féminine)', *The Social Service Review* 22:1 (1948), pp. 34–9

Delso, Ana, *Trescientos hombres y yo; estampa de una revolución*, translated by Antonia Ruiz Cabezas (Madrid: Anselmo Lorenzo, 1998)

Denes, Magda, *Castles Burning: A child's life in war* (London: Transworld, 1997)

Doherty, Muriel, *Letters from Belsen 1945: an Australian nurse's experience with the survivors of war* edited by J. Cornell and R. Lynette Russell, (Sydney, Allen and Unwin, 2000)

Dorgelès, Roland, *La drôle de guerre, 1939–40* (Paris: Albin Michel, 1957)

Downing, Rupert, *If I laugh: The Chronicle of my Strange Adventures in the Great Paris Exodus – June 1940* (London: George G. Harrap & Co, 1940)

Droz, Juliette, 'Les Evacués de Paris dans les départements-refuge', *Service Social Familial* 34:1 (Nov 1939), pp. 14–20

Duchesne-Cripps, Audrey M., *The Mental Outlook of the Displaced Person as Seen through Welfare Work in Displaced Persons Camps* (Cambridge: self-published, 1955)

'El Campesino' with Maurice Padiou, *Jusqu'à la mort* (Paris: Albin Michel, 1978)

Ezquerra, Miguel, *Berlín, a vida o muerte* (Granada: Garcia Hispan), 1999

Fabre-Luce, Alfred, *Journal de la France, mars 1939–juillet 1940* (Trévoux: Imprimerie de Trévoux, 1940)

Feldman, Valentin, *Journal de guerre* (Tours: Farrago, 2006)

Fittko, Lisa, *Escape Through the Pyrenees* translated by David Koblick (Evanston, Illinois: Northwestern University Press, 1991)

Flanner, Janet, 'Letter from Paris', in [no editor], *The New Yorker Book of War Pieces: London, 1939 to Hiroshima, 1945* (New York: Schocken Books, 1988), pp. 6–8.

Floore, Frances Berkeley, *The Bread of the Oppressed* (New York: Exposition Press, 1975)

Folcher, Gustave, *Les carnets de guerre de Gustave Folcher, paysan languedocien (1939–1945)* (Paris: Maspero, 1981)

Ford, Richard, *UNRRA in Europe, 1945–1947* (London: UNRRA European Regional Office, June 1947)

Frankl, Viktor E., *Man's Search for Meaning*, translated by Ilse Lasch (London: Rider, 2008 [1946])

Freeman, G. and D. Cooper, *The Road to Bordeaux* (The Cresset Press: London, 1940)

Friedmann, Georges, *Journal de guerre 1939–1940* (Paris: Gallimard, 1987)

Gargello Edo, Federico, *La Raison douleureuse* (Madrid: Anselmo Lorenzo, 1999)

Gaulle, Charles de, *Mémoires de Guerre: L'Appel* (Paris: Plon, 1994)

Gendreau, Georges, *Une jeunesse bretonne: an durzunell* (Rennes: Sareda, 1998)

Giraudoux, Hippolyte, 'Messages du Continental. Allocutions radiodiffusées du Commissaire Général à l'Information', *Cahiers Jean Giraudoux* 16 (1987), pp. 81–4

Gold, Mary Jayne, *Crossroads at Marseilles, 1940* (Doubleday and Co., New York 1980)

Gollancz, Victor, *In Darkest Germany* (London: Gollancz, 1947)

Goutalier, François-Xavier (ed.), 'L'exode de 1940', posted on http://perso.wanadoo.fr/fx.goutalier/120640.htm, accessed 27 June 2006

Goytisolo, Juan, *Señas de identidad* (Madrid: Alianza Editorial, 1999 [1966])

Gruber, Ruth, *Exodus 1947: the Ship that Launched a Nation* (New York and London: Union Square Press, 1999 [1948])

Grünbaum, Irene, *Escape through the Balkans*, translated and edited by Katherine Morris (Lincoln & London: University of Nebraska Press, 1996 [1949–50])

Guehenno, Jean, *Journal des années noires* (Paris: Gallimard, 1973)

Guérin, Raymond, *Lettres à Sonia, 1939–1943* (Paris: Gallimard, 2005)

Guest, John, *Broken Images: A Journal* (London: Leo Cooper, 1970 [1949])

'Gun Buster', *Return via Dunkirk* (London: Hodder and Stoughton, 1940),

Habrioux, Christian, *La Déroute (1939–1940)* (Paris: Aux Armes de France, 1941)

Heath, H., 'Two Years in UNRRA with Displaced Persons – II', *The Journal of the Association of Officers of the Ministry of Labour*, 25:10 (August 1948), pp. 10–13

Heymont, Irving, *Among the Survivors of the Holocaust, 1945: The Landsberg DP Camp Letters* (np: Hebrew Union College Press, 1982)

Hirschmann, Ira A., *The Embers Still Burn; an eye-witness view of the postwar ferment in Europe and the Middle East and our disastrous get-soft-with-Germany policy* (New York: Simon and Schuster, 1949)

Hoffman, Stanley, 'Témoignage' in Max Lagarrigue (ed.), *1940: La France du repli; l'Europe de la défaite* (Toulouse: Privat, 2001), pp. 15–19

Holowinsky, Ivan Z., 'DP Experience, Personality Structure and Ego Defence Mechanisms: A Psychodynamic interpretation', in Wsevolod W. Isajiw and Yury Boshyk (eds), *The Refugee Experience: Ukrainian Displaced Persons after World War II* (Edmonton: Canadian Institute of Ukrainian Studies, 1992), pp. 480–8

Howard, Donald S., 'UNRRA: A new venture in international relief and welfare services', *The Social Service Review*, 18:1 (March 1944), pp. 1–11

Hulme, Kathryn, *The Wild Place,* (London and New York: Shakespeare Head, 1954)

Humbert, Agnès, *Notre guerre: Souvenirs de résistance* (Paris: Emile-Paul Frères, 1946)

Jahn, Gunnar, 'Presentation Speech', Nobel Peace Prize 1945, http://nobelprize.org/cgi-bin; accessed 5 Nov 2009

Jamet, Claude, *Carnets de Déroute* (Paris: Sorlot, 1942)

Joffo, Joseph, *Un sac de billes* (Paris: Librairie Générale française, 1973)

Junod, Marcel, *Warrior without Weapons,* translated by Edward Fitzgerald (London: Non-Fiction Book Club, nd)

Kermadec, Roland de, *1937–1946; De l'Orne au Finistère; ma drôle de guerre* (Spézet: Keltia, 1995)

Kernan, T., *Report on France* (London: The Bodley Head, 1942)

Kibbutz Buchenwald, 'Homecoming in Israel', in Leo W. Schwarz (ed.), *The Root and the Bough: the Epic of an Enduring People* (New York: Rinehard, 1949), pp. 308–45

Kimche, Jon and David, *The Secret Roads: The 'Illegal' Migration of a People* (London: Secker and Warburg, 1954)

Kingscote, Flavia, *Balkan Exit* (London: Geoffrey Bles, 1942)

Klemme, Marvin, *The Inside Story of UNRRA; An Experience in Internationalism* (New York: Lifetime editions, 1949)

Klemperer, Victor, *I Shall Bear Witness: the Diaries of Victor Klemperer, 1933–41,* abridged and translated by Martin Chalmers (London: Phoenix, 1999)

Klemperer, Victor, *To the Bitter End: The Diaries of Victor Klemperer, 1942–45,* abridged and translated by Martin Chalmers (London: Phoenix, 2000)

Kluger, Ruth, *Landscapes of Memory: A Holocaust Girlhood Remembered* (London: Bloomsbury, 2003)

Koestler, Arthur, *The Scum of the Earth* (London: Jonathan Cape, 1941)

Kyte, George W., 'War damage and problems of reconstruction in France, 1940–1945', *The Pacific Historical Review* 15:4 (1946), pp. 417–26

Lacroix, A., 'L'abandon de la terre', *Revue des Deux Mondes* (55) 1 February 1940 pp. 493–505

Lafitte, François, *The Internment of Aliens* (London: Penguin, 1988 [1940])

Le Bon, G., *The Crowd: a study of the popular mind* (np: Ernest Benn, 1896)

Le Comité Français de Service Social Historique de son action, 1927–41 (Bergeur-Levrault, 1947)

Le Gros Clark, F. and Richard W. Toms, *Evacuation: Failure or Reform* (London: The Fabian Society, 1940)

Lesourd, P., 'L'Action Catholique au service de la nation', *Revue des Deux Mondes* (56), 1 April 1940, pp. 634–58

Levi, Primo, *The Periodic Table* translated by Raymond Rosenthal (London: Abacus, 1995)

Lewis, Norman, *Naples '44: An Intelligence Officer in the Italian Labyrinth* (London: Eland, 2002 [1978])

Lewis, Norman, 'The Cossacks Go Home', in Norman Lewis *A View of the World: Selected Journalism* (London: Eland, 1986), pp. 230–46

Liebling, A. J., 'Letter from Paris', in [no editor], *The New Yorker Book of War Pieces: London, 1939 to Hiroshima, 1945* (New York: Schocken Books, 1988), pp. 9–10

McClelland, Grigor, *Embers of War: Letters from a Quaker Relief Worker in War-torn Germany* (London and New York: I. B. Tauris, 1997)

MacDonald, Nancy, *Homage to the Spanish Exiles: voices from the Spanish Civil War* (New York: Insight Books, 1987)

MacMaster, Neil, *Spanish Fighters; An Oral History of Civil War and Exile* (London: MacMillan, 1990)

Marti, Vicente, *La Saveur des patates douces; histoire de ma vie, 1926–76* (Lyon: Atelier de Création Libertaire, 1998)

Meifredy, Françoise, *Mission sans frontières* (Paris: Editions France Empire, 1966)

Mesnil-Amar, Jacqueline, *Ceux qui ne dormaient pas: Journal, 1944–46* (Paris: Stock, 2009 [1957])

Mexandeau, Louis, *'Nous, nous ne verrons pas la fin': un enfant dans la guerre (1939–1945)* (Paris: Cherche-Midi, 2003)

Ministère de l'Air, *La Défense passive en Allemagne* (Paris: Imprimerie Nationale, 1938)

Miquel, Pierre, *Histoires vraies de la Seconde guerre mondiale* (Paris, Fayard, 1988)

Montherlant, Henry de, *Textes sous une occupation, 1940-44* (Paris: Gallimard, 1940)

Montseny, Federica, *Pasión y muerte de los españoles en Francia* (np: Espoir, 1969 [originally published 1945–50])

Moral i Querol, Ramon, *Journal d'Exil, 1938–1945,* translated by N. Besset and M. Prudon (Paris: Eole, 1982)

Morgan, KCB, Lieutenant-General Sir Frederick, *Peace and War: A Soldier's Life* (London: Hodder and Stoughton, 1961)

Morgenstern, Soma, *Errance en France,* translated by Nicole Casanova (Paris: Liana Levi, 2002)

Morize, André, *France: Eté 1940* (New York: Editions de la Maison Française, 1941)

Morrow, Christine, *Abominable Epoch* (privately published, nd. [1972?])

Mosley, Leonard O., *Report from Germany* (London: Victor Gollancz, 1945)

Némirovsky, Irène, *Suite française* (Paris: Denoël, 2004)

Nizan, Paul, *Intellectuel communiste, 1926–40, Vol II* (Paris: Maspero, 1979)

Orlin, Zippy, 'What it's really like in a DP Camp: A South African Girl in Belsen', in Erik Somers and René Kok (eds), *Jewish Displaced Persons in Camp Bergen-Belsen, 1945–1950* (Seattle: University of Washington Press and Netherlands Institute for War Documentation, 2004), pp. 154–83

Orwell, George, 'Not Counting Niggers', in *Collected Essays, Journalism and Letters, Vol I* (London: Secker & Warburg, 1969), pp. 394–8

Orwell, George, 'My Country Right or Left, in *Collected Essays, Journalism and Letters, Vol I* (London: Secker & Warburg, 1969), pp. 535–40

Orwell, George, 'London Letter', in *Collected Essays, Journalism and Letters of George Orwell*, Vol II (London: Secker and Warburg, 1968), pp. 286–92

Oz, Amos, *A Tale of Love and Darkness* (London: Vintage, 2005)

Palencia, Isabel de, *Smouldering Freedom: the Story of the Spanish Republicans in Exile* (London: Gollancz, 1946)

Paz, Abel, *Viaje al Pasado (1936–1939)* (Madrid: Anselmo Lorenzo, 2002)

Paz, Abel, *Entre la Niebla (1939–42)* (Barcelona: EA, 1993)

Pétain, Philippe, 'Discours', 20 June 1940; reproduced at http://ww3.ac-poitiers. fr/hist_geo/lp/bep1/sommdocs/pagedoc/guerrmond/tpeta20ju.htm; accessed 20 June 2010

Pettiss, Susan T. and Lynne Taylor, *After the Shooting Stopped: the Story of an UNRRA Welfare Worker in Germany 1945–1947* (Crewe: Trafford, 2004)

Pinson, Koppel S., 'Jewish Life in Liberated Germany', *Jewish Social Studies* 9 (1947), pp. 101–26

The Political Warfare Executive, *Instructions for British Servicemen in Germany* (Oxford: Bodleian Library, 2007 [1944])

Ramati, Alexander, *Rebel Against the Light* (New York: Page, 1960)

Rebatet, Lucien, *Les décombres* (Paris: Denoel, 1942)

Remarque, Erich Maria, *The Night in Lisbon* translated by Ralph Manheim (London: Hutchinson, 1964)

Rice, Joan, *Sand in My Shoes; Coming of Age in the Second World War: A WAAF's Diary* (London: Harper Perennial, 2006)

Richardson, W. L., *Know Your Enemy: The UNRRA Infiltra(i)tors* (Aberfeldy: McKinlay, 1947)

Rist, Charles, *Une saison gâtée. Journal de la guerre et de l'occupation (1939–1945)* (Paris: Fayard, 1983)

Sadoul, Georges, *Journal de Guerre* (Paris: Français Réunis, 1977)

Sarraut, A., *Instruction générale à l'usage de messieurs les préfets sur les mouvements et transports de sauvegarde* (Melun: no publisher, 1938)

Sartre, Jean-Paul, *Carnets de la drôle de guerre* (Paris: Gallimard, 1995)

Sartre, Jean-Paul, 'Paris sous l'Occupation' in Jean-Paul Sartre, *Situations III: Lendemains de la guerre* (Paris, 1976), pp. 16–42

Sautreuil, Henri Alexandre, *J'avais dix ans en 1940* (Luneray: Bertout, 2000)

Sawyer, Wilbur A., 'Achievements of UNRRA as an International Health Organization', *American Journal of Public Health* 37 (Jan 1947), pp. 41–58

Schwarz, Leo W. (ed.), *The Root and the Bough: the Epic of an Enduring People* (New York: Rinehard, 1949)

Schwarz, Leo W., *The Redeemers: A Saga of the Years, 1945–52* (New York: Farrar, Strauss and Young, 1953)

Seghers, Anna, *Transit*, translated by Jeanne Stern (Paris: Autrement, 1995)

Semprun, Jorge, *Le Grand Voyage* (Paris: Gallimard, 1963)

Semprun, Jorge, *Literature or Life*, translated by Linda Coverdale (Harmondsworth: Penguin, 1998)

Serge, Victor, *Mémoires d'un révolutionnaire* (Paris: Stock, 1951)

Serge, Victor, *Les Derniers Temps* (Paris: Bernard Grasset, 1951)

Setzler, Lorraine, 'Nursing and Nursing Education in Germany', *The American Journal of Nursing* 45:12 (Dec. 1945), pp. 993–5

Shuval, Judith T., *Immigrants on the Threshold* (New York: Atherton Press, 1963)

Smith, Marcus J., *Dachau: the Harrowing of Hell* (Albany, N.Y.: State University of New York Press, 1995 [1972])

Spears, Major General Sir Edward, *Assignment to Catastrophe, Vol II: the Fall of France, June 1940* (London: Heinemann, 1954)

Somerset Maugham, W., *France at War* (London: William Heinemann, 1940)

Soriano, Antonio (ed.), *Éxodos; historia oral del exilio republicana en Francia, 1939–1945* (Barcelona: Crítica, 1989)

Spender, Stephen, *European Witness* (London: The Right Book Club, nd. [1946?])

Stone, Brian, *Prisoner from Alamein* (London: Witherby, 1944)

Stone, I.F., *Underground to Palestine* (London: Hutchinson, 1979)

Supreme Headquarters Allied Expeditionary Force, *Guide to the Care of Displaced Persons in Germany* (SHAEF, May 1945)

Syrkin, Marie, *The State of the Jews* (Washington: New Republic, 1980)

Szereszewska, Helena, *Memoirs from Occupied Warsaw*, translated by Anna Marianska (London: Valentine Mitchell, 2000)

Thomas, Edith, *Pages de Journal, 1939–1944* suivies de *Journal Intime de Monsieur Célestin Costedet* (Paris: Viviane Hamy, 1995)

Todd, Barbara Euphan, *Miss Ranskill Comes Home* (London: Persephone Press, 2003 [1946])

Torres, Dolores, *Chronique d'une femme rebelle* (Paris: Wern, 1997)

Torres, Tereska, *Une française libre; Journal 1939–1945* (Paris: France-Loisirs, 2000)

UNRRA, *Helping the People to Help Themselves: The Story of the United Nations Relief and Rehabilitation Administration* (London: His Majesty's Stationery Office, 1944)

UNRRA, *Welfare Guide to United Nations Nationals Displaced in Germany* (London: European Regional Office, February 1945)

UNRRA, *Fifty Facts about UNRRA* (London: European Regional Office of UNRRA, January 1946)

Vallotton, Gritou and Annie, *C'était au jour le jour. Carnets (1939–1944)* (Paris: Payot, 1995)

Vernant, Jacques, *The Refugee in the Post-War World* (London: Allen & Unwin, 1953)

Vida, George, *From Doom to Dawn: A Jewish Chaplain's Story of the Displaced Persons* (New York: Jonathan David, 1967)

Warhaftig, Zorach, *Relief and Rehabilitation: Implications of the UNRRA Program for Jewish Needs* (New York: Institute of Jewish Affairs of the American Jewish Congress and World Jewish Congress, 1944)

Werth, Léon, *33 jours* (Paris: Viviane Hamy, 1992)

Wickwar, W. H., 'Relief supplies and Welfare distribution UNRRA in retrospect', *Social Service Review* 21:3 (1947), pp. 363–74

Wilson, Francesca M., *Advice to Relief Workers* (London: John Murray and Friends Relief Service, 1944)

Wilson, Francesca M., *In the Margins of Chaos* (London: William Clowes and Sons, 1944)

Wilson, F., *Aftermath: France, Germany, Austria, Yugoslavia 1945 and 1946* (London: Penguin, 1947)

Wilson, F. M., *They Came as Strangers: The Story of Refugees to Great Britain* (London: Hamish Hamilton, 1959)

Wilson, Roger, *Quaker Relief: An Account of the Relief Work of the Society of Friends, 1940–1948* (London: George Allen & Unwin, 1952)

Woodbridge, G., *UNRRA: the History of the United Nations Relief and Rehabilitation Administration*, 3 Vols, (New York: Colombia University Press, 1950)

Wriggins, Howard, *Picking up the Pieces from Portugal to Palestine: Quaker Refugee Relief in World War II: A Memoir* (Lanham: University Press of America, 2004)

Ziff, William B., *The Coming Battle of Germany* (London: Hamish Hamilton, 1942)

Press and Periodicals
L'Action française
L'Aube
British Medical Journal
Bulletin d'Informations de l'Ille-et-Vilaine
Bulletin de la Société de Secours aux Blessés Militaires
Le Canard Enchaîné
Candide
La Croix
La Croix de Lyon
Cultura Proletariana
La Dépêche du midi

Est Républicain
Le Figaro
Gringoire
Hansard
L'Humanité
L'Illustration
L'Intransigeant
Le Lyon Républicain
Le Jour – l'Echo de Paris
Journal of the American Medical Association
Journal des Débats
Journal du Loiret
Le Messin
New York Herald Tribune
Notre temps
Le Nouvelliste
L'OEuvre
Ouest-Eclair
The Polish Refugee
Revue des Deux Mondes
Le Temps
Times
UNRRA Review of the Month
La Voix du peuple

Films
Clément, René, *Jeux interdits* (1952)
Curtiz, Michael, *Casablanca* (1942)
Fowler Jr, Gene, *Seeds of Destiny* (1946)
Legg, Stuart, *Now – The Peace* (1945)
Loubignac, Jean, *Sommes-nous défendus?* (1938)
Téchiné, André, *Les Egarés* (2003)

Secondary Sources
Ahonen, Pertti, Gustavo Corni, Jerzy Kochanowski, Rainer Schulze, Tamás Stark and Barbara Stelzl-Marx, *People on the Move: Forced Population Movements in Europe in the Second World War and Its Aftermath* (Oxford and New York: Berg, 2008)
Alary, Eric, *La ligne de démarcation 1940–1944* (Paris: Perrin, 2003)
Alary, Eric, *Les Français au quotidien, 1939–1949* (Paris: Perrin, 2006)
Aleinikoff, T. Alexander, 'State-centred Refugee Law: From Resettlement to Containment', in E. V. Daniel and J. C. Knudsen (eds), *Mistrusting Refugees* (Berkeley: University of California Press, 1995), pp. 257–78

Allard, Paul, *La guerre du mensonge. Comment on nous a bourré le crâne* (Paris, Les Editions de France, 1940)

Alted Vigil, Alicia, 'Le retour en Espagne des enfants évacués pendant la guerre civile espagnole: la Délégation extraordinaire au rapatriement des mineurs (1938–1954)' translated by H. Poutet in [no editor], *Enfants de la guerre civile*, (Paris: l'Harmattan, 1999), pp. 47–59

Alted, Alicia, *La voz de los vencidos: el exilio republicano de 1939* (Madrid: Santillana Ediciones Generales, 2005)

Arendt, Hannah, *Eichmann in Jerusalem: A Report on the Banality of Evil* (London: Penguin, 2006 [1964])

Armstrong-Reid, Susan and David Murray, *Armies of Peace: Canada and the UNRRA years* (Toronto: University of Toronto Press, 2008)

Azéma, Jean-Pierre, *1940 L'année terrible* (Paris: Seuil, 1990)

Bauman, Zygmunt, *Liquid Modernity* (Cambridge: Polity, 2000)

Bauman, Zygmunt, *Modernity and the Holocaust* (Cambridge: Polity, 2005)

Bédarida, F., 'Huit mois d'attente et d'illusion: la «drôle de guerre»', in J.-P. Azéma & F. Bédarida (eds), *La France des années noires*, Tome 1 (Paris: Seuil, 1993), pp. 37–67

Beevor, Antony, *Berlin: The Downfall 1945* (London: Penguin, 2002)

Benjamin, Natalia, *Recuerdos: The Basque Children Refugees in Great Britain* (Norwich: Mousehold Press, 2007)

Berkowitz, Michael, *The Crime of My Very Existence: Nazism and the Myth of Jewish criminality* (University of California Press, 2007)

Berkowitz, Michael and Suzanne Brown-Fleming, 'Perceptions of Jewish Displaced Persons as Criminals in Early Postwar Germany' in Avinoam J. Patt and Michael Berkowitz (eds), *We are Here: New Approaches to Jewish Displaced Persons in Postwar Germany* (Wayne State University Press, 2010), pp. 167–93

Berry, David, 'French Anarchists in Spain', *French History* 3:4 (1989), pp. 427–65

Bessel, Richard, *Germany 1945: From War to Peace* (London: Simon & Schuster, 2009)

Besselievre, J.-Y., 'La défense passive en France, 1930–44: l'exemple de Brest', *Revue Historique des Armées* 4 (1998), pp. 97–103

Best, Geoffrey, *Humanity in Warfare* (London, Weidenfeld and Nicolson, 1980)

Beverly, John, 'The Margin at the Centre', in S. Smith and J. Watson (eds), *Decolonizing the Subject* (Minneapolis: University of Minnesota Press, 1992), pp. 91–114

Boswell, Laird, 'Franco-Alsatian Conflict and the Crisis of National sentiment during the Phoney War', *Journal of Modern History* 71:3 (1999), pp. 552–84

Browning, Christopher R., *The Origins of the Final Solution: The Evolution of Nazi Jewish Policy, September 1939–March 1942* (Nebraska: University of Nebraska Press, 2007)

Burgess, Greg, *Refuge in the Land of Liberty* (London: Palgrave Macmillan, 2008)

Caesteker, Frank, 'The Reintegration of Jewish Survivors into Belgian Society, 1943–1947', in D. Bankier (ed.), *The Jews are Coming Back* (New York: Berghahn, 2005 & Jerusalem: Yad Vasher, 2005), pp. 72–107

Caestecker, Frank, 'Les réfugiés et l'Etat en Europe occidentale pendant les XIXe et XX siècles', *Mouvement social* 225 (2008), pp. 9–26

Caldwell, Christopher, *Reflections on the Revolution in Europe: Immigration, Islam and the West* (London: Penguin, 2010)

Capdevila, Luc and Fabrice Virgili, 'Guerre, femme et Nation en France (1939–1945)', *Institut d'histoire du temps présent*, Ressources en ligne (2000). http://www.ihtp.cnrs.fr/spip.php%3Farticle511.html, accessed 4 March 2009

Caron, Vicky, *Uneasy Asylum: France and the Jewish Refugee Crisis 1933–1942* (Stanford: California, 1999)

Català, Neus, *Ces Femmes Espagnoles: de la Résistance à la Déportation; témoignages vivants de Barcelone à Ravensbrück*, translated by Caroline Langlois (Paris: Tirésias, 1994)

Chaubin, Hélène, 'Une micro-Europe des défaites: le refuge héraultais de 1940', in Max Lagarrigue (ed.), *1940: La France du repli; l'Europe de la défaite* (Toulouse: Privat, 2001), pp. 125–32

Cohen, Daniel G., 'Naissance d'une nation: les personnes déplacées de l'après-guerre, 1945–51', *Genèses* 38 (2000), pp. 56–78

Cohen, Daniel G, 'The Politics of Recognition: Jewish Refugees in Relief Policies and Human Rights Debates, 1945–1950', *Immigrants and Minorities* 24:2 (2006), pp. 125–43

Cohen, Susan, *Rescue the Perishing: Eleanor Rathbone and the Refugees* (London: Vallentine Mitchell, 2010)

Consonni, Manuela, 'The Written Memoir: Italy, 1945–1947', in D. Bankier (ed.), *The Jews are Coming Back* (New York: Berghahn, 2005 & Jerusalem: Yad Vasher, 2005), pp. 169–85

Cousin, Damien, 'Le repli du gouvernement français à Bordeaux en juin 1940', in Max Lagarrigue (ed.), *1940: La France du repli; l'Europe de la défaite* (Toulouse: Privat, 2001), pp. 155–61

Crémieux-Brilhac, Jean-Louis, *Les Français de l'an 40 (I): La guerre oui ou non?* (Paris: Gallimard, 1990)

Crick, Bernard, *George Orwell: A Life* (Harmondsworth: Penguin, 1980)

Daniel, E. Valentine and John Chr. Knudsen (eds), *Mistrusting Refugees* (Berkeley: University of California Press, 1995)

Davies, Norman, *Rising '44: The Battle for Warsaw* (London: MacMillan, 2003)

Delacor, Regina, 'From Potential Friends to Potential Enemies: the internment of "Hostile Foreigners" at the Beginning of the Second World War', *Journal of Contemporary History* 35:3 (2000), pp. 361–8

Delporte, Christian, 'The Image and Myth of the "Fifth Column" during the Two World Wars' in Valerie Holman and Debra Kelly (eds) *France at War in the Twentieth Century* (Oxford: Berghahn, 2000), pp. 49–64

Derogy, Jacques, *La loi du retour: la secrète et véritable histoire de l'Exodus* (Paris: Fayard, 1969)

Diamond, Hanna, *Fleeing Hitler: France 1940* (Oxford: Oxford University Press, 2007)

Doughty, Robert, 'The Maginot Line', *Military History Quarterly* 9:2 (1997), pp. 48–59

Dreyfus-Armand, Geneviève, *L'exil des républicains espagnols en France* (Paris: Albin Michel, 1999)

Dyczok, Marta, *The Grand Alliance and Ukrainian Refugees* (London: Palgrave Macmillan, 2000)

Engelking, Barbara, *Holocaust and Memory: The Experience of the Holocaust*, translated by E. Harris (Leicester: Leicester UP, 2001)

Espinosa Maestre, Francisco, 'Julio de 1936: golpe militar y plan de exterminio', in Julián Casanova (ed.), *Morir, Matar, Sobrevivir* (Barcelona: Crítica, 2004), pp. 51–119

Esser, Raingard, '"Language No Obstacle": War Brides in the German Press, 1945–1949', *Women's History Review* 12:4 (2003), pp. 577–604

Evans, Richard J., *The Third Reich at War, 1939–1945* (London: Allen Lane, 2008)

Eychenne, Emilienne, *Pyrénées de la Liberté: les évasions par l'Espagne, 1939–45* (Toulouse: Privat, 1998)

Feinstein, Margaete Myers, 'Jewish Women Survivors in the Displaced Persons Camps of Occupied Germany: Transmitters of the Past, Caretakers of the Present, and Builders of the Future', *Shofar* 24:4 (2006), pp. 67–89

Feinstein, Margarete Myers, 'Jewish Observance in Amalek's Shadow', in Avinoam J. Patt and Michael Berkowitz (eds), *We are Here: New Approaches to Jewish Displaced Persons in Postwar Germany* (Wayne State University Press, 2010), pp. 257–88.

Fogg, Shannon L., 'Refugees and Indifference: the effects of shortages on Attitudes towards Jews in France's Limousin Region during World War II', *Holocaust and Genocide Studies*, 21:1 (2007), pp. 31–54

Fralon, José-Alain, *A Good Man in Evil Times: the story of Aristides de Sousa Mendes – the unknown hero who saved countless lives in World War II*, translated by Peter Graham (London: Viking, 2000)

Frances, Hywel, *Miners against Fascism: Wales and the Spanish Civil War* (London: Lawrence and Wishart, 1984)

Frank, Matthew, 'The New Morality – Victor Gollancz, "Save Europe Now" and the German Refugee Crisis, 1945–46', *Twentieth Century British History* 17:2 (2006), pp. 230–56

Frank, Matthew, 'Working for the Germans: British voluntary societies and the German refugee crisis, 1945–1950', *Historical Research* 82:215 (2009), pp. 157–75

Fussell, Paul, *The Boys' Crusade: American GIs in Europe: Chaos and Fear in World War II* (London: Weidenfeld & Nicolson, 2003)

Garcia, Gabrielle and Isabelle Matas, *La mémoire retrouvée des Républicains espagnols: Paroles d'exilés en Ille-et-Vilaine* (Rennes: Editions Ouest-France, 2005)

Garraud, Philippe, 'French rearmament policy, 1936–40: priorities and constraints', *Guerres Mondiales et Conflits Contemporains* 55 (2005), pp. 87–102

Garraud, Philippe, 'The Politics of Fortification of the Borders, 1925–40: logic, constraint, and the use of the *Maginot Line*', *Guerres Mondiales et Conflits Contemporains* 57 (2007), pp. 3–22

Gatrell, Peter and Nick Baron (eds), *Warlands: Population Resettlement and State Reconstruction in the Soviet–East European Borderlands, 1945–50* (London: Palgrave Macmillan, 2009)

Gehler, Michael and Wolfram Kaiser, 'Transnationalism and Early European Integration: The *Nouvelles Equipes Internationales* and the Geneva Circle, 1947–1957', *Historical Journal* 44:3 (2001), pp. 773–98

Gemie, Sharif, 'France and the Val d'Aran; Politics and Nationhood on the Pyrenean Border, 1800–25', *European History Quarterly*, 28:3 (1998), pp. 311–46

Gemie, Sharif, 'Re-defining Refugees: Nations, Borders and Globalization', *Eurolimes* 9 (2010), pp. 28–37

Gemie, Sharif and Laure Humbert, 'Writing History in the Aftermath of "Relief": Some Comments on "Relief in the Aftermath of War", a reply to a special issue of the *Journal of Contemporary History*', *Journal of Contemporary History* 44:2 (2009) pp. 309–18

Gemie, Sharif and Fiona Reid, 'Chaos, panic and the historiography of the *exode* (France, 1940)', *War and Society*, 26 (2007), pp. 73–97

Gervereau, Laurent, *La propagande par l'affiche* (Paris: Syros Alternative, 1991)

Gildea, Robert, *Marianne in Chains: in search of the German occupation of France 1940-45* (London, MacMillan, 2002,

Giovanni, Janine di, *The Place at the End of the World; Essays from the Edge* (London: Bloomsbury, 2006)

Goedde, Petra, *GIs and Germans: Culture, Gender, and Foreign Relations, 1945-49* (New Haven and London: Yale University Press, 2003)

Gold, Mary-Jayne, *Crossroads at Marseilles 1940* (New York: Doubleday and Company, 1980)

Goldman, Jasper, 'Warsaw: Reconstruction as Propaganda' in L. J. Vale and T. J. Campanella (eds), *The Resilient City* (Oxford University Press, 2005), pp. 135–48

Goodfellow, Samuel, 'From Germany to France? Interwar Alsatian national Identity', *French history*, 7:4 (1993), pp. 450–71

Gotovitch, José, 'Les Belges du repli: entre pagaille et organisation' in Max Lagarrigue (ed.), *1940: La France du repli; l'Europe de la défaite* (Toulouse: Privat, 2001), pp. 51–64

Gousseff, Catherine, *L'Exil Russe: La Fabrique du Réfugié Apatride (1920–1939)* (Paris: CNRS éditions, 2008)

Grabowicz, George G. 'A Great Literature', in Wsevolod W. Isajiw and Yury Boshyk (eds), *The Refugee Experience: Ukrainian Displaced Persons after World War II* (Edmonton: Canadian Institute of Ukrainian Studies, 1992), pp. 240–68

Gracia, Jordi, *La resistencia silenciosa: fascismo y cultura en España* (Barcelona: Anagrama, 2004)

Groot, Gerard J. De, ' "I Love the Scent of Cordite in Your Hair": Gender Dynamics in Mixed Anti-Aircraft Batteries during the Second World War', *History* 82 (1997), pp. 73–92

Grossmann, Atina, 'Trauma, Memory and Motherhood: Germans and Jewish Displaced Persons in Post-Nazi Germany, 1945–1949', *Archiv für Sozialgeschichte* 38 (1998), pp. 215–39

Grossmann, Atina, 'Victims, Villains and Survivors: Gendered Perceptions and Self-Perceptions of Jewish Displaced Persons in Occupied Postwar Germany', *Journal of the History of Sexuality* 11:1/2 (2002), pp. 291–318

Grossmann, Atina, *Jews, Germans, and Allies: Close Encounters in Occupied Germany.* (Princeton: Princeton University Press, 2007).

Grynberg, Anne, 'Des signes de résurgence de l'antisémitisme dans la France de l'après-guerre (1945–53)?', *Les Cahiers de la Shoah* 5 (2001), pp. 171–223

Guillon, Jean-Marie, 'La Provence refuge et piège. Autour de Varian Fry et de la filière américaine', in Max Lagarrigue (ed.), *1940: La France du repli; l'Europe de la défaite* (Toulouse: Privat, 2001), pp. 269–85

Haan, Ido de, 'Paths of Normalisation after the Persecution of the Jews: the Netherlands, France and West Germany in the 1950s', in R. Bessel and D. Schumann (eds), *Life after Death: Approaches to a Cultural and Social History of Europe during the 1940s and 1950s* (Cambridge: Cambridge University Press, 2003), pp. 65–92

Haggith, Toby, 'The Filming of the Liberation of Bergen-Belsen and Its Impact on the Understanding of the Holocaust' in Suzanne Bardgett and David Cesarani (eds), *Belsen 1945: New Historical Perspectives* (London: Vallentine Mitchell, 2006), pp. 89–122

Harouni, Rahma, 'Le débat autour du statut des étrangers dans les années 1930', *Mouvement social* 188 (1999), pp. 61–75

Harp, Stephen L., *Learning to Be Loyal: Primary Schooling as Nation Building in Alsace and Lorraine, 1850–1940* (Dekalb: Northern Illinois University Press, 1998)

Haushofer, Lisa, 'The Contaminating Agent: UNRRA, Displaced Persons and Venereal Disease in Germany 1945–1947', *American Journal of Public Health,* 100:6 (2010), pp. 993–1003

Healy, Lynne M., *International Social Work: Professional Action in an Interdependent World* (New York: Oxford University Press, 2001)

Henkel, Anne-Katrin, 'Bücher zum Trauern und zum Leben – Druckerei und Bibliothek im Displaced-Persons-Camp Bergen-Belsen (1945–1950)', *Zeitschrift für Bibliothekswesen und Bibliographie,* 56:1 (2009), pp. 20–9

Hilton, Laura, 'Cultural Nationalism in Exile: The case of Polish and Latvian Displaced Persons', *The Historian*, 71:2 (2009), pp. 280–317

Hitchcock, William I., *The Bitter Road to Freedom: A New History of the Liberation of Europe* (New York: Free Press, 2008)

Hoffmann, Stanley, 'Le trauma de 1940', in Jean-Pierre Azéma and François Béderida (eds), *La France des années noires* (Paris: Seuil, 1993), pp. 131–50

Hoffmann, Stanley, 'The Trauma of 1940: A Disaster and Its Traces', in Joel Blatt (ed.), *The French Defeat of 1940: Reassessments* (Oxford: Berghahn, 1998), pp. 354–70

Holian, Anna, 'Displacement and the Post-War Reconstruction of Education: Displaced Persons at the UNRRA University of Munich', *Contemporary European History* 17:2 (2008), pp. 167–95

Hondius, Dienke, 'Bitter Homecoming: the Return and Redemption of Dutch and Stateless Jews in the Netherlands', in D. Bankier (ed.), *The Jews are Coming Back* (New York: Berghahn, 2005 & Jerusalem: Yad Vasher, 2005), pp. 108–35

Hucker, Daniel, 'French public attitudes towards the prospect of war in 1938–39: "pacifism" or "war anxiety"?', *French History* 21:4 (2007), pp. 431–49

Hutchinson, J., *Champions of Charity: War and the Rise of the Red Cross* (Boulder, Colorado; Oxford: Westview Press, 1995)

Ilnytzkyj, Roman, 'A Survey of Ukrainian Camp Periodicals, 1945–1950', in W. W. Isajiw, Y. Boshyk, R. Senkus (ed.) *The Refugee Experience. Ukrainian Displaced Persons after World War Two* (Edmonton: Canadian Institute of Ukrainian Studies Press, 1992), pp. 271–91

Imlay, Talbot, 'Mind the Gap: the Perception and Reality of Communist Sabotage of French War Production during the Phoney War, 1939–40', *Past and Present* 89 (2005), pp. 179–204

Irvine, William, 'Domestic Politics and the fall of France in 1940', in Joel Blatt (ed.) *The French Defeat of 1940: Reassessments* (Providence and Oxford: Berghahn, 1998), pp. 85–99

Jackson, Julian, *The Fall of France: the Nazi invasion of 1940* (Oxford: Oxford University Press, 2003)

Jackson, Julian, *France: the Dark Years, 1940–44* (Oxford: Oxford University Press, 2003)

Jackson, Peter, 'Returning to the Fall of France: recent work on the causes and consequences of the "Strange defeat" of 1940', *Modern and Contemporary France* 12:4 (2004), pp. 513–36

Jacobmeyer, Wolfgang, *Vom Zwangsarbeiter zum heimatlosen Ausländer: Die Displaced Persons in Westdeutschland, 1945–1951* (Gottingen: Vandenhoeck & Ruprecht, 1985,

Jaroszynska-Kirchmann, Anna D., 'Patriotism, Responsibility, and the Cold War: Polish Schools in DP Camps in Germany, 1945–1951', *The Polish Review*, 47:1 (2002), pp. 35–66

Jaroszyńska-Kirchmann, Anna D., *The Exile Mission: The Polish Political Diaspora and Polish Americans, 1939–1956* (Athens: Ohio University Press, 2004)

Jockusch, Laura, 'A Folk Monument to Our Destruction and Heroism', in Avinoam J. Patt and Michael Berkowitz (eds), *We are Here: New Approaches to Jewish Displaced Persons in Postwar Germany* (Wayne State University Press, 2010), pp. 31–73

Kershaw, Ian, 'War and political violence in twentieth century Europe', *Contemporary European History* 14:1 (2005), pp. 107–123

Kinnear, Mary, *Woman of the World; Mary McGeachy and International Cooperation* (Toronto: Toronto University Press, 2004,

Knudsen, John Chr., 'When Trust in on Trial: Negotiating Refugee Narratives', in E. V. Daniel and J. C. Knudsen (eds), *Mistrusting Refugees* (Berkeley: University of California Press, 1995), pp. 13–35

Kochavi, Ariel J., *Post-Holocaust Politics: Britain, the United States and Jewish Refugees, 1945–48* (Chapel Hill: University of North California Press, 2001)

Kolinsky, Eva, *After the Holocaust: Jewish Survivors in Germany after 1945* (London: Pimlico, 2004)

Königseder, Angelika and Juliane Wetzel, *Waiting for Hope: Jewish Displaced Persons in Post-World War II Germany* translated by John A. Broadwin (Evanston: Northwestern University Press, 2001 [1994])

Kristel, Conny, 'Revolution and Reconstruction: Dutch Jewry after the Holocaust' in D. Bankier (ed.), *The Jews are Coming Back* (New York: Berghahn, 2005 & Jerusalem: Yad Vasher, 2005), pp. 136–47

Kushner, Tony, *The Persistence of Prejudice: Antisemitism in British Society during the Second World War* (Manchester: MUP, 1989)

Kushner, Tony, 'From "This Belsen Business" to "Shoah Business": History, Memory and Heritage, 1945–2005' in Suzanne Bardgett and David Cesarani (eds), *Belsen 1945: New Historical Perspectives* (London: Vallentine Mitchell, 2006), pp. 189–216

Laborie, Pierre, *Les Français des années troubles: de la guerre d'Espagne à la Libération* (Paris: Seuil, 2003)

Lagrou, Pieter, 'Victims of Genocide and National Memory: Belgium, France and the Netherlands 1945–1965', *Past and Present* 154 (1997), pp. 181–222

Lagrou, Pieter, 'Return to a Vanished World: European Societies and the Remnants of their Jewish Communities, 1945–47 in D. Bankier (ed.), *The Jews and Coming Back* (New York: Berghahn and Jerusalem: Yad Vashen, 2005), pp. 1–24

Lake, Marilyn, 'Female Desires: the meaning of World War II', in Gordon Martel (ed.), *The World War Two Reader* (New York and London: Routledge, 2004), pp. 359–76 [originally published in 1990].

Lawrence, Paul, '"Un flot d'agitateurs politiques, de fauteurs de désordre et de criminels"; adverse perceptions of immigrants in France between the wars', *French History* 14:2 (2000), pp. 201–21

Lewis, Mary Dewhurst, *The Boundaries of the Republic: Migrant Rights and the Limits of Universalism in France, 1918–1940* (Stanford, California: Stanford University Press, 2007)

Lewy, Guenter, *The Nazi Persecution of the Gypsies* (Oxford: Oxford University Press, 2000)

Llorens, Vicente, *Estudios y Ensayos sobre el exilio republicano de 1939* (Sevilla: Renacimiento, 2006),

Loizos, Peter, 'Ottoman Half-lives: long-term Perspectives on Particular Forced Migrations', *Journal of Refugee Studies* 12:3 (1999), pp. 237–63

Lowy, Vincent, *Guerre à la guerre ou le pacifisme dans le cinéma français, 1936–40* (Paris: L'Harmattan, 2006,

Loyer, Emmanuelle, 'La débâcle, les universitaires et la Fondation Rockfeller: France / Etats-Unis, 1940–41', *Revue d'histoire moderne et contemporaine* 2001–1, pp. 138–59

Lüdtke, Alf, 'Explaining forced migration', in R. Bessel and C. Haake (eds), *Removing peoples: Forced Removal in the Modern World* (Oxford: Oxford University Press, 2009), pp. 13–32

Manley, Rebecca, 'The Perils of Displacement: the Soviet Evacuee between Refugee and Deportee', *Contemporary European History* 16:4 (2007), pp. 495–509

Mankovitz, Zeev, *Life between Memory and Hope: The Survivors of the Holocaust in Occupied Germany* (Cambridge: Cambridge University Press, 2002.

Marrill, J.-M., 'French Military Doctrine between the two wars', *Revue Historique des Armées* 3 (1991), pp. 24–34

Marrus, Michael R., *The Unwanted: European Refugees from the First World War through the Cold War* (Philadelphia: Temple University Press, 2002)

Martin Casas, Julio and Pedro Carvajal Urquijo, *El exilio español (1936–1978)* (Barcelona: Planeta, 2002)

Martínez Ten, Carmen and Purificación Gutiérrez López, 'Prólogo', in Carmen Martínez Ten, Purificación Gutiérrez López and Pilar González Ruiz (eds), *El movimiento feminista en España en los años 70* (Madrid: Fundación Pablo Iglesias, 2009), pp. 7–15

Marx, Karl, 'The Eighteenth Brumaire of Louis Napoleon', in Karl Marx and Frederick Engels, *Selected Works in Three Volumes: I* (Moscow: Progress, 1977), pp. 478–9

Maspero, Julia, 'La question des personnes déplacées polonaises dans les zones françaises d'occupation en Allemagne et en Autriche: un aspect méconnu des relations franco-polonaises (1945–1949)' *Relations internationales,* 138 (2009), pp. 59–74

Mendelsohn, Farah, 'Denominational Difference in Quaker Relief Work During the Spanish Civil War: the Operation of Corporate Concern and Liberal Theologies', *Journal of Religious History* 24:2 (2000), pp. 180–95

Meng, Michael L., 'After the Holocaust: the History of Jewish Life in West Germany', *Contemporary European History* 14:3 (2005), pp. 403–13

Meunier, Sabine, 'Les Juifs de Belgique dans les camps du Sud-Ouest de la France', in Max Lagarrigue (ed.), *1940: La France du repli; l'Europe de la défaite* (Toulouse: Privat, 2001), pp. 33–49

Meyers, Margarete L. 'Jewish Displaced Persons reconstructing individual and community in the US Zone of Occupied Germany', *Leo Baeck Institute Year Book* 42 (1997), pp. 303–24

Michlic, Joanna, 'The Holocaust and Its Aftermath as Perceived in Poland: Voices of Polish Intellectuals, 1945–47' in D. Bankier (ed.), *The Jews are Coming Back* (New York: Berghahn, 2005 and Jerusalem: Yad Vasher, 2005), pp. 206–30

Mir, Conxita, 'El sino de los vencidos: la represión franquista en la Cataluña rural de posguerra', in J. Casanova (ed.), *Morir, Mater, Sobrevivir* (Barcelona: Crítica, 2004), pp. 123–95

Monnier, Michel-Acatl, 'The Hidden Part of Asylum Seekers' Interviews in Geneva, Switzerland: Some Observations about the Socio-Political Construction of Interviews between Gatekeepers and Powerless', *Journal of Refugee Studies* 8:3 (1995), pp. 305–25

Néilas, Thierry, *Des Français face à L'invasion: Mai-Septembre* 1940 (Paris: Pygmalion, 2008)

Neu, Marcel, *L'évacuation en Lorraine, 1939–40* (Sarreguemines: Pierron, 1989)

Nicault, Catherine, 'L'utopie du "nouveau Juif" et la jeunesse juive dans la France de l'après-guerre. Contribution à l'histoire de l'Alyah française', *Les Cahiers de la Shoah* 5:1 (2001), pp. 105–69

Nivet, Philippe, 'Les réfugiés de guerre dans la société française (1914–1946)', *Histoire, Economie et société,* 23:2 (2004), pp. 247–59

Noiriel, Gérard, *Réfugiés et Sans-Papiers; la République face au droit d'asile, XIX–XXe siècle* (Paris: Calman-Levy, 1998).

Nye, Robert, *The Origins of Crowd Psychology: Gustave Le Bon and the crisis of mass democracy in the Third Republic* (London and Beverley Hills: Sage, 1975)

Offen, Karen, *Signs: Journal of Women in Culture and Society* 14:1 (1988) pp. 119–57

Oldfield, Sybil, *Women Humanitarians: A Biographical Dictionary of British Women active between 1900 and 1950* (London: Continuum, 2001)

Ollier, Nicole *L'Exode sur les routes de l'an 40* (Paris: Culture, Art, Loisirs 1969)

Overy, Richard, *The Morbid Age: Britain and the Crisis of Civilisation, 1919–1939* (London: Penguin, 2009)

Ozouf, Jacques and Mona. '"Le Tour de France par deux enfants"', in Pierre Nora (ed.), *Les Lieux de Mémoire* Vol I (Paris: Quarto / Gallimard, 1997) pp. 277–303

Panchasi, Roxanne, '"Fortress France": Protecting the Nation and its Bodies, 1918–1940', *Historical Reflections* 33:3 (2007), pp. 475–504

Passerini, Luisa, 'Introduction' to Luisa Passerini, *Memory and Totalitarianism* (Oxford: Oxford University Press, 1992),

Peschanski, Denis, *La France des camps: l'internement, 1938–1946* (Paris: Gallimard, 2002)

Peteet, Julie, 'Unsettling the Categories of Displacement', *Merip* 244 (2007), http://www.merip.org/mer/mer244; accessed 7 March 2008

Plas, Pascal, 'L'encadrement administratif des réfugiés. L'exemple de la Haute-Vienne' in Max Lagarrigue (ed.), *1940: La France du repli; l'Europe de la défaite* (Toulouse: Privat, 2001), pp. 175–86

Polman, Linda, *War Games: The Story of Aid and War in Modern Times*, translated By Liz Waters (London: Viking, 2010),

Pons, Silvio, 'La diplomatie soviétique, l'antifascisme et la guerre civile espagnole', in S. Wolikov and A. Bleton-Ruget (eds), *Antifascisme et nation* (Dijon: Editions Universitaires de Dijon, 1998), pp. 59–66

Pons Prades, Eduardo, *Las guerras de los niños republicanos (1936–1955)* (Madrid: Compañía Literaria, 1997)

Ponty, Janine, 'Réfugiés, exilés, des catégories problématiques', *Matériaux pour l'histoire de notre temps* 44:1 (1996), pp. 9–13

Porat, Dan A., 'From the Scandal to the Holocaust in Israeli Education', *Journal of Contemporary History* 39:4 (2004), pp. 619–36

Poznanski, Renée, *Etre juif en France pendant la Seconde Guerre mondiale* (Paris: Hachette, 1994)

Poznanski, Renée, 'French Apprehensions, Jewish Expectations: From a Social Imaginary to a Political Practice' in D. Bankier (ed.), *The Jews are Coming Back* (New York: Berghahn, 2005 and Jerusalem: Yad Vashem, 2005), pp. 25–57

Prost, Antoine, *Les anciens combatants et la société française 1914–1939*, 3 volumes (Paris: Presses de la Fondation Nationale des Sciences Politiques, 1977)

Prost, Antoine, *Republican Identities in War and Peace: Representations of France in the Nineteenth and Twentieth Centuries*, translated J. Winter and H. McPhail (Oxford: Berg, 2002)

Proudfoot, M., *European Refugees, 1939–1952* (London: Faber and Faber, 1957)

Pruja, Jean-Claude, *Premiers Camps de l'exil espagnol: Prats-de-Mollo, 1939* (Saint-Cyr-sur-Loire: Alan Sutton, 2003)

Rahe, Thomas, 'Jewish Religious Life in the Concentration Camp Bergen-Belsen' translated by K.-M. Meyke in Tony Kushner, David Cesarani, Jo Reilly and Colin Richmond (eds), *Belsen in History and Memory* (London: Frank Cass, 1997), pp. 85–121

Rajsfus, Maurice, *Les Français de la débâcle: juin-septembre 1940, un si bel été* (Paris: Le Cherche Midi, 1997)

Reinisch, Jessica, '"We Shall Rebuild Anew a Powerful Nation": UNRRA, Internationalism and National Reconstruction in Poland', *Journal of Contemporary History* 43:3 (2008), pp. 451–76

Reiter, Andrea, *Narrating the Holocaust* translated by Patrick Collier (London: Continuum, 2000)

Rémond, René, 'L'opinion française des années 1930 aux années 1940. Poids de l'évènement, permanence des mentalités' in Jean-Pierre Azéma and Bedarida (eds) *Vichy et les Français* (Paris: Fayard, 1992), pp. 481–92

Rinke, Andreas, *Le Grand retour – Die französische Displaced Person-Politik (1944–1951)* (Krankfurt: Peter Lang, 2002)

Rioux, Jean-Pierre, 'L'exode: un pays à la dérive', *L'histoire* (1990), pp. 64–70

Sabbagh, Karl, *Remembering Our Childhood: How Memory Betrays Us* (Oxford University Press, 2009)

Sassen, Saskia, *Guests and Aliens* (New York: New Press, 1999)

Schaeffer, P., *Moselle et Mosellans dans la Seconde Guerre Mondiale* (Metz: Editions Serpenoise, Société d'Histoire et d'Archéologie de la Lorraine, 1983)

Schröder, Stefan, *Displaced Persons im Lankreis und in der Stadt Münster 1945–1951* (Munster: Aschendorff Verlag, 2005)

Seidler, Victyor Jeleniewski, *Shadows of the Shoah: Jewish Identity and Belonging* (Oxford: Berg, 2000)

Sen, Amartya, *Identity and Violence; the Illusion of Destiny* (London: Penguin, 2006)

Sevillano, Francisco, *Rojos: la representación del enemigo en la guerra civil* (Madrid: Alianza Editorial, 2007)

Shamir, H., 'The drôle de guerre and French public opinion', *Journal of Contemporary History*, 11:1 (1976), pp. 129–43

Siegel, Mona., ' "To the Unknown Mother of the Unknown Soldier": Pacifism, Feminism and the Politics of Sexual Difference among French Institutrices between the Wars', *French Historical Studies* 22:3 (1999), pp. 421–51

Sirinelli, Jean-François, *Génération intellectuelle. Khâgneux et normaliens dans l'entre deux guerres* (Paris: Fayard, 1988)

Skran, C. M., *Refugees in inter-war Europe: the emergence of a regime* (Oxford: Clarendon, 1995)

Skran, Claudena and Carla N. Daughtry, 'The Study of Refugees before "Refugee Studies" ', *Refugee Survey Quarterly* 26:3 (2007), pp. 15–35.

Smith, Leonard V., Stéphane Audoin-Rouzeau and Annette Becker, *France and the Great War, 1914–1918* (Cambridge: Cambridge University Press, 2003)

Snyder, Timothy, *Bloodlands: Europe between Hitler and Stalin* (London: Bodley Head, 2010)

Soo, Scott, 'Ambiguities at work: Spanish republican exiles and the organisation Todt in occupied Bordeaux', *Modern and Contemporary France* (2007), 15:4, pp. 456–77

Stern, Frank, 'Antagonistic Memories: The Post-War Survival and Alienation of Jews and Germans', in L. Passerini (ed.), *Memory and Totalitarianism* (Oxford: Oxford University Press, 1992)

Stone, Tessa, 'Creating a (gendered?) military identity: the Women's Auxiliary Air Force in Great Britain in the Second World War', *Women's History Review* 8:4 (1999), pp. 605–24

Strauss, Léon, 'Les associations de PRAF (Patriotes Réfractaires à l'Annexion de Fait) d'Alsace et de Moselle', *Cahiers du centre d'études d'histoire de la Défense* 31 (2007), pp. 109–118

Summerfield, Penny, *Women Workers in the Second World War: Production and Patriarchy in Conflict* (London: Routledge, 1989)

Summers, Julie, *Stranger in the House: Women's Stories of Men Returning from the Second World War* (London: Simon & Schuster, 2008)

Thomas, Hugh, *The Spanish Civil War*, third edition (Harmondsworth: Penguin, 1986)

Thomas, Ned, 'Two Cataclysms', *Planet: the Welsh Internationalist* 198 (2010), pp. 93–102

Toscano, Mario, 'The Abrogation of the Racial Laws and the Reintegration of Jews in Italian Society (1943–1948)' in D. Bankier (ed.), *The Jews are Coming Back* (New York: Berghahn, 2005 & Jerusalem: Yad Vasher, 2005), pp. 148–68

Vidalenc, Jean, *L'Exode de mai-juin 1940* (Paris: Presses Universitaires de France, 1957)

Vormeier, Barbara, 'La pratique du droit d'asile à l'égard des réfugiés en provenance d'Allemagne et d'Autriche en France (de septembre 1939 à octobre 1940)', in Max Lagarrigue (ed.), *1940: La France du repli; l'Europe de la défaite* (Toulouse: Privat, 2001), pp. 105–12

Wasserstein, Bernard, *Vanishing Diaspora: the Jews in Europe since 1945* (London: Hamish Hamilton, 1996)

Wettstein, Howard, 'Introduction' to his edited *Diasporas and Exiles: Varieties of Jewish Identity* (Berkeley, Los Angeles and London: University of California Press, 2002), pp. 1–17

Wicks, Ben, *No Time to Wave Goodbye* (London: Bloomsbury, 1988)

Wieviorka, Annette, 'Jewish Identity in the First Accounts of Extermination Camp Survivors from France', *Yale French Studies* 85 (1994), pp. 135–51

Wyman, Mark, *DPs: Europe's Displaced Persons, 1945–51* (Ithaca and London: Cornell University Press, 1998)

Zamajski, Jan E., 'The Social History of Polish Exile (1939–1945); the exile state and the clandestine state: Society, Problems and Reflections', in Martin Conway and José Gotovitch (eds), *Europe in Exile; European Exile Communities in Britain, 1940–1945* (New York and Oxford: Berghahn Books, 2001), pp. 183–212

Zertal, Idith, *From Catastrophe to Power: Holocaust Survivors and the Emergence of Israel* (Berkeley: University of California Press, 1998)

Reference Works

Le Grand Robert, Dictionnaire alphabétique et analogique de la Langue Française, Deuxième Edition entièrement revue et enrichie par Alain Rey, Vol VIII (Paris: Le Robert, 1992)

Le Littré, Dictionnaire de la Langue Française Vol IV, (Paris: Hachette, 1883)

Web-sites
InternetArchive.org
http://www.calisphere.universityofcalifornia.edu/

Unpublished Doctorates
Carson, Jennifer, 'The Friends Relief Service – Faith into Action: Humanitarian Assistance to Displaced Persons Camps in Germany, 1945–1948', Unpublished PhD thesis, University of Manchester, (2009)
Dombrowski, Nicole, 'Beyond the Battlefield: the French civilian exodus of May–June, 1940', Unpublished PhD, New York University (1995)
Holian, Anna Marta, 'Between National Socialism and Soviet Communism: the Politics of Self-Representation among Displaced Persons in Munich, 1945–1951', unpublished PhD thesis, University of Chicago (2005)
Roberts, Siân Lliwen, 'Place, Life Histories and the Politics of Relief: episodes in the life of Francesca Wilson, Humanitarian Educator Activist', unpublished PhD thesis, University of Birmingham (2010)

Index